STATECRAFT

ALSO BY DENNIS ROSS

The Missing Peace:
The Inside Story of the Fight for Middle East Peace

STATECRAFT

{ AND HOW TO RESTORE AMERICA'S
STANDING IN THE WORLD }

DENNIS ROSS

Farrar, Straus and Giroux

New York

Farrar, Straus and Giroux
18 West 18th Street, New York 10011

Distributed in Canada by Douglas & McIntyre Ltd.
Printed in the United States of America
Published in 2007 by Farrar, Straus and Giroux
First paperback edition, 2008

The Library of Congress has cataloged the hardcover edition as follows:
Ross, Dennis.
    Statecraft : and how to restore America's standing in the world / Dennis Ross.
        p.   cm.
    Includes bibliographical references and index.
    ISBN-13: 978-0-374-29928-6 (hardcover : alk. paper)
    ISBN-10: 0-374-29928-5 (hardcover : alk. paper)
    1. United States—Foreign relations—2001–   2. International relations—
Case studies.   I. Title.

JZ1480.R674 2007
327.73—dc22   2006035767

Paperback ISBN-13: 978-0-374-53119-5
Paperback ISBN-10: 0-374-53119-6

Designed by Robert C. Olsson

www.fsgbooks.com

1   3   5   7   9   10   8   6   4   2

To my mother, Gloria Cherin, who always encouraged me

CONTENTS

Contents

PREFACE

I planned, after writing my book *The Missing Peace*, to write another book exploring the practice of negotiations. The more I thought about negotiations and how to do them, the more I realized that such a discussion would serve as an effective way to say something more generally about American foreign policy. This was early in the second term of George W. Bush, and I was motivated in no small part by my disquiet over the superficial way the debate on American foreign policy was being conducted.

I had no problem with questions about American priorities. Should the White House and the Pentagon have shifted from a war of necessity in Afghanistan to one of choice in Iraq? Was the war on terrorism being enhanced or diminished by our efforts to oust Saddam Hussein? If the "axis of evil" was such a threat, why were we so focused on Iraq, which posed the least immediate danger with regard to weapons of mass destruction, and doing so little about North Korea and Iran, which posed the greatest?

These were all legitimate questions that needed to be thrashed out. But at the same time, the increasingly shrill debate tended less toward answering those questions and more toward becoming riveted on the issue of multilateralism versus unilateralism. As such, it seemed to miss the essential point about the Bush administration and its conduct of foreign policy.

I am a multilateralist, and in my view there is no doubt that in an era of globalization and transnational challenges ranging from terrorism and weapons proliferation to pandemics such as AIDS, the United

States' capabilities will always have limits, and we have no real choice but to work with other states. But the calls for multilateralism—and the criticisms of the Bush foreign policy—too often have seemed to treat collaborative diplomatic efforts as an end in themselves. The president's fiercest multilateralist opponents seem to think that if only we had consulted our allies and followed all the diplomatic protocols, we wouldn't have any problems in Iraq, South Asia, or the Middle East—and that just isn't true.

Multilateralism is important, even essential, but as a means, not an end. When we speak of multilateralism or unilateralism, we are speaking of the means or the tools we as a state need to employ to achieve our interests in the world. We are speaking of how we define our purposes, make assessments about what we can and must do, and then go about implementing our choices. And yet the debate seemed to miss all that.

In a word, what is missing from the discussion of American foreign policy today is an understanding of statecraft. What is statecraft? It is the use of the assets or the resources and tools (economic, military, intelligence, media) that a state has to pursue its interests and to affect the behavior of others, whether friendly or hostile. It involves making sound assessments and understanding where and on what issues the state is being challenged and can counter a threat or create a potential opportunity or take advantage of one. Statecraft requires good judgment in the definition of one's interests and a recognition of how to exercise hard military or soft economic power to provide security and promote the well-being of one's citizens. It is as old as conflict between communities and the desire to avoid or prevent it. Plato wrote about statecraft. Machiavelli theorized about it. And Bismarck practiced it, never losing sight of his objectives, and recognizing that his objectives should never exceed his capabilities.

Statecraft is more difficult than ever in a world of rapid change, and with fewer national boundaries; more actors (states, and non-state actors such as religious groups and terrorist organizations); more diffuse power (at least economically); the smoldering resentments of have-nots and failed states; continuing ethnic or intercommunal conflicts; and interested parties or groups in one state who are determined to try to affect the political and power realities in another. Gordon Craig and Alexander George, two of the more thoughtful observers of diplomatic history, have suggested that "adaptation to accelerated change has become the major problem of modern statecraft, testing the ingenuity and the fortitude of those charged with the responsibility both for devising means and controlling international violence and for maintaining the security of their own countries."[1]

In this situation, the practice of statecraft in U.S. foreign policy comes down to appreciating our power while also respecting its limits; to assessing more completely how the international landscape is changing and what new challenges we now face; and to understanding how to use all the tools in our toolkit of power and influence to maximize what we can achieve at manageable costs.

While it may be more taxing than in earlier epochs, statecraft has never been more important. And if one wants to know both what has been missing in our foreign policy in the last years and what is necessary to fix it in the coming years, the answer is statecraft.

Why has statecraft been missing (or certainly downgraded) lately? To answer this question, it is important to look at the George W. Bush administration and its approach to foreign policy—the first Bush term in particular. Where did it fit the pattern of past administrations and where did it depart from that pattern? What guided it ideologically, and why did that ideological basis tend to disregard the basic tools of the trade? (Or, in its second term, when the administration has been more ideologically willing to embrace at least the symbols of statecraft, why has it conducted it so ineffectively?) I will use a discussion of these questions and their answers as a basis on which to turn to a more serious examination of statecraft and why restoring its centrality and effectiveness is so important to shaping a more successful American foreign policy in the years ahead.

The starting point for such a discussion—indeed, for understanding American statecraft—must begin with a serious consideration of our ideological point of departure for foreign policy. How should we see our role (and our power) in the world? What vision both fits our national self-image and is likely to be sustainable? What challenges internationally should dominate our concerns, and how are they changing from what concerned us in the past? How do our means square with what we would like to see take shape internationally? And, therefore, how can we more effectively employ our means to protect ourselves and achieve our goals?

These questions are the basis for sound statecraft, but at the present they rarely get posed, much less answered. No one book is going to provide satisfactory answers to all of them. And I make no claims that this one will. But I will try to get at the nature of America's role in the world and the fundamental differences between those—neoconservatives versus neoliberals—who believe that the United States must play a leading role internationally.

The book begins with a look at the Bush administration's foreign policy and how it has been weakened by the absence of statecraft. It goes on to offer an overview of what statecraft is, why we especially need it today, and how it worked in the past. It proceeds to delve more deeply into two essential tools of statecraft (negotiations and mediation) in order to explain what they are and how to conduct them. Every aspect of statecraft depends on negotiation in some form. Negotiations are necessary to persuade or dissuade, and statecraft is ultimately the art of using the means of influence leaders have to affect the behavior of others. And because no discussion of statecraft can be purely historical or abstract, the book also applies a statecraft approach prospectively to four challenges in our foreign policy—the Israeli-Palestinian conflict, Iran, our global struggle with radical Islam, and the rise of China.

To conclude, I offer a guide to what a neoliberal American foreign policy—one that employs statecraft as its inspiration—ought to be. I hope to provide insight into why we have to adjust our sights in foreign policy and refocus and retool our approach. But if the book helps to trigger debate about America's role in the world and how to enhance it, I will have more than met the purpose I had in mind when I decided to write it.

STATECRAFT

1.

{THE BUSH FOREIGN POLICY AND THE NEED FOR STATECRAFT}

Even more than his actual conduct of our foreign affairs, George W. Bush's rhetorical approach to foreign policy has been criticized and caricatured. That he speaks in slogans and general principles hardly makes him unique. Every president tries to put his policies in a clear and understandable framework, and few succeed. It is not easy to find a slogan that encapsulates the U.S. role and interests in the world and, at the same time, offers a sense of direction about our foreign policy.

During the cold war, "containment" met all these tests. It provided an easy handle to describe U.S. foreign policy. It served as a guiding principle; it told us how to organize ourselves, our priorities, and our resources to deal with a global Soviet threat. It provided the logic for alliances, and the commonly perceived threat forged bonds that held those alliances together. With containment, wherever the Soviet Union was expanding directly or through proxy, we would meet and counter that expansion. It seemed logical, even compelling—until, of course, the Kennedy and Johnson administrations saw Vietnam as part of the global strategy of limiting Soviet or Soviet-backed advances. The cost of such a deterministic approach became all too clear. The reality of local nationalism unconnected to a global template was slowly and painfully understood.

Even though the Nixon, Carter, and Reagan administrations refined the practice of containment, it would take the collapse of the Soviet Union to prompt American policy makers to formulate a new approach to our role in the world. In the George H. W. Bush administration (in which I worked under Secretary of State James Baker) we sought to create a "new world order" developing new organizations in Europe to promote security and guide emerging states from the former Soviet Union, while also employing force collectively to undo the Iraqi aggression against Kuwait and demonstrate that the law of the jungle would not be permitted in this new era. In the Clinton administration (in which I was chief Middle East envoy), "democratic enlargement" became the new catchphrase, describing not only NATO's embrace of those in Eastern Europe and the former Soviet Union who would adopt democratic institutions and civil society but also others around the globe who would embrace democratic values and free markets. To be sure, force would be employed where rogue actors threatened regional stability and engaged in ethnic cleansing.

Of course, the guiding principles were observed generally and not always with great consistency. The Bush administration chose not to get involved as Yugoslavia disintegrated and Slobodan Milošević began to seize parts of Bosnia and Croatia, practice "ethnic cleansing," and expel the non-Serb populations to create a Greater Serbia. Similarly, during the Clinton administration, Hutu genocide of the rival Tutsi population took place in Rwanda without a significant American or international response.

In the two terms of George W. Bush, U.S. policy and national security interests have been governed by the war on terrorism. Defeating terrorism has been the preoccupation. But "promoting freedom" and "ending tyranny" have become the administration's rhetorical guideposts. President Bush has declared the promotion of freedom as the best way to ensure that terrorists such as Osama Bin Laden do not have fertile ground to exploit. Insofar as terrorism, which after all is an instrument not a philosophy or a belief system, depends on frustration and alienation to attract recruits, the president is right to focus on changing or removing oppressive regimes that generate so much anger and hopelessness among their people.

Here, again, we should not expect perfect consistency between rhetorical goals and foreign policy behavior. While it might be desirable to see greater consistency between our stated purpose and goals and our behavior, it is not easy for any administration always to meet this standard. After all, the world situation and our interests are not black and white, and hard choices, not so susceptible to a simple slogan or principle, have to be made. President Bush, much like his father and President Clinton, has decided that maintaining stability in oil-rich Saudi Arabia is more important than pushing the royal family to democratize. He has made much the same judgment about Pakistan and its president, General Pervez Musharraf. In this case, Pakistan's importance to the war on terrorism, and the dangers of a fundamentalist coup in a nuclear-armed state, have trumped the administration's concerns about Musharraf's authoritarian rule and his protection of the Taliban and of A. Q. Khan, the father of Pakistan's nuclear program.

When it comes to the gap between rhetorical slogans and actual policies, the Bush administration is not materially different from or worse than its predecessors. Similarly—caricatures notwithstanding—the Bush administration has not departed radically from its predecessors when it comes to unilateral versus multilateral behavior.

The conventional wisdom that the Bush policy is unilateralist is simply wrong. No administration is ever entirely unilateralist or multilateralist. No American president has ever been prepared to allow others to veto a pathway that he considered to be vital to U.S. interests. Nor has any American president, including George W. Bush, been unwilling to join with other states in responding to potential challenges and threats. Indeed, when it comes to the Iranian and the North Korean nuclear programs, the administration has been only multilateralist—answering charges during the 2004 presidential campaign about the growth of North Korean and Iranian nuclear capabilities during Bush's first term by pointing to its efforts with allies to address the problems.

The issue has never been unilateralist versus multilateralist. Rather it is effectiveness. The Bush administration's failing has not been its instinct for unilateralism and its disdain for multilateralism. Its failing too often has been how poorly it has practiced multilateralism. On Iraq, it tried and failed to persuade the UN Security Council to pass a second resolution endorsing the war in Iraq. It tried and failed to gain Turkey's permission for U.S. forces to operate from Turkey's territory and send U.S. ground troops across the Turkish-Iraqi border—a failing that allowed large parts of the Ba'ath regime and the Republican Guard forces to melt away, avoid destruction, and regroup as an anti-American insurgency. Even after Saddam Hussein was captured, the administration tried and failed to persuade our NATO allies to help deal with the Iraqi insurgency, reconstruct Iraq, and train indigenous security forces.

Whether on Iraq or on its efforts to blunt North Korean and Iranian nuclear development, the Bush administration has adopted a multilateral approach, but failed to achieve our national security objectives as it did so. If the administration has not eschewed multilateralism, why is it perceived as unilateralist?

Is it because of its style? Is it because of its ideology? Or is it because it has been weak in its use of diplomacy and the tools of statecraft? All three factors help explain both the perception and the costs internationally of that perception.

STYLE MATTERS

Style matters in foreign policy. It is easy to dismiss style, and focus only on the substance of what we do. But the "how" of foreign policy—meaning how we act—also matters. While the how of our foreign policy involves many different tools—all relating to implementation of policies once we've settled on them—the way in which we carry out our steps and apply the various instruments available to us is particularly important. In this sense, our "style," or our public positioning and packaging, creates the context in which we deal with others and they respond to us.

At times, different administrations might adopt similar approaches to a given situation but package their approaches very differently. Compare, for example, the style of the George H. W. Bush administration in advance of the first Gulf War and the style of the George W. Bush administration in the run-up to the second Gulf War. There was no difference in the readiness of each administration to go it alone if necessary, but the two Bushes' styles were very different—and got very different results.

George H. W. Bush said unequivocally that the Iraqi aggression would not stand, and then proceeded to put together an international coalition and gain passage of UN Security Council resolutions that imposed sanctions and then authorized the use of force against Iraq—resolutions that his son would use to justify military intervention against Saddam Hussein twelve years later.

How did the elder Bush build his coalition and gain UN support? Through statecraft—in this case, through intensive and extensive efforts to persuade other leaders, often in face-to-face discussions. At one point, in November 1990, his secretary of state, James Baker, met with the leader or foreign minister of every country on the Security Council in order to formulate and win support for the crucial UNSC Resolution 678, which authorized the use of "all necessary means" to end Iraq's occupation of Kuwait.

In public, Baker explained that he was consulting other national leaders on the best ways to respond to the Iraqi aggression. In private, his message was very different: he told the leaders that President Bush had said the aggression would not stand and we would do what was necessary to undo it; the resolution that was being drafted would authorize the use of military means to expel Iraq from Kuwait; we hoped this particular country and its leaders would support the resolution, and if there was something we could do to make it easier for them to do so, they should let us know what that might be. However, at the end of the day, we would act collectively as we desired or on our own if we had to.

The "style" of the approach was consultative, even if the "substance" was not. But in this case, style was substantial. By sending its top foreign policy official to many other countries, the United States demonstrated that the views of others mattered. America was signaling its respect for the positions and attitudes of foreign leaders enough to go to them and solicit their input, to give them an explanation for their publics as to what they were doing, and to enable those foreign leaders to show that they were part of an international consensus they had helped to shape. The U.S. public posture did not make the leaders defensive or put them in a political corner. On the contrary, by going to them, the administration was giving them an incentive to respond favorably.

Contrast this with the behavior of the younger Bush's administration in 2002. From the president's speech at the UN in September, in which he challenged the body to be relevant, to his failure to travel to other capitals to make his case or solicit views, to his challenging others on the

Security Council to "show their cards" as the president proposed a second resolution—and then declaring such a resolution unnecessary when it was clear the votes weren't there to adopt it—the administration's public posture was "give us the cover for what we plan to do anyway, or get out of the way."

My point here is not to address the issue of whether going to war in Iraq in 2003 was right or wrong. Rather, it is to show that two administrations that were equally committed to using force if necessary went about gaining support for their goals in two very different ways. One understood that how it went about positioning itself and framing its goals was very important; indeed, that the "style" of what it did would have an impact on whether others would join it in carrying out the "substance" of its goals. The other showed very little interest in the effect its style might have on others.

Did the younger President Bush not want others to join us? No, he has spoken often and with obvious sincerity about the international response to terrorism, and he has referred to the countries who joined us in Iraq as the "coalition of the willing." The issue was not whether he wanted partners for the war in Iraq, but what he was willing to do to get them—and here the impact of 9/11 on the political psychology of President Bush must be understood.

9/11 AND ITS IMPACT ON THE BUSH STYLE

With the terrorist attacks on the World Trade Center and the Pentagon, a president who seemed to lack his footing in the first eight months of his administration found his mission, his confidence, and his voice. He would combat the evil of terrorism and its emergence as the leading threat to the United States and our values. There was no alternative to fighting this war that had been imposed on us, and there could be no compromise with the terrorists or those who supported them. His blunt, no-nonsense manner of speaking seemed to fit the moment. This was not a time for nuance.

Striking a strong, determined pose was necessary to reassure the American public. It was also the right policy, particularly because Osama Bin Laden and his supporters had to understand that the United States would not shrink from this conflict. Bin Laden had fully expected that we would. In his eyes, an America that had fled Lebanon after losing 241 marines to a suicide bombing; withdrawn from Somalia after losing 18 soldiers during the Black Hawk Down incident; and failed to respond in any meaningful way to the bombings in Saudi Arabia in 1996, of our embassies in Kenya and Tanzania in 1998, and of the USS *Cole* in Yemen in 2000, despite the numbers of Americans killed, appeared weak and irresolute. In Bush's mind, Bin Laden and his adherents had to see that there would be a tough, sustained response and that they would know no peace and find no refuge.

This was not just the right approach to policy; it was also good politics at home. President Bush adopted a style that fit the moment but also reflected who he was. His speaking plainly and bluntly struck a chord with the American public. It gave the public confidence when that confidence had been badly shaken. It responded to our collective need to be defiant in the face of such an outrage, and to show support for a leader who would not surrender to such an evil but would confront it. It helped the president forge a bond with the American public at a time when one was crucially needed.

When any president finds his voice—and it is authentic—he is unlikely to depart from it. Moreover, in an age of instant communication, a president cannot have one voice for America and another for the world. Certainly Bill Clinton spoke in the same voice regardless of where he was. His capacity to feel pain, empathize, and connect with people was employed, as I witnessed, not only in this country, but also in Moscow, Budapest, Tel Aviv, and Gaza—and it worked everywhere. George W. Bush's blunt style would look cynically political if he used it in this country but not elsewhere.

Inevitably, then, Bush's blunt rhetorical style after 9/11 began to have consequences for his foreign policy. For him it was simply not a big leap to go from finding Osama Bin Laden "dead or alive" to challenging Iraqi insurgents to "bring it on"—to badgering prospective allies to get with the program. Was the tone going to be different with potential partners? Was he going to try to cajole others into dealing with the "evil" of Saddam Hussein or simply declare that others should not shirk their duty?

Of course, one might ask whether Secretary of State Colin Powell could have complemented the president by pursuing a James Baker–type solicitation and consultation mission—at once both providing others with reasons to join the coalition and softening the effect of President Bush's style. Clearly, Secretary Powell should have tried to follow the Baker example and did not. However, to be fair to him, no one in the administration was eager for him to do so; some actively discouraged him and others undermined his legitimacy as secretary, questioning whether he was authoritative and actually spoke for the president. To be sure, the reason he did not speak for the administration was that the president, Secretary Rumsfeld, and other key officials came to translate Bush's style (the bluster) into substance. They believed what they said and did not think that the United States had to depend on anyone else—indeed, to do so, they felt, would signal weakness.

Once President Bush won reelection, however, he began to temper this style and see the value of reaching out to others. Iraq had already created a sobering reality. The United States was tied down in Iraq and Afghanistan and had few forces available for other contingencies. The costs of almost reflexive opposition of others in the international community, including from many of America's European allies, had also become increasingly apparent, and argued for a new stylistic approach. According to one report, President Bush "began signaling foreign leaders visiting him in the Oval Office that he knew much had gone wrong in his first term, and that he had empowered Ms. Rice to put a new emphasis on consultation and teamwork with allies."[1] New secretary of state Condoleezza Rice embarked almost immediately on fence-mending trips to Europe and Asia. In Europe, she went out of her way to emphasize a common approach on the question of Iran's nuclear program. And President Bush, in his February 2005 trip to Europe, echoed the theme of consulting European leaders and listening to European attitudes on how best to stop the Iranians from going nuclear. After the trip, he authorized a change in the U.S. approach; previously the administration had kept its distance from the British, French, and German negotiations with the Iranians (even if it claimed otherwise in the 2004 presidential campaign), but following the president's European trip, the United States began to coordinate with the European trio, and permitted them to offer limited incentives to the Iranians on the United States' behalf.

If nothing else, the president began his second term exhibiting greater awareness of the impact of America's public approach on others;

his secretary of state appeared even more sensitive in this regard, going so far as to remark in her senatorial confirmation hearing, "The time for diplomacy is now." While I don't mean to reduce diplomacy to style, there can be little doubt that the failure of the Bush administration's multilateralism in the first term was largely the result of its style. But even had the administration adopted a George H. W. Bush style, policy ultimately still comes back to substance. By most European and American accounts, Secretary Rice had a very successful initial trip to Europe; however, the same day she flew home, Iran announced it would never forsake its right to have nuclear power, and North Korea declared that it had nuclear weapons. Fences had been mended in Europe with an effective style, but the reality of real challenges to U.S. national security had not been altered.

Style matters precisely because it can help us affect the substance of foreign policy. Style is part of an approach to foreign policy. Style gets at how we shape the instruments at our disposal for trying to make us safer in the world—both removing threats and building a world more comfortable for our values and purposes. But it is those threats and the international landscape that we are constantly trying to alter as we pursue foreign policy.

How we go about dealing with the substance of our foreign policy concerns has always been a subject of debate, and appropriately so. We may often wax nostalgic about the ideal of politics ending at the water's edge. And we have succeeded at times with a bipartisan foreign policy. But that tends to be on big issues where the country truly does come together, as it surely did with 9/11.

Partisanship in foreign policy did not emerge just during George W. Bush's tenure. Woodrow Wilson, a Democratic president, lost his vision of an activist League of Nations to opposition from the Senate and the Republican chairman of the Senate Foreign Relations Committee Henry Cabot Lodge. Henry Kissinger's pursuit of détente fell victim in the mid-1970s as much to the politics within his Republican Party as it did to opposition from Democratic senator Henry "Scoop" Jackson.

Ideology, more than partisan politics, drove Lodge's opposition to the League. He did not believe in limiting America's freedom of action or sacrificing it to an international body. Similarly, from different parties,

Ronald Reagan and Scoop Jackson opposed détente not to gain politically but because they believed that it was seriously flawed—accommodating a dangerous Soviet Union and reaching agreements with it when we should have been competing with it, exploiting its vulnerabilities, and demanding an end to the oppression of its people. The point is that differences in foreign policy goals and objectives may express themselves politically but are often based on ideological premises. And it is the ideological divide about the proper course for American foreign policy that needs to be understood; but it, too, tends to be oversimplified.

LIBERAL VERSUS CONSERVATIVE— WHAT HAPPENED TO THE DIFFERENCES?

Traditionally, a liberal foreign policy (associated generally with Democrats) was guided by a core set of principles: promote dialogue; restrain aggression through collective security mechanisms rather than through balance-of-power maneuvering; strengthen international institutions to manage international relations and mediate conflicts; foster human rights and support humanitarian interventions militarily; and engage in nation-building and the export of democratic values. By contrast, a conservative foreign policy (associated generally with Republicans) has historically preferred to stabilize countries rather than promote democracy; more carefully calibrate and narrowly define what constitutes areas of national interest; use force unencumbered by others or by international institutions; and engage in interventions guided by more hardheaded national, not strictly humanitarian, interests.

Conservatives saw liberals as too ready to go on foreign policy moral binges that taxed our resources—human and material—and that failed to recognize the realities of power and the costs of employing it badly. Liberals saw conservatives as managing a foreign policy devoid of American values and in danger of making us dependent on other states whose stability at home was imposed by coercion. For liberals, this suggested that the stability might be hollow and temporary, and that, in any case, it was contrary to American values of freedom and human and civil rights.

On the use of force, the divide was less on the utility of force and more on its purpose. True, liberals might have been more inclined than conservatives to shape U.S. interventions around collective responses, but that was more to lead the world to fulfill its responsibilities. For liberals, our responsibility was to rescue and remake the world. Conservatives saw only folly in such endeavors, and were convinced that alliances had value not for transformative purposes but for countering or defeating aggressors.

Has the world turned upside down? Are today's liberals, who shy away from ever using force, even for humanitarian purposes, taking on some of the attributes of traditional conservatives? And are today's conservatives assuming some of the impulses for interventionism that characterized liberals in the past? Perhaps there is some role reversal, but it is important to remember that the cold war began to blur the distinctions between the two.

The cold war produced convergences between some in the Republican and Democratic parties, such as Ronald Reagan and Scoop Jackson, who saw the competition with the Soviet Union in terms not just of dangerous weapons but also of values. While understanding the danger of gratuitous provocation, they saw the potential for defense against such weapons and ultimately believed that in promoting our values we would wear the Soviets down and eventually win the cold war. For others, the risk of mutual annihilation meant that survival, stability, and predictability in our relations with the Soviets had to supersede concerns about values and human rights. Direct confrontations were to be avoided, particularly because clashes over moralistic concerns could lead to inadvertent crises and catastrophic escalation. Republicans such as Henry Kissinger and James Baker had more in common with Democrats such as Warren Christopher and Madeleine Albright than they did with fellow Republicans such as Senator Jesse Helms.

Today we see echoes of some of the past debates that blurred the lines between liberals and conservatives and Democrats and Republicans. Some see the danger of terrorism, especially given the potential of terrorists being armed with nuclear devices, as requiring collaboration with those such as the Saudis and Pakistanis, even if it means sacrificing our values and ignoring their human-rights abuses. Others might not dispense with such collaboration but also believe that it should take place on our terms. They see little reason not to put much more pressure on the Saudis and the Pakistanis to democratize, believing that they need us even more than we need them, and that our interests will be better served over time if both regimes are transformed.[2]

Of course, what tempers the differences of policy makers in administrations is that they have to make hard choices in implementing policies, and, as noted earlier, they often opt for stability in the short run. The Bush administration has certainly done that, at least with both the Saudis and Pakistanis. But that does not make President Bush a traditional conservative or a "realist"—someone who cares little about the domestic character of other countries and their regimes. On the contrary, while being prepared to adjust to some realities, he is overall an "idealist," and more revolutionary than conservative. Rather than seeking to preserve the status quo, he has recognized that in too many parts of Africa, Asia, and the Middle East, the status quo and internal oppression have fed the anger that both produces terrorists and provides a basis for them to recruit new followers. As President Bush declared in his second inaugural address, "The best hope for peace in our world is the expansion of freedom in all the world."[3]

President Bush and many of the so-called neoconservatives of his administration favor transformation, not preservation. They think big, convinced that we can end tyranny and must spread democracy. They are Wilsonian in their moralistic view of foreign policy and their belief about the role the United States must play in the world. President Bush is reported to admire Theodore Roosevelt. But Roosevelt was much more of a realist than an idealist, much more a believer in preserving balances of power than in chasing the chimera of collective security, and much more a devotee of artful and supple diplomacy to counter threats to U.S. interests and meet U.S. needs. Woodrow Wilson, on the other hand, was the embodiment of idealism, and is in many respects a better guide to President Bush's instincts and attitudes.

Wilson believed in the transformative power of the United States. Unlike those European countries that in his view sought only selfish advantage and so had produced the catastrophe of the First World War, America was selfless. We did not seek national aggrandizement or colonies, and we would not engage in a mindless competition for power and arms. We would be an example to others and appeal to the basic goodness of man, and his freedom-seeking nature. We would lead a world in which there would be an end to imperialism and where self-determination would allow colonized people to enjoy their freedom and their god-given rights. Wilson saw the hand of divine providence in our role, our unparalleled resources, our decency—and our call to duty. One hears the echo of Wilson's beliefs in President Bush's words.

To be sure, there is one very profound difference between President Bush's approach and Wilson's. President Wilson, the driving force behind the League of Nations, the precursor to the United Nations, believed fervently in collective security and international law; both would limit national sovereignty, including ours, and would constitute a practical and a moral inhibition on the use of force. In his eyes, the United States, given our standing and unselfish purposes, had to lead the way. But America, too, would be bound by the international conventions that Wilson favored.

President Bush wants no limits on the exercise of American power or sovereignty—not from the United Nations, not from the International Criminal Court, and, as we have seen, not even from something like the Geneva Convention on the rules governing torture of those we seize as we combat terrorism. Ironically, because he shares Wilson's conviction in our goodness, our selflessness, he opposes any limits on the exercise of our might. For President Bush, our benevolence and our exceptionalism mean we will use our power only for good, and therefore that power should not be constrained by others. Traditional conservatives also don't want others to limit our exercise of power. But unlike them, President Bush seeks to use our power not for defensive but for transformative purposes.

Some might argue that Ronald Reagan, not Woodrow Wilson, is George W. Bush's real historical model. Certainly, here at home, there is a strong case to be made that Bush is a Reaganite. In foreign policy, Reagan, too, was a Wilsonian—speaking of America as that "shining city upon a hill"—and like Bush, he was instinctively opposed to external limitations on our exercise of power. However, unlike Bush, Reagan was not quick to use American military might. True, he would compete with the Soviet Union and drive up the costs of empire by raising defense spending, pursuing the Strategic Defense Initiative, or a "Stars Wars" defensive shield against missile attack, and supporting insurgencies against the Soviets in Afghanistan or Soviet proxies in Nicaragua. But he was not keen on using American military forces for foreign interventions. One cannot compare a low-cost venture in Grenada, where there was essentially no indigenous military force, to the war in Iraq.

Moreover, consider President Reagan's response in Lebanon: the United States initially went into Beirut to preside over the PLO's departure from Lebanon, and did so as part of a small multilateral force of which American forces were essentially an equal part. The mission of the multilateral forces subsequent to the PLO exit was to support the Lebanese as they reconstituted a new national compact and reached agreement with Israel on its withdrawal from Lebanon. But with intense Syrian opposition to the new Lebanese government's negotiation (and resulting agreement) with the Israelis and the emergence of Hizbollah as a new Shi'a militia, internal fighting in Lebanon escalated. Following the suicide bombing of the U.S. Marine barracks near the Beirut airport in the fall of 1983, in which 241 U.S. marines were killed, President Reagan withdrew the American forces in early 1984.

President Reagan was quick to cut our immediate losses. He did not let concerns about perceptions of our staying power prevent him from pulling forces out. Though willing to use U.S. military forces in limited circumstances, he was clearly wary of getting bogged down, and did not look at American forces as the vanguard for producing political and regional transformation. President Reagan was an idealist in terms of the American role internationally. But, for him, America could transform the world more through the force of its example and less through the force of its military.

Both Wilson and Reagan saw the power of our example. Both also reflected well the ethos of Americans. We see ourselves as selfless and willing to help others, eschewing any special gain for our country. Internationally, others may see us and our purposes quite differently. Our self-image, however, is one of sacrifice for a greater good. And Bush, like Reagan before him, knows how to speak to the American idiom in foreign policy—something, not surprisingly, that gave his approach a ring of authenticity to many Americans.

Again, however, policy comes back to substance, and while shaping a foreign policy that reflects our ethos is important, there are still real threats that must be dealt with and real interests or causes to pursue.

The ideological starting point is important, and certainly in the George W. Bush first term, it is fair to say that the neoconservatives defined the foreign policy agenda and how it was pursued.

NEOCONSERVATISM VERSUS NEOLIBERALISM

Like most caricatures, the description of the neoconservatives has been overly simplistic. Their current standard-bearers—such as Richard Perle, David Frum, William Kristol, and Robert Kagan—are serious thinkers with a clear worldview.[4] To be sure, those who might describe themselves as neoconservatives are not homogeneous, but they do share a number of general precepts: force and power remain highly relevant in a very dangerous world; the United States is the world's premier state and has the moral responsibility to use its power, including its unrivaled military force, for good; the internal character of regimes matters; malevolent leaders and terrorist groups (which usually have some connection) must be confronted and defeated; our readiness to do so will undermine all such entities and reduce their coercive effect on others; using our force can transform the political landscape, embolden democratic, reformist elements regionally and internationally, and hasten the day that democracy triumphs around the globe; though many of our traditional allies, particularly in Europe, instinctively oppose the use of force, we must not be inhibited by their reluctance—a reluctance that favors accommodation of those who can, in fact, never be accommodated in their opposition to our values and purposes.

In the eyes of many neocons, 9/11 resulted from our weakness in responding to threats. It was far less an intelligence failure than a failure of will over the preceding decade to confront those such as Saddam Hussein or the Iranians or Hizbollah or the Taliban or Al Qaeda. Terrorism was never seen primarily as a law enforcement problem; rather it was a first-order threat that required a strong response against not just the groups but also the countries that gave those groups support and sanctuary. Ultimately, the neoconservatives are far more optimistic about being able to transform human nature and international relations than traditional conservatives.[5] Like conservatives, they are not as a rule inclined to intervene strictly for humanitarian purposes; unlike conservatives, they tend to see our military power as an agent of change that can be used to create an environment in which our ideas are able to flourish.

While some neoconservatives such as Robert Kagan and William Kristol would put a high premium on marrying force and diplomacy, others seem to believe that force often creates its own diplomatic logic.[6] Creating new facts on the landscape seemed to infuse the thinking of leading officials of the new Bush administration as it assumed office in January 2001. There was a sense that respect for American power had been lost during the Clinton years, and it had to be reestablished. Others, it was believed, would adjust to the realities we might create, even if they expressed unhappiness about our behavior. Initially, withdrawal from the Kyoto Protocol, the ABM Treaty, and the Arab-Israeli peace process was as much a part of creating new realities as was putting far more pressure on Iraq or Iran to change the character of the Middle East. But as one of the neocons wrote prior to assuming a policy-making position, forced regime change in either Iraq or Iran was far more likely to transform the Middle East than continuing futile diplomacy between Israelis and Palestinians.[7]

Obviously, Iraq has not turned out the way the neocons envisioned or hoped. To be fair to them, the Bush administration did not prosecute the war and the aftermath of Saddam Hussein's fall the way many of them had argued for. Richard Perle believed that U.S. forces should have gone in, removed Saddam Hussein, and withdrawn—leaving Iraq for Iraqis such as Ahmed Chalabi to manage. Others, such as William Kristol, were highly skeptical of such an approach and instead saw the administration's reluctance to use sufficient force to liberate territory and be able to hold it as a major failing, particularly because it allowed the insurgency to take root and undermine the ability to reconstruct Iraq quickly.

Kristol's views converge, in part, with what might be described as a neoliberal view of Iraq.[8] While there is as yet no clearly acknowledged or identified body of scholars, policy makers, and commentators broadly described as neoliberals, I will use the label and define it. First, neoliberals believe in the weight and importance of the U.S. role internationally. Second, just as the neoconservatives tend to be Republicans, the neoliberals tend to be Democrats—though clearly not all Democrats are neoliberals (any more than all Republicans are neocons). Third, with regard to Iraq, there were some in Congress—such as Senators Joseph Biden and Joseph Lieberman—and many who served in the Clinton administration who believed that going to war in Iraq was the right choice.[9]

To be sure, not all those whom I would define as neoliberals—Francis Fukuyama and Joseph Nye, for example—believed it was right to go to war in March 2003. But those who did raised questions about force size and its appropriateness to the military and political mission. Unlike Kristol and other thoughtful neoconservatives, neoliberal supporters of the war were far more preoccupied with what would be needed in the aftermath of Saddam's demise. There was much less optimism about the ease of the mission and much greater concern about the messiness of the reconstruction or nation-building phase. Similarly, neoliberals were far more riveted on the dangers of a vacuum after Saddam, and the implications of this for security; the role of the former Iraqi military during a transition period; the importance of having an international, not American, administrator of Iraq to avoid the symbolism of U.S. occupation; the need to create an early Iraqi administration; the risks of sectarianism, the likelihood of a Sunni insurgency, and the long-haul nature of the responsibility we would be assuming.[10]

Neoliberals come to nation-building with an understanding that transformations are about not just removing regimes but also focusing on what takes their place. Unlike the neocons, who, Francis Fukuyama observes, defined the task in Iraq as simply "getting rid of the old regime," neoliberals understand that regime change in general, and specifically in Iraq, required a "slow and painstaking" process of constructing institutions to fill the vacuum.[11] It was the newspaper columnist Thomas Friedman, a self-styled neoliberal, who wrote a running stream of commentaries supporting the war but cautioning that if we did not have a serious "day after" strategy, we were in danger of creating a Balkan-type nightmare in Iraq. We could not simply destroy; we had a responsibility to construct—recognizing that this would be a complex and very difficult task. Still, in Friedman's eyes, the benefits of replacing a truly evil, malignant leader with a decent, roughly representative government in the heart of the Middle East might justify such a Herculean effort. Ultimately, neoliberals are optimists who are guided by their hopes but who also recognize limits.

Here we can see what neoliberals have in common with neoconservatives, as well as where they diverge from them and the liberals of today. Like the neocons, they see that power and force are inescapable parts of international relations. They see real threats that require military responses, and they understand that the United States must be able to project its power. Unlike many of today's liberals, neoliberals are not defensive when it comes to the use of American force. They are far more likely to see the need for engagement internationally and to believe, unlike many on the political left, that there are forces in the world that must be resisted. Indeed, they tend not to "think of Milošević and Saddam as victims," or to accept the "sort of affectless, neutralist, and smirking isolationism" that Christopher Hitchens says characterizes too much of the "left" today.[12]

Neoliberals know that the world can be nasty and that American power is one essential tool for dealing with it. Not surprisingly, they are not against the principle of preemption—attacking those who threaten us before they can succeed in doing so. They see new security challenges from murkier places, in which waiting until the threat is unmistakable may be too late to prevent it from killing large numbers of Americans. Ultimately, what separates neoliberals from neoconservatives is not their optimism and their commitment to fostering positive changes worldwide, but their doubts about where our use of force is likely to succeed. Neoliberals are more skeptical than the neocons that force can foster democratic transformations, though they are more inclined to use force for humanitarian purposes in places such as Rwanda or Darfur.

Neoliberals see peace and democracy as having to emerge from within, not as imposed from without. They are willing to make the effort—diplomatically, economically, politically, and militarily—to help promote both peace and democratic change, but they realize that all the instruments at our disposal must be employed and in a way that fits the local context. They have no illusions about the limitations and weaknesses of international institutions such as the United Nations, but they also understand the value and greater legitimacy that results from taking actions under such international umbrellas. Unlike neocons, neoliberals also see the cost to the United States when America defies international conventions, rejects what may be a broad international consensus on something such as global climate change, and offers nothing to take the place of that which it opposes.

Neoliberals believe, to use Joseph Nye's term, in the use of smart power—meaning the optimal mix of hard and soft power to achieve our objectives.[13] While they don't rule out the need to engage in regime change, they tend to favor the changing of the behavior of regimes, believing that can have a transforming effect.

Neoliberals as a rule are convinced that Iran must not be permitted to develop or acquire nuclear capability, and that the North Korean nuclear weapons must be dismantled. But, again, unlike the neocons, neoliberals believe that we are more likely to succeed by persuading, not compelling, others whom we may need to join us in countering these dangers. It is too simple to say that neoliberals are more likely than neoconservatives to employ diplomacy over the use of force. But it is fair to say that neoliberals are more attuned than the neocons to how to employ all the instruments of statecraft—at least at this stage in the articulation and implementation of neoconservative strategies. Indeed, I would argue that the neoliberals are much more preoccupied than the neoconservatives with statecraft—largely because they have less confidence in the consequences of using military force for political purposes.

WHAT IS STATECRAFT?

Statecraft is not simply another way of referring to diplomacy. While including all diplomatic procedures, it is much more than only exercising diplomacy. Some define statecraft generally as the "art of conducting state affairs."[14] Others describe it more specifically as the "organized actions governments take to change the external environment in general or the policies and actions of other states in particular to achieve the objectives that have been set by policy makers."[15]

As a former policy maker, I would describe statecraft as knowing how best to integrate and use every asset or military, diplomatic, intelligence, public, economic, or psychological tool we possess (or can manipulate) to meet our objectives. Statecraft involves influencing others—those who are already friendly and share our purposes, and those who do not. But statecraft requires more than simply orchestrating all the resources directly or indirectly at our disposal. It requires putting our means into a broader context of goals and capabilities.

Statecraft starts with understanding our role and our broad purposes. It requires a definition of objectives that are desirable, even ambitious, but also tied to an appreciation of what is possible. Strategies and tactics must be fashioned that create a match—not a mismatch—between aims and the means available for acting on those aims. As such, statecraft puts a premium on being able to assess a threat or an emerging threat wisely. Such assessments must evaluate the nature of the danger, its likelihood of materializing, its possible consequences, and its timing, as well as which other actors have the capabilities to be helpful in countering it. Often those who are not our allies may have the greatest leverage on a potential adversary, and statecraft involves determining and then employing the most effective means to bring those who are not our friends to exercise their influence constructively.

By the same token, statecraft is not only about fending off threats, but also about taking advantage of opportunities to alter the landscape and make the world safer and more responsive to our interests or goals. Richard Nixon and Henry Kissinger understood that an opening to China could be strategically beneficial, creating leverage vis-à-vis the Soviet Union and giving the Chinese a new stake in economic cooperation and stability regionally and internationally. Similarly, the Bush administration, especially in its second term, appears to recognize the growing strategic significance of India and how it may be integral to triangulating with China as the latter's weight is felt increasingly on the world stage. Recognizing a strategic opening is certainly one requirement of statecraft. Being able to marshal the wherewithal to act on an opening and exploit it, in the final analysis, is one of the better measures of effective statecraft. By the same token, missing opportunities or squandering them may be one of the better measures of statecraft poorly executed.

Chester Crocker, a scholar and former practitioner, describes "smart statecraft [as] what you get when wits, wallets, and muscle pull together so that leverage in all its forms is harnessed to a realistic action plan or political strategy that can be set in motion by agile diplomacy. Smart statecraft does not dispense with hard power; it uses hard power intelligently, recognizing the limits as well as the potential of purely military power, and integrating it into an over-arching strategy."[16]

Shaping, in Dr. Crocker's words, "an over-arching strategy," requires something else: the capacity to establish meaningful and feasible objectives. One should not assume that is a given with leaders and decision makers. Did Lyndon Johnson and his main advisors establish meaningful and achievable objectives in Vietnam? Did Bill Clinton and his major advisors (like me) understand what was possible so long as Yasir Arafat was the Palestinian leader and develop a strategy that fit that possibility? Did George W. Bush understand what he was getting into in Iraq, and would he have established such ambitious objectives if he had? Obviously, having flawed assessments about threats and opportunities will lead to misguided objectives. Failing to understand the local circumstances or the setting in which one is involving our forces or our national prestige is a failure of statecraft.

In other words, statecraft involves developing aims and strategies that fit both the context and the means available. Bad statecraft creates mismatches between means and ends; it also misreads what policies are likely to be sustainable domestically and what must be done to preserve domestic support. Vietnam was a classic example of failure on nearly every measure, with disastrous consequences for our standing in the world, our self-confidence, and our readiness to exercise power, as well as a colossal loss of life.

Will Iraq turn out to be different? It is hard to exaggerate the Bush administration's fundamental miscalculations on Iraq, including but not limited to unrealistic policy objectives; fundamental intelligence failures; catastrophically poor understanding of what would characterize the post-Saddam period, and completely unrealistic planning as a result; denial of the existence of an insurgency for several months; and the absence of a consistent explanation to the American people or the international community about the reasons for the war. Small wonder that after nearly four years of warfare, Iraq has been a disaster, costing thousands of lives, requiring the expenditure of hundreds of billions of dollars, stretching our forces and reserve system to the breaking point, and becoming a magnet for terrorists and hostility toward the United States throughout the Muslim world. Could the war yet yield a less disastrous and possibly more hopeful outcome?

It is possible. The removal of Saddam Hussein could yet represent a historic development in Iraq and the region. With Saddam gone, authentic, if messy and sectarian, politics may yet become manageable and permit a new Iraq to emerge that is a threat to neither its neighbors nor its own people. Such an outcome could, over time, have a liberating effect on reformers and even publics in the region, convincing them that the dangers of opposition to strongman rule need not be overwhelming.

But that is the best case, and few outside the Bush administration would bet on that being the outcome in Iraq. In the near term, sectarian violence threatens to tear Iraq apart. Unfortunately, a prolonged civil war and the fragmentation of the country may be a more likely outcome in Iraq than the best case still envisioned by President Bush. Even if we succeed in avoiding such an eventuality, we should have no illusions; in the best of circumstances, it will take time for Iraq to become stable and self-sustaining. Any such success will still have to be hard won, will require a U.S. presence for years to come, and will depend on giving the Sunnis of the country a stake in the new Iraq.

It will also require the Sunnis to adjust to a new reality: they are not the majority or dominant force in Iraq. They will have a role and a share, but others will dominate. Like the Maronites of Lebanon, who held the commanding heights of wealth and power for so long, the Sunnis will have to accept a far less exalted position in Iraq. To be sure, stability does not depend only on the Sunnis. Their readiness to accept a Maronite-type posture in Iraq also requires the Shi'a to be willing to grant them a share of the national assets and power.

National reconciliation has not yet taken place. A new national compact as embodied in the constitution has not been accepted by the Shi'a, Sunnis, or Kurds—with the amendments the Sunnis sought on distribution of oil revenues, provinces not having the right to secede, and an agreed role on Islam in law and society never having been adopted. Without a real national compact, Sunnis will continue to acquiesce in the insurgency and Shi'as will not give up the militias that they see as their protection from the Sunnis—militias that both exact revenge and inflict violent punishment while also preventing real national, not sectarian, security forces from emerging.

Perhaps seeing the abyss of unrelenting civil war and fragmentation of the country, the Shi'as, Sunnis, and Kurds will decide to reconcile and accept the burden of responsibility for security in Iraq that the United States continues to carry. Most Iraqis don't want American troops there, and yet nearly all Iraqis are afraid to have U.S. forces leave. Knowing we will withdraw in a way that does not leave them in the lurch but that requires them to assume responsibility could still save the day. But the transition won't be easy, and the insurgency won't immediately disappear. And so long as the insurgency goes on, a violent Iraq will not be an attractive model for others in the region.

Moreover, the new Iraq—with the Shi'a politically dominant—will not be especially close to its Arab neighbors such as Saudi Arabia and Jordan, with their Sunni leaders and populations. Nor will the new Iraq be hostile to Shi'a Iran. While not a puppet of the Iranians, the new Iraq will not be part of any American-led efforts to isolate the Iranians over their pursuit of nuclear weapons or their support of terrorist groups such as Hizbollah, Hamas, and Islamic Jihad.

How will the American public react at that point? If, given the sacrifices we have made for Iraq, we are faced with a leadership that opposes our policy toward Iran and on other regional issues, or with an Iraq that devolves into civil war or continuing civil strife, how will the Bush decision to go into Iraq be perceived? Even now a majority of the American public believe the decision to go to war in Iraq was a mistake. It is hard to escape the conclusion that the Iraqi experience, much like Vietnam before it, will make the American public far less willing to support the use of force in other contingencies.

Like other neoliberals, I share the doubts about too optimistically using force for effecting political change. But losing credibility in being able to use or threaten force is not good for the effective exercise of statecraft. Smart statecraft, as Chester Crocker observed, depends on being able to orchestrate hard and not just soft (meaning nonmilitary or coercive) power.[17] Sometimes the perception that we will use force if other forms of leverage won't work creates pressures on others (who fear our use of force) to act, when they otherwise might not, to resolve a problem or threat. If others doubt that we can use force because we are hamstrung—constrained by domestic realities or self-doubt or military forces stretched too thin—our capacity to counter a threat before it becomes far more dangerous and requires a response will be diminished. Statecraft is unlikely to be effective if it has to be conducted literally with our arms tied behind our back.

WHY IS STATECRAFT SO NECESSARY TODAY?

The challenges we face internationally today are different from those we had to confront in the latter half of the twentieth century. Since the United States has been a global power—certainly since the end of World War II—the main threats we have faced have come from nation-states. With nation-states, even those with a messianic, expansionist ideology, as the Soviet Union and China had at one time, there is an address. Traditional forms of deterrence work. Costs that matter to these states can be inflicted in response to certain behaviors. The leaders of these states have something to protect and something unmistakable to lose. Miscalculation is possible, and war through inadvertence can certainly occur. Nonetheless, leaders can be held accountable, and countering threats, while not easy—witness Iraq or Iran or North Korea today—falls in a familiar domain.

But what happens in a world where the principal, or at least increasingly serious, threats come from non-state actors? Where it is not so easy to find their addresses? Where traditional deterrence does not apply? Where our use of military power may actually increase the anger toward us and make terrorism more, not less, likely? Where threats of terror become increasingly destructive and know no borders? Where we are in a war but it is a war of ideas, and our moral standing and legitimacy may determine a struggle for hearts and minds that will affect who becomes a terrorist? In such a world, traditional standards and uses of power must be redefined, and all, not just some, of our instruments for affecting others must be brought to bear. In such a world, effective statecraft will be critical to securing our national interests.

Later I will discuss in greater detail what is new and different in the international landscape and how and why we need to apply statecraft to U.S. foreign policy. For now, suffice it to say that America's leaders will have to contend with the new reality of non-state actors (especially radical Islamists) who are driven not only by a deep sense of grievance and anger against the United States, but also by their desire to do great damage to America's interests and citizens—and by their belief that they can succeed in doing so. It is not just that they employ terror, but also that they seek weapons of mass terror. They are trying to acquire or develop nuclear or biological or chemical weapons, and the security of such weapons and their components worldwide—especially in the former Soviet Union—leaves much to be desired. Ensuring the security of such weapons or potential weapons stocks is not something the United States can do on its own, any more than America alone can prevent the spread of weapons of mass destruction to rogue regimes or terrorist groups.

America needs partners in a new world to win the struggle with radical Islamists and also to develop joint strategies for stopping acts of terror and for limiting the appeal of the Islamists to those throughout the Muslim world who are alienated from corrupt and nonresponsive regimes. Similarly, our leaders must know whom to work with and how to forge a division of labor to respond to the increasing phenomenon of failing and weak states, particularly in Africa, that are breeding grounds for conflict and havens from which the radical Islamists base themselves and operate.

And if these challenges weren't already daunting, America's foreign policy must also now be able to marshal the means to manage the emergence of rising powers on the international stage such as China and India. The world as we have known it was dominated by the transatlantic relationship of the United States and Europe. In the years ahead, three of the four dominant powers, at least economically, are likely to be Asian—China, Japan, and India. China, in particular, is becoming more assertive and, unlike Japan and India, is not democratic. How likely is it that the Chinese will view the international order the way Americans do? If not, what tools can the United States wield, on its own and with others, to shape Chinese choices and exert leverage in a way that creates incentives for China to play by familiar and acceptable rules of the game?

Whether dealing with the qualitatively new non-state actor threats or winning the battle of hearts and minds with the radical Islamists or finding ways to integrate the Chinese into a more open and congenial international system, American foreign policy will need to be guided by a statecraft mentality. Our leaders will need to know how to conduct statecraft effectively. And ultimately that is what this book is about.

While not ignoring *what* our policies must be, I want to focus as well on *how* to pursue our needs and interests. Knowing *what* our policies should be matters little in the end if we don't know *how* to do what is necessary.

With an eye toward learning how best to do what is necessary, I want to turn now to a survey of several historical cases of statecraft.

2.

{CASES OF STATECRAFT}

German Unification in NATO

There is no better way to grasp statecraft done well or not so well than to look at a number of historical examples. I have chosen to examine more recent cases for several reasons. First, since each of the cases either straddles or follows the end of the cold war, each has particular relevance to the international landscape that we are dealing with today. Second, in several of the cases, I was either directly involved with or in a position to talk to key decision makers and, thus, have a good understanding of what was driving the American decisions at the time. Third, the stakes in each case were high, and there is no better basis on which to measure the effectiveness of statecraft than in cases where different administrations believed that a great deal was riding on the achievement of their objectives.

With those reasons in mind, I will offer an overview of what happened in each case, why we developed the objectives we did, what obstacles we faced, and what were the means we used to overcome them. One way to measure the effectiveness of statecraft is to ask: were the objectives difficult to achieve? In many of the cases, the objectives were seen by many internationally—and even by some within the administrations—as desirable but unachievable. And yet we did achieve them. Surely, statecraft had something to do with it.

In the first case, German unification in NATO, it is safe to say that almost no one initially thought it conceivable that Germany could be unified and integrated into NATO. Indeed, had one queried leaders in Europe or most of those in the State Department or in the Washington punditry class, they would have insisted that the Soviet leadership could never accept such an outcome. Yet the application of statecraft made it happen.

BACKGROUND AND CONTEXT

Nothing more clearly embodied the cold war than the division of Germany into Western and Eastern nations. It took on a life of its own, and the so-called Four Powers at the time—the United States, the Soviet Union, France, and the United Kingdom—assumed rights and responsibilities at the conclusion of World War II as a result of their victory. The victorious powers became the supreme authority over Germany, and their inability to come to an agreement on a final peace treaty or on the fate of a reconstituted political authority in Germany led in time to the creation of two states.

In reality, the Soviets, the British, and the French—having paid such a horrific price in wars with Germany—feared the revival of German power in Europe and had little interest in any early reconstitution of a united German state. American attitudes were shaped less by history and more by the fear of Soviet power spreading west into Germany. Successive American administrations thus pressed the British and French to accept the need for prosperity in our zone of control in Germany, and for the advent of self-government. This, in turn, created the basis for the establishment of the Federal Republic of Germany (West Germany). Berlin remained under direct Four Power control, and in effect, the Federal Republic had the legal status of an interim state whose "final structure and borders" would be determined in an eventual peace settlement.[1] The Soviets, having subsequently set up a state in the area they occupied, argued that Germany as a country had ceased to exist and that it had been replaced by two states: the Federal Republic (West Germany) and the German Democratic Republic (East Germany).

The position of the United States, Britain, and France, as embodied in their 1952 treaty with the Federal Republic, was that international conditions precluded the reunification of Germany. Until a peace settlement could be negotiated, the Four Powers would retain their rights and responsibilities and the final borders of the German state would remain unresolved. The presumption of the treaty was that "Signatory States [would] cooperate to achieve, by peaceful means, their common aim of a reunified Germany enjoying a liberal-democratic constitution, like that of the Federal Republic, and integrated within the European community."[2]

While reunification (to be achieved through all-German elections) might have been the stated goal, no one acted to promote it. On the contrary, the division of Germany came to be an accepted fact. American policy makers, more sympathetic to the Germans than any of the other Four Powers, nonetheless came to see the German question as "secondary to the overall management of the U.S. relationship with the Soviet Union."[3] In time, West German leaders also adapted to this reality. Even Helmut Kohl, who more than other West German leaders maintained a public commitment to resolving the German question, dismissed the idea that Soviet leader Mikhail Gorbachev might offer unity to Germany at some point by saying as late as October 1988, "I do not write futuristic novels . . . What you ask now, that is in the realm of fantasy."[4]

And yet the fantastic became quite real, and in short order. Gorbachev introduced "new thinking" in 1986, and by 1988 there were profound stirrings in Poland and Hungary testing the limits of Soviet control and tolerance for increasing independence in Eastern European countries.[5] By the summer of 1989, Hungary set in motion a train of events that led to the Berlin wall coming down. When Hungary opened its border with Austria, essentially lifting the iron curtain there, East Germans began streaming into Hungary in order to get to Austria and flee to the West. Initially, the reformist Hungarian government would not allow the East Germans to cross the Austrian border, but it was also unwilling to force them to return home. Soon Hungary let them cross into Austria, triggering a virtual hemorrhage of East Germans seeking asylum. Even as the East German government blocked direct transit to Hungary, other routes were exploited, and soon swelling numbers of other asylum-seeking East Germans camped out in the West German embassy in Prague. Fearing contagion to their own population, the Czech government worked out a deal with the help of the West German foreign minister, Hans-Dietrich Genscher, in which the asylum seekers were allowed to go to West Germany after returning first to East Germany.

(The East Germans accepted this deal, hoping to end the embarrassing image of large numbers of asylum-seekers prior to the celebrations planned for the fortieth anniversary of the state.)

Rather than staunching the flow of East Germans trying to get out of their country, however, the deal gave it new impetus. And at this point, the Kohl-led government of West Germany began to drop all pretenses of working with the East German government and seeking only legal, controlled emigration. Though the Soviets began to issue warnings to the West German government of the danger of not respecting "postwar realities," Gorbachev was not prepared to countenance a draconian, violent crackdown in East Germany. Only such a crackdown might have blunted what were now daily demonstrations demanding change. Erich Honecker, the aging East German leader, knowing he could not get Soviet backing for such a crackdown, hesitated and was, himself, removed from power in mid-October, barely a week after Gorbachev had visited the GDR for the fortieth-anniversary celebrations. The reformers who took his place sought to end the crisis in East Germany by promising a new course. With repression no longer an option, pent-up frustrations gave way to continuing demonstrations, with five hundred thousand turning out on the streets on November 4. Hoping to demonstrate responsiveness and gain popularity, the reformist government eased restrictions on foreign travel.

There was no intention to remove the need for an exit visa. Nonetheless, on the night of November 9, Günter Schabowski, one of the new reformist leaders, gave a rambling press conference and, near the end of it, read the text of a new travel law that had just been approved by the Central Committee: "Requests for private trips abroad may be submitted from now on even in the absence of special prerequisites."[6]

Rumors quickly spread that all restrictions had been lifted, and huge crowds almost immediately assembled at the Berlin wall. The guards simply gave way and opened the wall. Crowds poured into West Berlin, and the next day—November 10—was a day of euphoria in Berlin. The unthinkable was now thinkable. The wall came down figuratively and then literally on the night of November 9–10, 1989, and by September 12, 1990, there was a ceremony in which Germany formally was reconstituted and Four Powers rights and responsibilities ended.

How did it happen with Soviet opposition and with low expectations from nearly every quarter? As late as October 25, the American embassy in Bonn was reporting to decision makers in Washington that "virtually no one believes reunification is the first order of business on the German-German agenda."[7] Only three days before the wall came down, Mikhail Gorbachev told his ambassador in East Germany, "Our people will never forgive us if we lose the GDR."[8] Yet, less than two weeks later it was unquestionably on the agenda, and the Bush administration fashioned a strategy to make sure that a reunified Germany would be a member of the NATO alliance.

THE BUSH ADMINISTRATION MAKES GERMAN REUNIFICATION IN NATO ITS OBJECTIVE

If it had been up to the State Department, the United States would not have embraced German reunification in NATO as a goal. The State bureaucracy was conditioned to think that unification would create instability and that the notion had few supporters even in the two Germanys. When Robert Zoellick, the politically appointed counselor and confidant of new secretary of state James Baker, asked a visiting West German general in early 1989 about German attitudes toward reunification, Roz Ridgway, the then assistant secretary of state for European affairs, rebuked him, saying unification was "the subject that all Americans are interested in and no German cares about."[9] The October 25 embassy cable cited earlier signaled a similar hesitancy even when the march toward reunification had clearly begun.

President Bush and his senior advisors saw it differently. As early as May 1989—well before the wall had come down—the president said in an interview that he would "love to see" Germany reunified.[10] The president and those around him believed that the new Soviet glasnost would lead to a far-reaching transformation in Europe and that no such transformation would be complete without the reunification of Germany. The cold war began there and it would end there. In the words of Robert Zoellick, an architect of the policy, "President Bush, Secretary Baker, and National Security Advisor Brent Scowcroft and their colleagues recognized that their decisions would shape Europe for decades to come . . . The U.S. aim was to unify Europe in peace and freedom, while seeking to avoid a 'Versailles victory' that invited its own destruction."[11]

The analogy to Versailles is critical for understanding how Bush's advisors applied statecraft to German reunification. It meant that Germany could not be singled out for special treatment—that there could not be "restrictions on German sovereignty" as a price of the country's unity. In Zoellick's words, "any limits imposed from the outside would create the potential for future grievances"—just as they had after Versailles, when the Allies required reparations that bankrupted Weimar Germany and set the stage for the Nazi accession to power.[12]

At the same time, Germany's history of violent conquest could not be ignored. The president and his advisors believed that if Germany was not embedded in NATO, it would be a source of danger. If neutral, it would seek security by gaining its own nuclear capability, which would put Europe on a nuclear hair-trigger and cause the nuclear nonproliferation regime to unravel as other states capable of developing nuclear weapons chose to do so. How could we ensure this would not happen and that Germany would be unified and in NATO?

Two considerations guided us. First, if we identified from the beginning with German aspirations and coordinated literally every step together with German leaders, they would not opt to remain neutral and make a separate agreement with the Soviets. Second, to win the confidence of others and lessen their fears of a German revival, Germany should be embedded in European institutions.

Ironically, it was the political leadership of the administration (not the mid- or working-level foreign affairs specialists) who had the broader, more historic perception of the far-reaching changes in Europe and tried to position us in advance of them. In fact, the most senior officials read Chancellor Kohl correctly and succeeded in winning his trust. Kohl saw almost instinctive U.S. support, came to count on it, and saw the United States removing the numerous obstacles to unification.

OBSTACLES TO ACHIEVING THE
BUSH ADMINISTRATION'S OBJECTIVE

To begin with, the Soviets, the British, and the French were not enthusiastic about reunification. For the Soviets, the division of Germany symbolized that Germany could never again threaten the Russian people. For the British and the French, a unified Germany rekindled harsh memories of German domination, and they worried that their respective weight in Europe would be diminished. While they might favor an end to the cold war and the division of Europe, they believed it should occur only gradually and in stages.

The British and French preferred stability, and they saw Mikhail Gorbachev as a Soviet leader in whom the West had a very high stake because he would make cooperation, not conflict and confrontation, a new reality. Margaret Thatcher and François Mitterrand, the British and French leaders, believed that German unification in NATO would be a political disaster for Gorbachev and would look like an unmistakable defeat, thus destabilizing Europe as well as the USSR.

Bob Blackwell, the national intelligence officer for the Soviet Union in the CIA, shared this concern and wrote that "if it were to appear that Soviet troops were being forced to retreat from the GDR, he [Gorbachev] had 'lost' Germany, and the security environment for the USSR was now more threatening, the domestic fallout—when combined with other complaints—could pose a threat to his position. Gorbachev at least has to have one eye on this contingency."[13]

Gorbachev apparently did. In late November 1989, he told Mitterrand that the day Germany unified, "a Soviet marshal will be sitting in my chair."[14] When movement toward unification began to gain momentum, he bluntly responded to a question about Soviet attitudes toward a united Germany being in NATO, saying "We cannot agree to that. It is absolutely ruled out."[15]

Some of Gorbachev's harsher public statements came after high-level meetings with either President Bush or Secretary Baker in which the actual discussions, even while reflecting Soviet disquiet over unification, were far more measured. Clearly, Gorbachev was under domestic internal pressure, and for understandable reasons.

No matter how you sliced it, the Soviet Union seemed to be losing. As Vadim Zagladin, a Gorbachev advisor, said, "There used to be two Germanys—one was ours and one was yours. Now there will be one and you want it to be yours."[16] But this was only part of the story. The Soviet position in Eastern Europe was unraveling, and there were increasing challenges emerging within the Soviet Union as Lithuania was pressing for independence. Everywhere Gorbachev looked, perestroika was causing problems, not providing salvation. In such circumstances, he could hardly appear to be acquiescing in a defeat of historical proportions— the removal of one of the major vestiges of the Soviet victory in the Great Patriotic War and its incorporation into the alliance that was arrayed against the USSR.

Moreover, Gorbachev knew he had leverage: the hesitancy of others in Europe and what he presumed would be German fear of Soviet opposition to unification. His conversations and communications with Thatcher and Mitterrand made clear that he knew where the British and French stood on unification. Thatcher told Gorbachev that "although NATO had traditionally made statements supporting Germany's aspiration to be reunited, in practice we were rather apprehensive."[17] Mitterrand was dubious, saying, "Reunification poses so many problems that I shall make up my mind as events occur."[18]

In reality, Thatcher was afraid (as she warned President Bush) that Germany would be "the Japan of Europe, but worse than Japan." She (and Mitterrand too) even worried that "the Germans will get in peace what Hitler couldn't get in war."[19]

Thatcher urged President Bush to focus on democratizing the GDR, not reunification, and after Helmut Kohl unveiled a ten-point plan for unification, her foreign minister, Douglas Hurd, said, "I believe that there is a need for an eleventh point which says that nothing will be done to destroy the balance and stability of Europe or create anxiety in the minds of people who have a right to be worried."[20]

In Germany such fears were bound to resonate domestically. The Social Democratic opposition was particularly sensitive to the anxieties of the neighbors and the Soviets. But it was not just the opposition; Foreign Minister Genscher was also uneasy. In fact, after Soviet foreign minister Eduard Shevardnadze publicly posed seven, obviously negative, questions about reunification, Genscher approvingly cited responses that the newspaper *Bild Zeitung* offered to the Shevardnadze queries—responses that called on Germany to consider abolishing NATO and the Warsaw Pact or reducing the American presence in Germany to a "symbolic contingent."[21] Genscher's ministry was convinced that the Soviets could not accept full NATO membership for a united Germany, and Genscher shared the view of Thatcher and Mitterrand that it was not in our collective "interest to defy Gorbachev if success meant the reformer's downfall and the end of perestroika."[22]

If Soviet, British, and French concerns were not enough, there was also the unease of the Poles over the issue of Germany's eastern border. The Poles worried that their western border, which included areas that had been annexed from Germany after the war, might now be part of claims a newly reunified Germany in NATO would make on Poland. They certainly added to the obstacles the Bush administration faced if it was going to achieve its objective.

THE MEANS TO OVERCOME THE OBSTACLES

The obstacles were formidable, but even in such circumstances, those who seize the initiative can shape the reality. The Bush administration was poised to do so, and had a partner in Helmut Kohl.

Seizing the initiative, however, requires more than just anticipation. It also requires a clear objective that reflects a good reading of the situation and of all the players. And it requires the ability to get out in front on the issue and force others to respond to your formulations and actions.

The day after Helmut Kohl presented his ten-point plan—a plan that would create unification in the form of a federation following a period of confederation—Secretary Baker laid out four principles to guide the approach to unification. The four principles had been drafted by Francis Fukuyama, who was my deputy on the Policy Planning Staff in the State Department. They were: (1) Self-determination for the Germans must be pursued without prejudice to its outcome. We should not endorse or exclude any particular vision of unity. (2) Unification should occur in the context of Germany's continued commitment to NATO, to an increasingly integrated European Community, and with due regard for the legal role and responsibilities of the Allied [Four] powers. (3) Unification should be gradual and peaceful. (4) The inviolability of borders must be respected as stated in the Helsinki Final Act.

This formulation was important and savvy from several standpoints: It addressed the perceived causes of potential instability: timing, pace, and the inviolability of borders. It also addressed at least implicitly a role for the Soviets, as one of the Four Powers, by referring to their "legal role and responsibilities." And yet it did so before anyone else could shape a definitive response to what Kohl had called for and also just prior to the summit with Gorbachev in Malta—a summit that was extremely important to Gorbachev and one he had no interest in ruining. (Two days after the Malta Summit with Gorbachev, President Bush, with an eye to cementing the four principles as guidelines for unification, repeated them with a slight modification in a speech to a summit of NATO leaders in Brussels.) By framing the issue, the administration provided the basis for how to resolve the unification question and also began a necessary conditioning process for transforming attitudes.

But the administration was not just framing the issue for leaders and senior officials in private. German unification was a very public issue. East Germans essentially rallied around unification and made it a public movement. History made unification a matter of concern for other publics in Europe and the Soviet Union. And no leaders could be indifferent to public concerns or interests. As such, transforming attitudes was an obvious key to overcoming the psychological obstacles to German unification in NATO; our words and actions had to be able to reach out and affect different publics.

Public diplomacy was a crucial tool for identifying with aspirations in Germany, addressing concerns elsewhere, and pointing the way to resolution. Framing was involved but so was presenting new ways to think about the changes taking place in Europe, particularly in Germany, ways that highlighted new, hopeful possibilities while also taking account of concerns about security and freedom. That was the meaning of Secretary Baker's speech in Berlin ten days after the Malta Summit, in which he offered a new architecture for Europe. Baker called for NATO to become more of a political and less of a security alliance, and for new forms of cooperation to make European integration—East-West— a new reality. Later in February, the same logic drove Baker to issue a high-profile public statement to explain the mechanism that had been privately hammered out to manage the unification process. The process, called "Two Plus Four," was designed in part to show Germans the practical means for making unification real, and to assure the Soviets that they would have a place at the table and that any outcome would be shaped by their participation and input.

"Framing" and "public diplomacy" represented one set of tools for overcoming the obstacles. They, of course, were a complement to the necessary forms of personal and private diplomacy that were required to orchestrate every move with the Germans, manage the hesitancy of the British and French, and bring the Soviets along to see that their needs would be addressed, particularly as they joined a train that they would not be able to stop.

The diplomatic efforts at the highest levels of the administration were remarkable for their extensive, intensive, and time-consuming nature. The president and the secretary of state conducted a highly personal diplomacy that involved an extraordinary number of face-to-face meetings with other leaders. Certainly phone calls were made, especially in the interim between meetings or to brief other leaders on the meetings that had just taken place with their fellow leaders. This was especially true with both Kohl and Gorbachev. Following a meeting with one, President Bush would place a call to brief the other on where things now stood. These were not perfunctory phone calls; they were highly substantive and were designed to move the process along or undo a false impression that might otherwise become rooted and create problems. Though these calls, and meetings at lower levels, were an essential part of the diplomacy, there can be no doubt that the face-to-face meetings at the president's and secretary's level were the heart of the effort.

To give an idea of the scope and intensity of the personal diplomacy of the president and the secretary of state, it is worth noting that President Bush met Chancellor Kohl in either strictly bilateral settings or on the margins of broader multilateral events nine times over a period of roughly one year. (Four of those meetings were in only bilateral settings.) He saw Prime Minister Thatcher eight times during the same period, of which three of the meetings were for exclusively bilateral purposes. He also saw President Mitterrand eight times at many of the same multilateral events, and had two meetings set exclusively for their bilateral discussions. With Gorbachev, he held two high-profile summit meetings during this period.

The Baker meetings were far more numerous, totaling close to thirty separate encounters with each of his German, British, French, and Soviet counterparts—many on the margins of multilateral events during this same time period. Of course, in many cases he visited their capitals for meetings, or they visited Washington. When he visited foreign capitals, he would see not only the foreign minister but also the president or prime minister—and, of course, he would have opportunities to speak publicly in each locale.

I cite the number of meetings—which was extraordinary and certainly has no parallel with any other president—only to give an indication of the scope of what was involved. But it was the quality of the meetings, and what was accomplished in them, that mattered. Because we were operating on the premise of identifying with the German aspirations even as we managed the fears of the other parties, both the president and the secretary put a premium on coordinating closely with the Germans before dealing with others.

The president's private meetings with Kohl did much not only to win the confidence of the German chancellor but also to bring him along on core questions. Their discussions in Germany in May 1989 (prior to a speech the president made in Kohl's home province) began a process in which President Bush showed his sympathy for unification and German aspirations. Their meeting in Brussels after the president's December 2–3, 1989, summit with Gorbachev deepened Kohl's appreciation for the president's conditioning efforts with Gorbachev, whose negative remarks had triggered similarly negative comments from Thatcher and Mitterrand at the summit. Finally, inviting Kohl to Camp David in February 1990—the first time a German chancellor had ever been a guest there—was critical for solidifying the Two Plus Four negotiating process (involving the two Germanys plus the United States, Russia, France, and the United Kingdom), and for gaining an unmistakable commitment from the chancellor that unification must take place with the new Germany a full member of NATO.

Meanwhile, the Americans feared the Soviets would trade their support of unification for strict German neutrality—which the president and his most senior aides believed would produce an enduring source of instability and competition between the blocs. Kohl looked to the United States, arguing that Gorbachev would concede on NATO only directly with Bush.[23]

In fact, the American-German consultation on the approach to the Soviets was remarkably close. When Baker went to Moscow to see Shevardnadze and Gorbachev in the middle of February 1990, we informed the Germans about what Baker planned to do and say prior to his arrival.

With Kohl scheduled to see Gorbachev immediately after our visit, I drafted (before we left Moscow) a detailed letter from Baker to Kohl that summarized what had transpired in the meeting: the key arguments Gorbachev used against unification; Baker's rebuttal; his explanation of why Germany in NATO was in Soviet interests and why a neutral Germany that might feel the need for its own nuclear deterrent was not; and, finally, our suggestions for how Kohl should handle his meeting with Gorbachev both in terms of tone and substance. Kohl was to tell President Bush that hearing from Baker prior to seeing Gorbachev had been extraordinarily helpful.

While Bush lobbied Kohl, Baker was working on each of his counterparts—Genscher, Hurd, Dumas, and Shevardnadze. Baker used his meetings and phone calls with Hurd and Dumas to mitigate Thatcher's and Mitterand's opposition. Mitterrand was keen to transform the European Community into the European Union, creating real integration that would allay French fears of German unification: in his eyes, a European Union, with a common currency and common policies, would create a European-Germany, not a German-dominated Europe. Here, too, Baker and Bush emphasized their support for European integration, provided Germany was a full member of NATO.

The Soviets required a special effort. The challenge was to balance two conflicting needs: winning Gorbachev's and Shevardnadze's confidence by showing that their concerns about unification would be addressed, while also leaving no doubt that it would be futile and counterproductive to try to prevent unification. Too much emphasis on one part of the equation would undermine the other.

Baker worked intensively to balance these messages for the Soviets. From February to August 1990 Baker saw Shevardnadze nearly every other week at some venue around the world. Of course, a full array of issues—ranging from arms control to bilateral economic relations to the internal changes taking place in the Soviet Union and Eastern Europe—were on the table. But German unification was a centerpiece of nearly every discussion. Bush saw Gorbachev less often, but made a point of calling him—sometimes to brief him after seeing Kohl, sometimes to go over an initiative such as putting a ceiling on U.S. and Soviet conventional forces in Europe. And this effort paid off, with Gorbachev telling Bush during the president's call to describe his conversations with Kohl at Camp David, "That is twice [you have called me], and I am in debt. I will have to draw some conclusions from this."[24]

The conclusion Gorbachev drew was that Bush and Baker were committed to helping him make perestroika succeed. This was Gorbachev's highest priority, and he staked everything on it. He understood this could not be achieved without moral support and enormous economic assistance from the West.

Not surprisingly, he had initially worried that President Bush might see the changes taking place in the Soviet Union and Eastern Europe as a sign of weakness that could be exploited. But at the Malta Summit, Bush began by presenting twenty different initiatives on U.S.-Soviet relations, including new proposals for arms control and economic cooperation. Gorbachev responded by saying he had been looking for tangible expressions of U.S. support—and now he saw it. Bush made a point then (and in subsequent meetings with Gorbachev) to emphasize how he had deliberately understated the U.S. response to the fall of the Berlin wall—drawing some domestic U.S. criticism for it—so as not to "complicate your life." And Gorbachev said he had noted that and appreciated it.[25]

Similarly, in his much more extensive meetings with Gorbachev and Shevardnadze, Baker dealt at length with Soviet fears. One time, in Moscow, Shevardnadze arrived directly from a Central Committee meeting in which he and Gorbachev had come under personal attack for "weakening" the Soviet Union and bringing great "joy" to Soviet enemies. Baker listened sympathetically and, on this and other occasions, talked of ways to take on the hard-liners.

But Baker was not just offering sympathy and advice. He was also working hard to persuade, explaining why it was important not to single out the Germans or to appear to be trying to deny them their aspirations; why a neutral Germany would feel the need to guarantee its security by having its own nuclear weapons—a result that no Soviet or American leader could want; why we should transform the institutions in Europe to take account of new realities; and why NATO, in these new circumstances, would not be a threat to the Soviet Union.

Sympathy and persuasion, while important, would likely have fallen on deaf ears if they had not also been accompanied by a serious effort to respond to Soviet needs. And here Baker went to great lengths both to be responsive and to show Gorbachev and Shevardnadze how we were being responsive: (1) We proposed and produced the mechanism, Two Plus Four, which gave Gorbachev an "explanation," permitting him to show that nothing was being decided without the Soviets or being imposed on them, and that they had a hand in shaping the outcome of unification. (2) We put together a package of nine assurances that addressed Soviet concerns on security, political, and economic issues in Europe and Germany. (3) We worked with the Germans to convey a promise from them on the ceiling of forces they would maintain even prior to the round of conventional arms talks in which these limits would be adopted as part of a broader reduction of forces in Central Europe. (4) We announced a trade agreement at a time when Gorbachev desperately needed one.

More than anything else, Shevardnadze told Baker that Gorbachev must be able to show his critics that Germany, the United States, and NATO were no longer threats to the Soviet Union. In July, when the Communist Party Congress would be held, Gorbachev would need to be able to show that the European landscape had been transformed and German unification in NATO could not become a new danger to the USSR.

With that in mind, the administration at the most senior levels formulated a declaration for the NATO Summit that would be held in parallel with the Communist Party Congress. President Bush decided to share the draft declaration only with other NATO leaders on the eve of the summit and to have Secretary Baker work on the draft at the summit itself. It would not be in the hands of bureaucrats, and Baker told his NATO counterparts, "We do not need to water down this document. It would be a mistake. We have one shot at this. These are different times. This is not business as usual."[26] Accordingly, the declaration was written in direct political language—not security or bureaucratic jargon. It pronounced a new pathway for NATO and Europe, making nuclear weapons "truly weapons of last resort"; eliminating U.S. nuclear artillery; proposing a new, less offensive military strategy; offering further cuts in conventional weapons; inviting the members of the Warsaw Pact to open liaison missions in NATO; and unveiling a declaratory commitment to nonaggression that invited the Warsaw Pact to reciprocate. Years of policy were being reversed in recognition of Gorbachev's needs. To make sure the declaration was produced intact, President Bush had raised the stakes by making leaders responsible for finalizing it and by having his secretary of state preside over the process for adopting it.

Proclaimed during the Party Congress, the declaration had the desired effect of undermining Gorbachev's challengers. Leaving little to chance, Baker had shared the draft with Shevardnadze even before it was adopted so that the Soviet foreign minister could use it internally to discredit the arguments of the hard-liners. Shevardnadze reported back to Baker that the NATO Declaration had been decisive in holding off their critics on Germany, saying, "Without the declaration, it would have been a very difficult thing for us to take our decisions on Germany . . . If you compare what we're saying to you and to Kohl now with our Berlin document, it's like day and night. Really it is heaven and earth."[27]

The Berlin document that Shevardnadze referred to was actually a speech he made at a ministerial meeting of the Two Plus Four on June 22, 1990 (the forty-ninth anniversary of the German invasion of the Soviet Union). In it, he retreated from understandings on unification that had been reached over the preceding three weeks: a Soviet agreement to respect German sovereignty upon unification, and Soviet acknowledgment that Germany was free to choose which, if any, alliance it wanted to join. In Berlin, Shevardnadze declared the opposite: the Four Power rights would remain even after unification, and for a five-year transition period Germany would remain split between NATO and the Warsaw Pact, with the alliance issue remaining open after that.

How was it possible to manage the situation, given such a reversal? By using one other mechanism or tool that was critical to maintaining and lubricating the high-level personal diplomacy of the president and the secretary—special back channels. In this case, my relationship with Sergei Tarasenko—Shevardnadze's chief assistant and confidant—proved indispensable. Normally I would coordinate with Tarasenko before the meetings to avoid surprises or to find out where there were problems that would have to be managed; in this case we had not had the opportunity to do so. When I rushed to see Tarasenko after the speech, to find out what had happened, he explained that Shevardnadze had been forced to present a Politburo-drafted statement, and that he and Gorbachev would act on the previous understandings as long as we were tough in response to this statement and could deliver clearly on the changed nature of NATO by the time of the Party Congress.

On this and other occasions, the back channel with Tarasenko made it possible to understand a Soviet move and how U.S. or German responses might affect the maneuverings in Moscow; it allowed us to explain what we could and could not do; and it also permitted us to design the words and actions that each of us could use to help the other, knowing when the timing was right to take a new step or respond to a challenge. There were other back channels with the Germans—Robert Blackwill, at the National Security Council, worked discreetly with Horst Teltschik, Chancellor Kohl's national security advisor, and Robert Zoellick built a relationship of profound trust with Frank Elbe, Hans-Dietrich Genscher's right-hand man. (At certain junctures, we would put Tarasenko and Elbe together to try to ameliorate German-Soviet problems and prepare for crucial meetings.)

The back channels enabled us to prevent misunderstandings, to manage them when they occurred, and to condition attitudes of decision makers in private. Without the back channels, the trust that was required to manage the process would have been far more difficult to achieve.

Of course, the ability to build trust also depended on the character of the personal diplomacy conducted by the president and the secretary, who were each active in solving problems that emerged at different points. President Bush secretly mediated the German-Polish problems on their border, problems created by Kohl's hesitancy, for political reasons prior to Germany's election, to recognize openly the existing border. To defuse the issue, President Bush called Kohl prior to Polish prime minister Tadeusz Mazowiecki's visit to the White House and worked out language on the border issue that Kohl would discreetly commit to and that Bush would privately show Mazowiecki, with the American assurance that this language would be incorporated into a German-Polish treaty after unification. Mazowiecki accepted Bush's assurance.[28]

CONCLUSIONS

American statecraft in producing German unification in NATO was successful for multiple reasons: The administration at the highest levels anticipated the issue and put it in the larger context of sweeping changes in the landscape of Europe; it developed a clear objective and forged deep trust with the main driver in the process, the German chancellor; it moved quickly to gain control of the agenda and it framed the issue for all to deal with; it used public diplomacy not to shape our image abroad but to reinforce how we framed the problem by appealing to different European publics in terms they could understand; it reflected the enormous time and the energy the president and the secretary of state spent in personal diplomacy with their counterparts; it used back channels to underpin and smooth the personal diplomacy and to avoid misunderstandings; it developed a mechanism (Two Plus Four) to steer the unification issue and create a basis for resolving the legal and political problems; and it managed those parties most likely to be able to derail the process (principally the Soviets) by combining responsiveness and firmness, and ensuring that Gorbachev and Shevardnadze had a public and private "explanation" for the process and the outcome.

Notwithstanding all this, the process of German unification relied on good fortune and luck, too. While the administration certainly read Gorbachev well, and as in all good statecraft, developed and used its leverage effectively, Gorbachev was indecisive and failed to use Soviet leverage to force us to change or modify our objectives. He made tough statements from time to time, but he assumed the British and French would do more to oppose unification, and certainly not give a unified Germany full membership in NATO. He overestimated their readiness to resist the American president and slow the diplomatic onslaught that the United States created. And he was reluctant to create a crisis with the United States or Germany because his priority was perestroika and he needed our support.

Luck and timing will be a part of dealing effectively with any issue. The more effectively leaders position themselves, the more effectively they anticipate events and read circumstances, the more likely they will be to take advantage of moments and the "luckier" they may be. And, here, timing is to foreign policy as location is to real estate. Seizing moments is critical. By definition, they don't last and can easily be lost. The very concept of a window of opportunity is bound by time; fail to act, and the window closes.

Nowhere was this "truth" more clearly revealed than in the case of German unification. The critical Party Congress and NATO Summit came in July 1990. On August 2, Iraq invaded and seized Kuwait. Had the invasion come on May 1, would the president of the United States and his secretary of state have been able to devote the time, effort, energy, and resources to German unification? There can be little doubt about the answer to this question. As it happened, the pursuit of unification and the trust that was developed with Gorbachev and Shevardnadze strengthened our hand in dealing with what has become known as the first Gulf War. Before turning to that case and its contrasts with the lead-up to the ongoing war in Iraq, let me first discuss another European case: the collapse of Yugoslavia, the war in Bosnia, and the war's resolution.

3.

{ CASES OF STATECRAFT }

Bosnia

During the cold war, Yugoslavia was a unique Communist country in Europe. It did not share a border with the Soviet Union; it fought Nazi occupation during the Second World War, led by a partisan—Josip Broz Tito, who subsequently became its leader—and it was not liberated by the Soviet army. Tito broke with Stalin after the war, unwilling to be simply a tool of the Soviet leader. As the leader of Yugoslavia, Tito was a fierce nationalist, determined to keep Yugoslavia intact as a country and free of Soviet domination. While his strongman and strong-arm rule might have held Yugoslavia's diverse ethnic groups together in their respective republics, the pressures for disintegration grew in the decade following Tito's death in 1980.

Serb nationalism, in particular, became an increasingly potent force and was used by Slobodan Milošević to build his power and his following in Serbia. His language invoking a greater Serbia incited passions among Serbs who had historically felt victimized and it played on the fears and the separatist impulses of the Croats, Slovenians, and Bosnian Muslims. But his actions weren't limited only to orations; using the Yugoslav National Army (a force that came to be dominated by the Serbs), he began to arm ethnic Serbs and form large paramilitary forces, especially in the Serbian parts of Croatia and Bosnia. By early 1990, there were frequent skirmishes in Croatia and a strong independence movement in Slovenia.

Independence in Slovenia could not be viewed in isolation. Should Slovenia declare itself independent, it would trigger other cascading developments: Croatia would likely follow suit; Serbia would undoubtedly try to separate the Serb part of Croatia and join it to Serbia and act to do the same in Bosnia. For its part, Croatia might also seek to take the part of Bosnia dominated ethnically by Croats. In short, Slovenia's declaration of independence would set in motion not just the unraveling of Yugoslavia but also a widening civil conflict. And yet in early 1990 when visiting Belgrade, Lawrence Eagleburger, deputy secretary of state, in commenting on how the United States would respond to a Slovenian declaration of independence, said that while we hoped Slovenia would not leave the federation, we would not do anything to force it to reverse its policy.[1]

Eagleburger was well aware of the consequences of a Slovenian move toward independence, but was also dubious that much could be done to stop an unfolding tragedy, and highly fearful that Yugoslavia would become a quagmire. Earlier in his career, Eagleburger had served as the American ambassador in Belgrade, so his views on Yugoslavia carried special weight. But he was not operating in a vacuum, and he understood this very well. He was well aware that the unfolding drama in Yugoslavia was more a sideshow for the president and the secretary of state than a main event. Their preoccupation was managing the transition in the Soviet Union and ending the cold war; they focused on Gorbachev and how to respond to his needs even while they worked with the states of Eastern Europe newly freed from the Soviet grip. They looked to develop a new security architecture to shape a world no longer governed by the realities of the cold war.

Perhaps the disintegration of Yugoslavia, with the potential for civil war, ethnic cleansing, refugee flows, and even the spread of conflict, should have been seen by the administration as a threat to the institutions they hoped to construct in a new Europe. However, this presupposed a full appreciation of what was going to unfold in Yugoslavia. While Deputy Secretary Eagleburger believed the situation was bad and was going to get worse, he and the administration's decision makers viewed the conflict as localized. It might have tragic consequences for the Bosnians in particular, but the war was unlikely to spread and engage our broader stakes in Europe; given our other priorities, it was not worth the investment.

Secretary Baker shared the view that, unlike in the Persian Gulf, our vital national interests were not at stake. He later wrote, "The Yugoslav conflict had the potential to be intractable, but it was nonetheless a regional dispute. Milošević had Saddam's appetite, but Serbia didn't have Iraq's capabilities or ability to affect America's vital interests, such as access to energy supplies. The greater threat to American interests at the time lay in the increasingly dicey situation in Moscow, and we preferred to maintain our focus on that challenge."[2] So our focus remained elsewhere as Yugoslavia moved toward disintegration and then, in 1991, devolved quickly into conflict.

LIMITED OBJECTIVES, MANY OBSTACLES

In the case of the Bush administration's response to the breakup of Yugoslavia and the war in Bosnia, the obstacles to American involvement largely shaped the administration's determination to stay on the sidelines of the conflict. Aside from rhetorical support for efforts to stop the fighting, there was no real stomach for a serious intervention, even one that was only diplomatic. Five factors drove the Bush administration's approach to Bosnia.

First, as Secretary Baker indicated, we had other priorities. The Soviet Union, our main preoccupation and rival for more than forty years, was going through a transition. Its leader who sought partnership with us, was under increasing threat, and the country itself appeared on the verge of unraveling. With thousands of nuclear weapons in Soviet arsenals, it was understandable that President Bush and Secretary Baker would be focused on the USSR. It was the "dicey situation in Moscow," with its "global ramifications" that constituted a greater threat than Yugoslavia's disintegration.[3] Besides the concern of what would happen in the Soviet Union, there was also the sense of possibility in the Middle East, and as Baker was to say, "in the summer of 1991, we were already consumed by the Middle East peace process and close to getting the parties to the table."[4]

Second, the administration's leaders felt that Yugoslavia was a European problem and should be handled by the Europeans. With the cold war ending, the Europeans were looking to solidify a separate European identity and to assume clear responsibilities on the continent at a time when plans for European integration (known as "EC 92") were in the offing and presaged the transformation of the European Community into the European Union. If European leaders were anxious to demonstrate their capacity through the existing EC mechanisms to handle problems, the Bush administration was only too happy to let them deal with the Yugoslav crisis. John Shalikashvili, who served as chairman of the Joint Chiefs of Staff following his stint as the American four-star general commanding NATO, later described this reality very clearly: "We forget this now, but everywhere you went in Europe in 1991 and 1992 there was this enormous optimism about what the new Europe could do . . . The Europeans would handle this one, they were saying, and the Americans, who had just finished the Gulf war and were playing out their role as the overseer in the end of the Soviet empire, were only too glad to accommodate them."[5]

Third, the administration feared that to prevent Yugoslavia's disintegration and conflict would take a military intervention, and for Larry Eagleburger and Colin Powell, Shalikashvili's predecessor as the chairman of the Joint Chiefs of Staff, it looked like Vietnam all over again. Each saw us being dragged into an ethnically driven conflict that would know no end, that would inflict high casualties on our forces, and that the American public and political leaders would tire of very quickly.[6] While there were some in the military, such as Chief of Staff of the Air Force Merrill McPeak, who believed that American air power could make quick work of the Serbs as they escalated the conflict in 1991, they were in the minority. Powell, especially, viewed airstrikes as the first step on a slippery slope toward a quagmire. The last thing he wanted after the Gulf War, which seemed to have ended the Vietnam syndrome, was to be sucked into a messy civil war again. As he wrote in a *New York Times* op-ed in 1992, "You bet I get nervous when so-called experts suggest that all we need is a little surgical bombing or a limited attack. When the desired result isn't obtained, a new set of experts then comes forward with talk of a little escalation. History has not been kind to this approach."[7]

Fourth, the administration's leaders had been going full bore, moving seamlessly from one crisis to the next from the onset of the Yugoslav conflict. When Larry Eagleburger was in Yugoslavia in February 1990, the president and Jim Baker and their teams were in the midst of working intensively on German unification. The high point of that German unification process passed just prior to Saddam's invasion of Kuwait, which kept them all absorbed until the spring of 1991, when the internal pressures and economic and political challenges to Gorbachev became far more acute. When the Serbian siege of Dubrovnik occurred in the beginning of October 1991, Secretary Baker was consumed with the aftermath of the failed coup against Gorbachev and putting together the Madrid peace conference. In short, it was not only other preoccupations that precluded involvement in the unfolding Yugoslav disaster, it was also fatigue. Taking on a conflict that was seen as largely localized, someone else's problem, and too hard in any case, was simply more than the Bush administration—whose leaders were already emotionally and intellectually drained—was ready to contemplate.

Fifth, there were also domestic political realities. By 1992, with his poll numbers dropping in no small part because he seemed interested only in foreign policy and not domestic needs, the last thing President Bush needed was to look like he was going to go to war over another distant problem.

THE BUSH ADMINISTRATION'S LIMITED MEANS

Notwithstanding the many factors limiting the Bush administration's involvement in Bosnia, it did make a belated effort to stem the violent breakup of Yugoslavia. As violence grew in 1991, and efforts by the EC to mediate the conflict yielded little, Secretary Baker made a one-day trip to Belgrade to see if it was possible to forestall the impending scenario of unilateral declarations of independence and the almost certain civil war that would ensue. In what amounted to a shuttle in one building, he met with the leaders of each of the republics and found either a strange fatalism from some of his interlocutors or outright lying from those such as Milošević, who denied arming paramilitary Serb forces and fomenting ethnic conflict. While Baker pleaded to avoid unilateral actions and warned Milošević of the consequences of promoting violence, there were no teeth in the warnings.

One day's commitment to discussions was unlikely to have much effect on any of the leaders, and it did not. Still, it was not too late to prevent Milošević's ethnic cleansing, even though he was becoming increasingly brazen in spelling out his intentions. During the same month of Baker's visit, Milošević had lunch with the EC ambassadors and told them that if Yugoslavia broke up, he would carve out a new Serbia. He explained that he cared little about Slovenia but he would join the Serb-populated areas of Bosnia, Croatia (especially Krajina), and Montenegro into a Greater Serbia.[8] Milošević undoubtedly was testing what the likely response would be to taking territories from his neighbors as Yugoslavia dissolved, and he soon found out that egregious actions on the part of the Serbs would provoke little reaction.

In early October 1991, Serb forces imposed a siege and inflicted a prolonged artillery and naval bombardment on Dubrovnik. It was a signal event, a test for Milošević to see what he could get away with before facing an international reaction. Though Dubrovnik did not present a difficult military problem, with Serb artillery and naval guns highly vulnerable, there was no Western military reaction. Soon a more cruel and brutal Serbian assault against the Croat city of Vukovar set in motion a deepening pattern of ethnic cleansing.

As violence between Serbs and Croats worsened in 1991, the UN Security Council adopted a resolution calling for an end to the conflict and imposing an arms embargo on all parties in Yugoslavia—a response that put the aggressor and victim in the same category. When the UN negotiators worked out a cease-fire in Croatia in early 1992, with Krajina under Serbian control, the Yugoslav National Army moved its armor and artillery forces from Croatia to Bosnia. While Croatia was not landlocked and could get arms, the same was not true for the Bosnian Muslims— who remained largely at the mercy of both Serbs and Croats.

When the Slovenian and Croatian declarations of independence came in 1992, with the encouragement of the Germans and the Italians, the conflict widened. By late spring, the signs of ethnic cleansing became more apparent and more gruesome, especially in Bosnia. With the systematic bombings of the Bosnian capital, Sarajevo, and the exposure by journalists of Serb-created concentration camps, the killings of all Muslim males in some Bosnian villages, and the expulsion of Muslims in others, the Bush administration supported efforts by the UN to rein in the Serbs, impose economic sanctions on them, and provide some protection and humanitarian assistance to the Bosnians.

But the UN forces that were sent were small in number (twelve thousand in all), and their mandate was weak and very limited. The so-called UN protection force (UNPROFOR) offered little protection in practice, and the U.S. military remained deeply averse to any involvement in Bosnia. By late 1992 the Serb irregulars and the Bosnian Serb army that Milošević had created had seized a great deal of Bosnian territory and forced 750,000 Muslims from their homes.

With the atrocities no longer hidden from public view, and shocking pictures of the concentration camps appearing in the summer of 1992, presidential candidate Bill Clinton denounced the Bush administration for standing by and doing little in the face of gross human rights violations and Serb aggression. He called for a change in policy, and supported air strikes against Serbs and an end to the arms embargo against the Bosnian Muslims, the main victims at this juncture of Serb aggression.

In effect, Clinton the candidate was calling for a policy of "lift and strike": lift the arms embargo that had been voted by the UN Security Council but punished the weak Bosnians far more than the arms-laden Serbs, and strike the Serb forces using significant air power. However, not only did the Bush administration and the U.S. military oppose such a policy, but also our allies, particularly the British, French, and Dutch, who made up the bulk of UNPROFOR, were dead set against any such posture. Their forces were on the ground and were too small to protect the Muslims, and unfortunately too weak even to protect themselves from retribution by Serb forces.

Nonetheless, after the 1992 election, then secretary of state Lawrence Eagleburger sought to get the Bush administration to adopt a lift-and-strike policy and was authorized to sound out the Europeans on the idea. They rejected it, but there was one final warning—this time one that implied real coercion—before President Bush left office. In what became known as the Christmas warning, President Bush, in a message to Milošević, warned that "In the event of conflict in Kosovo caused by Serbian action, the United States will be prepared to employ military force against Serbians in Kosovo and in Serbia proper."[9] Kosovo, an enclave along the Albanian border with a population that was 90 percent Albanian and 10 percent Serb, had deep historic meaning to the Serbs. It was the place where in 1389, Serbs had committed suicide rather than surrender to the Turks. It was where Milošević had played on the Serbian sense of injustice to build his own following around a Serb nationalist calling. But it was also a place that could easily trigger a war with Albania and a broader conflict in the Balkans as a whole.

Here the Bush administration drew a clear red line. Had such a warning been made over Bosnia, Milošević might have contained his ambitions and spared his people and the Muslims enormous pain and suffering. Instead, the Clinton administration inherited the Kosovo warning and a Bosnia increasingly controlled by Serb forces with atrocities and ethnic cleansing continuing against the Muslims.

It also inherited the so-called Vance-Owen plan for ending the conflict in Bosnia. Former secretary of state Cyrus Vance and former British foreign secretary David Owen were UN envoys who made an effort to negotiate an end to the fighting. They put together a plan that would have created ten cantons in Bosnia: three with a Serb majority, two with a Croat majority, three with a Muslim majority, one mixed Croat-Muslim, and a special canton for Sarajevo. The Bush administration had quietly supported the plan, seeing it as the best possible solution available and one likely to stop the bloodshed at a time when no one was prepared to take tough measures against the Serbs.

In the end, what guided the Bush administration was an objective of "avoidance." We would support the efforts of others to stop the fighting, but would minimize our own involvement. The administration left the heavy lifting to the international community, which was similarly disinclined to protect Bosnia. The Christmas warning indicated that had the Bush administration viewed Bosnia in a different light, perhaps a different outcome could have occurred. But since it didn't perceive Bosnia as a serious problem, and didn't have the political will to intervene, it behaved uncharacteristically in this case, lacked effective statecraft, and left the cleanup to the next administration.

THE CLINTON ADMINISTRATION'S APPROACH:
NEW OBJECTIVE, SIMILAR MEANS

The new Clinton administration, however, did not like the Vance-Owen plan. For Clinton and those around him, the plan legitimized Serb gains made through a genocidal policy. While the administration was unwilling to attack the plan publicly, its coolness to it was unmistakable, and when the State Department spokesman, Richard Boucher, refused to comment on whether the Vance-Owen plan ratified ethnic cleansing, Owen later wrote that the no-comment answer was the equivalent of rubbing "salt in the wound."[10]

But if the president and his team wanted to change the policy, they failed to devise a plan for achieving the objective of ending the fighting in Bosnia. Confronting many of the same obstacles or constraints that had faced their predecessors, the Clinton administration lacked the will to act effectively in the Balkans. Implementing any kind of change on the ground would have required a pronounced diplomatic initiative to organize our European allies behind such action, willingness to deploy America's own military assets into the theater of conflict, and bureaucratic unity within the administration to implement decisions. From 1993 to 1995, the Clinton policy toward Bosnia contained none of these components at a level necessary to counter the increasingly deadly civil war in that country.

Our military was against any U.S. involvement, and our allies, who had troops on the ground, opposed the lifting of the arms embargo, fearing their forces would bear the brunt of more severe fighting in escalating confrontation. An American call for greater military pressure against the Serbs rang hollow, as the new administration was not prepared to put our forces at risk and the European forces were the ones exposed to the expected Serb retaliation. Our allies would be open to a shift in policy only if we wanted to assume the military burden and cost.

It might have been one thing to talk about such a shift in the campaign; it was another to implement it in office. Rather than launch a new policy, the Clinton administration launched a review of our policy in the Balkans. The review took three months and reflected the old divisions within a new administration. Some, most notably at the State Department and at the National Security Council, saw the stakes in moral and national security terms of allowing Bosnian Serb ethnic cleansing to go unchecked, and favored using force against the Serbs. Others, most notably the military, led by the chairman of the Joint Chiefs, Colin Powell, opposed any use of force, citing the likelihood of a quagmire. The compromise at the end of the review sounded much like the policy that candidate Clinton had appeared to embrace: lift and strike. Lift the arms embargo and provide Bosnian Muslims the arms to defend themselves, and using air power, strike decisively at Bosnian Serb and Serbian forces and infrastructure as necessary.

In May 1993, Secretary of State Christopher went to Europe to sound out the Europeans on such a policy shift. The operative words are *sound out*; he went to consult and try to persuade, not to present a policy that the United States was prepared to implement, particularly if it meant any U.S. military involvement. Perhaps, if he had gone to inform the allies of our new approach and how we intended to carry it out, the reaction might have been different. But if he was asking and not telling, then the answers were bound to be starkly negative—and they were. At every stop starting in London, Secretary Christopher heard clear rejections of lift-and-strike. Lifting the embargo would require revoking a Security Council resolution, and an increased flow of arms would only lead to an escalation in fighting that the British, French, and Dutch feared would ensnare their troops already on the ground. Adding air strikes against Serbs to that mix would only ensure Serb retaliation against the international contingent in Bosnia. If the United States wanted to shift the policy, it would have to take the lead with its own military forces being exposed to the consequences.

Secretary Christopher returned, declaring to President Clinton that lift-and-strike as a policy could be implemented only if the president were prepared to insist on it with the allies and enforce it with American forces. But at this stage of his administration, the president had other priorities. It was his domestic agenda that mattered—"it's the economy, stupid" was the refrain that had elected Clinton—and he was not about to squander his political capital on an issue in which he faced the very clear opposition of the U.S. military and the chairman of the Joint Chiefs of Staff, Colin Powell. Powell, the hero of the Gulf War, was in his last year as chairman and he, not Clinton, had stature on national security issues.

If anything, Clinton's reluctance to invest capital in Bosnia—notwithstanding his posture during the presidential campaign—made Christopher even more reluctant to press for greater U.S. involvement. Instead, after Christopher's European trip, the policy became one of containment of the conflict, even as the rhetoric remained tough toward the Serbs.

LIMITED OBJECTIVE, LIMITED MEANS

Unfortunately, Serb aggression against Bosnian Muslims continued, with the sieges and bombardment of Muslim cities and towns. The administration's options remained very constrained. Unwilling to risk alliance cohesion for the sake of Bosnia, hamstrung by the Pentagon's opposition to any role for U.S. forces, stung by the imagery of Black Hawk Down in Somalia and an inglorious American withdrawal of forces, and by the president's increased hesitancy to invest in Bosnia, the administration looked for ways to increase leverage on Serbia at a low cost.

One mechanism for doing so was the forging of a Croat-Muslim federation, and the administration succeeded in facilitating such a union in 1994. In the words of Secretary of State Christopher, "The two sides needed to turn their energies against the stronger and more threatening adversary, the Bosnian Serbs."[11] The federation was designed to create common cause between Croats and Muslims, both of whom had lost or were losing ground to Serb offensives, but the Croatian president's dislike of the Muslims made this a difficult basis on which to build leverage against the Serbs. Nonetheless, it did make a difference over time as Franjo Tudjman, the president of Croatia, permitted arms to reach the Muslims—of course, with the Croats keeping some of them for themselves. Later in 1995, with the Bihać pocket in Bosnia surrounded by the Serbs and with a slaughter of Muslims in the offing, the Muslims and Croats forged a common front. They fought against the Serbs, with the Croats, in particular, taking advantage of the Serbs' being overextended, and began to turn the tide of battle on the ground.

The administration sought to build leverage in other ways as well. In an effort to improve coordination and present a more united front against Serbia, the administration created a new forum called the Contact Group. It consisted of the United States, the United Kingdom, France, Germany, and the Russians. If nothing else, the messages to Milošević and the Serbs would be more in sync and would include the Serbs' traditional friends and protectors, the Russians. By July 1994, the Contact Group developed a peace plan, with a detailed map that placed 51 percent of Bosnia under the Croat-Muslim federation and 49 percent for the Bosnian Serbs. The Muslims and Croats accepted the plan—

after all, they would be recovering roughly 20 percent of the territory that had been lost—and the Serbs rejected it. Nonetheless, the plan remained a focal point of Contact Group efforts.

In addition to forging the Croat-Muslim federation and the Contact Group, the administration also sought to pressure the Serbs through at least limited use of air power. While not being able to persuade the Europeans to accept a policy of lift-and-strike, the administration did win support for NATO air strikes in response to Serb threats against the six safe areas in Bosnia—Muslim enclaves protected by UNPROFOR. There was a price, however: in order to support the U.S. proposal, the Europeans required the creation of a dual-key arrangement whereby both NATO and the UN had to sign off on when, where, and how such air strikes would occur before they could be authorized. In reality, dual-keys became an inhibitor, not a facilitator, of air strikes, as the UN machinery was rarely willing to go along with the proposed strikes. Even when they were agreed upon, as in the case of Serb threats and the shelling of Bihać, one of the safe areas, in November 1994, the air strikes were so limited as to be described as "pinpricks."

If it wasn't the difficulty of reaching agreement in NATO and with the UN high command, it was the concern about triggering retaliation against the British, the French, or the Dutch forces that limited the application of air power even when air strikes might have been approved in response to Serb threats. By 1995, the fear of Serb retaliation was replaced by the fear of the Serbs' taking UNPROFOR troops as hostages— which the Serbs did in the spring of 1995 when air strikes against Serb ammunition dumps and weapons were authorized in response to renewed Bosnian Serb shelling of Sarajevo. The Serbs seized more than 350 UN peacekeepers and chained them to ammo dumps and bridges— the possible targets of the air strikes. Rather than being frightened by very limited air strikes, which basically signaled how little the international forces were prepared to do, the Serbs began to turn the UN peacekeepers into human shields to protect what they valued from any such attacks. That ended the air strikes, since protecting UN forces became more important than protecting the Bosnians and made the safe areas safe only for Serb attacks.

As the humiliation of UN forces became more pronounced, the frustration within the administration became more acute. When Jacques

Chirac, the new president of France, declared that the humiliation of French forces was unacceptable, there was pressure from the French to increase the number of troops on the ground—at least to be able to protect themselves. Chirac's insistence at the G-7 meeting that a new policy must be implemented in Bosnia helped to foster a new look at options within the Clinton administration.

Both Warren Christopher and National Security Advisor Tony Lake began looking at alternatives built around not pulling the UN forces out but rather securing them, and tying a more secure presence to a push for a comprehensive diplomatic solution in Bosnia. Lake, in particular, generated options for producing an endgame diplomatically.

Any serious diplomatic effort to solve the Bosnian problem, however, required having serious leverage on the Serbs, and that was still missing. But that was about to change, as the Serbs overplayed their hand and the Croats began effectively using their military forces for the first time.

MORE AMBITIOUS OBJECTIVE, MORE AMBITIOUS MEANS

President Clinton's frustration had grown with a policy that left us appearing weak and irresolute; in response to his increasing anger over the choices he was being left with, the administration began to wrestle with possible ways to change what Secretary Christopher described as the "problem from hell." Coincident with the administration exploring new options, on July 6, 1995, the Serbs launched a brutal new assault, on Srebrenica, a "safe area" protected by a Dutch contingent of UNPROFOR, and on its population of forty thousand Muslims. As the onslaught worsened, the Dutch forces initially watched, and then fled. NATO belatedly bombed a few Serb sites, but it was too little and too late. By July 11, the Serbs had seized Srebrenica, and five days later they had killed seven thousand Muslim men and boys. Not satisfied with having absorbed Srebrenica, the Serbs seemed poised to go after two other supposedly protected areas—Žepa and Goražde.

Srebrenica was too much to swallow. The Pentagon's civil and military leaders—Secretary William Perry and Chairman of the Joint Chiefs John Shalikashvili—both saw the massacre as a decisive turning point. Now each felt that for the United States and NATO not to respond would put the alliance and our standing in the world at risk. For

Shalikashvili (or Shali, as he was known), the moral fabric of the West and NATO was literally at stake. If, before, we were reluctant to act because it might tear NATO apart, now Shali feared our failure to respond would threaten NATO's future. Perry saw the challenge in similar terms, saying, "The issue was not taking [UN] peace-keepers hostage, the issue was taking the whole policy of the international community hostage."[12] Previously, it was the Pentagon's leadership that resisted more aggressive policies in Bosnia; now they were prepared to take the lead in creating new rules, with Perry saying that the answer to a threat to Goražde or any other safe area must not be pinpricks but a "massive air campaign."

John Major called a conference to respond to the shock of Srebrenica, and the Clinton administration prepared the ground for a new approach militarily, with President Clinton telling French president Chirac that any attack on the safe areas should be met by a sustained air campaign designed to "cripple" the Serb military capability. The London conference, with some administration arm-twisting still required, produced a new consensus on what became known as the "Goražde rules": any Serb attacks against the safe areas would be met by sustained and decisive use of air power throughout Bosnia. To facilitate such responses, the "dual-key" system would be modified by removing civilian UN officials from the decision-making process.[13]

Although ironing out how the Goražde rules would work in practice still proved difficult, involving a thirteen-hour meeting of the NATO foreign ministers to nail down the specifics, a clear threshold had been crossed. Srebrenica in this sense triggered a profound change in how Serb aggression would be dealt with by the United States and its allies. Two other factors combined to transform the realities in Bosnia fundamentally.

First, the fortunes of the war changed dramatically on the ground. The Serbs not only overplayed their hand before the world, finally going too far and triggering a response, but they were also overstretched with their forces. When the Croats came to the defense of Bihać on July 25, they made quick work of the Bosnian Serb forces. Soon thereafter, the Croats launched an offensive against the Bosnian Serb forces in Krajina, the Croatian area taken by the Serbs in 1991; even though the State Department had urged the Croats not to widen the war, the latter soon successfully forced the Serb forces and civilians to flee Krajina. By early

August, "for the first time in the four-year Balkan conflict, the Serbs had suffered a significant military defeat."[14] Suddenly, the balance of forces on the ground had changed.

Second, the administration also decided to go for a diplomatic solution to the conflict. Almost simultaneously with the Croat offensive, the administration considered certain "endgame" papers for bringing the conflict to a conclusion. The president saw an opening and believed, in his words, that we needed to "bust our ass to get a settlement in the next few months . . . We've got to exhaust every alternative, roll every die, take risks . . . If we let this moment slip away, we are history."[15]

From July to August 1995, the dynamics in Bosnia were transformed. Instead of the Muslims being on the brink of defeat in Bihać, with other safe areas about to fall and with talk increasing of having to withdraw UNPROFOR in humiliation, suddenly the Serbs were on the run, losing territory; the West for the first time was ready to threaten the meaningful use of force; and the Clinton administration was about to present a comprehensive plan for settling the conflict.

Not only did the administration formulate a seven-point plan for ending the conflict, but National Security Advisor Tony Lake took an interagency delegation with him to Europe to present the plan. Unlike Christopher, Lake was not going to consult on the virtue of the plan; he was going to inform Europeans of what the United States had decided and how we would proceed. Like James Baker during the first Gulf War, he would ask in private for their support of a plan that would go ahead whether or not European countries were prepared to go along with us.

This time the European leaders, given four years of warfare, with 300,000 deaths and 1.2 million refugees, were ready to admit that they could not deal with Bosnia and were ready to follow the American lead. Everywhere the Lake team went they found strong support for a plan that drew on the Contact Group's 51:49 solution: a unified Bosnian state with two autonomous entities involving the Croat-Muslim federation and the Bosnian Serbs who had a special relationship with Serbia; and a readiness to end the sanctions regime against Serbia and produce a broad economic reconstruction plan as part of a diplomatic settlement.

Moreover, for the first time, embedded in the plan was a serious combination of carrots and sticks to be employed with all sides. If the Muslims cooperated and the Serbs blocked an agreement, the embargo on arms to the Muslims would be lifted and the Serbs would face massive air strikes in support of the Muslims; if the Muslims didn't negotiate in good faith and the Serbs did, there would be a lift-and-leave policy—namely, there would be a lifting of the embargo and sanctions against the Serbs, no training or arms for the Muslims, and no air strikes against the Serbs.

This new American policy had to be implemented. Richard Holbrooke, the assistant secretary of state for European affairs, was chosen to carry out the American commitment to its new policy. He had long called for a serious U.S. intervention to stop Serb aggression, the atrocities, and the war itself. Now he would lead a small team to do so. He launched a series of shuttle missions to make an all-out effort to end the war.

MEANS TO A DIPLOMATIC END: THE HOLBROOKE SHUTTLES

During the first of his shuttles, his team could not fly to Sarajevo, given the siege, and had to travel on the winding, narrow Mt. Igman Road to get there. In trying to maneuver around a truck on the narrow mountain road, the French armored personnel carrier in which a number of the team members were riding went over the side of the road and rolled down a cliff. Ambassador Robert Frasure, Deputy Assistant Secretary of Defense for European Affairs Joseph Kruzel, and U.S. Air Force colonel Nelson Drew were killed in the accident. The loss of three key members of the team—representing the State Department, the National Security Council staff, and the Pentagon—redoubled the sense of mission and obligation to finish what the team had started.

Holbrooke embodied the president's attitude of pulling out all the stops in trying to forge an agreement that would end the war. The first shuttle mission was geared toward probing each side's intentions and interests. The second mission would be designed to outline the broad parameters of a settlement. It was preceded by a Bosnian Serb mortar attack on Sarajevo that killed thirty-seven people. Holbrooke understood that he would have no credibility with either the Muslims or the Serbs if the "Goražde rules" were not implemented. President Clinton agreed, giving the command that "we have to hit 'em [the Bosnian Serbs] hard."[16]

To avoid the hostage-taking of the past, ninety-two UN troops were withdrawn from Goražde, and a massive bombing campaign started before the Holbrooke team arrived in Belgrade. Though Holbrooke expected Milošević to be tough in their meeting, the Serb leader surprised the team by providing them with a letter signed by the seven members of the Bosnian Serb leadership and by the patriarch of the Serb Orthodox Church agreeing to join a negotiating delegation in which Milošević would have the final word. In addition, Milošević agreed in the meeting to the 51:49 ratio for Bosnia as the basis for negotiations. For one year, Milošević had resisted representing the Bosnian Serbs and the 51:49 ratio—yet now, under the pressure of intensive bombing of the Bosnian Serbs, he was showing how responsive he could be. Only two hours into the meeting did Milošević ask for a bombing halt to help the negotiations; Holbrooke responded that the shelling of Sarajevo must first stop and that the Bosnian Serb guns must be withdrawn from around the city.

Holbrooke used the second shuttle mission to get an agreement on a general legal and political framework for Bosnia. He proposed that the three foreign ministers—Serb, Muslim, and Croatian—meet within a week in Geneva to endorse this framework, and succeeded in getting them to do so. While it took nonstop talks to make sure all would show up, and there were crises up to the last minute, on September 8, 1995, the three foreign ministers came and signed what became known as the Geneva Principles: Bosnia would be one state with shared power between the Croat-Muslim federation and the Serbs; there would be free elections, human rights standards, binding arbitration of disputes, and parallel special relations with neighbors.

All this had been agreed in the context of a massive bombing campaign against the Bosnian Serbs. Coercion unmistakably worked, and Holbrooke was a master of knowing how to employ it. When the Bosnian Serbs subsequently betrayed their promises to pull artillery back from Sarajevo as part of the bombing pause Holbrooke had been working to negotiate, he pushed to resume the intensive bombing—and still pulled off the agreement on the Geneva Principles.

The third shuttle mission began with increasing pressure from within NATO and from the Russians to stop the bombing campaign. Both had objected to the use of American Tomahawks, with the Russians particularly angered over what they saw as coordination between the Croat-

Muslim ground offensive against the Bosnian Serbs and the Tomahawk attacks against Bosnian Serb infrastructure. NATO allies were also upset over targets being struck that they felt went beyond those that had been agreed upon. Within the Pentagon, our military was also saying we were running out of the "Option Two" targets that had been agreed upon, and they favored a bombing halt. Holbrooke and his team did not want to bring the bombing to an end but understood that, given the circumstances, it might be difficult to sustain it. At the outset of the third shuttle mission, therefore, they knew they might have to see what they could get from Milošević in exchange for a suspension of the bombing.

Once again the team was pleasantly surprised to see that if the bombing stopped, Milošević was ready to produce an end to the siege of Sarajevo by the Bosnian Serb forces. He asked Holbrooke and his team to meet the Bosnian Serb leaders, and after difficult discussions, they accepted an American plan in which they stopped all their offensive operations around Sarajevo, began to relocate their heavy weapons, allowed road access to Sarajevo, and permitted the opening of the city's airport for humanitarian missions —all in return for a halt to the bombing.

The Muslim leadership, believing that they were on the brink of decisive military victories, were not happy over the bombing halt. But even though the bombing was halted, the ground offensive led by the Croats continued. The Holbrooke team saw value in not stopping it prematurely, particularly because it was changing the realities on the ground and making the eventual negotiations on the map easier to conduct. Washington might favor an end to the Croat offensive, but Holbrooke and his team did not. They would press for restraint only at a juncture when the Croats and Muslims might turn on each other; otherwise, Holbrooke was reluctant to surrender leverage on the Serbs, and at one point he even urged Tudjman to take more towns in order to have land to give away once the negotiations commenced.[17]

As part of this same shuttle mission, Holbrooke and the team negotiated "further agreed principles" that fleshed out the Geneva Principles and were concluded in a second meeting of foreign ministers in New York. Much like the run-up to the Geneva meeting, this, too, came down to the last minute. The question of whether the Bosnian elections had to be direct and whether the office of the presidency would have "exclusively" foreign policy powers created a crisis, requiring nonstop negotiations not only in New York but also in Belgrade and Sarajevo. When Sacirbey, the Muslim foreign minister, appeared to back out of an agreement at the last moment, Secretary Christopher told him that if he did not relent and go along with the original understanding, President Clinton would announce the failure of the New York meeting and blame the Muslim government for it. With that, the further agreed principles were adopted by the three foreign ministers on September 26, 1995. In what became known as the "New York Principles," the powers of the joint presidency, the parliament, and the constitutional court were agreed.

Two days later, Holbrooke and his team set out on their fourth shuttle mission to the Balkans in six weeks. The purpose of this mission was to get an agreement and set a firm date for a peace conference and to produce a cease-fire throughout Bosnia. Milošević had already indicated that he wanted to come to a summit and was ready to deal; he had indicated as much by leaning on the Bosnian Serbs, pushing them to give up the siege of Sarajevo, and recognizing Bosnia as an independent state. Milošević wanted an end to the sanctions on Serbia and wanted to be accepted internationally. Tudjman was also keen for an agreement, having gained back most of the territory that mattered to the Croats and now beginning to see the Bosnian Serbs regrouping militarily. Only the Muslims were resistant; their leadership was divided and feared that any settlement might be a trick.

The peace conference was designed to have all the leaders and their delegations colocated and to conduct proximity talks, with the Holbrooke team acting as the principal go-between. Holbrooke wanted the talks to take place in the United States so that we would be able to control the setting, agenda, and course of the talks. Dictating the process would, in Holbrooke's eyes, give us more leverage to make the negotiations succeed. Holbrooke faced nearly united opposition to this from President Clinton's top advisors, who all feared that an American venue for the talks would magnify the costs of failure if they did not work. However, Holbrooke's argument soon carried the day within the administration, with the help and advice of Deputy Secretary of State Strobe Talbott and Tom Donilon, Secretary Christopher's chief of staff, on how best to craft his points. Concerns over European sensitivities about having the United States running everything resulted in instructions that Holbrooke work with the Contact Group on follow-up meetings or ceremonies to be conducted in a European capital. And, of course, the Contact Group would have a team at the site of the negotiations.

Holbrooke also wanted to be able to announce the cease-fire at the same time that he announced the peace conference. The Muslims, who were the most chary of the cease-fire and the peace conference, laid down stiff conditions for the cease-fire: restored utilities to Sarajevo, a demilitarized Banja Luka, and road access to Goražde. In addition, Alija Izetbegović, the president of Bosnia, wanted ten more days before a cease-fire would go into effect. Holbrooke used both the Croats and the Serbs to pressure the Muslims, and also exerted his own pressure, reminding Izetbegović of the risks he was running by letting the fighting continue too long, warning, "If you continue the war, you will be shooting craps with your nation's destiny."[18]

Finally, Izetbegović agreed that if the gas lines to Sarajevo were functioning and there was an open road to Goražde he would accept a ceasefire in five days, and he wanted Milošević's commitment to this. Holbrooke went to Belgrade but left two members of his team in Sarajevo. As Holbrooke worked to get Milošević's acceptance, he had an open phone line to Izetbegović to be sure he would not change his mind, and one to Washington for consultations; and over a period of three hours an agreement was reached on the cease-fire.

With that in hand, Holbrooke then worked the agreement on the announcement of the peace conference. This was October 5. The cease-fire was agreed to take hold on October 11, and the conference would begin two weeks later.

PEACEMAKING IN ACTION: THE DAYTON CONFERENCE

Prior to the beginning of the peace conference, intensive work was needed on several fronts. First, Holbrooke directed that a full-draft peace treaty be completed. He had had a small team in the State Department begin drafting in September on all legal questions, but now he had them working on a framework agreement and seven annexes that addressed disengagement and the cessation of hostilities, constitutional structure, arbitration, human rights, refugees and displaced persons, national monuments, and implementation. By October 15, they had put together at least the first cut of such a draft agreement. Soon thereafter, three annexes were added on the elections, public corporations, and NATO's implementation forces (IFOR) for carrying out any agreement that was concluded.

Second, discussions on IFOR needed to be conducted, and were complicated not only by different views within the administration on how extensive the role and missions of the forces might be, but also by the Russian desire to take part but not in a capacity subordinate to NATO.

Holbrooke's team took a maximal view on what would be required for the forces in terms of assisting refugee return, providing security for the elections, arresting war criminals, ensuring freedom of movement, and the like. In the Pentagon, fear of mission creep (the expansion of a project or mission beyond its original goals) led to a minimalist preference. The minimalists wanted to be only peacekeepers; the maximalists were far more geared toward state-building. General Shalikashvili eventually offered a compromise that would grant IFOR the "authority" to work in all such areas but not the "obligation" to do so—giving the forces great discretion on the scope of the mission. As for dealing with the Russians, this was managed by both Strobe Talbott on a general level—helping to ensure that Bosnia would neither spoil more general U.S.-Russian relations nor subvert the reformers in Russia—and on the military level by Secretary of Defense Perry. Though it took time, working with Russian defense minister Pavel Grachev, Perry was eventually able to finesse the participation of the Russian forces in a way that had the local Russian commander answering to the American general in charge of IFOR and not technically to NATO. (The former was acceptable to the Russians; the latter was not.)

Third, the Holbrooke team worked with the Europeans on all implementation issues—civil and military—while also trying to condition the different Balkan parties on what would happen once the peace conference convened. In the last and shortest shuttle mission prior to the conference, Holbrooke brought Carl Bildt of the EU and Russian foreign minister Igor Ivanov to meetings that started in Belgrade, where he announced that the peace conference would take place at Wright-Patterson Air Force Base, in Dayton, Ohio.

Throughout this period, the American effort effectively required managing three parallel sets of negotiations involving the Balkan parties, the NATO allies, and the Russians. All this, while also preparing the choreography of a major peace conference.

The peace conference represented a roll of the dice. Holbrooke saw it in "all or nothing" terms, understanding that it was essential to build the sense of what was at stake for all those involved. Ending this war would require a very clear awareness on the part of Milošević, Tudjman, and Izetbegović of not just what they could gain by success but what they would be certain to lose by failure. Ultimately the conference succeeded.

It went through different phases, with the first week designed to build some basis for progress by formalizing the federation agreement between the Croats and Muslims while also working out the one territorial issue that mattered to President Tudjman of Croatia, Eastern Slavonia, which was solely a Serbia-Croatia issue. In the first week, there was no movement on the core issues of the map or the constitution. Progress was very painful and slow throughout the second week—with most of the work being done by the American team shuttling between the sides after direct meetings of the parties proved to be counterproductive. Divisions within the Bosnian team were paralyzing them, and most of the movement tended to be driven by Milošević, who was anxious to reach agreement.

On the key issue of control over Sarajevo, it was Milošević who broke the stalemate, on day sixteen, by simply conceding the issue to the Muslims, telling them that after three years of shelling by the cowardly Bosnian Serbs, the Muslims had "earned" the city. With Dayton hovering on the brink of failure on day twenty-one, Milošević again acted: First, in conversations with Haris Silajdžić, he sought to resolve the key territorial stumbling block of getting the Bosnian Serb territory up to 49 percent, and then, when overcoming the differences on the status of the city Brčko became the only way to work out the territorial questions, he offered the compromise of arbitration by an international mediator to resolve the issue. He did not want Dayton to fail. He was ready for the conflict to end, and to gain the economic benefits that would result from that.

One of the factors that contributed to Milošević's concessions was Holbrooke's use not just of coercive means but also of positive inducements. Holbrooke wanted to suspend sanctions against Serbia at the beginning of the peace conference, believing that Milošević also needed to see the rewards at the right moment. While he faced opposition within the administration, Holbrooke read Milošević's desire for economic relief and manipulated it well.

The Bosnian Muslims on the last day exasperated Secretary Christopher and Holbrooke as they appeared unable to take yes for an answer, putting at risk all they had achieved through the agreement that was available. In the final hour, as the United States grew frustrated with the Muslims, Christopher told Izetbegović that there were no more deadlines and the United States needed an answer immediately. Izetbegović reluctantly agreed, and the Bosnian war was over—at least on paper.

For a conflict that the United States had wanted no part of during the Bush administration, and for which it had shown reluctance to assume any military obligations during the Clinton administration, America now was prepared to commit twenty thousand troops—one third of the IFOR troops—to help implement an agreement that U.S. leadership had produced.

CONCLUSIONS

The Bosnian case represents both ends of the spectrum in statecraft. During the Bush years, it was a conflict that was avoided. Fatigue from German unification and the first Gulf War reduced the inclination to be involved, and the president and his senior advisors rationalized our noninvolvement by convincing themselves that this was a conflict that Europe should manage. When ethnic cleansing became unmistakable, with the gruesome images of concentration camps in the summer of 1992, the administration supported the development and deployment of UNPROFOR; later, when Serb actions in Kosovo risked a possible expansion of the war, President Bush warned Milošević, but this came at the end of the administration.

For the Bush administration, this was the wrong war at the wrong time in the wrong place. Could more have been done to deter Milošević and his Greater Serbia ambitions? Almost certainly, but that required active involvement and a readiness to use coercive diplomacy that Milošević would have believed credible. It was not in the cards for an administration that did not believe in the stakes and that seemed guided by an objective more of avoiding involvement than of solving the conflict.

But the Clinton administration arrived in January 1993 with a sense of outrage over what Serbia was doing. Ethnic cleansing was decried, Serb aggression was not to be tolerated, arming the Muslims was called for, and stopping a conflict in the heart of Europe was certainly seen as an important American national security interest. And yet it took until the summer of 1995—and the massacre in Srebrenica—to finally move the administration to transform the situation and produce the use of force and diplomacy to end the war.

What is remarkable about the period from August 1995 through the end of the Dayton negotiations is that in many ways it is a model of effective statecraft. The objective was finally defined in a clear way and with a strategy to pursue it. The Clinton administration not only framed the objective in a way that generated support internationally, but also acted in a unified, disciplined fashion even when some differences remained internally. The marriage of force and diplomacy was carried out masterfully, particularly as we resisted alliance pressures to stop NATO's bombing of the Serb positions prematurely, and we also held off the calls to seek a cease-fire before the realities on the ground had changed to a point where they served the prospects of a negotiated settlement. The diplomacy itself was intense and nonstop, with coordination taking place simultaneously with the Contact Group, the Europeans, the UN, the Russians, and the various Balkan parties (including within the Muslims, between the Croats and the Muslims, and with Milošević and the Bosnian Serbs). And a sequence for negotiations was developed and implemented, culminating in the marathon of Dayton.

Throughout the course of Holbrooke's involvement, coercive means were exploited to build leverage, inducements were employed to render rewards for good behavior, and communication channels were used to inform, explain, and assuage. More than anything else, the Holbrooke team worked constantly to deal with Muslim fears and internal divisions, intervened whenever potential fissures between the Croats and Muslims threatened to erupt, acted to build Milošević's interest in managing the Bosnian Serbs, and spent time briefing the Europeans when the potential for their resentment at the Americans' running the show might have become a problem.

The assessment of the different parties, their stakes, and the incentives and disincentives that could be orchestrated to affect the parties was done well and often on the run, befitting an intensive effort. Could it have worked in 1995 without the Serb leader Slobodan Milošević's wanting an end to Serbia's isolation, an end to the sanctions, and international acceptability for himself? Probably not, but give credit to Richard Holbrooke and his team for reading him correctly and for understanding the dynamics of the Bosnian Muslim leadership. And give credit to President Clinton for backing this all-out effort and for deciding to commit twenty thousand American troops to implement the agreement.

Presidential leadership and involvement play a far greater role in the first Gulf War in 1991, but are managed very differently before and during the run-up to the Iraq war, in 2002–2003. To those two cases, we will now turn.

4.

{ CASES OF STATECRAFT }

Undoing Iraqi Aggression in Kuwait

On August 2, 1990, Iraq invaded neighboring Kuwait and seized a country Iraqi leaders began referring to immediately as the "nineteenth province" of Iraq. The Bush administration condemned the invasion and called for the immediate, unconditional withdrawal of Iraqi forces. It moved swiftly to get the UN Security Council to adopt a resolution in which the invasion was unanimously condemned, and by Sunday, August 5, President Bush declared that "This will not stand—this aggression against Kuwait."

With that statement, the president was declaring that the United States, either on its own or with others, would act to ensure that the Iraqi seizure of Kuwait would be undone. It was a remarkable declaration, particularly because the United States had no preexisting commitment to Kuwaiti security, and had done little before the invasion to signal any serious American interest in the fate of Kuwait. Moreover, U.S. relations with Iraq had steadily improved since the Reagan administration had taken Iraq off the terrorism list in 1982.

U.S.-Iraqi relations were restored in 1984, and American policy had tilted toward Iraq, favoring it in the war it launched against Iran. Even though Iraq had invaded Iran, the American view of the threat posed by the revolutionary mullahs ruling Iran (and American antipathy to Iran in the wake of the 1979–1981 hostage crisis) led us to support Iraq and its secular Ba'athist regime, led by Saddam Hussein. Adopting the traditional realist posture that the "enemy of my enemy is my friend," Ronald Reagan—hardly a disciple of the realpolitik school of foreign policy—offered very tangible and meaningful support to Iraq. America provided the Iraqi regime with intelligence and advanced radars that had a significant force-multiplying effect. And in 1987, when Iran was attacking oil tankers to cut Iraq's oil revenues, we "reflagged" neutral tankers and protected them with U.S. warships to prevent such a loss. In addition, the Reagan administration offered extensive credit guarantees to the Iraqi government to buy agricultural goods from the United States, and maintained that program even after we began receiving reports that the Iraqis were misusing the credits to free up funds for military purchases. Even the use of chemical weapons against the Iranians and Iraq's own Kurdish population did little to affect our relations.

With the end of the Iraq-Iran War in 1988, the policy of seeking to improve relations with Saddam Hussein continued, and was embraced by the Bush administration in its first year. It was only in 1990 that American policy began to waver, as Saddam pressured his neighbors to increase oil prices and threatened Israel, even implying a readiness to employ chemical weapons against it. In response to Iraq's increasingly bellicose posture against its neighbors, the Bush administration began a review of the agricultural credit program, which eventually led not to its revocation but to the suspension of a second tranche of five hundred million dollars in credits. In May 1990, Saddam charged that Kuwait was engaging in economic warfare against Iraq and demanded that it provide Iraq with billions of dollars and territorial concessions; in late July, these threats escalated as Saddam declared that Kuwait and the United Arab Emirates were guilty of direct aggression against Iraq and declared that if words had no impact, "something effective must be done."[1]

Throughout the spring and summer of 1990, America's Arab friends in the Middle East counseled restraint in the face of Iraq's threats, and the Bush administration did little. For the most part, the policy was being handled in the administration by second-tier officials as the time and attention of the president and the most senior level remained riveted principally on German unification. Much like the Saudis, Egyptians, and Jordanians, those American officials felt that Saddam was posturing because of increasing economic troubles; even when the verbal threats became more pronounced and Iraq moved heavy concentrations of troops to the Kuwaiti border in the second half of July, Arab regimes and the U.S. ambassador to Iraq assured the administration's leaders of Saddam Hussein's benign intentions. Hosni Mubarak, Egypt's president, after seeing Hussein, declared on July 25 that "I believe he ... has no intention of attacking Kuwait or any other party." And on July 29, King Hussein of Jordan told President Bush in a phone call, "Nothing will happen."[2] But the attack came four days later, and America's policy was transformed.

WHY DID WE SEEK TO UNDO IRAQI AGGRESSION?

The Iraqi seizure of Kuwait came as a shock. Even when Iraqi troops crossed the border, the initial assumption was that the action might be a limited land grab (perhaps the Rumaila oil field) as a way of extracting economic concessions from the Kuwaitis. Though even a limited seizure of territory would have been deeply disturbing, few in the neighborhood or in the administration foresaw the possibility of Iraq actually seizing all of Kuwait. Their assessments were guided by wrongheaded assumptions about Saddam Hussein.

The administration had to scramble in response. Certainly the shock of the invasion affected the administration's mind-set. But what shaped the adoption of its objective to reverse the invasion was the early recognition that far more was at stake than the future of Kuwait. Iraqi forces stood poised on the Kuwaiti-Saudi border, only 275 miles from the Saudi capital of Riyadh, and little separated the Iraqi forces from advancing into the kingdom. Suddenly the specter of Iraq seizing Saudi northern oil fields and the Saudi capital conjured up the image that a hostile power could gain a stranglehold over the flow of oil from the Middle East, with potentially devastating consequences for the economies of the Western industrialized world. Preventing that outcome had long been defined as a fundamental U.S. interest. Previously, the Soviets were seen as the prime threat; the Khomeini revolution in Iran indicated that such a threat could be more localized. And now Iraq's absorption of Kuwait could enable it to dominate the Gulf States, determine the flow of oil, and use its leverage on the oil supply to blackmail our allies and pursue its pan-Arab objectives in the region—including its anti-Israel agenda.

The Iraq seizure of Kuwait thus posed an unmistakable threat to America's interests in the Middle East.

For President Bush, it was not just the threat to oil and our vital interests in the Middle East that were at stake—as important as they might be. The president believed that Iraq's actions threatened the structure of international relations after the cold war. With the fall of the Berlin wall, one era had ended. Would this new one be governed by the rule of law or the law of the jungle? Would it be characterized by order or disorder? In James Baker's words, the president's instinctive sense from the beginning was that "this was no ordinary crisis, that it truly would become a hinge point of history," and how we responded would have a great influence on whether there would be a new world order—terminology that President Bush now began to use.[3]

This concern for shaping the post–cold war world was why Iraq's aggression could not stand and why *how* we undid it was so important. President Bush was prepared, in his words, "to deal with this crisis unilaterally if necessary," but he did not want the United States going it alone and making this a confrontation between America and Iraq.[4] Rather, for President Bush and Secretary Baker, it must be the world against Saddam. There must be a coalition that would signal that the world would not tolerate this kind of behavior. Indeed, for Bush and Baker, the United States should lead an international coalition to counter this aggression and undo the Iraqi occupation of Kuwait.

Consequently, President Bush, in his words, "wanted the United Nations involved as part of our first response. . . ." He was convinced that "Decisive UN action would be important in rallying international opposition to the invasion and reversing it."[5] Secretary Baker affirmed that "Almost by definition, the first stop for coalition building was the United Nations."[6]

Forging an international consensus would make our action legitimate and define the ground rules of this new era. It would show that aggression would not be permitted and that those who engaged in it would unmistakably lose.

While President Bush defined our objective in these terms, it was no simple task to fashion a strategy for achieving it. Deterrence of further Iraqi military thrusts, especially into Saudi Arabia, had to be the first order of business, and the development of a coalition to undo the aggression could not simply be mandated; it had to be nurtured and constructed. Practically speaking, it would take time to put military forces in place to counter the Iraqis, and the Saudis would have to accept the deployment of large American forces in the kingdom—something they had always been loath to consider, fearing that admitting large numbers of "nonbelievers" to defend the "custodians" or protectors of the holy places might affect the very legitimacy of the royal family.

Building forces for deterrence was one thing; being able to put together an international coalition would be another. Each phase required time. Notwithstanding the president's declaration that the Iraqi aggression would not stand, the early strategy of the administration as outlined by the president and his senior advisors in the NSC meeting of August 4 was geared to deterrence and the gradual buildup of pressures on Iraq designed to make the occupation of Kuwait untenable. Coercive diplomacy, starting with political isolation and leading to economic sanctions, was designed to "make Saddam Hussein pay such a high price" that he would realize the need to withdraw from Kuwait. It was hoped that this would be sufficient, but the president understood that if isolation and sanctions failed, Saddam would have to be expelled by military force.[7]

The strategy depended on establishing an international consensus and a broad-based coalition. "Having decided on building a coalition, we turned our attention," Secretary Baker said later, "to the practical and arduous task of actually putting one together and maintaining it throughout the crisis . . . In retrospect, I believe maintaining the coalition's solidarity was even more difficult than assembling it in the first place."[8]

WHAT OBSTACLES DID WE FACE?

The obstacles to achieving the objective established by the president were formidable. Some of them stemmed from a structural reality: influential countries such as the Soviet Union would find it difficult to be a part of a coalition designed to exert great pressure on Iraq, its principal client state in the Middle East. Other obstacles grew out of the inherent complexities in the process the administration sought to use to apply pressure on Iraq—namely, the adoption of resolutions in the United Nations Security Council. Even assuming that consensus could be developed among the five permanent members of the Council on escalating the pressure on Iraq (certainly not a given by any means), the nonaligned bloc might balk over coercing a country in the developing world, and, if nothing else, could prevent resolutions from appearing to have broad support.

Still other obstacles were bound to arise given the incremental nature of the strategy, which by definition meant that there would be different phases. Gaining support first for political isolation might not be demanding. But getting it again for sanctions, and then for enforcement of a sanctions regime to inflict genuine penalties on Iraq, and finally again for the actual use of force to expel Iraq, was bound to be very difficult. Necessarily, each go-round would re-create opposition from those who were instinctively hesitant, opposition that would have to be managed and overcome.

If these structural obstacles were not sufficient, there were others that were certain to be daunting: employing sanctions that imposed an effective boycott against the Iraqi economy would damage those, such as Turkey and Egypt, whose economies depended on commercial ties or subsidized oil from Iraq. They would find it difficult to go along with embargoes if they were not compensated for what they were losing financially—and that "bill" would rise very quickly into the billions of dollars. Who was going to provide that money to sustain the effectiveness of the embargoes on all Iraqi trade? Moreover, would we find it so easy to sustain the costs of our own military buildup in the Gulf, particularly given our sudden turnabout in policy toward Iraq that inevitably raised questions about how we could go from trying to improve relations with Iraq to coercing it?

In this sense, the economic costs would trigger political costs as well. Bear in mind that the administration had done little or no conditioning to change the public perception of Iraq. In addition, few looked at Kuwait as a country that was worth fighting for. So domestic opposition was yet another important obstacle the administration would have to contend with if it was to achieve its objective of forcing Iraq to disgorge Kuwait.

In retrospect, it appears that Saddam counted on creating a fait accompli to which the world would have to adjust. He apparently assumed that the international community would criticize but accept a reality that it could not undo. He expected that the Soviets, his longtime patron and supplier of the bulk of his heavy armaments, would block any meaningful pressures on him. He had strong ties to the Soviet military establishment, and the Soviets had a large military support presence in Iraq that they were unlikely to jeopardize for the sake of the Americans. Similarly, Saddam probably believed, with some justification, that the French, who had very large commercial interests in Iraq—and defense industries heavily dependent on large arms sales to the Iraqi military—would understand how much they had to lose by imposing any significant economic sanctions on his regime.

Saddam was right to see impediments to what we would try to do from these two permanent members of the Security Council, each with a veto. Beyond this, the Iraqi leadership apparently also believed, again with some justification, that Arab countries would not be able to sustain support for external pressure on Iraq. Joining with an outside power to try to impose on a brother Arab would conjure up all the imagery of a history of colonialism that the people of the region rejected—and local regimes would be fearful of domestic reactions as a result. To make Arab involvement in any international coalition against Iraq less likely, the Iraqis also sought early on to make this an Arab-Israeli, not a world-against-Iraq, issue. Seeing initial condemnations of the Iraqi invasion even in the Arab world, Saddam on August 12—ten days after the seizure of Kuwait—offered a "peace plan," suggesting that he had invaded Kuwait for the Palestinians, and declaring that the issue of Kuwait could be discussed in the context of ending the Israeli occupation of Palestinian territory. Later, Iraqi foreign minister Tariq Aziz began to say that if there were an attack against Iraq, Iraq would retaliate by firing missiles at Israel, something the Iraqis assumed would trigger Israeli retaliation and make it impossible for Arabs to act in a way that made them appear to be siding with the Israelis.

Aziz told Secretary Baker at their January 9 meeting in Geneva that the Arabs would defect from any coalition with the United States for essentially atavistic reasons: "Once a people enter battle and fire prevails and blood is spilled, then people go back to their origins and behave instinctively. If you were to attack an Arab state, you will be the enemy in many Arab countries."[9] Many American experts on the Arab world echoed Aziz's words in warning the Bush administration about the consequences of using force against Iraq. One such expert, Christine Helms, in a fall meeting with President Bush, declared that if we went to war against Iraq to oust it from Kuwait, "no American would be able to do business or set foot in the Arab world for the next twenty years."[10] It matters now not whether such experts were profoundly wrong; what matters is what the administration had to contend with at the time in terms of real or perceived obstacles.

One last set of obstacles to achieving the president's objective should be noted. Within the administration (and even with British prime minister Margaret Thatcher) there were doubts at certain key junctures about going to the United Nations Security Council. The fear was that the Security Council might not agree to the resolutions we sought, and if we tried for them and failed, our ability to then use Article 51 of the UN Charter (the "self-defense" provision) to justify our use of force would be seriously undermined. But for a president who believed that unmistakable international backing for our actions was important both for legitimizing our steps and for establishing a crucial precedent for shaping a new international order, gaining UN endorsement was necessary even if there were obstacles.

Similarly, gaining UN endorsement but lacking congressional and popular backing at home would create questions about our ability to sustain the policy we had adopted. And yet, when the administration in November 1990 (three months after the invasion) began to move from a deterrence-and-sanctions approach to dramatically building up our forces to give us the offensive capability to expel Iraq from Kuwait if necessary, leading figures in the Congress, such as Senators Sam Nunn and Bob Kerrey—both centrist Democrats and credible on security issues—became openly critical of our policy. Moreover, polls at the time indicated that 47 percent of the U.S. public felt that the administration was "too quick to get American military forces involved rather than seeking diplomatic solutions."[11] With Nunn holding hearings in which former military officials such as retired admiral William J. Crowe, Jr., Bush's first chairman of the Joint Chiefs of Staff, argued against the use of force and for the maintenance of a sanctions-only approach, the administration had a congressional problem, and ameliorating it was yet another obstacle to overcome.

HOW COULD WE USE STATECRAFT?

President Bush was very clear in establishing his objective and his desire to have an international consensus for backing it. Effectively, the administration sought to "frame" the issue by building the international consensus around the objective of the intolerability of the Iraqi seizure of Kuwait and the need to see it reversed. Personal diplomacy was again employed very intensely and at very senior levels, much as with German unification. But in this case, the personal diplomacy, including the use of back channels, was geared toward putting together a broad coalition to demonstrate that Iraq was isolated; keeping key players on board as the process of ratcheting up pressure on Iraq unfolded; sustaining the coalition over time while managing problems as they emerged or could be anticipated; and agreeing on who would play what roles in the event of war—whether sending forces and/or financially supporting the effort.

While the UN Security Council remained the critical forum for expressing the international consensus, and President Bush was to call our UN ambassador, Tom Pickering, shortly after the invasion to convene an emergency session of the Security Council, the real starting point for producing the coalition that the president sought was getting the Soviets on board. They might be on the decline, but they were still a military superpower and Iraq's principal military patron.

Without the Soviets, there would be no clear international consensus. Soviet opposition to our objective would provide protection and cover for Saddam Hussein; it would give Arab nationalists a reason to stay on the fence; and it would give the French an excuse to assume a posture midway between us and the Soviets. Conversely, a joint U.S.-Soviet approach would make it impossible for the French to be softer on Iraq than the Soviets. Additionally, should the Soviets join us in opposing and pressuring Saddam, the realities at the UN would be transformed: a much stronger basis for agreement among the permanent five members would be created, and the nonaligned, who, belying that description, typically voted with the Soviets, would be much more likely to support resolutions we might now author.

No wonder President Bush thought that "Soviet help in particular was key, first because they had veto power in the Security Council, but also because they could complete Iraq's political isolation."[12] We thus moved quickly to forge a common approach with the Soviets.

GETTING AND KEEPING THE SOVIETS ON BOARD

The first step—and our first essential "means"—for overcoming the obstacles to the administration's objective was forging a joint statement with the Soviets in response to the Iraqi invasion.

At the time of the Iraqi invasion (August 2, 1990), Secretary Baker was meeting with Foreign Minister Shevardnadze in Irkutsk, Siberia, and I was with him.[13] When Baker reported to Shevardnadze on the morning of August 2 that we had intelligence reports that suggested an Iraqi invasion of Kuwait now appeared imminent, Shevardnadze doubted them but instructed Sergei Tarasenko to check and see what "our people" know. Tarasenko reported back shortly that the Soviet "system" believed that nothing would happen. Shevardnadze was plainly embarrassed when, less than two hours later, Baker told him that Iraqi forces had crossed into Kuwait; he was the foreign minister of a country with thousands of its citizens (military and civilians) on the ground in Iraq, and he was blindsided by his national security establishment, requiring the visiting American secretary of state to inform him of the Iraqi invasion.

Shevardnadze's embarrassment may well have contributed to his readiness to work with us in setting up a joint response initially. With Baker leaving Irkutsk for a scheduled trip to Mongolia, I had previously arranged with Sergei Tarasenko to fly back to Moscow on Shevardnadze's plane, so Sergei and I could hold policy planning talks. While we had felt such talks would be useful, the real reason for holding them at this time was that I wanted to get home for the weekend and had planned the trip back to Moscow as an excuse to avoid going with Baker to Mongolia.

Regardless of my less-than-altruistic motivations, the joint U.S.-Soviet statement grew out of my presence in Moscow. Peter Hauslohner, a member of my staff, met us in Moscow and suggested I push for such a statement in response to the invasion. But such a statement, while useful for putting the Soviets on record with us and for "framing" the issue internationally, would have far greater impact if it were mutually announced at the political level. That would leave no doubt that this was a common policy and would send an extraordinary signal to the world. Such an announcement, of course, would require Baker to leave Mongolia and come to Moscow to stand with Shevardnadze and make the statement.

Naturally, before raising this idea with Tarasenko, I needed to know that Baker would come. I reached the secretary in Ulan Bator. He immediately understood the value of the statement, and authorized me to pursue the idea with Tarasenko and Shevardnadze—with the proviso that the joint announcement must have enough "meat" in it to justify his unexpected presence in Moscow.

Over the next twenty-four hours, I rode an emotional roller coaster. Initially, I was on a high as both Tarasenko and then Shevardnadze agreed that here was an opportunity to show the world that the cold war was over and the United States and the USSR were no longer adversaries but rather partners in trying to develop a world of greater peace and stability. That, of course, required a joint statement that did more than merely condemn the Iraqi invasion; in addition, it had to call for an arms embargo on Iraq and further punitive measures if Iraq's withdrawal were not forthcoming. Our first draft reflected these points—and even implied a readiness to go beyond strictly economic sanctions if the Iraqis did not withdraw. The statement was written in blunt language, but Tarasenko was confident he would be able to get it approved. On this basis, I told Baker, and he made plans to come to Moscow; I also reached National Security Advisor Brent Scowcroft, who was with President Bush, and he was surprised and pleased, believing this was very significant and telling me that now he knew the cold war was over.

Only one problem: Tarasenko's confidence was misplaced. The Soviet bureaucracy fought back, seeing the draft as serving America's interest, damaging a client central to the Soviet position in the Middle East, and putting the Soviets on the ground in Iraq in potential danger— and the draft was completely emasculated. We went back and forth, with me threatening to tell Baker not to come and arguing to the Soviets that we must not have a weak statement devoid of actions that would demonstrate to the world how little we could do together in response to the Iraqi aggression. In the end, Shevardnadze took it upon himself to overrule the Soviet traditionalist establishment and agreed to a forceful statement, even acknowledging (as he stood with Baker and spoke to the assembled media) that deciding to make this joint announcement had been no simple undertaking: "Let me tell you that it was a rather difficult decision for us . . . because of the long-standing relations that we have with Iraq. But despite all this . . . we are being forced to take these steps . . . because . . . this aggression is inconsistent with the principles of new political thinking and, in fact, with the civilized relations between nations."[14]

Here was the Soviet foreign minister not only issuing a joint statement with his American counterpart but also framing the issue publicly the way we wanted the world to see and respond to it. In private, he was determined to stick with us, but he did ask Baker to promise that the United States had no intention to use force anytime soon. Baker agreed, with the caveat that this assumed no American citizens were being threatened or harmed in Kuwait.

Why did Shevardnadze do it? He and Gorbachev believed that our relations (and international relations more generally) needed to reflect a new basis, and the secretary of state was going to make an unscheduled trip to Moscow to demonstrate this. Having seen how the German unification issue and the transformation of NATO were handled, Shevardnadze and Gorbachev trusted Bush and Baker. But that did not mean we were over the hump with them on how to respond to Iraq. Literally every subsequent decision point on Iraq had to be managed carefully, particularly because of Gorbachev's opposition to the use of force and because of the political backlash that began increasingly to brew in Moscow over the image and reality of declining Soviet power.

In this sense, managing the Soviets and keeping them in the coalition was an ongoing challenge. In late August, the Soviets opposed stopping an Iraqi oil tanker heading toward Aden, even though the Security Council had passed a resolution imposing a trade embargo on Iraq. Gorbachev felt that an additional UN resolution was necessary to authorize military enforcement of the embargo—and he wanted one more chance to try to get Saddam Hussein to withdraw before enforcing the embargo and adopting such a resolution. Other than Secretary Baker, all of the president's senior advisors wanted to stop the tanker, believing that the credibility of the embargo was at stake. But as Secretary Baker told President Bush, "We're going to be much worse off losing the Soviets than losing the ship," and the president gave Baker a few days to work the issue with the Soviets.[15] Baker did so. He spoke daily to Shevardnadze, seeking to affect the Soviet calculus by explaining not only the pressure he was under but also the importance of having the mandatory Security Council resolutions mean something. He used the phone conversations to move Shevardnadze and Gorbachev, and effectively put Gorbachev in a position in which his desire for delay became a test of Soviet abilities to change Saddam's behavior. Since they could not, the Soviets stayed in the coalition and supported a new resolution.

Later, in the fall, the political counterattacks and pressure within the Kremlin against Shevardnadze led Gorbachev to allow Yevgeny Primakov, a longtime Soviet Arabist with a close relationship to Saddam, to come to Washington to try to persuade us to alter our approach away from pressure on Saddam to an engagement strategy in which Saddam might be given something in order to get him to withdraw. My back-channel relationship with Tarasenko, which had proven so instrumental during German unification, again was useful at this point and in the later stages, when we became primed to use force. At this juncture, Tarasenko sent me an extraordinary message through a secure channel, showing both desperation and the extent of his trust in this relationship:

Dennis,
Primakov is coming over Shevardnadze's opposition. He is against
Saddam paying a price. He wants to reward him. His mission has
been pushed on Gorbachev and if he succeeds, he will replace
Shevardnadze as foreign minister and end everything we have been
working for. He must be seen as failing and creating problems with
the United States. This is a desperate situation.

Sergei

Needless to say, the president made sure that Primakov was seen as failing. President Bush rejected Primakov's strategy and then sent Gorbachev a message, saying Primakov's approach would offer Hussein "face-savers" that would inevitably be seen as "rewards," and would undo the principles that he and Gorbachev had agreed upon in their own joint statement issued in Helsinki in September.[16]

Primakov and the traditional elements in the Soviet national security apparatus were stymied for the moment. But to move from sanctions enforcement to a resolution that would authorize the use of force to expel Iraq was a big leap for Gorbachev. It took an intense lobbying effort by Baker and the president, reminiscent of that on German unification, and Shevardnadze again proved instrumental in persuading the Soviet leader.

However, in this case, what did the trick was less the provision of rewards—although we would help respond to urgent Soviet economic needs at one point—and more the readiness to bring the Soviets into our confidence and be responsive to Gorbachev on the crafting of the most important UN Security Council resolution. During a day in and around Moscow in which Baker would spend nearly thirteen hours with Shevardnadze and then Gorbachev, explaining the need for a new resolution to authorize force against Iraq, Baker offered something previously unimaginable: a confidential military briefing by Lieutenant General Howard Graves to Shevardnadze on how the U.S. military would fight the war if Iraq did not withdraw from Kuwait. Given the sensitivity of the subject, only Baker, Graves, and Shevardnadze were present, and both Tarasenko and I were asked to leave the room. Shevardnadze was so impressed by this demonstration of our readiness to treat the Soviets as a partner that after Graves left the room and Sergei and I had returned, he asked Baker to delay his meeting with Gorbachev to give him some time to "lobby" Gorbachev on the importance of the resolution.

Later, upon listening to Gorbachev's concerns, Baker revised the language of the draft resolution to take account of Gorbachev's reluctance to mention "force" explicitly, and instead inserted language that would authorize the use of "all necessary means"—which legally meant the same thing. He also incorporated into the resolution a forty-five-day clock before the ultimatum in the resolution would be operative and "all necessary means" would be authorized. Baker did this to accommodate Gorbachev's concern about an ultimatum that ruled out one last effort at diplomacy. Gorbachev suggested that there be two resolutions: one with an ultimatum for withdrawal and a second one to then authorize force;

Baker said two resolutions would render the first meaningless, but one resolution with a clock would address the Gorbachev concern.

WORKING THE SECURITY COUNCIL

The "all necessary means" Security Council resolution transformed our posture from deterrence and containment of Iraq in Kuwait to one of being able, with international sanctions and backing, to expel Iraq from Kuwait. Even though we had successfully orchestrated the adoption of five Security Council resolutions at this point, Prime Minister Margaret Thatcher did not favor pursuing this one—and National Security Advisor Scowcroft and Defense Secretary Dick Cheney supported her view. They worried that we would not be able to garner a consensus on actually going to war without some crippling amendments; to try and fail would make it appear that we were using force over international opposition. Better simply to rely on the previous resolutions and Article 51 of the UN Charter. But as Secretary Baker said,

> I agreed with all of them that it would be extremely damaging to lose such a crucial vote. *It made no sense to try for the resolution unless we were certain the votes were there for approval.* I believed, however, that intensive diplomacy could enable us to obtain the necessary support. I argued that it could be done in such a way that we would never submit the issue to the Security Council for a vote unless we were certain we had sufficient commitments to know the ultimate result. In the end, the President agreed it was a risk worth pursuing.[17] (Emphasis added)

Though it took a special effort to produce this resolution, with Secretary Baker meeting either the leaders or leading officials of every sitting member of the Security Council, the diplomatic effort exemplified the unusual means that were employed from the outset to move the Security Council to adopt resolutions against Iraq. The administration operated at three different levels in managing the Security Council. Tom Pickering, the U.S. ambassador to the United Nations, worked his counterparts in New York; in Washington, the ambassadors from the countries on the Security Council were called in for meetings at the State Department; and in the foreign capitals of the countries on the Security

Council, our ambassadors discussed every resolution with their host countries. The message was that each of these resolutions mattered and could affect the relationship of that country with us, and that there would be no "free" votes.

To reinforce the seriousness of our consultations, each resolution was drafted first in Washington and then shared with other capitals before negotiations in New York even took place. Little was left to chance on the resolutions, especially on the "all necessary means" resolution.

Baker had promised the president that the resolution would not be brought up if we did not have the votes; while Baker took an extended trip every month to see the Soviets, our NATO allies, and the Saudis, Egyptians, Kuwaitis, and Syrians, to manage the coalition (and its Soviet, European, and Arab constituent parts) and to move it from one phase to another, it was his trips to see a senior representative of every sitting member of the Security Council that were his most arduous.

Starting on November 3, he spent eighteen days traveling to twelve countries on three continents. In Baker's words, "I met personally with all my Security Council counterparts in an intricate process of cajoling, extracting, threatening, and occasionally buying votes. Such are the politics of diplomacy."[18]

With the Chinese, who were anxious to end the chill in relations with the United States after the breakdown triggered by the Tiananmen Square massacre in 1989, the question was whether there would be a senior-level visit to China by an American official. Even though Baker would meet every one of his Security Council counterparts, he met the Chinese foreign minister, Qian Qichen, in Egypt, not in China. Qian wanted a presidential visit in return for support for the resolution; Baker promised only a visit by the undersecretary of state to prepare for a visit by him the next year. The Chinese ultimately abstained, permitting passage of the resolution. With the Ivory Coast, Baker promised to explore G-7 debt forgiveness. With Malaysia, he made clear that our bilateral relations would be seriously affected by a "no" vote.

Such were the means that Baker used to produce the necessary votes, and he succeeded in doing so.

PERSONAL DIPLOMACY IS USED
TO SUSTAIN THE COALITION

From early on in the crisis, the president and his senior advisors understood that sustaining support for the coalition and for sanctions on Iraq would be costly, not just politically but also financially. Countries such as Turkey and Egypt in particular would be exposed to extreme economic hardship for respecting the embargo. Turkey would have to close down the Iraq oil pipeline, an extremely expensive proposition for Turkey. To meet both our needs and the needs of those who could not sustain the embargo, Baker launched what came to be known as his "tin-cup" trips to raise money. He focused principally but not exclusively on the Saudis, Kuwaitis, Germans, and Japanese; at the time, the latter two were prohibited by their constitutions from contributing any military forces.

Baker used his leverage effectively with these four, explaining that our costs would eventually be measured in blood and it would be impossible for him to defend to Congress countries that would gain immensely from our expelling Iraq if those countries were not paying their fair share. The logic was compelling, and we eventually collected $53.7 billion from these four countries and other allies, leaving us to absorb only $7.4 billion of the costs of the war.[19] Aid packages were put together for Turkey and Egypt and were also instrumental in building Gorbachev's stake in staying the course: privately at one point, Gorbachev asked Baker if he could ask the Saudis to provide a four-billion-dollar credit line to the Soviets to manage urgent economic needs. Baker did so, and the Saudis, understanding how critical the Soviets were to the coalition, responded.[20]

Much as in the German case, the intensity and scope of the personal diplomacy conducted by the president and the secretary of state were extraordinary. While he held fewer face-to-face meetings than during the German unification process, President Bush nonetheless met all the key leaders in the coalition (including Gorbachev twice), and his telephonic diplomacy earned him the nickname the "mad dialer."[21] From the outset he was on the phone, calling our ambassador at the UN to give him instructions or speaking to the Saudi king Fahd and Egyptian president Mubarak to make sure they would be responsive. These were not "check the box" calls; he sought to gain support or to reinforce the positions and confidence of those who might be wavering. And at certain key junctures, especially on the eve of transition from air war to ground war, he held long phone conversations with Gorbachev and others.

For his part, Baker's travels were exhaustive and exhausting. Consider that after issuing the joint statement with Shevardnadze, he returned home to take part in an NSC meeting with the president and then turned around almost immediately and flew to Turkey to work out several understandings with Turkish prime minister Ozal. We required an agreement with Turkey over cutting the Iraq oil pipeline and using Turkish bases in the event of war with Iraq. The meeting also provided the Turks the opportunity to outline what they needed to sustain these positions, and we agreed to consult on each step should additional pressure need to be brought to bear against Saddam Hussein. Next, Baker flew to Brussels to gain NATO endorsement of our steps vis-à-vis Turkey—a NATO member—and put the alliance on record against Iraq.

Baker's subsequent trips, most of which involved going first to the Middle East and then to Moscow and back to Europe before returning home, focused on holding the coalition together even as he pursued different purposes: first the tin-cup exercise; then the effort discreetly to explain to coalition members why we were moving from a deterrence-only posture militarily to one that would enable us to use force offensively if necessary—and the additional monies and bases we would need for such an increase in forces; then the around-the-world effort to garner support for the "all necessary means" resolution; and, finally, one last set of visits to Middle Eastern and NATO countries both before and after the meeting with Tariq Aziz in Geneva to hold the line and prevent any backsliding or division in the coalition in the days leading up to the end of the ultimatum period.

Between the trips and visits to Washington and the phone calls, holding the coalition together was a daily effort. The president and his most senior advisors were riveted on the Gulf crisis and in Richard Haass's words, "Everything else was secondary. The U.S. government, for better or worse, revolved around this set of issues."[22]

New ground could be broken for the sake of the coalition. In addition to the unprecedented focus on the Soviets as the core of the coalition, and getting the Saudis to accept a massive U.S. military presence in the kingdom to deter and later defeat the Iraqi army, Baker also met with Hafez al Asad in Damascus to enlist him as an active member of the coalition aligned against Saddam Hussein. While I had felt that there was no need to have the secretary of state travel to Damascus and give this kind of recognition to a leader whose country was on our terrorism list, particularly when Asad's own enmity with Saddam would generate his support, the president and the secretary saw Syria's overt inclusion in the coalition as essential for gaining credibility in the Arab world. In retrospect, they were probably more right than I was: Asad brought Arab nationalist credentials to the coalition, making Saddam's isolation appear much more complete, even in the Arab world.

More than anything else, the readiness to reach out to Syria demonstrated the priority the administration assigned to having a very broad based coalition. Baker made Damascus a regular stop on his Middle Eastern trips in the run-up to the war; ironically, Israel was never a stop in advance of the war. The fear of Saddam's being able to exploit Arab hostility to Israel and to make it harder for the Arab partners in the coalition to preserve their anti-Saddam position led to this anomalous situation.

That did not mean, however, that the administration was indifferent to Israeli concerns. It simply did not want Saddam to be able to transform the crisis from his seizure of Kuwait and the world's determination to undo it into an Arab-Israeli imbroglio. But as part of the effort to keep the coalition intact, Baker used his trips starting in November to raise the threat of Iraq striking Israel if it came to war to oust Iraq from Kuwait. With the Saudis, Egyptians, Syrians, and others in the Middle East, he raised this contingency and elicited from the leaders of all those Arab states a commitment that they would stay in the coalition, provided Israel did not strike first but only retaliated after an Iraqi strike.

Notwithstanding the conditioning and preexisting commitments, when the Iraqis did launch Scud missiles against Israel on the second night of the war, the administration was convinced that the coalition might be jeopardized if Israel retaliated, particularly because an Israeli air strike would involve overflying one of its Arab neighbors—most likely Jordan. An Israeli military action would, in Brent Scowcroft's words, "change the entire calculus for the coalition."[23]

To prevent such an escalation, Baker and the president spoke to Prime Minister Yitzhak Shamir, and Secretary Cheney to Defense Minister Moshe Arens, to persuade Israel not to strike back. Arens felt that Israel must retaliate for the credibility of its own deterrent, but Shamir was more understanding of the American entreaties not to transform the war and thus play into Saddam's hands. However, the administration offered more than words to persuade the Israelis: we promised to target western Iraq to prevent the Scuds from being fired, claiming that we could employ far more assets for such targeting than Israel; we sent Patriot missiles immediately to Israel, which we believed were effective in shooting down the Scuds; we created a new downlink to give the Israelis a few extra minutes of early warning on the firing of Scuds from western Iraq; and the deputy secretary of state, Lawrence Eagleburger, and a team of senior officials were sent to Israel as a sign of American support and to be sure Prime Minister Shamir held the line in the face of pressures from the Israeli military to respond.

In fact, notwithstanding the American efforts to prevent them, there were thirty-nine Iraqi Scud attacks against Israel. Material damage was limited, and Israel did not retaliate, though the pressure to do so was intense. Shamir withstood the pressure—in large part because of the American assistance, reassurance, presence, and pressure.[24]

MANAGING OUR DOMESTIC REALITIES AND GOING THE EXTRA MILE

The administration had been quick to frame the issue internationally and had been successful in producing an international consensus based on our core objective. Its effort to produce UN Security Council resolutions that isolated Iraq and then imposed sanctions on it also won it public and congressional support. The focus of the administration's work was international, geared to forming and sustaining the coalition.

The Congress was asked to do little, and no senior official in the administration made any effort throughout the first month after the Iraqi invasion to put what we were doing in the context of a larger explanation. Standing with Shevardnadze and offering a joint statement that condemned the Iraqis and called for countermeasures, and getting off a helicopter and declaring that this aggression would not stand—as the president did—signaled intent and resolve but did not offer a deeper public explanation of what we were doing and why. The focus of the effort was on diplomacy—private, not public. Unlike with German unification, when we were highly conscious of public sentiments in Germany, the Soviet Union, and Europe, and felt a need to address those sentiments and try to shape them, the focus was different in this case. Here the concern was to win the support of foreign governments with the assumption that the publics would follow.

Thus, the very first effort to craft a broader conceptual explanation for our response to the Iraq invasion took place only in September, when Secretary Baker had to testify before the Senate Foreign Relations Committee. The secretary and the president were not giving speeches; they were working their counterparts to keep the pressure on Saddam. The two efforts need not have been mutually exclusive, but in this case the effort to talk clearly, consistently, and coherently about our response and our strategy for undoing the Iraqi aggression tended to be made mostly in private.

That did not become a problem until we sought to shift course from deterrence and sanctions to the possible use of force—and at that point we did not have a built-in reservoir of support domestically. On the contrary, we faced serious domestic opposition. When a bipartisan congressional delegation came to see President Bush on October 30—two days after Congress had adjourned for the midterm elections—Speaker of the House Tom Foley gave the president a letter signed by eighty-one Democratic congressmen that reflected deep concerns about reports that the "United States has shifted from a defensive to an offensive posture and that war may be imminent." The letter went on to say that the members believed "that the UN-sponsored embargo must be given every opportunity to work and that all multinational, non-military means of resolving the situation must be pursued."[25]

The public conditioning had been limited to this point. As President Bush later explained, "part of our problem was that so much was happening away from public view, and few people outside of the top echelon in the White House were paying attention to what was going on in Kuwait."[26] While certainly true, the problem was also that the administration was simply not giving a clear, coherent explanation to the public of what was at stake and why force might prove necessary. The problem both was seen as and became more acute when Secretary Baker, near the end of his global tour to drum up support for the "all necessary means" resolution, answered a press question about our stakes in the Gulf by saying, "jobs, jobs, jobs."

Why did Secretary Baker, probably the most attentive of any of the senior leaders of the Bush administration to the need for domestic and congressional support for our policy, offer this rationale? Because, in his words:

> for weeks I'd been frustrated by the administration's collective inability to articulate a single coherent, consistent rationale for the president's policy. Our public pronouncements had ranged from the principled to the esoteric. At times we talked of standing up to aggression and creating a new world order. At others we called Saddam the new Hitler and cited the threat to global stability from rising oil prices . . . we had done a lousy job of explaining not only the fundamental economic ramifications of Iraq's aggression but also the threat to global peace and stability . . . and we were beginning to pay a political price at home as a result of our rhetorical confusion.[27]

Baker was, of course, correct, but his public response had made it appear that we had only narrow commercial reasons for going to war and putting American lives at risk. "Why not let sanctions play out?" was the response of a growing chorus of critics in the Congress and in the punditry class. The answer that sanctions were not working and Saddam was simply digging in and fortifying his position in Kuwait was an appropriate response rhetorically but not politically.

Politically, given increasing public doubts, it was important to gain a congressional resolution of support to go to war—or so Secretary Baker believed. Most of his senior colleagues—especially Defense Secretary Cheney—did not share his views. Much as they feared the risk of pursuing a Security Council resolution on "all necessary means" and failing, so, too, did they worry about the consequences of seeking and then losing a congressional vote on a resolution that backed going to war. President Bush sided with Baker, not because he felt he lacked the legal authority to commit our forces to war. He understood that the war might prove to be costly, and that to launch it amid domestic opposition and without congressional blessing would make it very difficult to sustain the effort.

The administration ultimately succeeded in winning a congressional vote on the war by employing two basic means: first, it got the UN on record authorizing such a mission, and second, it proved that we had, in fact, exhausted every means available short of war for trying to get Saddam to withdraw from Kuwait.

With regard to the UN, the logic was essentially to build momentum for dealing with Congress's doubts by obtaining an international mandate for using force. In effect, the administration could then pose the question, were members of Congress less willing to confront aggression than the United Nations? Certainly questions about the legitimacy of using force were bound to be fewer in Congress once the Security Council had adopted the "all necessary means" resolution. While this was undoubtedly true, both President Bush and Secretary Baker felt that something more was needed—some further demonstration of the lengths to which the administration had gone to use diplomatic means to produce Iraqi withdrawal. And, in fact, they acted to show they had gone "the extra mile" the morning after the passage of the "all necessary means" resolution at the UN.

The president, Secretary Baker, and National Security Advisor Scowcroft met, and the president then went out and announced, on the morning of November 30, one last initiative to avert war: he invited Saddam Hussein to send his foreign minister to Washington, and he was offering to send Secretary Baker to Baghdad anytime between December 15 and January 15 for face-to-face discussions. This was a dramatic announcement that caught everyone by surprise, including senior staff. I was appalled, and told Baker so afterward, saying that this initiative was bound not only to be seen by our coalition partners as a sign of wavering on our part, but even worse, it would give Saddam Hussein a perfect opportunity to render the forty-five-day clock and deadline in the Security Council resolution meaningless. After all, that clock ran out on January 15, and now Saddam merely had to accept the president's initiative by offering talks at or near the deadline.

After additional consideration and some pointed conversations with Saudi ambassador Bandar bin Sultan, the president withdrew the offer and dropped the idea of an exchange of visits, though Secretary Baker did meet Tariq Aziz in Geneva. Without getting into a discussion of some of the external consequences of the announcement, the point here is that our domestic needs as perceived by the president and the secretary produced this going-the-extra-mile initiative. And to be fair to Bush and Baker, they were correct in terms of its impact. The president's announcement changed the dynamics in the Congress, and while the vote on the subsequent resolution was close, the administration did gain a congressional resolution endorsing the use of force.

The president's initiative had one other salutary effect: it headed off other possible bad ideas in the final period leading up to the war. With a forty-five-day clock and the certainty of war if Saddam did not pull out of Kuwait by January 15, a wide variety of initiatives or intermediaries might well have leaped into the vacuum created during this period. But with the president's announcement and the expected direct U.S.-Iraqi discussions, there was no vacuum to be filled. While some of his advisors might not have fully appreciated what the president was doing, he used his unique "means" to answer a genuine domestic problem and preempt potentially unhelpful international interventions.

CONCLUSIONS

Before Saddam Hussein invaded Kuwait, the Bush administration, at least at the highest levels, was consumed with managing German unification in NATO. It was certainly not sending the kind of signals that might have deterred the invasion; to be sure, given Saddam's enormous capacity for miscalculation, that might not have mattered. Some may argue that because it was not paying attention before, and because it defined its objectives basically as undoing Iraq's occupation of Kuwait and not as destroying the power of Saddam's predatory regime, the George H. W. Bush administration left problems that had to be attended to later—a view that many in the George W. Bush administration came to believe.

But George H. W. Bush was quick to settle on a clear objective and to frame it in a way that was embraced internationally. He settled on a basic strategy for achieving the objective and built an international coalition for carrying it out. Our objectives once the war began remained Iraq's expulsion from Kuwait and not the destruction of Saddam Hussein's regime. This was the basis on which the international coalition had been constructed and maintained. Yes, our military would destroy much of the infrastructure Saddam had developed for weapons of mass destruction during the war, and the international coalition would agree that the resolutions for a cease-fire should include inspections so Iraq would not be able to develop WMD and threaten its neighbors.

The essence of the objective, however, remained the same, and the determination to act on the basis of an international consensus guided the administration's policy. Its communications with those in the coalition were clear and ongoing. Problems were anticipated and dealt with using intensive personal diplomacy at the highest levels. Hand-holding when useful, pressure when necessary, and high-level attention at all times with the key members of the coalition was the norm, particularly when moving from one phase to the next.

Notwithstanding all the attention and effort, luck still played a part in developing and sustaining the coalition. Indeed, there can be little doubt that having Saddam Hussein as the adversary made achievement of the administration's objective easier. Would the coalition have remained intact had Saddam Hussein been smarter? Could he not have undone the coalition or at least made it difficult to launch the war if he had announced a partial withdrawal shortly before the January 15 deadline imposed in the "all necessary means" resolution? We constantly assumed he might do this and then declare a readiness to withdraw further once negotiations commenced—and we tried to condition those coalition partners we thought most vulnerable to such an initiative. But we had little doubt about the impact such an initiative by Saddam would have had. And yet, Saddam never took any real conciliatory steps to create fissures within the coalition. Only by striking Israel did he try to drive a wedge in the coalition, and we managed that by getting the Israelis not to respond.

In truth, Saddam Hussein had it in his power to make it far more difficult for us to achieve our objective. But being the master of miscalculation, he assumed he would win more by a war in which he believed he could hold his own and force us eventually to give up the effort. Once again, we see a case of statecraft done well—perhaps with the exception of poor framing of our stakes and rationale for action domestically. But the ultimate success, measured in terms of an objective achieved, was made easier by good fortune or luck—in this case, the luck of having an adversary who could not use the leverage he had.

Perhaps the administration's agility in anticipating contingencies and conditioning its coalition partners to them would have permitted it to manage more adroit moves by Saddam Hussein. Certainly, President Bush's sensitivity to the coalition, and its sustainability, made this more likely.

So did his determination not to expand the objectives in Iraq. He felt we had built the coalition on one basis and could not alter that basis as victory was in our grasp. Was his reluctance to expand our objectives also driven by his desire not to have the coalition come apart as our mission was being completed? That was certainly a factor in his thinking. However, other considerations led him to resist the impulse either to go after Saddam Hussein or even to crush the Republican Guard and make Saddam's regime more susceptible to being overthrown. First, the president and those immediately around him felt that if U.S. forces went to Baghdad, they could trigger a long, messy war with an uncertain outcome. Second, they worried about Iraq fragmenting and becoming both a source of greater instability in the Middle East and creating an opportunity for Iranian/Shi'a expansion into the Arabian peninsula. Third, the leadership of the U.S. military was dead set against continuing the war. They had a neat, clean victory and wanted nothing to detract from that or to prolong their presence in southern Iraq. This desire led to a profound reluctance to shoot down Iraqi helicopter gunships that effectively destroyed the Kurdish and Shi'a uprisings after the war, and after President Bush had called on the Iraqi people to unseat Saddam Hussein.

Our unwillingness to come to the aid of the Shi'a in particular, as they were being ruthlessly suppressed by Saddam after the war, plagues us to this day. For some, it makes the Gulf War a case in which statecraft may have been exercised well during the run-up to the war itself but done poorly at the end, particularly because of the legacy that was left.

While some criticism may be warranted, especially for not at least stopping the Iraqi military from using its helicopters against the Shi'a and the Kurds, the larger question is whether the administration had the right objective for the Gulf War. An essential part of statecraft is defining objectives and making them feasible and achievable. Inevitably, there could and should be questions raised about whether an objective responds only to near-term needs or is also shaping a longer-term future effectively. To the extent that the administration reversed Saddam's aggression and won international support for disarming his regime of its weapons of mass destruction, its definition of objectives responded not only to the near term. Whether more was achievable is debatable.

The president made a judgment call. All major foreign policy decisions come down to that. In cases when statecraft is done well, all factors are carefully considered. Sometimes, with the passage of time, the judgments turn out to be wrong. So long as they reflect careful consideration, with thorough internal discussion, one cannot ask for more. In this case, the tools of the trade were skillfully employed, and the consideration of objectives—even at the end—was serious. It is not possible to say the same about the approach to the Iraq war.

5.

{CASES OF STATECRAFT}

Saddam, George W. Bush, and the Iraq War

The Iraq war is ongoing, yet the Bush administration's decisions and style provide a strikingly different approach to statecraft from that seen in the case of the first Gulf War. Because of the contemporary nature of the case and the importance of understanding why the administration's policy evolved as it did, I have chosen to spend more time in this chapter reviewing the background and context of the administration's approach.

BACKGROUND AND CONTEXT

In 1991, Saddam Hussein's seizure of Kuwait was undone, but America's conflict with Iraq did not end. Regime change was explicitly rejected as an objective by President George H. W. Bush, who resolved early on to stick to the terms of the international coalition he had helped to forge. There was agreement on expelling Iraq from Kuwait; however, there was no consensus on expelling Saddam Hussein from Iraq.

President Bush encouraged Iraqis to remove Saddam Hussein, but he would not intervene when Shi'a in the south and Kurds in the north openly rebelled against Saddam's regime. Fear of mission creep and the disintegration of Iraq led the administration to stand aside and allow the Republican Guard forces (which had emerged largely unscathed from the war) to use their superior firepower to decimate the uprisings.

While President Bush had been determined not to redefine the mission to permit intervention internally in Iraq, he was not prepared to permit Iraq to threaten its neighbors or destabilize the region after the war. And here the administration was successful in also getting the UN Security Council to embrace two additional objectives. First, the Iraqi army's assault against the Kurds in the north triggered a massive refugee flow to—and in some cases across—the Turkish border. Given its own delicate relationship with Turkey's Kurdish population, Turkey would not permit a massive influx of refugees. To prevent a humanitarian disaster, a protected area under UN control was established in the north, and most of the Kurdish refugees were able to return at least to this area. In time the Kurdish zones were stabilized, rebuilt, and became largely autonomous from the rest of Iraq—with a "no-fly" zone for the Iraqi air force adding to the area's quasi-independence. Second, the Security Council agreed that Iraq's capacity to develop or possess weapons of mass destruction must be eradicated. The Security Council adopted an inspection and monitoring regime and mandated that economic sanctions could not be lifted until inspectors certified that all such capability had been destroyed. According to the terms of the cease-fire resolution 687, Iraq was to cooperate with the inspection regime and to furnish within fifteen days all information in any way connected to its WMD programs, labs, or even scientists.

But Iraqi cooperation was not forthcoming. Instead, a pattern of partial, grudging responses began. Only under great pressure would the regime reluctantly respond and belatedly permit the inspectors to go to the facilities they sought to investigate. The Iraqi approach came to be described as one of "cheat and retreat." Iraqis would seek to block, inhibit, stall, and deceive the inspectors, making their work as hard as possible. Eventually, when the pressure grew and threats were made by the United States, the Iraqis would acquiesce to particular inspections. Notwithstanding the Iraqi-imposed impediments to their work, the inspectors succeeded in finding and subsequently destroying far more WMD-related material during the period 1991–1998 than did our forces during the 1991 war.

Certainly Saddam remained unrepentant and continued to try to defy the international community. In 1993, he was responsible for an assassination plot to kill former president Bush and the Kuwaiti emir during President Bush's visit to Kuwait. President Clinton authorized a nighttime cruise missile attack against Iraqi intelligence headquarters in Baghdad in response. In 1994, Saddam again threatened Kuwait, requiring a U.S. buildup of forces before he backed down.[1] Several years later, in 1998, Saddam prevented inspectors for several months from monitoring sensitive sites, and the Clinton administration, following a number of warnings issued from the Security Council, was poised to carry out massive air strikes against Iraq in early November. Only a last-minute retreat in a letter from Saddam to Kofi Annan prevented the U.S. air campaign at that time. Within a month, Saddam had walked away from the promises he made to the secretary-general. As a result, the United States carried out four days of intensive, far-reaching air and missile strikes that inflicted heavy damage on all suspected WMD and related military targets.

In response, Saddam refused to allow the reentry of inspectors and declared the end of the inspection regime. While that precluded any further inspections, it also prevented the lifting of economic sanctions on Iraq. The sanctions had imposed terrible costs on the Iraqi public, without staunching the flow of money Saddam used to maintain his omnipresent security system and the lavish lifestyle of his ruling clique.

The toll that sanctions took on the Iraqi population was very grim. The standard of living plummeted, health care deteriorated dramatically, and the country was generally impoverished. The suffering of the Iraqi public—an image Saddam sought to cultivate and exploit—increasingly raised questions about the costs of the sanctions regime internationally. To sustain it, and to ease the impact on the Iraqi public, the Oil-for-Food program was developed at U.S. instigation, adopted by the Security Council and managed by the UN. But corruption and Saddam's manipulation of the program helped to bolster him without doing much to change the image worldwide of Iraqi suffering.

Saddam's capacity to sustain the regime—while inflicting greater suffering on most Iraqis—helped to foster competing pressures in the international community and within the United States. Internationally, concern for the plight of the Iraqi people triggered increasing pressure to lift the sanctions. Domestically, there was a chorus of voices beginning to demand that it was time for regime change. Those lobbying for such a posture were driven by the fears that the mood internationally would make sanctions unsustainable and that once Saddam escaped the sanctions, he would again become a source of grave danger in the region. For domestic critics of the Clinton administration, this promised to produce the worst of all worlds: Saddam free of sanctions and free to accumulate the monies necessary to feed his appetite for WMD.

In January 1998, the Project for a New American Century sent President Clinton a letter stating that "The current policy, which depends for its success upon the steadfastness of our coalition partners and the cooperation of Saddam Hussein, is dangerously inadequate." The letter emphasized the need for regime change, and its signers included Donald Rumsfeld, Paul Wolfowitz, and Richard Armitage—all of whom would come to have leading positions in the new Bush administration.[2]

This group played a pivotal lobbying role with the Congress, which a few months later adopted the Iraqi Liberation Act. Regime change thus acquired a bipartisan character, even though little practically was done to act on it. But for those who would be around George W. Bush as he prepared to run for the presidency, there was a deep-seated preoccupation with Iraq and a shared perception that, in the words of Richard Perle, "the feebleness of the Clinton Administration" was appalling.[3]

The legacy of how the war ended, and the conviction that Saddam was an ongoing threat, certainly shaped the views of key Bush advisors such as Paul Wolfowitz. Did they shape candidate Bush's views or did they simply reinforce what he already believed? It is difficult to answer this question with any certainty, but one thing is clear: during the presidential campaign, one of the very few foreign policy issues Governor Bush would address and often highlight was Iraq and Saddam Hussein. Following the election, when he met President Clinton at the White House on December 19, 2000, the outgoing president told him that it appeared from the campaign that the incoming president's national security priorities were missile defense and Iraq, and President-elect Bush acknowledged that this was correct.[4]

THE NEW BUSH ADMINISTRATION AND IRAQ

Upon becoming president, however, George W. Bush (and his White House staff) was not riveted on Iraq, and the initial policy was developed and managed largely by the State Department. "Smart sanctions" defined the policy, a policy designed not to accelerate regime change but to make sanctions much more sustainable. The idea was to loosen the sanctions regime on nonmilitary, non-dual-use technologies and allow much more trade and investment with Iraq. The logic was to ease the dire economic situation in Iraq while still making it difficult for Saddam to develop weapons of mass destruction. In this way, Saddam would still be "in the box," but the pressure for lifting all the sanctions would dissipate—or so the theory went.

September 11 changed all this. The world was transformed for the Bush administration in terms of threats, priorities, preoccupations, and missions. Both Secretary of Defense Rumsfeld and Deputy Secretary Wolfowitz quickly focused on Saddam Hussein. Within hours of the attack, Rumsfeld wrote notes in which he contemplated attacking Saddam Hussein in response: "best info fast. Judge whether good enough [to] hit S.H. at same time."[5]

They were not alone. President Bush was also thinking of Saddam Hussein. On September 12, when he was in the Situation Room, he told his counterterrorism team to "See if Saddam did this. See if he's linked in any way." Richard Clarke replied by saying, "But, Mr. President, al-Qaeda did this." And the president responded, "I know, I know but . . . see if Saddam was involved. Just look. I want to know any shred."[6]

Even though the president in the September 15 meeting at Camp David with his national security team did not accept Wolfowitz's preference for making Iraq the focus of America's initial military response to 9/11—emphasizing instead that Afghanistan would be first—he did not take his eye off of Iraq. At the end of the Camp David meeting, he privately asked the outgoing chairman of the Joint Chiefs, Hugh Shelton, if it was a mistake to focus on Al Qaeda and not Saddam.[7] The next day he told National Security Advisor Condoleezza Rice that he wanted plans drawn up if it turned out that Iraq was implicated in the 9/11 attacks, and the following day, September 17, he stated to his senior advisors that "I believe Iraq was involved."[8] And, as early as November 21, the president privately asked the secretary of defense, "What kind of a war plan do you have for Iraq? How do you feel about the war plan for Iraq?" After Rumsfeld expressed his concern about the state of war plans in general, President Bush—seventy-two days after the destruction of the twin towers—told Donald Rumsfeld, "Let's get started on this. And get Tommy Franks looking at what it would take to protect America by removing Saddam Hussein if we have to."[9]

At a press conference on November 26, five days after asking Rumsfeld to get started on a war plan for Iraq, the president declared that Saddam Hussein needed to let inspectors back into Iraq to prove he was not developing WMD. When asked what the consequences would be if Saddam did not do so, Bush replied, "He'll find out." On December 28, 2001, General Tommy Franks, the head of Central Command, briefed the president at the president's ranch in Texas on the initial plans for Iraq, and by February of 2002, the president ordered General Franks to begin shifting troops from Afghanistan to the Gulf.[10] The next month, President Bush joined a meeting Condi Rice was having with three senators. Mr. Bush left little doubt about his intentions: "Fuck Saddam. We're taking him out."[11]

While the president would say he had no war plans on his desk, he not only directed the preparation of war plans but also expected to go to war to remove Saddam Hussein a full year before we went to war. Richard Haass, then director of the policy planning staff in the State Department, has described a meeting he had in June 2002 with Condi Rice, then national security advisor, in which he began to raise some of the hard questions about going to war in Iraq, and she cut him off, saying, "Save your breath. The President has already decided what he's going to do on this."[12]

For Haass, the decision to go to war simply "happened," it was never actually made. Momentum built up behind the presumption of war and took on a life of its own. During the summer of 2002, unease about the drift toward war began to build outside of the administration. At a time when the administration seemed to assume that it had a blank check to do whatever it deemed necessary in the war on terror, and presumed that a war with Iraq could simply be mandated accordingly, questions began to percolate about the wisdom of such a war. But among many in Congress and the foreign policy cognoscenti, these questions remained largely inchoate until Brent Scowcroft, the former national security advisor, wrote an article in *The Wall Street Journal* on August 15. In the article, entitled "Don't Attack Saddam," Scowcroft argued that there was "scant evidence to tie Saddam to terrorist organizations, and even less to the September 11 attacks." Besides observing that Saddam had little incentive to make common cause with Al Qaeda—our real target—Scowcroft asserted that "There is a virtual consensus in the world against an attack on Iraq at this time," and warned that "so long as that sentiment persists, it would require the U.S. to pursue a virtual go-it-alone strategy against Iraq, making any military operations correspondingly more difficult and expensive."[13]

For a variety of reasons the Scowcroft article energized questioning about the administration's course on Iraq. First, it was August, and there was a virtual news vacuum, and here was a story: the national security advisor to the elder President Bush, someone known to be very close to the former president and unlikely to adopt a position that president would reject, was seemingly challenging the course on which the younger President Bush was launched. Second, the president and his advisors had offered little public explanation or justification for a path that seemed inexorably to be leading to war with Iraq. Third, Scowcroft's argument created a focal point for others to embrace and yet not be accused of being soft on fighting terrorism or defending an indefensible figure such as Saddam Hussein—after all, Scowcroft had been the national security advisor to two Republican presidents.[14]

But it was not only those outside the administration who seized on the Scowcroft article. The leading official who had doubts about the march toward war with Iraq, Secretary of State Colin Powell, used it to marshal greater support for going through the UN to deal with the Iraqi threat. His argument effectively was, we will need bases, over-flight rights, and access if we believe war is going to be necessary; if nothing else, Powell argued that we could not simply go it alone. If we were to gain what was necessary from others in warfare we would, at least, have to try for a diplomatic solution first, and that argued for going through the UN.[15]

While Bob Woodward reports that Powell called Scowcroft *after* the article appeared to thank him for providing the secretary "some running room" to move on what was now his "opportunity," I know from my own conversations with Scowcroft that he spoke with Powell about their mutual misgivings about where the administration was headed on Iraq *prior* to writing the article, and Powell encouraged him to speak out.[16] Secretary Powell was trying to steer the president toward the United Nations, believing this might create an alternative to war by redirecting us more toward an international effort to restore inspectors in Iraq.

With the president slated to address the United Nations General Assembly on September 12, a year and a day after the 9/11 attacks, Powell was hoping to use the speech to focus on Iraq and the need for a new Security Council resolution. According to Bob Woodward, the president made the decision to make Iraq the focal point of his address to the UN the day after the Scowcroft article appeared. In doing so, Bush instructed Condi Rice and his speechwriter Mike Gerson to "tell the UN that it's going to confront this problem or it's going to condemn itself to irrelevance."[17]

Vice President Cheney may not have been enthusiastic about going through the UN, but he certainly favored the idea of challenging it to be relevant if the president was going to speak there about Iraq. He doubted that the UN could be a vehicle for dealing with Saddam Hussein, and feared that gearing ourselves to getting inspectors back into Iraq was potentially dangerous. As he said in a speech on August 26, ten days after the president's instruction to Mike Gerson on his UN address, "A return of inspectors would provide no assurance whatsoever of his [Saddam Hussein's] compliance with UN resolutions. On the contrary, there is a great danger that it would provide false comfort that Saddam was somehow 'back in his box.'" And, for the vice president, there was "no doubt that Saddam Hussein now has weapons of mass destruction. There is no doubt he is amassing them to use against our friends, against our allies, and against us."[18]

Here was a call to action. The vice president was not just setting the stage for the president's challenge to the UN or trying to counter the secretary of state's preference for inspections as the way to contain Saddam. He was also responding to increased public questioning triggered by the Scowcroft article about the administration's policy toward Iraq. No one from the administration had countered the burgeoning view that Saddam was not the prime threat and, in any case, could be handled by putting the UN and inspectors on the case.

The vice president was mindful of the need to preserve a domestic base for our actions, including his presumption—like the president's—that war would be necessary to remove Saddam Hussein as a threat. Even with the president slated to go to the UN, Vice President Cheney was instrumental in developing a political strategy that focused on getting a congressional resolution authorizing whatever means might be necessary for dealing with Saddam Hussein before getting a UN resolution. He wanted every member of Congress to be forced to go on record on where they stood on Saddam Hussein and his dangerous regime before the midterm elections in early November.

In fact, throughout the fall, it was the domestic strategy that was uppermost in the minds of the White House. Unlike in 1991, forging a domestic, not international, base of support required and received the greatest attention. A full-court press with congressional leaders began the day after Labor Day; the next day, two dozen senators from both parties were invited to the Pentagon for briefings on Iraq with the vice president, the secretary of defense, and George Tenet, the director of Central Intelligence. As one senior administration official said, the White House lobbying campaign with the Hill included "not-so-subtle mentions of the regrets experienced by those lawmakers . . . who did not vote for the 1991 'use of force' resolution before the Persian Gulf war."[19]

The domestic strategy was built around getting a congressional resolution authorizing the president to use force to deal with the Iraqi threat, while the UN strategy was geared toward getting inspectors back into Iraq, and if Iraq failed to comply with all the requirements, then force could be authorized. The President's speech to the UN did catalyze a great deal of activity, with the secretary of state in New York trying to strike quickly to develop a consensus on action to follow up on the president's call for showing that the UN could be relevant.

The two strategies could easily have meshed, with broad-based congressional support being a useful lever for American diplomats to use with the Security Council. But the strategies tended to diverge in terms of their objectives. With Congress, the administration was focused on the use of force to be rid of Saddam Hussein and his weapons of mass destruction. With the UN, the focus necessarily became disarmament, not regime change or even necessarily the use of force. The difference was significant insofar as the French, the Russians, and others on the Security

Council saw the return of inspectors as a device to produce Iraq's disarmament.

Secretary Powell's initial flurry of activity—he held a dozen meetings with foreign ministers on September 13 at the UN—cemented the consensus for pressure on Iraq. But when Iraq, working with Kofi Annan, announced its readiness to have inspectors return, our efforts to produce a clear, unequivocal Security Council resolution quickly ran into difficulty. Neither the French nor the Russians were prepared for a strongly worded resolution that created an automatic trigger on the use of force if the Iraqis were not in compliance with the demands of a new resolution.

Following nearly two months of discussions, Secretary Powell succeeded in producing a unanimous Security Council resolution, 1441, which mandated unconditional and unfettered access for inspectors and promised "serious consequences" if Iraq failed to comply. The "consequences" were, however, understood differently by France and the United States. The French, as their ambassador to the United Nations declared in his explanation of his vote on 1441, understood that this resolution created a "two-stage approach," and that noncompliance would lead "the Council [to] meet immediately to assess the seriousness of these violations . . . [and] France welcomes the fact that . . . all elements of automaticity have disappeared from the resolution."[20] By contrast, even though Powell made a critical concession to produce the resolution—namely that the Council would be convened to discuss what to do if Iraq rebuffed the inspectors or was shown to have illegal weapons—the American posture was that a failure to comply meant Saddam Hussein was once again in "material breach," and that that was sufficient to trigger the use of force.[21]

A month prior to the adoption of UN Security Council Resolution 1441, the Congress voted to authorize the president to use force "as he determines to be necessary and appropriate" to defend the nation against "the continuing threat posed by Iraq." When it was clear that congressional authorization would be forthcoming, a senior White House official asserted that "Once Congress acts, that's final—that's all that has to happen in our system."[22] The point was that this is what was going to govern the president's behavior, not the resolution in the Security Council. The administration saw action at the Security Council as falling in the desirable, not necessary, category.

When Security Council Resolution 1441 passed, it was hailed by the president: now the world must not, President Bush declared, "lapse into unproductive debates over whether specific instances of Iraqi noncompliance are serious . . . If Iraq fails to fully comply, the United States and other nations will disarm Saddam Hussein."[23]

The president was clear, and the administration's efforts to seek support for military action, especially as it related to over-flight rights and access for our forces, became more pronounced. At the same time, our buildup of forces in and around Iraq also became more visible. For the administration, all this activity simply underscored that Saddam had to comply or else; for others, it signaled an American intent not to give the new inspection regime a chance.

The difference in perception—or the "ambiguity," as Wolf Blitzer called it in an interview with Secretary Powell shortly after 1441 was adopted—came back to haunt the administration as it saw Saddam's initial response being one of noncompliance.[24] Iraq was given one month to provide a full accounting of its WMD capabilities and infrastructure, and no one—including the French and Russians—believed the Iraqi report was responsive. But France and Russia felt that the inspectors had to be given a chance to go to Iraq and offer their findings.

And it was not only the French and Russians; most members of the Security Council felt that UN weapons inspectors in Iraq must be given the time to complete their work, even "if it means delaying the onset of hostilities."[25] On January 20, at a Security Council meeting ostensibly held on terrorism, in Secretary Powell's presence, the French and German foreign ministers came out strongly against any early resort to force. Dominique de Villepin, the French foreign minister, who had specifically asked for the January 20 session to be held at the ministerial level, went so far as to declare, "Nothing justifies envisioning military action."[26]

From seemingly driving the train at the Security Council and being in control of events, the United States looked increasingly to be in the minority. Even our most important ally, British prime minister Tony Blair, who was under increasing domestic pressure not to rush to war, declared that the weapons inspectors must be given "time and space" to finish their work, and that the January 27 date for Hans Blix, the chief of the UN inspection team in Iraq, to report to the Council "shouldn't be regarded in any sense as a deadline."[27]

The American plan had, in fact, been to use the Blix report as the deadline for decision. Tony Blair's opposition made that impossible. To make matters worse, Blair now made clear to President Bush that he needed a second resolution at the Security Council to actually authorize the use of force. The fear of those such as Vice President Cheney that going to the UN could become a trap was now materializing. Nonetheless, President Bush, appreciating the importance of Blair and his domestic needs, agreed to go for a second resolution. Here, again, however, French opposition proved particularly troublesome.

The French, particularly President Chirac and his foreign minister, Villepin, were far more active in framing the issue and lobbying for votes than we were. Chirac produced a trilateral statement with the Russian and German leaders, calling for "the substantial strengthening" of the "human and technical capabilities" of the weapons inspectors in Iraq.[28] The answer to the Iraqi WMD program was to have the inspectors do their job and carry out Iraqi disarmament—or, at least for the French, Russians, and Germans, to see that the inspectors were given enough time to do the job and to resort to force only when it became clear that Saddam Hussein would never permit them to do the job.

In response to Secretary Powell's presentation to the Security Council on February 5, Villepin, who was to travel to Africa to persuade key nonaligned members on the Security Council, declared, "If this approach fails and leads us to an impasse, we will not rule out any option, including, as a last resort, the use of force . . . For now, the inspections regime, favored by Resolution 1441, must be strengthened, since it has not been completely explored . . . Why go to war if there still exists some unused space in Resolution 1441?"[29]

To be sure, the administration made an effort to persuade the Council and others. Secretary Powell's February 5 presentation to the Security Council highlighted Iraq's continuing deception and presented evidence of ongoing Iraqi WMD programs. Powell and the administration were persuasive with what Secretary of Defense Donald Rumsfeld called "new Europe," the countries of Eastern Europe, and with a number of members of "old" Europe: the British, Italians, Spanish, Portuguese, and Danish. But with the exception of the British and Spanish (and Bulgarians), most of our supporters were not on the Security Council. Soon after the second resolution was introduced, it became clear that the American and British positions were in the minority. With the head of the International Atomic Energy Agency, Mohamed ElBaradei, and chief UN inspector Hans Blix reporting that at least some progress was being made with the Iraqis, efforts to persuade several nonaligned members on the Security Council, including Mexico, Chile, Cameroon, and Guinea, became more difficult. These members began to insist they would support a second resolution only if it gave the inspectors more time and if it also included benchmarks on Iraqi performance or nonperformance.

The administration was unwilling to go along with such a phased resolution, believing that new reasons for delay would be found—and the debating of noncompliance would rule out our ability to use force. Even though we introduced the second resolution, and President Bush even proclaimed at one point that he wanted all members to "show their cards," we did not have the nine (out of fifteen) votes needed to pass a resolution, and therefore chose not to bring our resolution to a vote.

Unfortunately, having presented a second resolution, our failure on it created the impression that we were going to war over the opposition of the UN Security Council. Nonetheless, President Bush believed he had the legal basis needed to launch the war against a regime that had defied the international community since 1991. In speaking to the country on March 19, 2003, to announce the beginning of war, he explained, "Our nation enters this conflict reluctantly—yet our purpose is sure. The people of the United States and our friends and allies will not live at the mercy of an outlaw regime that threatens the peace with weapons of mass murder."[30]

THE END OF MAJOR COMBAT OPERATIONS AND THEIR AFTERMATH

The military campaign to take Baghdad and oust Saddam Hussein took three weeks. Cobra II, the military plan for the campaign, depended more on technology, high mobility, precision-guided weapons, and information dominance on the battlefield than on massive forces. Bypassing areas and not fully subduing them fit the plan of getting to Baghdad quickly and forcing a collapse of the regime. It was Secretary Rumsfeld's concept of warfare, reflecting what he saw as the revolution in military affairs. For Rumsfeld, technology and surprise made much more sense in this era than employing large forces. He pressed Tommy Franks, and Franks in turn pressed his senior officers, such as General David McKiernan, to reduce the number of forces used, keep their buildup time to a minimum, and not count on forces continuing to flow to Iraq once Saddam was ousted.

Anthony Zinni, a Marine Corps general, had been the previous head of Central Command. He developed a war plan for Iraq that provided for a minimum of 380,000 troops to stabilize the country, minimize chaos, subdue any remaining opposition, control all provinces in the country, and safeguard the borders. His plans were rejected in favor of a significantly smaller force. Rumsfeld had been determined to transform the military, its structure, and its approach to war fighting, and the military plan for Iraq reflected his thinking.[31]

He similarly wanted to transform the concept of what to do after the end of major combat operations. In mid-February, one month before the war, Rumsfeld gave a speech entitled "Beyond Nation-Building"; in it, he described how the postwar reconstructions of the 1990s bred a culture of dependency and were, therefore, wrongheaded. The Bush administration would do things differently in Iraq, reflecting the minimalist approach of Afghanistan. Unlike in the Balkans, where U.S. forces were tied down in a long-term commitment, we would have a smaller presence and be "enablers"; we would limit our presence and assistance and "enable" the indigenous people to shape their own future. We would not rebuild or reconstruct; we would not create a massive bureaucracy to run a country after warfare—as in Bosnia or Kosovo. Much like the use of massive force in military campaigns, the Balkans represented the "old" way of thinking about what needed to be done after conflict.

As Lawrence Di Rita, Rumsfeld's spokesman, told Jay Garner—the retired general Rumsfeld selected to manage the period in Iraq after the "war"—the secretary was determined to avoid the mistakes that the State Department had made in the Balkans, and we would not be creating a long-term military or reconstruction effort: "DoD would be in charge, and this would be totally different than in the past . . . We would be out very quickly."[32] (De Rita explained to Garner and his team, "All but twenty-five thousand soldiers will be out by the beginning of September.")[33] To reduce our troop level from more than 160,000 troops in April to 25,000 in four months suggested a very rapid withdrawal of our forces.

Rumsfeld's insistence on limiting the number of troops available and on a rapid drawdown led Garner to tell General McKiernan, "There was no doubt we would win the war, but there can be doubt we will win the peace."[34] Unfortunately, Garner, who was replaced by L. Paul "Jerry" Bremer in May 2003 as the civilian running what became the Coalition Provisional Authority, proved to be far closer to predicting reality than his boss, Donald Rumsfeld.

CHANGING OBJECTIVES

The administration's goals in Iraq appeared straightforward. Regime change was clear; Saddam Hussein had to go. From the time President Bush gave instructions to Secretary Rumsfeld to develop the war plans for Iraq in November 2001, the purpose had been to remove Saddam Hussein.

On a number of occasions, including with visiting leaders, the president made the point publicly that Saddam Hussein represented a danger to the international community, had developed WMD in violation of UN Security Council resolutions, and had used them against his own people and his neighbors—and that after 9/11, we understood that we could not risk the danger of Saddam's giving such weapons to terrorists. We would not let him do that; we would certainly not wait to be hit. The logic of the post-9/11 world demanded that we remove such dangers before they were inflicted on us. The president's new national security doctrine of "preemption" provided a conceptual rationale for such a policy.[35]

As President Bush was also keen to point out, removing Saddam Hussein's regime predated preemption as our national security strategy. The policy of the Clinton administration toward Iraq had also been regime change—and President Bush often noted this as a way of suggesting that his determination to deal with Saddam was not a departure for American policy.

However, in August 2002, as questions began to be raised about the administration's seeming march to war, and President Bush decided to go to the UN for an additional resolution, the administration's objective began to morph into one of disarmament of Iraq. While the fear that terrorists might get their hands on WMD—and that Saddam Hussein might be the one to give them such capabilities—was certainly part of President Bush's continuing rationale for pressing for action against him, the focus for the United Nations was disarmament and not regime change.

This created an inevitable tension in terms of what we were saying and what we would be seeking. Tim Russert raised the apparent contradiction with Vice President Cheney in an interview on the eve of the president's address to the United Nations General Assembly:

RUSSERT: If Saddam did let the inspectors in and they did have unfettered access, could you have disarmament without a regime change?

VICE PRESIDENT CHENEY: Boy, that's a tough one. I don't know. We'd have to see. I mean, that gets to be speculative, in terms of what kind of inspection regime and so forth.

RUSSERT: But what's your goal? Disarmament or regime change?

VICE PRESIDENT CHENEY: The president's made it clear that the goal of the United States is regime change. He said that on many occasions. With respect to the United Nations, clearly the UN has a vested interest in coming to grips with the fact of Saddam Hussein's refusal to comply with all those resolutions . . .

RUSSERT: So you don't think you can get disarmament without a regime change?

VICE PRESIDENT CHENEY: I didn't say that. I said the president's objective for the United States is still regime change. We have a separate set of concerns and priorities with the UN.[36]

Russert was to raise the same basic question again with Secretary of State Powell a month later on his show:

RUSSERT: So he [Saddam Hussein] can save himself, in effect, and remain in power?

SECRETARY POWELL: All we are interested in is getting rid of those weapons of mass destruction. We think the Iraqi people would be a lot better off with a different leader, a different regime, but the principal offense here are weapons of mass destruction, and that's what this resolution is working on.[37]

Here Secretary Powell is describing regime change as something that would benefit the Iraqi people, but it is clearly secondary to the objective of eliminating Saddam's weapons capabilities. Leaving aside the obvious difference in tone and content between the secretary and the vice president, the two different objectives had very different implications in terms of U.S. action. Regime change by definition required the use of force; disarmament did not. The objective shaped the means. Our confusion on objectives was likely to create confusion on means as well.

Of course, such confusion could have been avoided had there been a clear and agreed-upon sequence of steps. For example, disarmament through inspection and UN-run weapons destruction would be the initial objective, and only if this was frustrated by the Iraqis would we then produce disarmament through the use of external force—which presumably meant removing the Saddam Hussein regime as well. That certainly appears to be what Secretary Powell had in mind.

President Bush, however, appears to have had much more in mind. The president appears to have set his sights on goals that went well beyond only disarmament and even regime change. Regime change, in the president's eyes, would unleash much more far-reaching transformations in Iraq, internationally, and in the war on terrorism more generally. In a speech to the American Enterprise Institute one month before the war, President Bush declared that liberating Iraq would be part of a broader approach to democratizing the Middle East. Iraq, the president said, would become a democratic model for the region. The president's objective was to win the war on terrorism not only by military means but also by implanting democracy in the heart of the Middle East. When anger and alienation no longer existed in the Middle East because oppressive regimes were replaced by democratic ones, Jihadists would no longer find it so easy to recruit terrorists; in this way, removing Saddam not only would deal with the WMD threat but would also change the balance fundamentally in the Middle East and in the war on terrorism.[38]

The goals were lofty and visionary. Within Iraq, there would be liberation, an end to tyranny, and the emergence of a society based on moderation, pluralism, and democracy. Outside Iraq, the removal of the regime would mean that Iraq was no longer a threat to its neighbors; a safe haven for terrorists would disappear; an object lesson for Iran and even North Korea would be created on the danger of going nuclear and resisting us; and the emergence of a new model of democracy in the midst of the Arab world would likely have a domino effect throughout the area. The president's optimistic view of what would be achieved by regime change even extended to the Israeli-Palestinian conflict: on the eve of the war he told one group that the liberation of Iraq would produce peace between the Israelis and the Palestinians.[39]

These were the goals and expectations. Much later, in 2006, President Bush began to explain the difficulties we faced in achieving our objectives in Iraq by saying that no military plan survives contact with the enemy. It would have been far better had the administration seen the obstacles in 2003.

OBSTACLES TO ACHIEVING OUR OBJECTIVES

The obstacles the administration faced ranged from the absence of international support for its most important objective to the realities within Iraq itself. Leaving aside what it might face in Iraq, the first problem the Bush administration had to confront was opposition to our objective of regime change. There was consensus on forcing Iraq to live up to UN Security Council resolutions and disarming it as a consequence. But on the Security Council, very few of the countries were prepared to support regime change.

France and Russia were both against it, and France, in particular, was very energetic in mobilizing others to oppose regime change and the use of force. And, here, the tension in objectives between disarmament and regime change was bound to make even an attempt at producing a sequenced approach problematic. After all, there were basically different mind-sets as to what constituted giving an inspection process a fair chance. Our position was that Saddam was already in material breach of Security Council resolutions, and the first sign that he was resisting 1441 justified the use of force. The French and Russians—and most of the members of the Security Council—took a different view. Patience was called for in their eyes, and represented a major problem for the administration in terms of the time and content of any inspections process. The ambiguity of 1441 only served to blur these differences and make a unified approach more difficult when subsequent negotiations took place.

But even if the administration had been prepared to be more patient, there was an additional problem with a sequenced approach: while France was willing to support the use of force for purposes of disarmament if it became unmistakable that inspections could never work, it did not necessarily follow that such a use of force automatically meant regime change. In fact, though President Chirac was not convinced that force would ever prove necessary, even if it did, he still believed that, much as in 1991, force could be used against the WMD and not necessarily against the regime itself. In other words, it was possible to forcibly disarm Iraq of WMD without having to change the regime, which could be very messy and create untold consequences.[40]

Two factors also compounded our readiness to work the UN process. President Bush was mindful of the political difficulties his father had faced, and was determined not to repeat them. Once he realized there might be a domestic problem in acting against Iraq, his administration focused a great deal of energy and effort on mobilizing domestic support for military action. That is why his approach in the fall of 2002 was geared to the Congress first and to the Security Council second. Whereas his father sought to get a UN Security Council resolution to create a domestic base to support our use of force, George W. Bush worried first about a congressional resolution and saw it as the base for action at the UN. But generating congressional authorization to use force against Iraq before achieving a Security Council resolution on inspections raised red flags at the UN on what the real purpose of that force was. While certainly generating greater pressure on the Security Council to produce a resolution on fostering disarmament through inspections, congressional authorization also produced even greater determination among members of the Security Council to give inspections a chance and not create a rush to war.

Our buildup of forces, however, left us with little interest in having a drawn-out process of inspections—or even a second resolution that might give Saddam more time and create benchmarks on performance for the Security Council. Even if the forces involved were much smaller than in 1991 or than General Zinni had envisioned, they still would number more than 150,000 and the administration was loath to leave them in the area for an extended period of time. (Ironically, in 1990, we had nearly 250,000 troops in the Gulf region by the end of October, but did not go to war until January 16; a larger presence created far less pressure in the minds of administration leaders to use the force, lest we not be able to sustain that presence.)

To be sure, there were other force-related obstacles. Tommy Franks's war plan counted on a northern front, and that required being able to muster an invasion force from Turkey. But the newly elected government there, led by the Muslim party—the Justice and Development Party—was quick to join the chorus that a second Security Council resolution authorizing force was absolutely essential. The Turkish foreign minister, Yasar Yakis, not only emphasized that such a resolution was necessary from Turkey's standpoint, but also called attention to a more fundamental problem of public opposition to Turkey's playing the role envisioned for it: "If we are talking about the extensive presence of American forces in Turkey, we have difficulty in explaining this to Turkish public opinion. It may be difficult to see thousands of American forces being transported through the Turkish territory into Iraq or being stationed or deployed somewhere in Turkey and then carrying out strikes in Iraq."[41]

In addition to the international obstacles we faced, there were, of course, the sectarian realities within Iraq itself. Saddam's rule had cemented the historical advantages for the Sunnis in Iraq, and probably generated one million people who depended on and benefited from his Ba'ath regime. Shi'as became more of an underclass during his rule and, after the 1991 uprising, had been subjected to even greater deprivation and brutality. Kurds faced Saddam's deliberate Arabization of areas that had traditionally been Kurdish, especially in the city of Kirkuk. Several consequences flowed from Saddam's sectarian policies: Sunnis, if Saddam lost power, would resist losing their dominance to a traditionally Shi'a underclass. The Shi'as, who were the numerical majority, would feel that they were finally entitled to receive their due within Iraq. And the Kurds, who had enjoyed a protected status of nearly complete autonomy since the creation of the northern zone in 1991, would not simply retain a strong interest in preserving their quasi-independent status from the rest of Iraq, but would also be determined to undo the Arabization of Kirkuk and repatriate the Kurds who had been expelled.

Two last obstacles to achieving the administration's objectives should be noted. First, while the administration sought to make postwar Iraq a model for the rest of the region, this was bound to face problems. Shi'as were certain to emerge as the leaders of post-Saddam Iraq, given their strong numerical majority, and most of the Arab world is Sunni. Wouldn't others in the region find this a source of threat and not attraction? If so, that would undercut the credibility and appeal of Iraq as a model. Making Iraq nonsectarian and an economic success would, thus, be an imperative.

However, success in Iraq also depended on the administration's being able to draw on all its resources in a coherent, systematic fashion. Unfortunately, here there was another problem. The administration was plagued by poisonous relations that pitted the Defense Department and the vice president's office against the State Department and the CIA. The former saw the great evil of Saddam Hussein and believed deeply that his ouster would have a transformative impact on the region. The latter tended to see Iraq in terms of its divisive, "Balkan" character, retained great skepticism about the region's potential socially and culturally for democratic change, and favored stability over transformation as a result. Such an analytical divide might have fostered a creative tension that permitted a wider variety of problems to be anticipated and dealt with. But that assumed an ability to take each other's concerns seriously and respond to them. Instead, what emerged in the administration was the perception that those who were on the other side of the ideological divide were not to be trusted. Their concerns were not to be taken seriously, their motivations were suspect, and therefore the questions or problems they raised shouldn't be considered.

This reached absurd lengths: The Pentagon forbade officials from taking part in a simulation the CIA ran before the war on what would happen in Iraq when Saddam Hussein's regime fell—believing that the problems that would surface would give credibility to those who argued against going to war in the first place.[42] In addition, Tom Warrick, who ran the Future of Iraq Project at the State Department, was fluent in Arabic, and had great familiarity with Iraq, was kept off of Jay Garner's team—notwithstanding Garner's strong desire to have him—because he was opposed by Secretary Rumsfeld and the vice president's office. And, even though a consortium of think tanks offered the administration a panel of experts to provide facts and options for postwar planning—and National Security Advisor Rice told them, "this is just what we need"—the effort was vetoed because it implied "nation-building," and that was an unacceptable doctrine in the White House and the Defense Department.[43]

Divisions within the administration were simply never resolved. The attitudes differed fundamentally on what was needed both to conduct the war and manage Iraq in the aftermath of Saddam's demise. Secretary Powell, in particular, raised concerns about insufficient troop size and difficulties with the postwar planning, but his concerns were not addressed. In the secretary's farewell meeting with President Bush, he told the president that the national security decision-making process—meaning, principally, the NSC process—was broken.[44]

MEANS USED TO OVERCOME THE OBSTACLES

The administration certainly recognized some of the obstacles and sought to deal with them. Secretary Powell made an effort at the Security Council to forge an international consensus on objectives. He worked hard to produce Resolution 1441 and did deliver a 15–0 vote in its favor. Along the way, he made an estimated 150 phone calls between September 12—the day of President Bush's speech at the UN—and November 10, the day the resolution was adopted. He had countless meetings at the UN in New York and Washington. While he did not travel to capitals, he worked hard to produce the resolution, and succeeded.

His success, however, did not bridge the differences on objectives; it simply masked them. Perhaps the secretary believed that the resolution would create a new reality. If so, he was bound to be disappointed. The French and the Russians interpreted his key concession to produce the resolution—namely, that the Council must be reconvened for a discussion if Iraq were found to be in noncompliance—as mandating that there could be no automatic resort to force. They felt confident that they were raising obstacles to the use of force, while the secretary believed that he was creating a path that would either obviate the need for force because Saddam would comply or justify it because he had not done so.

The secretary's judgment that the UN route provided him his only real means to try to reconcile the difference in objectives was understandable. However, the only way the UN path could have succeeded is if the inspectors had immediately reported that Saddam Hussein had changed his behavior. Given Saddam's desire to preserve ambiguity about his WMD for deterrence purposes against Iran and for coercive purposes domestically, that, unfortunately, was never in the cards.

What about the means used to get a second resolution? After all, achieving a second resolution would have created a Security Council–backed basis on which to use force against Iraq. Prime Minister Blair felt that a second resolution was essential, and even though the administration believed 1441 to be sufficient authorization and said so publicly, President Bush understood his partner's needs, and instructed that we make the public effort to secure a second resolution. The same basic technique used for the first resolution was applied. The secretary of state made numerous calls to his counterparts and also had meetings in Washington and at the UN in New York. In addition, the president telephoned those most recalcitrant, such as Presidents Putin and Chirac.

To try to persuade members of the Security Council—and the international public more generally—Secretary Powell, who was considered the most credible of administration leaders on the world stage, also made a detailed, televised presentation before the Council, offering evidence that Saddam Hussein was continuing to develop his WMD programs and obstructing the work of the inspectors in defiance of Resolution 1441.[45]

The secretary and his key aides also discussed in New York, or on the phone, different ways to accommodate the concerns of countries such as Mexico and Chile—each of whom, if persuaded, might have swung enough votes to cross the threshold of having at least nine Council members supporting the resolution. Had that been the case, then either France or Russia would have had to veto the resolution, and the French strategy, according to their ambassador to the UN, was to block the resolution, not necessarily to veto it.

Additional efforts were made to gain international support; the administration won the support of most of the Eastern European countries to back military action in Iraq and to garner both limited logistic and in some cases small combatant force contributions to the effort. Statements of support were also orchestrated to show that the United States did have international backing for going to war.[46]

The administration also used offers of financial assistance to try to win support from those whose involvement was seen as critical. In the case of Turkey, the administration, trying to persuade the Turkish government to permit American forces to operate from and through the country, offered a sizable package of potential assistance: three billion dollars in aid, three billion dollars in financing, and promises to secure one billion dollars in free oil, and access for Turkish companies to reconstruction contracts in both Iraq and Afghanistan.[47] With the Russians, there were also hints of inducements, at least with regard to Russian oil companies not losing out on the existing contracts they had to develop Iraqi oil fields—assuming, of course, the Russians played ball on the second resolution. And with Chile, there was the suggestion that a Free Trade Agreement could be reached quickly.

Whether on trying to forge an international consensus on objectives or to produce support or important backing of others, the administration made an effort politically and economically to demonstrate that it was not acting alone. The secretary of state worked the phones and the environs of the Security Council in New York. The deputy secretary of defense was sent to Turkey to win Turkish support, and the undersecretary of state for political affairs went to Moscow and Paris to gain Russian and French acquiescence. Though the president and the secretary took one trip to Russia, as we will see in discussing why the administration's efforts and the means employed failed, the level of the effort tended to be too low, lacked intensity, and had to overcome other policies that soured the atmosphere.

How did the administration deal with the obstacles related to the internal realities in Iraq and the consequences of warfare? It planned to deal with contingencies that it found most likely and dangerous. In a briefing at the White House on February 24, 2003, less than a month before the war, the interagency preparations for providing "humanitarian support in Iraq in the event of any military action" were outlined. The displacement of people, a breakdown in the distribution of food, and the destruction of oil wells and infrastructure were uppermost in the list of concerns. The need to ensure the quick provision of humanitarian supplies was a clear priority. Two guiding principles for shaping our response to these contingencies were (1) to rely primarily on civilian relief agencies, and (2) to ensure effective civil-military coordination.[48]

Representatives of several governmental agencies explained the nature of the planning to deal with the expected contingencies.[49] What is unmistakably clear is that planning for contingencies was geared toward the disruptive humanitarian consequences of the war. Perfectly sensible but not particularly related to sectarian realities and the consequences of the collapse of the regime and the vacuum that might result from that.

To be sure, the administration was mindful of minimizing the human impact of the war and the disruption of services, and it tended to see its strategy as cutting off the head of the snake but leaving the body intact. In the words of Elliott Abrams—the lead briefer at the White House on February 24—the military campaign would be designed to "minimize the displacement and the damage to the infrastructure and disruption of services."[50] The assumption was that with Saddam and his cronies gone, a new Iraq could rapidly emerge, provided we did limited damage to the infrastructure and the Iraqis had their oil intact to finance their recovery and reconstruction.

It was not unreasonable to worry about the contingencies that the administration considered and to develop the means to deal with them. It is interesting, however, that destruction of oil wells and refugee flows and displaced persons reflect contingencies seen in the 1991 Gulf War, when Saddam set the Kuwaiti oil fields on fire and triggered a massive Kurdish refugee problem. While generals are often accused of preparing to fight the last war, it appears that Secretary Rumsfeld planned to fight a different war of "shock and awe," with much smaller forces, but prepared for the contingencies of the last war.

The fact that Saddam had set Kuwait's oil fields on fire but not his own was a distinction considered not to be important. The assumption was that if Saddam was going down he would bring everything down with him. The problem was that Saddam thought he would survive, and he wasn't going to destroy the financial source of his power. Similarly, who were going to be the refugees of 2003? They would not be the Kurds, because they remained protected. Displaced people from fighting could certainly be created, but massive refugee flows were unlikely, particularly given the plan for the war, which was to move rapidly toward Baghdad and bypass areas without fully subduing them.

And here we see the gap in military and civilian planning. Notwithstanding the claim that there would be close civil-military coordination on relief, the military plan made that difficult, at least in the early going. We would be bypassing areas, not acting to control them. Relief agencies would not be able to get into Basra and other areas throughout southern Iraq because the military aim was to get to Baghdad quickly, not facilitate the entry and security of those providing relief in areas our forces had already gone through on the way to the north.[51]

There were certainly other inconsistencies: one of the avowed purposes of the war was to deal with Iraq's WMD and ensure that they could not be given to or fall into the hands of terrorists. Yet the shock and awe plan did not provide for the forces necessary to find and control WMD sites or to control the borders in a way that would have prevented terrorists from either going to such sites or smuggling what they acquired out of the country.

Perhaps the reason this inconsistency did not figure highly in the minds of the administration planners is that the overriding objective was getting rid of Saddam. Get rid of Saddam, produce regime change, and everything would *fall into place, not fall apart.* That was the critical assumption, and it was based on a flawed assessment. Statecraft must start with assessments based on reality, and not on faith. If we are to understand the failures in Iraq, this is the starting point.

UNDERSTANDING THE FAILURES IN IRAQ

The greatest single failure in Iraq is related to the assessments. Certainly the intelligence failure on WMD created a major problem; had we been able to display the WMD to the world, the region, and the Iraqi public, there would have been far greater acceptance of the legitimacy and importance of the U.S. mission. With displays of truly awful biological toxins and weapons, who would have challenged the need or the merits of the mission? President Bush was sensitive to this, wanting there to be camera crews with forces who would seize the WMD to show the world what we were uncovering in Iraq.[52]

Ironically, however, we were lucky that there turned out to be no WMD, because we were so ill-equipped to control all the possible sites and to prevent terrorists from getting their hands on them.[53] And here, again, we see flawed planning and flawed assessments. It is not just that the assessment that we would be greeted as liberators proved to be wrong; we also failed to anticipate the chaos, the looting, and the complete breakdown of law and order.

Each of these latter events had a devastating impact on the nature of our task in Iraq. The chaos and the looting made the challenge of reconstruction vastly more difficult. One estimate of the cost of the looting was twelve billion dollars, the equivalent of the revenues Iraq was projected to generate in the first year after the war.[54] Quite apart from the cost of repair, the materials lost and destroyed greatly complicated the task of providing electricity and reconstituting oil production, and further vitiated American credibility with the Iraqi people. After all, in a region in which conspiracy is like oxygen and breathed by everyone, Iraqis asked how we could remove the seemingly all-powerful and untouchable Saddam Hussein in three weeks and yet we could not prevent looting or get the electricity resumed? We must not want to; we must *want* to occupy Iraq.

Was looting something that was hard to imagine or prepare for? No, outside humanitarian groups that met with administration officials warned of it. Similarly, in the State Department's Future of Iraq Project, there were also warnings of it. And when Jalal Talabani, today the president of Iraq, came with other Iraqi opposition leaders to meet with Vice President Cheney and Secretary of Defense Rumsfeld in August 2002, he called attention to the danger of looting, observing that there were many poor people in Baghdad, and with no authority in Baghdad, they would take the law into their own hands.[55]

Moreover, there were those both within the administration and outside who were focused on the need to establish law and order quickly. One official in the Justice Department proposed a plan that called for five thousand international police advisors to be rushed to "Iraq to fill the law enforcement vacuum after the collapse of Saddam's government."[56] Robert Perito of the United States Institute for Peace briefed the Defense Policy Board on February 28, 2003, only weeks before the war, calling for a civilian constabulary to keep order, and telling the board that the United States would not be able "to rely on local authorities" to meet the needs of providing law and order, and that "prior experience indicates the regular Iraqi police will be unavailable, intimidated or unprepared to act in the chaotic postwar environment."[57]

But such warnings and proposals flew in the face of the administration's image of what would happen in Iraq after Saddam fell. Our problems were seen as largely humanitarian; without Saddam, Iraqis would no longer be oppressed and could assume their responsibilities no longer impoverished and inhibited by a brutal dictator and his corrupt elite. Looting, disorder, lack of security, and insurgency were not part of the administration's assessment or planning. While the CIA did not warn of insurgency, its National Intelligence Council did warn that the "building of an Iraqi democracy would be a long, difficult, and probably turbulent process, with potential for backsliding into Iraq's tradition of authoritarianism."[58] After generations of being oppressed, it would not be easy to share power.

In the world of division and distrust in the administration, such warnings were interpreted as an indication of opposing the enterprise of liberating Iraq and bringing it democracy. For those who were driving the policy, and who were convinced of what would be achieved in Iraq, there was every reason not only to dismiss the doubters as wrongheaded but also to dismiss and ignore the problems they raised. Secretary Rumsfeld might speak of planning, but such planning was limited, came late in the process, and gave short shrift to the very problems that would plague us once we were in Iraq.

To make matters worse, once we were in Iraq, there was a continuing denial of what was happening on the ground. During the phase of major combat operations, the attacks of fedayeen Saddam were not seen as a precursor of an insurgency that required dealing decisively with these forces and that demanded they not be allowed to melt away. Afterward, Secretary Rumsfeld denied that we were facing a guerrilla war, refused even to use the word *insurgents*, and continued to refer to violent incidents as being the work of dead-enders who, by implication, could not amount to much.

Though an insurgency should have been anticipated, and was not by the administration policy makers, there were those who foresaw it as a certainty. They saw Sunnis finding it difficult to accept losing their status of dominance in Iraq—a status they had enjoyed since Ottoman times—and they suggested that rather than submit to the Shi'a, whom they saw as an underclass, the remnants of the regime would find sanctuary in the tribal areas of the Sunni triangle and fight an insurgency from there.[59] Had such warnings been heeded, the administration would have understood not only that it needed more forces, especially to pacify Anbar province (an area where the absence of forces made it easy for the insurgency to take root), but also that we had to avoid any possibility of becoming the symbol of occupation in Iraq. Once we became such a symbol, the insurgency was bound to become far more sustainable.

Perhaps, if the administration had seen that it would be facing an insurgency and needed to avoid the insurgents' acquiring legitimacy and sustainability, it would have understood the importance of having UN backing for the war. We did not need the Security Council backing to remove Saddam, but we certainly needed it afterward. It was essential that the United States not be the administrator of Iraq after Saddam lest we be seen as an occupier. We needed a UN administrator or an international administrator (such as Carl Bildt), but not an American administrator. But this was our victory and we, not others who did not share our vision—whether at the UN or in the State Department—would shape the post-Saddam Iraq.

We did not foresee an insurgency; we foresaw a rapid movement toward a model democracy, and we would be its enablers. We would de-Ba'athify the system and we would disband the military—strategic blunders on par with the decision to have an American administrator guide post-Saddam Iraq to the promised land. Our assessments were shaped by an ideology, not by the realities of Iraq. The first task of statecraft is to have objectives that are clear and not confused. They can be ambitious, but they must fit the world as it is, not as we wish it might be; it takes well-grounded assessments to refine objectives and shape them so they fit reality.

Clearly the Bush administration failed in the first task of statecraft. Unfortunately, it also failed in the second task of statecraft: frame the objective in a way that gets others to accept its legitimacy. Colin Powell's effort to reframe the objective as "disarmament" was successful to a point. It might even have been successful in overcoming the gap between disarmament and regime change—the administration's real objective—if Powell could have persuaded his boss and his colleagues to give the inspection process enough time to make it appear credible to others on the Security Council, especially swing votes such as Mexico and Chile. In such circumstances, he might have been able to produce a second resolution at the UN that would still have won backing for the use of force.

But the failure on the second resolution, no doubt partly the result of the context in which the Bush administration was not willing to allow more time for the inspection process, also resulted from what can only be described as a failure on the third task of statecraft: effective use of diplomacy. The diplomatic effort made by the administration was extremely limited. Where was the high-level attention? Where was the intensity of the effort? Where was the constant working of issues and readiness to preempt problems or to reassure at critical moments? Where was the travel by the most senior officials to the critical foreign capitals to show our concern for the political needs of others and give them an explanation with their publics?

This is not to say there was no effort, but rather that a limited number of phone calls by the president, and a secretary of state who made only one trip to Russia and China, are simply not sufficient in circumstances where we have to convince others of what we are seeking to do. The higher our stakes, the greater our effort should be. However, in this case, as we raised our stakes to get ready for the use of force, and such use became even more controversial, our effort varied little. Certainly, Secretary Powell did not travel or even match the number of phone calls he made in advance of gaining support for Resolution 1441. Perhaps he felt that such efforts could not pay off.

But with Turkey so critical to our having a northern front, how is it possible that the secretary of state would not visit that country? True, the deputy secretary of defense went and, true, the incoming Turkish leader was invited to the White House and, true as well, a very significant package of assistance was offered. But the vote in the Turkish parliament went down by 3 votes out of 514 cast. Had a major public effort in Turkey been made by the United States, showing sensitivity to Turkish concerns, demonstrating publicly (not only privately) our responsiveness to Turkish economic needs, giving interviews in Turkey to the electronic and print media, would the vote still have gone down?

Maybe the mood in Turkey would have ruled it out. However, when you barely lose in parliament with a relatively weak diplomatic effort, it is at least arguable that raising the profile of what we were doing and reaching out much more visibly to the Turkish public—and thereby strengthening the hand of those Turkish leaders arguing for responsiveness—might well have made the difference. To prove the point, contrast the effort of the Bush 43 administration with that of the Bush 41 administration in the first Gulf War. In the six months leading up to the war, Secretary Baker made three trips himself to Turkey; the president called Turkish prime minister Ozal nearly sixty times—phone calls that became part of the public domain in Turkey, so that Ozal could speak credibly about his talks with his "friend" President Bush. Acting in this way with an ally builds their stake in being responsive, even on those issues that are difficult, and in 2002–2003, we simply did not make an effort that either helped produce a new dynamic within Turkey or even raised the costs to the Turks of turning us down.[60]

Of course, the limited diplomacy cost us not only with Turkey. Secretary Powell seems to have believed that visits to capitals couldn't accomplish much more than meeting at the UN or talking on the phone with his counterparts. Phone calls have utility, especially if there is already a strong personal relationship. But face-to-face meetings with counterparts will always be critical in any negotiating process. Face to face, one can read the body language as well as the verbal responses; face to face, there is more opportunity to persuade or dissuade; over the phone it is always easier to say no. Face to face, there always seems to be more time to explore the nature of differences and find ways to overcome or manage them; and face to face, there is a more natural tendency to do real strategizing: anticipating emerging problems, determining where someone in a possible coalition will need to be shored up, and comparing notes on who else may be helpful in persuading recalcitrant parties to come along.

While meetings in New York could have overcome the limitations of phone calls, they were bound to have some disadvantages. Almost by definition, the number of meetings with different foreign ministers is certain to limit the time for each. Of course, there is great value in having multilateral settings for meetings, because coordination can take place far more easily. It was not wrong for Secretary Powell to see the utility of operating at the UN. But such meetings could not take the place of going to capitals, where time, outreach, and context would have created more opportunity to achieve our desired end.

Unfortunately, the administration's statecraft failings were not limited to confused objectives, disastrous assessments, misguided planning, weak diplomacy, and poor communication and framing of the issues. Perhaps the least understandable failing of its application of statecraft was in its approach to the second resolution at the UN. True, Tony Blair insisted on the need for a second resolution, but it is hard to imagine that Blair thought he would be better off with a very visible public failure in trying to produce it.

Contrast the administration's approach with Secretary of State James Baker's effort to produce the "all necessary means" resolution in 1990. Baker believed the resolution was necessary and yet was opposed in this by Prime Minister Thatcher and then secretary of defense Cheney—both of whom argued that we had the necessary legal basis for war already and that we would undercut our position politically if we went for such a resolution and failed. Baker responded that he would not go for the resolution in public unless he knew without question he could produce it.

Baker explored the issue with the other members of the Security Council in private, determined not to go public until or unless he was certain he had the votes. In 2003, the Bush administration should have done the same—and Blair would certainly have been better off with an outcome in which we were not going to war after having failed to win backing for a new UN resolution giving us the authority to do so.

In the end, the Iraq case stands as a model for how not to do statecraft. Could statecraft effectively employed have made for a different situation with far better prospects in Iraq? I believe so. Given the sectarian reality and likelihood of a vacuum after Saddam, Iraq was bound to be difficult. However, a realistic assessment of what we were getting into, a military plan that covered the full array of missions, a Baker-type management of the UN Security Council, and an international, rather than

American, administration of Iraq, would have avoided many of the mistakes we made. The insurgency didn't have to take on roots the way it has. And bolstering an effective and indigenous Iraqi administration that did not rely on exiles would have diminished the sectarian divide and weakened Iranian influence. Ultimately, statecraft done well never guarantees success but certainly creates the best chance for it—and that definitely would have been true in Iraq.

6.

{LESSONS OF STATECRAFT FOR TODAY}

Several lessons emerge from a review of the German unification, Bosnia, Gulf War, and Iraq cases. In the German unification and the Gulf War cases, the objectives were shaped clearly and at the highest levels. The administration leaders believed the stakes were very high and they mandated an intensive effort that they often led. In addition, the national security bureaucracy—the State Department, the Defense Department, and the NSC—worked in harmony.

In Bosnia, this was generally not the case until the summer of 1995. Prior to that time, the objectives were clear in terms of our wanting to shape the outcome, end Serb aggression, stop ethnic cleansing, and bring the war to a conclusion. But certainly in the first two years of the Clinton administration, there was no consensus on the stakes, and the administration was internally divided. As a result, there was a very clear gap between objectives and means. This changed in the summer of 1995, when the stakes were suddenly seen as very great and the means employed reflected that understanding.

Once that point was reached, statecraft in Bosnia had much in common with the statecraft conducted on German unification and the first Gulf War. In these cases, the objective, stakes, and means were clearly harmonized. Not surprisingly, the national security apparatus was generally unified and the administrations were fixated on achieving the objective. The diplomacy was intensive and continuous, and there was an ongoing and accurate assessment of the environment, the openings, the problems, the sources of leverage, and the role and effectiveness of potential partners. Finally, there was deep presidential interest and effective follow-through.

In the case of German unification, the Gulf War, and Bosnia from August 1995, one sees policy not by slogan but by determined action. Nothing is left to chance or to hopeful assumptions. The case of Iraq reflects wishful thinking, and the confusion of objectives there leads to confusion of means. The divisions within the administration are so poisonous that they make reality-based assessment impossible. Those who know the most about the realities on the ground in Iraq are relegated to irrelevance because of their perceived opposition to the war and its purposes. The military's preferences for force size and requirements—especially for creating law and order, controlling the borders, and subduing the area most likely to give rise to an insurgency—are rejected by the secretary of defense. He believes the military's mind-set on warfare is outdated in an era of mobility, precision weapons, and the force-multiplying effects of intelligence and information technologies.

Planning for postwar reconstruction is not taken seriously by those given the responsibility for implementing it. Small wonder that with weak planning, there was weak follow-through. That, unfortunately, has been a hallmark of the George W. Bush administration. Iraq in foreign policy and Katrina in domestic policy are the poster children of an administration that too often fails when it comes to planning and follow-through.

Statecraft done well requires both. It requires administrations not at war with themselves. It requires effective assessments and accountability, with someone taking the lead and acting or ensuring that things are not left to chance. In the cases of German unification, the first Gulf War, and Bosnia beginning in the summer of 1995, we saw all of those elements in action. There is one factor that separates Bosnia in 1995 from the other two cases. The very apex of the Clinton administration was not consumed by Bosnia, the way the apex of the Bush 41 administration was completely preoccupied and absorbed in dealing with German unification and the Gulf War.

To be sure, Secretary Christopher played a pivotal role at certain

strategic moments, especially in New York and at Dayton, where his interventions were decisive. But his involvement was episodic, not perpetual. The same is certainly true of President Clinton. Episodic involvement did not signal his lack of interest—far from it. Nor did it prevent him from making critical strategic decisions, one of which was to empower Richard Holbrooke and his team to do the job.

And that is the point. The continuous, intensive effort made in Bosnia is carried out by a level below the president and secretary of state. As such, it showcases a different model of statecraft from the German unification and Gulf War cases insofar as it employs a small interagency team that runs the policy in a way that certainly requires presidential and secretarial involvement but does not demand nearly all of the president's and secretary's time and attention.

Holbrooke had access to the secretary of state whenever he wanted or needed it, and had the latter's backing for what he was doing. Of course, he had access to the national security advisor whenever necessary, but their relationship was complicated. Don Kerrick, a brigadier general serving on the National Security Council staff, was on Holbrooke's team and he kept National Security Advisor Lake informed but also on board—getting him to back what the team was doing. The other members of the team played the same role with the other essential bureaucratic players. Wesley Clark, a three-star general, represented the Joint Chiefs of Staff and kept the chairman apprised of what was going on and what the team needed to succeed—including keeping up the bombing when most of the allies (and our own military) were second-guessing it. James Pardew, who represented the secretary of defense, did the same, maintaining William Perry's support for what the team needed.

Without this team functioning in this way the same bureaucratic divisions that hampered and at times paralyzed the policy from 1993 to 1995 would have continued. Instead, the team, under Holbrooke's leadership, thrashed out what needed to be done on the road, and then got their home agencies to back them. The value of having checks and balances was preserved because the team itself debated every issue; they preserved a group dynamic but never fell victim to a dangerous "group think"—where other points of view are discredited and ignored, as was the case with the Iraq war of 2003.

One additional factor helped to make this work: Holbrooke had the trust and active support of key people around Secretary Christopher, who also played an essential role in making the decision-making process work. Strobe Talbott, the deputy secretary, who was also close to the president and to Tony Lake, would often make the case for Holbrooke or tell him when he would need to do more to overcome the opposition to the decisions he might be seeking. Tom Donilon, the secretary of state's chief of staff, with ties to the White House, also frequently acted to make sure the process did not fall apart.

Given this team concept, and the active intervention of leading players in Washington to back the team, the president and the secretary of state played their roles and contributed to a success. They did not have to be the central players in this process the way they were in German unification and the first Gulf War. In those cases, their internal discussions and high-level meetings, their travels and phone calls, left them little time for anything else. Would it have been better for the leaders of the administration and those immediately around them to be less consumed by German unification? Yes. They might have paid more attention to Saddam Hussein prior to his invasion of Kuwait. Similarly, if the run-up to the Gulf War had not been so all consuming, the leaders of the administration might have had more energy and inclination to deal early with issues such as Yugoslavia's falling apart or the need to secure Soviet weapons and scientists as the USSR collapsed.

The issue of fatigue—physical and emotional—in carrying out the duties of statecraft has received far too little attention. It is not just preoccupation and having little time for anything else that were certainly factors in German unification and the first Gulf War. But, especially in the case of the first Gulf War, the president and his senior advisors (the so-called "group of eight") rode an emotional roller coaster from the time of the Iraqi invasion until the end of the war. Over an eight-month period, which followed immediately on the heels of the German unification effort, they were involved with an exhausting process of responding to the invasion, building an international coalition, and holding it together to see if pressure could force Saddam out of Kuwait or if war would be required to do so. Compounding the exhaustion was a gnawing uncertainty about the likely costs of war both politically and militar-

ily. The burden that the president and his team bore was immense, particularly with the unknowns about the scope of American casualties and with the very real fears that they could be high.

It should come as no surprise that the success of the war produced exhilaration and relief—but also a letdown. It was not conscious, but it was unmistakable. There was simply no energy, intellectually or emotionally, to tackle new and different challenges. True, Secretary Baker was prepared to launch an effort on Arab-Israeli peace, but that was seen as a continuation of the effort, and in any case had been one of the promises made as we built the coalition. And one deeply ingrained trait of President Bush and Secretary Baker was a profound commitment to living up to their word. They had given it as part of the coalition development and had actively planned an initiative after the war.

Given the timing, tackling something such as Yugoslavia—given its messiness and our military's reluctance even to contemplate involvement—was a nonstarter. One could argue that that might have been true even if we had not just gone through an emotional binge at the top of the administration on Iraq. Perhaps, but there would have been more of a debate, more of a discussion of our stakes and the consequences of letting a conflict emerge in Europe with the potential for ethnic cleansing, large refugee flows, and a widening of the war. There just wasn't the energy for such a thrashing-out.

When there isn't the energy, when there is such fatigue, it is going to affect "assessments" that are made and the will to act more generally. And that, too, was seen at this time in the Bush administration, and not only in its dealing with other potential conflicts. For example, there was little energy available to persuade the Congress that with the collapse of the Soviet Union we would have to mobilize resources on our own and internationally to secure the Soviet weapons sites and Soviet scientists. Safeguarding the sites, converting weapons materials to civilian purposes, making sure nuclear scientists were not becoming destitute and, therefore, vulnerable to being paid by the Iranians or the Libyans to hand over their nuclear know-how were all critical needs. To be fair, they were understood by the administration and some effort was made to address each of these issues. But there was simply no energy to mobilize the world, launch a major campaign, or actively work the Congress to finance what would be needed. In the end, the initiative on these challenges came not from the administration but from Senators Sam Nunn and Richard Lugar.[1]

The point here is not to criticize the Bush administration for neglecting what needed to be done or even to raise questions about the effectiveness of its statecraft. The fact is that in the George H. W. Bush administration statecraft was conducted with extraordinary skill and effort. All the tools of the trade were understood and exploited. Rather, the point is to note that when the most senior leadership of an administration is consumed for extended times, there is bound to be a cost. And sometimes the cost is borne afterward. Certainly, there are times when there is no alternative to this kind of involvement by the leaders of the administration. If war is involved, it is not a choice but a requirement for the president and those closest around him to be deeply involved on an ongoing basis. And, in any case, the greater the stakes, and the more we want to persuade the political leaders of other countries to make hard choices and join us on tough issues, such as Iranian nukes, the more the president and the secretary must be the only ones to make the case. In some circumstances other political leaders need to hear directly from our political leaders about why certain choices are necessary.

The question is not whether the president and secretary of state should be involved; they have to, and they also need to travel. The question is, can their involvement be made more strategic and not so perpetual that they have little time for anything else? I would argue that it can. Perhaps the Bosnia-Holbrooke case provides the model for those cases where the stakes are high or where we have a keen interest in conflict resolution. The essence of the model is the creation of an interagency team that is senior and has access to the top leadership when it needs it; is capable of managing bureaucratic divisions and yet can call on all necessary bureaucratic resources for support; is seen as having authority not only domestically but with those it deals with internationally; and is able to bring in the president and secretary not just for decisions but also for persuasion of others at decisive moments.

I don't offer this assessment only as an observer of the Holbrooke team. I led a team in managing our approach to Middle East peacemaking for nearly all of the Clinton administration. The team was not as high-level as Holbrooke's, but it did involve the senior experts from the

National Security Council staff, and when I needed support from the Defense Department, I had it—even taking lieutenant generals with me on trips to Syria when I felt it was required. When not on the road, I had daily meetings in my office at 10:00 a.m. to plan what we were doing and to make sure that nothing was going on in the administration that might be inconsistent with what our diplomacy required. I had authority across the administration and access to the secretary at all times and to the president when necessary. Bureaucratic impediments were managed in this fashion, and support across the administration, including from the intelligence communities, was something I could always call on.

If nothing else, this shows that a Holbrooke-type model with lower-level officials is sustainable over time and not only for short, intense bursts of activity. It is a model at least mechanically for how to make statecraft effective. Clearly, statecraft is not just about defining objectives, assessing how to relate our means to those objectives, and then acting on them. Statecraft must necessarily also involve organizing our bureaucratic agencies so they work together and can be managed effectively to maximize the tools we have. Presidential leadership is needed to mandate such harmony and select cabinet officials with that in mind. When there is bureaucratic disagreement, presidents must be prepared to make decisions, or at least authorize a Holbrooke-type model that can contend with the problem.

President George H. W. Bush did much of the former. President Bill Clinton certainly did the latter, authorizing Holbrooke-type envoys and teams to lead our efforts on the Middle East, Russia, and North Korea. Unfortunately, President George W. Bush appears to have done none of the above, with bureaucratic dysfunction often being the result. The administration spent its first term without a policy toward Iran largely because the Pentagon and vice president's office advocated isolation and regime change while the State Department preferred engagement. Unwilling or unable to resolve this internal conflict, President Bush and his National Security Council deferred the issue and wasted valuable time as Iran continued to progress in its quest to acquire nuclear weapons.

When it comes to exercising statecraft, the starting point, at least organizationally, is to prevent bureaucratic dysfunction or paralysis. To ensure that the executive branch functions well and maximizes the full potential of our assets, it is essential to be able to integrate all our bureaucratic tools and have someone responsible for spearheading them in a way that responds to our strategic aims. As Joseph Nye points out, this is no simple task, since many of the "official instruments of soft power—public diplomacy, broadcasting, exchange programs, developmental assistance, disaster relief, military-to-military contacts—are scattered throughout the government, and there is no overarching strategy or budget that ever tries to integrate them with hard power into an overarching national security strategy."[2]

This remains a challenge for all presidential administrations. At a minimum, statecraft done well demands having a keen eye for organization and knowing how to gain control over all the relevant means we have in order to employ them synergistically. The president must designate someone—presumably the national security advisor or the White House chief of staff—to make sure that all of our bureaucratic assets are being used in a complementary or reinforcing fashion to help achieve our policy objectives.

Of course, statecraft is not just about the orchestration of the means or the tools of the trade. Ultimately, to be effective, statecraft is about identifying and acting on the right objectives. And that is rarely a given.

One can certainly argue—and I have publicly—that given who Arafat was and his inability to make peace, we pursued the wrong objective; rather than a conflict-ending agreement, we should have focused on increasing the scope of Palestinian independence from Israeli control and on broader cooperation between the two societies until after Arafat passed from the scene. That could have created the conditions for peacemaking for the post-Arafat period.

Here we are reminded that if the objectives are wrong, we can employ our tools and our leverage effectively and still produce bad outcomes. Sometimes we might identify the right objectives in the near term, but not necessarily the right objectives for over time. Margaret Thatcher was convinced that German unification in NATO was the wrong objective because it would cost us Mikhail Gorbachev; perhaps we would win the new "battle" for Europe but lose the war by losing a reformer in Moscow who would serve our longer-term aims of genuine partnership with the Soviet Union. The Bush administration made the judgment that shaping a new architecture in Europe, with Germany embedded in Western institutions, was a surer way to safeguard our long-term interests than letting Gorbachev's needs be the arbiter of what was possible in Europe.

This is not to say the Bush administration was indifferent to Gorbachev's needs—far from it. But the president and his advisors, while wanting Gorbachev to succeed, made an assessment that his success over time was in many ways beyond our control to affect. We might have done all we could to help him, and still he might not have succeeded. If we had mortgaged the future of Europe by accepting a neutral Germany as the price of helping Gorbachev, we might have ended up losing on both counts—and with disastrous consequences as a result.

In other words, the Bush administration made a judgment. It focused on the most important objective even as it sought to minimize the costs to Gorbachev, and worked with him to do so. The administration also made a judgment call on how to end the first Gulf War. Would it have been better to alter the objective either to regime change or even to the destruction of the Republican Guard, the main forces that protected the regime? Would having done so have prevented the war in 2003?

Looking at the enormous difficulty and costs of our involvement in Iraq from 2003 to the present, and at the sectarian nature of the conflict there, the veterans of the George H. W. Bush administration would answer that their judgment of ending the war as they did has been vindicated. Others might argue that altering the objective at least to destroying the key military forces underpinning Saddam's rule would have been the wiser course when thinking about the future.

Is the answer in such a debate obvious? I think not. And that is also going to be true for every administration as it conducts statecraft. Defining the right objectives is enormously important, but also enormously difficult if one is trying to find a balance between near and longer-term objectives. Choices have to be made. Oftentimes there will be tension between objectives, and leaders and their advisors have to choose based on the best assessments they can make. The point is to make assessments so that at least the choices are conscious. Decision makers must at least consider which objectives are ultimately the most appropriate for now and for over time.

And that argues for assessments that bring all factors into consideration. Faith-based or ideologically driven assessments will exclude what needs to be considered. The Bush administration in 2002–2003 proved the folly of such an approach.

So what does all this mean for how to think about statecraft? To be effective, statecraft starts with being able to define clear, understandable, and meaningful objectives. Hardheaded assessments are essential for refining the objectives to fit reality, our relevant ambitions, and our means, including the means we can marshal with others. It is also critical to be able to "frame" what is at stake in a way that not only can mobilize and sustain domestic support but also does so in a way that makes our objective "legitimate" internationally and raises the costs to those who would oppose it. Active diplomacy (including back channels) and the orchestration of inducements and penalties—including threats and coercion—in a way that promotes our defined objectives is also a necessity.

To this point, I have defined statecraft, explained in general terms why it is necessary, showed how it has worked effectively in some cases and not in others, and drawn some general lessons. Before exploring when and how to use some of its tools (negotiations and mediation) more precisely, it is important to discuss the new international landscape in which statecraft must be conducted. There are familiar features of international relations today that reflect continuity with the past and also unfamiliar challenges that pose new threats and make new demands on statecraft.

7.

{STATECRAFT IN A NEW WORLD}

Statecraft can never be effective if its practitioners are divorced from reality. Our practitioners today must understand how the international landscape is changing. Sticking to assumptions that fit the international system of the 1980s would certainly mislead us on what our foreign policy priorities ought to be today. While some of the developments of the past twenty years have shaped today's realities, especially with regard to burgeoning sectarian conflicts, there can be little doubt that the landscape of a globalized world presents its own set of challenges.

Secretary of State Condoleezza Rice has acknowledged that the United States faces new challenges, but she finds parallels with the post–World War II period. The United States emerged from the war as a dominant global power for the first time, stronger than any other state economically and militarily. There was, however, a new competitor ideologically and militarily, and we had to adjust to a different reality that also required a new American role. At that time, the advent of the cold war required new thinking and new institutions, both domestically and internationally. Secretary Rice compares the early years of the cold war era to the current period in terms of the need to develop a new architecture and new approaches. In no small part, she finds the analogy apt because in those early years of the cold war, there was not instant success. It took several years to build institutions such as NATO, and to trans-

form Germany and Japan into stable countries that could become real
partners.

While one can quibble over whether new institutions are being built
today or whether the occupations in Germany and Japan offer much insight into what we face in Iraq—where there is an insurgency led by
those who do not consider themselves defeated—the comparison is useful insofar as it reminds us that at certain junctures in international relations we must refashion assumptions about our role in the world and the
means necessary for carrying out that role.

Walter Russell Mead has observed that the United States confronted
two challenges in the postwar period. First, we had to stop the spread of
communism in Europe and Asia while containing the Soviet Union. Second, we had to replace the British world system with a set of political
and economic institutions and practices. If containment failed, the economic system and alliances would also fail, but if the economic system
failed, impoverishment would be the result, the Soviets would exploit it,
and we would find it difficult to contain the USSR. We needed to succeed in both areas or we would fail everywhere.[1]

Mead points out that we face two similarly intertwined challenges
today: we must deal with fanatical terrorists, potentially armed with
weapons of mass destruction, and we must build an effective economic
and political system for a globalized world. If we fail to deal with the terrorists, there could be a collapse of the global economic and political order, but if we fail to develop ways to manage that new order, many of the
world's people will suffer and the terrorists will be able to recruit new
allies.[2]

In drawing this comparison, Mead highlights both the similarities
and the differences between the eras. What's similar is that security challenges cannot be separated from economic and social challenges. What
is different is that during the cold war we had a great power competitor,
and states were the main source of danger—and the vast thermonuclear
arsenal of the Soviet Union made the threat existential. Today, it is not
clear that any nation-state truly threatens our survival; the main danger
comes from non-state actors; and while our very existence is not at stake,
the threat of violence is always around the corner.

So what is familiar in the international landscape of today and what
is not? Terrorism is not a new phenomenon. Nor is the danger of the

spread of weapons of mass destruction to rogue or irresponsible regimes, or the emergence of new powers that seek influence to match their new capabilities. Historically, the rise of one power has come at the expense of existing or dominant powers, and produced conflict. That is obviously what worries many today about China. Each of these phenomena is familiar and requires the effective use of statecraft and the tools of the trade.

What is different, clearly less easy to grasp, and far more complex to deal with is the new reality of threats from non-state actors (i.e., terrorist groups that don't depend on state sponsors). The new phenomenon of fewer and fewer being able to threaten more and more became a stark reality on September 11, 2001. Today, even small numbers can inflict mass casualties, and it is clear that terror groups such as Al Qaeda and its offshoots are trying hard to do so. It is the possible marriage of the worst weapons in the worst hands that makes these apocalyptic terrorist groups so catastrophically dangerous.

Given the complexity of the challenge and the need to defeat not just the tools but the ideology of the new purveyors of terrorism, we necessarily will be called on to use all of the tools of statecraft—all the imagination and capability to work with others that we can muster. Statecraft will thus be in great demand.

STATECRAFT AND THE FAMILIAR CHALLENGES ON THE INTERNATIONAL HORIZON

STATE-SUPPORTED TERROR

Terrorism is not new. In the past, state support facilitated the ability of such groups to carry out terrorism. The Soviets saw terrorism, particularly when carried out by Palestinian rejectionist groups, as a means to threaten our friends and the established order in the Middle East. The KGB and its sister security organizations in Eastern Europe gave extensive, if covert and deniable, support—training, financing, intelligence, fake documentation, logistical help, and sanctuary and protection—to many of the leading terrorist groups in the Middle East and Europe from the 1950s until the collapse of the Soviet Union.

State support of terrorism still exists today. Both Syria and Iran continue to provide operational and material support to Hizbollah, Hamas, and Islamic Jihad, pressing them to carry out terrorist attacks against Israel. They seek to subvert any possibility of peace between Israelis and Palestinians and to foment conflict more broadly in the region—which they certainly did in Lebanon in 2006. Similarly, Syria—and Iran, to a different extent—has sponsored the operations of the insurgents in Iraq. (Though declaring otherwise, Pakistan's support for Islamist groups carrying out terrorism against India over the disputed territory of Kashmir does not appear to have ended.)

The Syrians have treated terrorist groups as "cards," designed either to show enemies the costs of not responding to Syrian interests or to disrupt developments that they find threatening. The Iranians have sought, through Hizbollah, to promote a Shi'a-led Islamic state in Lebanon. Iran fomented war between Hizbollah and Israel by providing roughly 7,500 rockets to Hizbollah *after* Israel withdrew from Lebanon in 2000. In the eyes of the Revolutionary Guard, who continue to dominate the national security apparatus in Iran, polarization and confrontation serve Iranian interests in the Middle East more than efforts toward peace, stability, and reconciliation.

Where terrorist groups remain primarily dependent on states, the states can be held accountable. Leaders in states such as Syria, Iran, or Pakistan can be made to understand that their governments will be held responsible if groups operating out of their countries carry out attacks in other states. Historically, the fear of the reaction probably limited the scope and character of the terrorist operations that Syria, Iran, Libya, or other states have historically supported or countenanced. They, no doubt, would always deny any involvement, making it harder for us (or others) to justify attacks or reprisals against them, but they also knew that if we suffered an egregious loss we would feel driven to respond.

Deterrence of state-supported terror will continue to be an essential aim and requirement of statecraft. A related goal must be changing the behavior of those states that sponsor terror. The Bush administration has sought to do so with Pakistan. Its efforts immediately after 9/11, when it communicated directly to President Musharraf that he had a choice to make, worked to a certain extent: at the time, Musharraf made a choice against Al Qaeda, and seemingly also the Taliban in Afghanistan. There was both a threat that the administration conveyed and also the promise of benefits in the form of increased aid—much of which has been delivered. To date, President Musharraf has been helpful in terms of arresting members of Al Qaeda, but Pakistan's record on the Taliban is, at best, very mixed—and, of course, there has been a similar ambivalence on rooting out the groups who carry out terrorism in Kashmir and India. U.S. fears of who might replace Musharraf and our continuing stake in his help have led the administration to try to encourage his positive moves and convince him that for his own reasons he needs to do more against the Taliban and the groups who operate against India. (India, to be sure, also applies its own pressure and inducements on Musharraf in this regard.)

While it is not easy to change the behavior of those states that sponsor terrorism—and the Bush administration's posture has often tended to emphasize regime change over changed behavior—it can be done, and should be seen as one of those areas in which we need to practice statecraft. The administration's record on Pakistan is mixed. Its record on Libya has been much better; here it had the benefit of a leader who had sought since the 1990s to get sanctions lifted. Qadhafi suffered not just from American sanctions for his support of terrorism but also from collective sanctions imposed by the Security Council after Libya was held responsible for the bombing of Pan Am flight 103 in December 1988. Throughout the Clinton administration, Qadhafi used all sorts of intermediaries—including the Palestinians with me—to offer to change his ways if the sanctions were lifted.

The problem was that Qadhafi was willing to meet only some but not all of the Clinton conditions: assuming responsibility and paying damages to the families of the victims of Pan Am 103, stopping all support for terrorist groups, and giving up Libya's WMD programs. Not surprisingly, Qadhafi tried to see if he could go partway. Keeping the pressure up, while also making clear how he would be rewarded if he changed his behavior, characterized the Clinton approach, and over time also came to govern the Bush administration effort. President Bush and others in his administration have claimed that the war in Iraq persuaded Qadhafi genuinely to turn over a new leaf—which he has done with respect to his

WMD program. Martin Indyk, who participated in the Clinton administration's effort to wean Qadhafi away from his terrorist-supporting and WMD ways, has pointed out that Qadhafi had a change of heart only when he finally came to understand that he would not get sanctions relief until he gave up terror and his WMD program.[3]

There is probably merit in both arguments. The ongoing pressure (including the Bush administration's interdiction of a shipment of nuclear components to Libya), the image of Saddam Hussein being swept out of power by the U.S. military, and the promise of restoring ties and lifting sanctions combined to produce the turnabout in Qadhafi's behavior. Much as with Milošević before him, the sanctions created domestic pressures on Qadhafi. They took time but there were painful consequences, and to get relief and the promise of ties and economic investment, Qadhafi was ready to shift course dramatically.

The wielding of important sticks that raised the price of bad behavior was combined with the offer of meaningful carrots—carrots that could become available only with demonstrative steps to prove that bad behaviors were, in fact, being stopped. It worked with Qadhafi—and also Milošević, at least as far as settling the Bosnia conflict was concerned. Here is the essence of statecraft in terms of changing the behavior—not necessarily the regime—of a state supporting terrorism. In the case of Libya, it required patience, real pressure with a real and meaningful price, and partners who were prepared to join the sanctions regime and sustain it, while also going along with the promise of inducements at the right time and in the right way. (In the case of Qadhafi, the Bush administration might not have succeeded without the British, who were ready to be tough but who initially conducted and drove the talks in which the potential for gains for the Libyans were also conveyed.)

PREVENTING THE PROLIFERATION OF
WEAPONS OF MASS DESTRUCTION

Trying to prevent the proliferation of nuclear, biological, or chemical weapons has been a central feature of American foreign policy for the last forty years. In the past, the effort focused on stopping the spread of such weapons to new states, particularly those in volatile regions. The

Nuclear Non-Proliferation Treaty (NPT) and other multilateral instruments (e.g., the Australia Group focused on the supply of chemical weapons and precursors, the Missile Technology Control Regime, etc.) have been used to forestall proliferation. There have been successes. In the last fifteen years, a number of countries have renounced their nuclear ambitions and deactivated their programs (South Africa and Argentina) or returned weapons based on their soil (Kazakhstan, Belarus, and Ukraine in agreement with Russia).

The challenge today on proliferation is more complicated than before. We must be focused not only on states but also on non-state actors. We must try to strengthen the security of a large number of sites that have components, materials, or actual weapons—that could be exploited by states or non-states. We must strengthen the nonproliferation regime to make it more difficult and costly for those who might be tempted to acquire or develop such weapons. And we must find ways of imposing a price on those who are defying the international community now to affect their behavior and to be sure that others don't recalibrate their own interests on the merits of acquiring such weapons.

The danger of unsecured WMD sites. Consider that a ten-kiloton nuclear warhead could be highly portable, and in the words of one study "if set off in mid-town Manhattan on a typical workday could kill half a million people and cause over $1 trillion in direct economic damage."[4] It is essential that neither states seeking such weapons (Iran) nor terrorist groups (Al Qaeda) be able to gain access to unsecured facilities housing nuclear warheads or artillery shells through penetration or bribery.

How big is the problem of unsecured sites? At the beginning of the Bush administration, in 2001, a bipartisan task force assessed the threat of "loose nukes" and concluded that "The most urgent unmet national security threat to the United States today is the danger that weapons of mass destruction or weapons-usable material in Russia could be stolen and sold to terrorists or hostile nation states and used against American troops abroad or citizens at home."[5]

Notwithstanding the Nunn-Lugar legislation of 1991 (devoted to the destruction and decommissioning of thousands of nuclear warheads), CIA director George Tenet told Congress that "Russian WMD materials and technology remain vulnerable to theft or diversion."[6] Unfortunately, there are still plenty of unsecured sites, and "thousands of kilograms of military plutonium and highly enriched uranium (HEU) in the countries of the former Soviet Union (FSU)."[7] As Graham Allison has trenchantly pointed out, even after thirteen years of the Nunn-Lugar program, there were still "44,000 potential nuclear weapons' worth of HEV and plutonium vulnerable to theft; terrorist groups would have until the year 2018 to be able to shop in Russia and its former Soviet neighbors for nuclear weapons.[8]

The problem, of course, is not limited to the sites in the former Soviet Union. Worldwide it is estimated that there are 20 metric tons of highly enriched uranium at 130 operational civilian research reactors in forty countries. Since only 26.4 pounds of enriched uranium ore are needed to make a nuclear bomb, the scope of the potential problem even outside Russia is daunting.[9] And the fact that there is now an underworld of "stealthy black market procurement networks of brokers, intermediaries, and front companies" only too ready to supply nuclear materials for reasons of greed or ideology means that it has become immeasurably easier for states or terrorist groups to gain access to a nuclear weapon.[10]

Securing nuclear sites remains a major challenge. The Bush administration has made efforts in all these areas, but the issue of unsecured sites needs to be an even higher priority. The Nunn-Lugar Cooperative Threat Reduction program, which, as noted above, has worked effectively in securing nuclear weapons and materials in the former Soviet Union, needs vastly more funding to accelerate its work.[11] Similarly, the Megaton to Megawatts program, which takes highly enriched uranium from Soviet nukes and turns it into low-enriched fuel for nuclear reactors, has also been effective, but it, too, needs to be accelerated. The G-8 Global Partnership initiated in 2002 supports an array of nonproliferation initiatives; here again, more money and a higher priority is needed.

Private-sector NGO (nongovernmental organization) initiatives have also been effective in beginning to deal with the problem of securing sites where biological agents have been developed. Former senator Sam Nunn, the cochairman and CEO of Nuclear Threat Initiative, has been especially active with the Russians, initially in finding ways to tackle security problems associated with nuclear weapons sites but more recently in trying to deal with biological and chemical sites. Biological sites are especially sensitive, with the Russians denying access to potential production sites; at times NGOs may be a less threatening and more politically sensitive vehicle for approaching governments and should be integrated into a comprehensive strategy for dealing with the security of WMD sites.

Strengthening the nonproliferation regime. Steps have been taken to strengthen the barriers to the acquisition of WMD. The Bush administration conceived and launched the Proliferation Security Initiative, which has created an umbrella for countries acting in concert to openly interdict WMD supplies or components going to rogue countries. Under this rubric, the United States seized a ship with a cargo that included centrifuges heading to Libya, and, as noted above, that was certainly a key factor in influencing Qadhafi's decision to give up his WMD program.

Other steps have been taken to prevent the proliferation of nuclear weapons, including through the more conventional means of closing loopholes in the existing regime. For example, the Additional Protocol to the NPT was designed to provide for much more expansive monitoring and verification of all related sites. This is especially useful, as the NPT permits monitoring and inspection of only declared (not undeclared) sites of nuclear-relevant activity. The Additional Protocol closes that loophole. It does not, however, address the most fundamental problem of the treaty: any signatory of the treaty is entitled to pursue and develop civilian nuclear power and receive technical help to do so. In practice, this means that signatories are allowed to complete the fuel cycle of enriching uranium and reprocessing it, which puts them in a position of being able to produce either fuel for nuclear reactors or fissile cores for nuclear bombs. Having developed this capability under full monitoring, any country could then exercise its legal right to withdraw from the treaty and produce nuclear weapons—and not be in violation of the treaty.

One way to deal with this problem is straightforward: amend the treaty to make it a violation (in which the violator is subject to Security Council sanctions) to acquire nuclear technology under the aegis of the NPT, use it to develop nuclear weapons, and then withdraw from the treaty. If some countries fear that amending the treaty would require opening it up with unclear consequences, an alternative approach might be to produce another protocol outside the treaty that picks up on a French suggestion raised in preparation for the last NPT review conference in 2005—namely, that any signatory that acquired nuclear technology and then withdrew from the treaty would be required to return the technology, destroy it, or seal it—and be declared in violation of the treaty if it did not do so. This proposal received little support but could be revisited.

Another way to deal with the fuel cycle problem could be to provide a guaranteed source of nuclear fuel at subsidized rates to any country that forewent the acquisition of sensitive fuel cycle facilities and returned the spent fuel to the suppliers. This would be economically attractive for those who genuinely sought nuclear power for strictly energy-generating purposes and would effectively make it impossible for anyone to use the treaty to acquire nuclear weapons legally.[12] Nongovernmental organizations represent another tool available to help in this regard. Warren Buffett, working through the Nuclear Threat Initiative, has offered fifty million dollars to help set up an international nuclear fuel bank that aspiring countries could use to receive reactor fuel rather than having to make it on their own.[13] With many countries now declaring that they need nuclear power, including Egypt, the United States had better find a way to create widely accepted and fully legitimate alternatives to countries acquiring the means to complete the fuel cycle, lest we face a world of states capable of converting their nuclear power to nuclear weapons.

All this will not mean much if we do not also organize a new international effort to deal with the "large secretive networks of brokers, middlemen, scientists, engineers, manufacturers and front companies" who circumvent the existing controls on the export of nuclear-related materials.[14] Clearly, states (such as Iran) and non-state actors will continue to exploit this nuclear black market unless more is done to disrupt it. Perhaps the United States could take the lead in getting the G-8 plus China to adopt new standards and techniques for making export controls more effective. Working groups might be created and asked to report back to the political leaders with proposals for enhancing existing controls at both national and multinational levels.

To be sure, it will be easier for the United States to lead in this area, to mobilize others to take on the challenge of dealing with proliferation with greater urgency, if we are also setting a moral example. The more we act to reduce the importance of nuclear weapons and to resist the temptation to constantly modernize our own nuclear arsenal, the easier it will be to set an example. I am not saying that if we only reduced our nuclear capabilities, quantitatively and qualitatively, pressures would be inexorably created on others to follow suit. But it is surely hard for us to make the case that others should not have nuclear weapons when we keep improving our own; when we are one of the very few who have not ratified the Comprehensive Nuclear Test Ban Treaty; and when we research low-yield nuclear weapons, seemingly with an eye to making it easier to employ such weapons.

True, there may be military utility in using these weapons, but our objective—particularly if we are not ready to seriously reduce our own nuclear stockpile in any appreciable way—must be to give others a reason not to go nuclear. And it is undoubtedly easier to foster greater collective pressures on regimes such as those in Iran and North Korea if our own behavior is seen as more defensible and less provocative to others. Framing our policies and explaining them in a more compelling and credible fashion is a must; so, however, is adopting policies that seem to promote international goods such as paying for the conversion of warheads to nuclear fuel and supporting, not opposing, the Comprehensive Nuclear-Test-Ban Treaty.

Preventing Iran from going nuclear, and reversing North Korea's nuclear posture. Nothing would reinforce our efforts to strengthen the NPT regime more than success in preventing Iran from going nuclear or getting North Korea to change its course. We need to show that the prohibitions remain strong on crossing the nuclear threshold and that there is a price to be paid where those prohibitions are violated. Others who might be tempted to go nuclear—or acquire other WMD means—must see that they pay an unacceptable price, and rather than becoming more secure, they become less so.

Iran and North Korea have been a focal point of concern in the acquisition and spread of nuclear weapons, in part because of the possibility that they might provide terrorist groups with these means, but also because of the threats they might pose in their regions. Each in its own way represents a "tipping point" in which their acquisition of these weapons creates an inexorable dynamic where others feel they must also have the capability. Isn't it likely that Japan and South Korea will feel the need to offset North Korean capability? And, with Iran, won't Saudi Arabia and also Egypt respond to the Iranian capability with one of their own? The Saudis almost certainly were one of the beneficiaries of the A. Q. Khan nuclear network and will want the Iranians to see that they are not coercible.[15]

In these cases, the tipping point, that is, having whole regions go nuclear, will make these areas more dangerous and uncertain. A nuclear Asia may not ineluctably devolve into war, but can we be so confident in the Middle East? When the Iranian president Ahmadinejad calls for wiping Israel off the map, what kind of threshold are the Israelis likely to have vis-à-vis potential Iranian threats, especially if Iran develops nuclear capability? As one leading Israeli defense official said to me, "We think the Iranians intend to use nuclear weapons against us, and we won't wait for that to happen." The Israeli impulse toward preemption is likely to be on a hair trigger should its leaders come to believe that Iran is on the verge of producing fissile material by itself.

That, alone, argues for preventing Iran's acquisition of such a capability. The international community has been seized with the Iranian nuclear program since 2002, when Iranian opposition groups revealed that Iran had been engaging in secret, illicit nuclear activities and that the nuclear watchdog agency, the IAEA, knew nothing of these efforts. International opposition expressed in votes of the thirty-five-nation board of the IAEA notwithstanding, Iran has made it clear that it is determined to create an independent fuel cycle. To date, Iran has continued to develop the infrastructure to be able to produce nuclear weapons, and yet it has paid no real price.

Will the United States have to threaten the use of force to prevent Iran from going nuclear—or actually have to use force to prevent it? Has our position in Iraq made us less credible and capable in Iranian eyes, particularly given Iran's potential to make life even more difficult for everyone in Iraq? Can we gain an international consensus for the use of force or, lacking that, for significant economic sanctions against the Iranians? And even if we can, will that raise the costs of going nuclear in Iran sufficiently high that the Iranian government will defer its efforts? In chapter thirteen, I discuss the prospects of changing the Iranian calculus and how to go about doing so.

But one point should be very clear: should Iran cross the threshold and become a nuclear weapons state, the international landscape will be affected profoundly. Not only could it make the Middle East far more dangerous and less stable, but it may also contribute mightily to taking what has been the "redline" against countries going nuclear and turning it to "pink." Whatever the flaws and limitations of the Nuclear Non-Proliferation Treaty (NPT), it has created a regime that has been remarkably successful. Many predicted that the NPT would never work, and that within a decade or two after its adoption in 1968 there would be twenty to thirty nuclear powers. Yet nearly forty years after the NPT entered into force, there are only eight nuclear weapons states. The NPT has provided a prohibition on going nuclear; however, should the NPT redline become pink, we will be looking at a new landscape internationally, one that is far less predictable and far more prone to miscalculation and preemption in crisis.

It is not clear whose interests would be served by such a development. Emerging powers such as China and India, who need stability, especially in terms of access to energy supplies to maintain their high economic growth rates, should not look favorably on such a development. Given its ties to North Korea and Iran, and its status as a permanent member of the UN Security Council, China is in a good position to affect the decisions of both the North Koreans and the Iranians on nuclear weapons.

In the case of the North Koreans, the Chinese have more influence and leverage than anyone else. They border North Korea, they can relieve or cement its isolation, and they provide the bulk of the fuel and food North Korea consumes. The Chinese are very mindful of the problems North Korean nukes present, and are certainly keen on ensuring that Japan does not feel the need to go nuclear in response. Similarly, the Chinese relationship with, and desire to affect the behavior of, South Korea is also an important factor in China's posture. China has taken the lead in the six-country talks and been far more active diplomatically than ever before. But the limits of China's readiness to pressure North Korea must also be understood. China fears a North Korean collapse that might trigger millions of North Korean refugees streaming across the border. Kim Jong Il is adept at exploiting Chinese fears.

Perhaps he became overconfident in this regard. Kim embarrassed the Chinese leadership when, over their public and private objections, he conducted a nuclear test. The Chinese, in turn, applied much more pressure on North Korea than ever before, producing resumption of the six-party talks and, clearly, a readiness on the part of North Korea to reach agreement in them. The real question now is whether the agreement (meaning full denuclearization) will be implemented. No doubt, the North Koreans will test the limits of the agreement and whether China will side with them if we appear too insistent that North Korea open up its system. China's fear of North Korea's collapse may still supersede its concerns about North Korea preserving hidden nuclear weapons if it has closed down its nuclear reactor and allowed inspectors to return. Our own strategy must take account of this possibility, just as our approach to South Korea needs to be understood as greatly affecting our leverage in general and on China in particular.

For the Iranians, the Chinese are also a critical factor in their considerations. A Chinese veto in the UN Security Council could protect them either from international economic sanctions or from a Security Council resolution to use force against them. The Chinese have been reluctant to use their veto at the UN, but they also have contracted with the Iranians for more than a hundred billion dollars' worth of energy-related contracts for the coming decade, and given their seeming desire to lock in their energy supplies, they may be inclined to block any oil-related or economic sanctions against the Iranians. For now, the Iranians, who see the strategic benefit of their growing economic ties with China, seem to believe that China will protect and not pressure them.

In effect, China may have a choice to make: try to enforce certain international rules of behavior that in general promote greater stability, or deviate from an international consensus against a country violating a broad norm because of its preoccupation with its own oil supplies. It is an interesting choice, and may reveal where China is headed in the coming years. Is it a rising power whose political ambitions and reach will expand inevitably to match its economic might in a way that threatens others, or is it a rising power that will integrate itself into the existing international system? Or is there a third alternative that combines both integration and transformation? The answers to these questions remind us that China is a major new factor on the world stage and will significantly influence issues as diverse as the proliferation of nuclear weapons, the fate of rogue regimes, and the protection of the planet's environment.

Given the increasing importance of China, I will discuss how to contend with its rise internationally in chapter fourteen. My purpose here has been to highlight China as one of the familiar challenges we face in the new global landscape. Let me now turn to the unfamiliar challenges that confront us in the new international setting.

A NEW INTERNATIONAL LANDSCAPE, UNFAMILIAR THREATS

TERRORISTS AS NON-STATE ACTORS

Non-state actors such as Al Qaeda that carry out terrorism, including mass acts of terrorism, are different from previous terrorists (individuals and groups) in one important respect. Those groups almost invariably were backed by nation-states. Those states had something valuable to lose and could be held accountable. They could and often would choose to control the groups, and as such, we could deter the state-backed terrorist groups by deterring the states in which those groups resided. But in a world of non-state actor threats, who are we deterring and how do we do it? Can we still make deterrence effective? Our response to 9/11 has already demonstrated our readiness not only to hit Al Qaeda very hard but also to preempt Al Qaeda, and keep up a constant effort at preemption, by still making war on states we believe sponsor terrorism. That may have worked to some extent in Afghanistan, but has it worked in Iraq?

While the war in Iraq has diverted at least some capabilities that might have been better deployed in Afghanistan to finish the job against the Taliban and root out Osama Bin Laden, our intelligence efforts have been ongoing against Al Qaeda. Our intelligence organizations have sought to find Al Qaeda operatives and to disrupt their operations—and that helps to account, in part, for why there has been no successful terror act in the United States since 9/11.

However, our actions against Al Qaeda represent more of a strategy of "denial" in which we are trying to defeat it and stop or inhibit its capability to conduct terrorist acts. Deterrence is hard to achieve, because our threatened military reprisals are not necessarily something that imposes a price on Bin Ladenism or its adherents. They are not troubled by tough military responses, particularly because many of them have been socialized to believe that martyrdom is their religious duty and that nothing is more glorious. Moreover, the more violent our response, the more we are likely to kill noncombatants—spreading an image that Al Qaeda constantly seeks to exploit, of the U.S. killing and inflicting pain on Muslims. They want to promote an image of America being at war with Islam and with all Muslims. Hizbollah, though Shi'a and not necessarily an ally of Al Qaeda, has had very much the same strategy vis-à-vis the Israelis. In their war with Israel, they fired rockets from populated areas not only to try to use civilians as shields and to complicate Israeli targeting, but also to trigger great anger throughout the Islamic world against the Israelis—and by extension the United States—when their bombings killed women and children.

Fomenting anger against the United States is essential for Al Qaeda and others to produce new recruits and to persuade those recruits to carry out acts of suicidal terrorism. This is not an argument against using force against these groups. There is very little alternative to doing so. But it is a reminder that deterrence as we have always known it is not going to work with these groups and that military responses have to be shaped with political objectives in mind.

Deterrence remains relevant for dealing with states such as Iran or Syria. In a world of shadowy non-state actors, however, the United States will need different approaches and will need to employ other tools or forms of statecraft. Indeed, to deal with this threat, America must be able to work with others, and to find new ways to convince those in the Islamic world that the United States can be a partner in defeating the radical Islamists who represent a threat to us both. Moderate Muslims must take the lead in competing with the radical Islamists, discrediting their claims of religious purity, and showing how they represent a threat to Islam itself.

The United States doesn't need to invent reasons for moderate Muslims to take on the radical Islamists; they are the ones most immediately threatened by them. We do, however, have to recognize why there has been reluctance and hesitancy on their part to take on this task, and develop our responses accordingly. One important factor in the hesitancy of local moderates is that leading regimes, whether in Egypt or Saudi Arabia, have often viewed them as more of a threat than the Islamists. The regimes have wanted to keep the alternatives available limited to themselves or the Islamists, believing the Islamists would scare their publics and the outside world. Secular, reform-minded figures might look too attractive as an alternative. In the end, these regimes have felt vulnerable and have appeared neither to want real political alternatives to emerge nor to be ready to take on those who claim to be religiously pure and devout. Lacking in legitimacy, these regimes have been too quick to take on the trappings of religious orthodoxy and too slow to condemn the radical Islamists in any but very narrow terms.

These regimes have also been very defensive about their ties to the United States, and moderates throughout the region have often found that their calls for reform are caricatured, to make them appear to be serving an American, not a national, agenda. In this connection, we also have to recognize how America's behaviors and policies have frequently made it harder for moderates to do what we want, and that often, the United States, not the Islamists, has been the source of the anger in the Islamic world.

Traditional approaches won't work in this new struggle. The use of force, while necessary, will not be the key to our eventual success. In a world of non-state actor threats, persuasion more than coercion will be necessary for wielding influence and getting others to join us in the essential task of discrediting and delegitimizing the radical Islamists.

Moderate Muslims can do that; the United States cannot. The task of statecraft in such a context is at least two-fold: first, use our leverage with, for example, the Egyptian and Saudi regimes to get them to stop pressuring moderate reformers; and, second, use our means and the means of others who share our interests and concerns to help empower or strengthen the hand of Muslim moderate regimes (Jordan, Morocco, Gulf Cooperation Council states) and reformers who are prepared to take on the radicals. Whether they need security, economic, educational, or technical means of assistance, we must find a way to create an effective international division of labor to help them in their societies and enhance their readiness and their capacities to compete with the radical Islamists. I have more to say about why and how to do this in chapter thirteen. For now, however, it is important to explain what makes the non-state actors—especially the apocalyptic terrorist groups—so dangerous.

TERRORISTS AND MUSLIM ANGER

Earlier, I spoke of WMD materials and components being far too accessible, both for the states seeking them and for non-state actors. There can be little doubt that Al Qaeda and its global network of like-minded radical Islamists certainly have the motivation to acquire and use them. These terrorist groups are far more dangerous than their predecessors because their ambition, particularly as it relates to inflicting destruction, dwarfs anything previous terrorist groups ever imagined. Osama Bin Laden has spoken often of a global war against America and the need to inflict pain and suffering on the United States and its allies in the same way he charges the West with having inflicted pain and suffering on Muslims worldwide. On at least one occasion, Bin Laden has even borrowed from the image of the cold war that was so often invoked between America and the Soviets: "Just as they're killing us, we have to kill them so that there will be a balance of terror. This is the first time the balance of terror has been close between the two parties, between Muslims and Americans, in the modern age. American politicians used to do whatever they wanted with us. The victim was forbidden to scream or to moan."[16]

Bin Laden has charged that America was leading "the most dangerous, fierce and savage Crusade advanced against Islam," and that "a nation of 1,200 million Muslims is being butchered from its east to its west every day in Palestine, Iraq, Somalia, the south of Sudan, Kashmir, the Philippines, Bosnia, Chechnya, and Asam."[17] His is a call "to sacrifice for the sake of the one God." As Bin Laden has proclaimed, the "youth of Islam are waiting for their scholars to say such words."[18] He even says, "Whether Osama is killed or remains, thanks be to God that the *awakening* has begun."[19]

In the face of such an "awakening," military responses or traditional forms of deterrence are not only irrelevant but probably also counterproductive. We must use the instruments of statecraft in a new way. But to use statecraft effectively, we had better understand this awakening and how the means of globalization promote it.

Globalization, the Internet, terrorism's new recruits, and using intelligence effectively. Globalization clearly has a dark side. It is not just that borders are increasingly porous, it is that images of what "have-nots" lack and what "haves" possess can be seen in any Internet café, and that mythologies of Western insults or impositions against Islam can be spread instantaneously around the globe, spawning anger and deepening alienation.

The power of the Internet is especially significant given the demographic trends in the greater Middle East, where as much as 70 percent of the population is under the age of thirty. This younger population is susceptible to demagogic appeals. They see corrupt regimes that are largely unresponsive to them. They are impatient and dissatisfied, with few employment prospects and little expectation that life will become better. They thus have little hope, and the absence of hope feeds their twin impulses of frustration and anger.

There is something contagious about these feelings. Youthful Muslim populations in Europe may not be growing as fast as in the Middle East, but their sense of grievance and social isolation is probably greater. They are in societies that make them feel different; they face discrimination and exclusion even as they see the possibilities offered to others. They find connections with one another and often a sense of belonging in the mosque—and the mosque in Europe, unlike in the Middle East, is not tied to the social and religious fabric of the state and the larger community, with its traditions and habits. And that, as Francis Fukuyama has observed, adds to their alienation.[20]

The Muslims who planned and carried out the July 2005 bombings in London came from families living in segregated and lower-middle-class neighborhoods. At one time, they had been largely aimless, often on drugs, committing petty crimes, and then they found a sense of purpose, however diabolical, in the radical Islamist mosques and chat rooms.

Violence gives power to those who have felt bereft of it. They can strike back at whomever they hold responsible for the ills and the sense of grievance they feel. Like Bin Laden, they can stand up and show that they will no longer give in.

The French "intifada" of November 2005 was carried out largely by teenagers (and those in their twenties); they were typically unemployed and generally living in segregated, largely Muslim areas they called "cages." Having felt legitimately neglected by French society, they found that violence provided a sense of liberation and got them attention and even respect. Such a phenomenon is neither new, nor unique to Muslims. But using cell phone text messages and blogs to organize arson attacks, as the French police report the rioters did, is clearly new.[21]

Paradoxically, youthful Muslim populations that feel disconnected in Europe and left out in their home countries in the Middle East are "wired" and connected by the Internet to one another. And Al Qaeda and the groups that take their inspiration from it know how to use the Internet to fight their fight and inspire actions with explosive potential.

Look at how the cartoon controversy over the portrayal of the Prophet Muhammad in European newspapers entered the world of cyberspace and triggered violent protests as a result. Radical Islamic websites incited violence, with many calling for an "embassy-burning day" to protest the Muhammad cartoons and with one—alghorabaa.net— urging people to throw Molotov cocktails and storm embassies. Many of the same websites spread wild rumors that are taken at face value and often feature pictures of beheadings and glorify acts of terrorism.[22]

In Iraq today there are few, if any, traditional training camps teaching the insurgents how to build improvised explosive devices; instead, there are "virtual" terrorist training camps over the Internet that teach how to build the bombs and conduct operations.[23] On websites one finds not only master bomb makers offering instructions on how to build bombs but also videos of successful bomb attacks, including those where secondary bombs have killed American soldiers who came to respond to the initial explosion. Having seen these videos, I can say that the message is always the same: our faith is superior; we are heroic; you are one of us; we will impose on those who have humiliated us for so long; we will prevail, and they will suffer the way they have forced us to suffer.

Terrorist training camps in the Libyan desert or outside of Damascus or in the Bekaa Valley in Lebanon represented the old landscape, with state sponsors of terror. These may not have completely disappeared, but the new landscape, with homegrown Al Qaeda–type groups and cells and an army of "shahids," or martyrs, ready to sacrifice themselves, is increasingly growing out of this virtual training reality.

Of course, old-school training and direction still remain important. The lead plotters in the aborted effort in August 2006 to bomb multiple airliners flying from London to New York, Washington, and Los Angeles traveled to Pakistan to meet operators with much more know-how.

These kinds of connections create openings for intelligence organizations to disrupt such terror operations. In this case, the British, American, and Pakistani intelligence agencies worked together to preempt the airliner attacks, sharing information and making arrests in the United Kingdom and Pakistan. Developing formal and informal relationships between intelligence organizations and their leaderships is an essential form of statecraft and one of the key ingredients in any strategy for countering terrorism.

George Tenet has described how important it was for him to have a close, often informal, working relationship with each of his counterparts heading intelligence organizations, and not only among formal American allies but also with states with whom we had no treaty relationships.[24]

In the Middle East, I saw Tenet's capacity to do business with his counterparts in the region based largely on their trust in him. Such trust existed because he invested in building personal ties, spending the time to compare views on what was going on in the region, sharing his understanding and information on threats to his hosts, demonstrating the benefits of coordination, and even having frank discussions on our areas of disagreements or where he believed internal change in the host country was needed for reasons of their self-interest. Having developed the relationships in Saudi Arabia, Egypt, Jordan, the Palestinian Authority, and Pakistan, he could be frank even on issues sensitive to his hosts.

Such relationships will pay big dividends in the new international landscape. They are one important measure of statecraft that leaders in every American administration must be sure to develop. Unfortunately, after Tenet left as CIA director, his successors no longer preserved or sought to nurture the relationships with their counterparts the way he had.

This form of statecraft takes for granted that non-state terrorists are here to stay. At the same time, we must take up the more fundamental challenge of cutting off the ability of the radical Islamists to recruit new followers. This is obviously not just an intelligence problem. In its essence, it is a problem of hearts and minds.

The awakening and the battle for legitimacy and the moral high ground. Zbigniew Brzezinski, who was President Carter's national security advisor, argues that the terrorist "awakening" has explosive potential among youth throughout the developing world, Muslim and non-Muslim alike, and is creating "revolutionaries-in-waiting."[25]

Al Qaeda seems to understand this, and while its focus is on Muslims, its effort and certainly Bin Laden's is to undermine our behavior among non-Muslims as well. In this environment, we have a major disadvantage: American power and purpose are deeply questioned, and the war in Iraq, fairly or not, has magnified the anger toward and rejection of American policies.[26]

To much of the Sunni Muslim world and beyond, the war seems to confirm the American readiness to kill Muslims and subjugate them to U.S. interests. Notwithstanding claims that the Sunni-Shi'a split in the Islamic world is exaggerated, there has been a deafening silence throughout much of the Arab Sunni world in response to suicide bombings that have taken, and continue to take, a horrendous and daily toll on the Shi'as in Iraq, including when they are worshipping in mosques. Where is the outcry from Arab leaders or leading Sunni clerics? It is essentially nonexistent. Instead, we hear criticism of what the United States is doing to the Iraqi people and the costs its campaign is imposing on them—certainly not an illegitimate concern, but where is the outrage about the suicidal bombing campaign that targets primarily Iraqi civilians?

Similarly, much of the rest of the world, especially among those revolutionaries-in-waiting, see us as the cause of the problem. In their eyes, we have imposed a war on Iraq that is widely considered to be unjust, perceived as inflicting great suffering on the Iraqi population, and seen as guided by narrow, selfish, oil-related interests.[27] In addition, the Israelis' extensive bombing and destruction of Lebanon in the war of 2006, which many internationally and especially in the Muslim world believed was not only sanctioned but also encouraged by the United States, has deepened the sense of resentment toward America.

As a result, we must compete in an environment in which America is *not* viewed as morally superior to terrorists. As hard as it is to accept this, we must face reality if we are to succeed in changing it. And we can change it, because this vast younger population has aspirations; they want to be part of the modern world, not left behind. They don't want a new dark age or a dictatorship of religious intolerance. But we must find ways to address them on their terms. We must demonstrate that we are prepared to tackle broader issues of social justice. We must prove we are not indifferent to the plight of Palestinians. We must show that on issues that affect the international community—such as global warming, health pandemics, and poverty—we are on the right side of the issues and leading the way. It won't be easy; we will have to work with others, including those in the Muslim world who may be critical of us but who also reject the Islamists. We will also need to work closely with the Europeans, and this, too, will be complicated by the internal challenges they face—challenges that if not dealt with effectively will affect whether we collectively are seen as holding the moral high ground.

The French and the Germans may believe that they are viewed differently than we are because they did not support the war in Iraq; because, together with their European partners, they commit much more material assistance proportionately and collectively to fighting global poverty; because they are much more open to favoring international law, institutions, and limitations on their own sovereignty; and because, particularly in the case of the French, they identify much more with the Palestinian cause than with the cause of Israel. And yet, how these nations treat their Muslim populations is increasingly going to be a factor internationally. As I have already noted, and as Daniel Benjamin and Steven Simon catalog, jihadist dogma has found a fertile breeding ground among alienated, marginalized Muslims in Europe.[28] How attractive can liberal democracy be as a model if the Europeans fail—as they are now failing—to integrate culturally diverse populations into a single, cohesive national community? Francis Fukuyama persuasively argues that "violence linked to unassimilated second- and third-generation Muslims in Holland, France, and Britain represents a political time bomb."[29]

Won't the problems the Europeans are having with their Muslim populations have an effect on the struggle with the radical Islamists? If it is likely to do so, should we promote a dialogue among and with the Europeans on issues of societal integration? Would we have any credibility doing so? In an era in which domestic issues may be an integral part of the struggle internationally with the radical Islamists, we may have to address questions that traditionally seemed outside the scope of foreign policy. And when we do so, we will have to bring all our tools and all our skills to the task. Anything less, and we may find it very difficult to transform the psychological and social terrain on which the struggle with the radical Islamists is waged.

UNFAMILIAR THREATS: THE NEW DANGERS OF WEAK AND FAILING STATES

Weak and failing states are not necessarily new, but in today's world they create new opportunities for penetration by radical Islamists and criminal networks. One definition of a failed state is that it has lost control over most of its territory and has stopped providing even the most rudimentary services to its people. Many states, particularly in Africa, fit this category and are essentially powerless to stop terrorist groups from setting up shop in their territory.

Globally, the World Bank identifies close to thirty countries as essentially failing, describing them as "low income" and "under stress." The UK Department for International Development identifies forty-six such "fragile" states, with these countries described as impoverished and susceptible to terrorism, armed conflict, and epidemic disease.[30] Regardless of how one counts, the problem is growing, not receding. In a 2006 report, the World Bank identified nine additional countries as becoming "fragile" in the three years since it last issued such findings.[31]

In speaking of dealing with terror, it has become popular to refer to "draining the swamp"—meaning undoing the conditions that have helped to spawn terrorists. One part of the strategy for defeating terrorism depends on recognizing how terrorist networks can be developed in states that lack capabilities, institutions, and infrastructure. Failed or failing states such as Somalia or Côte d'Ivoire (which was recently added to the World Bank's list of failing or fragile states) simply

don't have the means—law enforcement or military or border controls—
to prevent terrorist groups from situating themselves in their territories.

Afghanistan remains a failing state, but under the Taliban it was not
the weakness of the state that permitted Al Qaeda to operate there; instead, it was the Taliban's conscious choice to support Al Qaeda and give
it the benefits of sanctuary and support. The Taliban believed in what Al
Qaeda stood for and was doing, and also benefited from Bin Laden's
largesse.

The Taliban's support, then, constituted state-sponsored support for
terrorism and could have, and arguably should have, triggered much
tougher responses from us prior to 9/11. But what does one do when Al
Qaeda or others (Lashkar-e-Taiba, the Taliban) operate in places such
as Somalia or even in the hinterlands of Pakistan, which seem beyond
the reach of the national governments? Pakistan is clearly a more ambiguous case. It has much greater capability, with a professional army
and a strong central government. However, it previously supported
Lashkar-e-Taiba over the Kashmir (and to some extent may still be doing so). It also continues to demonstrate ambivalence and hesitancy in
going after Al Qaeda and Taliban elements along its Afghan border, for
fear of igniting internal difficulties. In theory, Pakistan could be held
accountable either by the United States or by NATO over the Taliban,
operating now from the hinterlands of the country, but concerns over
preserving the stability of the Pakistani government, and not pushing it
too far, limit our collective willingness to pressure the Musharraf government.

In most cases of weak or failed states, there is simply no government
to hold accountable. The existing government can simply plead weakness, claiming that it just cannot control terrorist groups operating from
its territory; certainly the president of the Palestinian Authority (who
heads a government and not a state) has argued since his election in January 2005 that his government was powerless to stop Hamas, the Islamic
Jihad, and the Al Aqsa Martyrs' Brigades from carrying out acts of terror. (After Hamas won the greatest number of seats in the Palestinian
Legislative Council, this became more believable.)

From the standpoint of terrorist groups, weak or fragile states may be
even more desirable than already failed states as a place to base themselves. Their relatively more developed infrastructure may provide a

more hospitable place in which to operate, and yet the absence of good governance and the presence of extensive corruption offer terrorists easy access to these countries and some protection. In either case, criminality is likely to be rampant in either weak or failing states and local mafias may offer additional means of support for movement and for meeting the needs of groups such as Al Qaeda.

If the United States is serious about "draining the swamp," we have to find ways to strengthen weak or failing states and also to ameliorate or settle the local or regional conflicts that keep them weak. Targeted material assistance from the international community is, of course, necessary. However, such assistance is almost certain to be squandered if it is not tied to the development of institutions for good governance: customs and tax collection, port and maritime security, air traffic control, law enforcement, judicial reform, and the delivery of health care and education. No one outside country, even one as capable as the United States, has the means or the wisdom to develop and promote good government on its own.

There is no magic solution; no shortcut is available. To restore failed states, other governments and nongovernmental organizations will have to share the labor. There can be a natural division of labor between governments who have greater experience in particular regions (e.g., the French in Africa) or in particular forms of assistance for institution or capacity development (the Norwegians) or in peacekeeping and nation-building missions (the European Union). Similarly, NGOs (such as the Bill and Melinda Gates Foundation, the Clinton Global Initiative, FAFO) and the World Bank must coordinate in order to tackle, for example, the health-related problems that undermine the capacity of failing or weak states to function because sickness literally saps their strength and resources.

There is no shortage of those internationally who are committed to trying to deal with the challenges of weak and failing states. But this area more than others cries out for effective statecraft carried out with a sense of urgency and commitment. This means orchestrating the efforts of many different nations and NGOs in a way that takes account of their respective strengths and eliminating redundant and uncoordinated assistance efforts, which often detract rather than complement one another. As one example, the World Bank reports that in Afghanistan, the

Ministry of Finance receives *competing* "technical assistance for customs modernization from the Bank, USAID, and the European Union," all without these entities effectively talking to one another or ensuring that they are tackling different slices of the problem.[32] Apart from potentially vitiating the effect of the aid, uncoordinated donor assistance, in the words of one developmental specialist, also constitutes "a massive managerial burden on low-capacity states."[33] Too often donor efforts contribute to the very problem they are trying to overcome by, among other things, forcing local beneficiaries and the most talented local people to spend far too much time dealing with the needs of the donor bureaucracies and consultants.

It is not just that new approaches are necessary. Leadership is, too. Someone must take the lead internationally in providing impetus, direction, coordination, follow-through, feedback, evaluation, and the pressure to act rapidly in dealing with the needs of failing states in conflict-ridden regions.

Can the United States do it? Presently, it is unlikely, for several reasons. For one thing, we rank lowest among leading industrial nations (on a per capita basis) in our developmental assistance for poverty reduction. For another, we lack the moral authority. Having opposed Kyoto and the International Criminal Court, appeared to suggest that the Geneva Convention on torture did not apply to our forces in the war on terrorism, and gone to war in Iraq over the apparent opposition of the Security Council, the United States too often appears to be outside the international consensus on what serves the public good. What adds to our problems is that the reality of our power (and our way of wielding it) also breeds resentment.

In the post–cold war world, the use of our power created anxiety among our allies in Europe even before the Iraq war. Then, as Francis Fukuyama has observed, the Bush administration's "contemptuous brush-off of most forms of international cooperation," and its public commitment to a security doctrine of preemption fostered the growth of anti-Americanism.[34] Josef Joffe, an Americanophile German intellectual, believes that the United States must restore its identification with good works internationally.[35]

Perhaps the end of the Bush administration will create an opening and ease the resentment of American hegemony. If so, a new U.S. effort to show that we are willing to lead the way on issues such as global warming, environmental degradation, and poverty reduction—in other words, to adopt the Joffe recommendation—might well have a great effect.

But I prefer not to wait. Even now, I suspect that if the United States were to set a new tone and define capacity building as central to reducing poverty and also to dealing with those who exploit poverty for purposes of terror, the Bush administration might find it easier to attract others to a common strategy. Of course, President Bush and Secretary Rice would have to do much more than change their tone. Putting our money where our mouth is on capacity building in weak states would certainly add to our credibility. Lebanon is an interesting case in point. The administration committed $230 million to the reconstruction effort after the 2006 war. It spoke of launching a major donor initiative. What we have seen, however, is that Iran was more effective in getting monies immediately to Hizbollah, and the Western international community, which has the means to produce much more assistance than Iran (especially given the willingness of the Gulf oil states to contribute), took far longer to get launched and then to ensure that donor monies got to those who needed and could use them. Taking the lead in the donor efforts is fine, but there must be follow-through and a continuing level of interest. Onetime events that get attention seem too often to drive the Bush administration; outside of Iraq, it is difficult to see where the administration has sustained the effort.

CONCLUSION

Needless to say, I have not sought to discuss every challenge to statecraft we are now facing. With polar ice caps shrinking and oceans rising, global climate change will affect our need to work with others. Oil dependency and consumption have an impact not only on global warming but also on the security problems America faces with Iran, Venezuela, and increasingly Russia. The higher the prices and the dependency, the more confident, assertive, and irresponsible these oil-producing states are likely to become. At a time when alternatives to oil are cost-effective, it is irresponsible for the U.S. government (using a judicious mix of subsidies, imposed emission standards on utilities and cars, and possibly a gas tax) not to make the end of oil dependency a national security priority over the coming decade.

However, resolving these issues depends less on statecraft and more on leadership. Surely there is no more important objective for our national security than making leaders such as Presidents Ahmadinejad and Chavez less relevant to the United States and the rest of the world.

Clearly, there are a number of issues and countries I have not discussed in this chapter. As important as China is, India is also a large emerging power that will affect the international landscape and create interesting openings for U.S. statecraft.

Russia, too, remains a colossus on the world stage. I certainly recognize that Russia can be a pivotal player when it comes to ameliorating or compounding transnational threats and dangers such as proliferation and climate change. While seeking to gain Russia's cooperation where we can—certainly on an issue like Iranian nukes—we need to understand that Russia will frequently try to stake out a posture that suits its desire to be an alternative to the United States internationally. Psychologically, Russia will strive to recoup its lost standing as a global power, and certainly not one inferior or beholden to the United States. Without deliberately playing on Russian feelings of insecurity and loss of stature, American statecraft in the years ahead will need to find ways to show the Russians that they can be effective on the world stage when their behaviors are responsible and cooperative but will become far less relevant when they are not. If nothing else, this argues for coordinating very closely with the Europeans on how best to deal with the Russians, ensuring our maximum leverage for either including the Russians or excluding them when their behavior warrants doing so.

The international realities we face in the early twenty-first century demand our understanding, effective assessments, the ability to match our objectives and our means, the know-how to wield influence well and to get others to do what we want, and the skillful application of all the policy instruments at our disposal. In a more complicated world, in which knowledge is more widely shared, resentments are more intensely felt, and the use of our hard power is more likely to be constrained— especially after Iraq—we have little choice but to become far more adept in exercising every aspect of statecraft.

Ultimately, there is no aspect of statecraft that in one way or another does not depend on negotiations. War is a form of statecraft, but its termination usually involves negotiations. Preventing war surely involves negotiations—or mediation; building collective approaches to security does too. Promoting more enduring structures for peace requires negotiations; and so, of course, does convincing others to work together to defuse potential conflicts, build capacity in failing and weak states, or find ways to empower moderate Muslims. In effect, negotiations are the lifeblood of statecraft. It is through negotiations that one persuades, dissuades, induces, threatens, and presents choices. It is through negotiations that one often discovers and exerts one's points of leverage. Having described cases of effective and ineffective statecraft and the landscape that U.S. foreign policy must now contend with, let us turn to a discussion of when, why, and how to negotiate and mediate.

8.

{ NEGOTIATIONS AS AN INSTRUMENT OF STATECRAFT }

Negotiations are probably the most essential tool of statecraft. Problems or crises can be resolved through negotiations. Wars might be averted through negotiations, and when not averted, are oftentimes brought to an end by negotiations. Every single instrument of statecraft in one way or another involves negotiations. Indeed, even in those cases in which we declare that we will not talk to another country, communication still takes place—and with objectives clearly in mind.

Take, for example, the U.S. approach to Iran. Although we are not talking, much less meeting directly, we send messages through other countries, designed to affect the Iranian calculus—and, of course, those countries transmit messages back to us. While in the past we might have said we would not negotiate over American hostages being held in Iran or Lebanon, we did negotiate through third parties. Some may confuse our stated declaration of never "bargaining" over the release of hostages as meaning that we would not negotiate. But, through the Algerians, we did negotiate with Iran to resolve the hostage crisis in 1980, and through the Red Cross and other private intermediaries, we held indirect discussions with Hizbollah about the American hostages held in Lebanon during the George H. W. Bush administration. When we tried to find out why hostages were being held or the circumstances in which they might be released, when we were conveying what might happen positively if they were released or more ominously what would happen if they were not, we were certainly negotiating.

Negotiations are employed not just to reach mutual understanding but also to achieve particular ends. Whether we are trying to conciliate or coerce, negotiations are typically the mechanism we use for doing so. When Prussian military thinker Carl von Clausewitz observed that war is an act of violence designed to achieve political ends, he was saying that countries go to war to achieve particular goals. If those goals can be achieved at a lesser cost through diplomacy, then so much the better. But coercion works best, using the threat or application of hard power to make clear to an adversary what he is losing and what he might yet lose through his actions. Negotiations don't have to take place between equals—indeed, in international relations, they rarely do. Sometimes countries will go to war to shake up the status quo and give their adversary an incentive to change behavior through a negotiated process.

Anwar Sadat went to war in 1973 not because he expected Egypt's army to vanquish Israel's but because he thought he might alter the Israeli calculus (and perhaps also the American view of the status quo) and produce a negotiating process that would eventually yield the return of his country's land. Later, knowing that there would be only losses from the further employment of force and frustrated by the diplomatic stalemate, Sadat went to Jerusalem—believing that through a dramatic gesture of conciliation, he would induce the Israelis to enter into negotiations that would rapidly lead to their withdrawal from the Sinai.

As the United States surveys the international landscape and pursues its interests, it will employ negotiations with adversaries, with friends, and with countries with whom it would like to improve relations. It will negotiate in international forums to produce certain desired outcomes, to alter the behavior of those it sees as a threat, or to produce international sanction for its use of force where diplomacy has failed. In 2003 the Bush administration succeeded in negotiating one Security Council resolution, 1441, that it thought would give it the backing to use force if Saddam Hussein did not comply with its demands. It miscalculated in that respect, and a second resolution was required to achieve such international support. The administration's effort to negotiate the second resolution failed not because it was impossible to achieve such a resolution but because the administration was not willing to meet the terms of the key swing voters (Chile and Mexico) who would accept the resolution only if the administration gave UN inspectors another thirty to sixty days to determine whether Saddam Hussein had weapons of mass destruction.

Regardless of whether we are trying to head off threats or build new alliances or alter the terms of international trade or answer the broader challenge of contending with poverty and the AIDS pandemic in Africa, any American president will preside over a number of negotiations. While Americans like to think of themselves as always willing to negotiate, a closer look at our self-image and ethos suggests that our attitudes toward negotiations have often been ambivalent. We have not always embraced negotiations enthusiastically and have frequently ruled out talks with certain countries and leaders. In a more complicated international landscape, our need to negotiate may increase, forcing us to get past our ambivalence and prepare to negotiate in circumstances we might have excluded in the past.

THE AMERICAN APPROACH TO NEGOTIATIONS

One reason Woodrow Wilson was not an effective negotiator is that his principles were inviolable. There could be no concession on principle or adjustment to others that required compromise with basic beliefs. Such beliefs and principles are important. They reflect basic values and should inform thinking and behavior. And our values and our belief in freedom, individual rights, respect and protection for minorities, and the rule of law should not be compromised.

But negotiations are about mutual adjustment. That is the essence of compromise. Our values do not get in the way of negotiations, but our self-image does. We see ourselves as selfless, as adopting positions that represent only a higher good. American "exceptionalism" is deeply embedded in our national psyche. It creates an ethos that also informs how the American public considers its behavior internationally. If we act only out of a higher purpose, how easy is it to compromise with those who don't?

Because of our self-image, we have often been attracted to concepts that seem to require minimal diplomacy and negotiation. Containment of the Soviet Union was straightforward—align with those who would oppose the Soviets and provide them the military and economic support to do so. Certainly statecraft was involved, but the negotiation was limited to seeing what military and economic payoffs were necessary to induce or protect our potential partners. Negotiations to change the behavior of those who did not so easily fit into our cold war division of the world were not given much priority. Only the Kennedy administration made a serious effort in this regard. Its Alliance for Progress in Latin America reflected an understanding that other factors—poverty and resentment of America's power and patronizing posture—might influence who would be willing to align with or against us. Similarly, Kennedy's pursuit of a new relationship with Gamal Abdel Nasser of Egypt—one of the leaders of the "nonaligned movement"—was driven by a belief that the world was not black and white and that our cold war division unnecessarily made enemies of those who might not be hostile to us. However, the complicated and ultimately futile negotiations with Nasser were a reminder that those with regional ambitions were themselves keen to exploit superpower competition for their own purposes.[1]

Détente, unlike "containment," required mutual adjustment and even accommodation with our adversary. We were changing our behavior to change theirs, confident that talking, as opposed to containing, could create greater payoffs for our interests and make us more, not less, secure. Not surprisingly, such a shift in course faced domestic criticism. While the American public has supported negotiations, at least in the abstract, skepticism and fear of what we might be trading away have always created constraints on policies that seemed to depend heavily on negotiations with adversaries. As noted in chapter 1, Henry Kissinger came under severe domestic criticism for his negotiations with the Soviet Union and was clearly constrained by it.

Similarly, conducting negotiations or a dialogue with certain adversaries has been seen as legitimizing them and weakening us. Unquestionably, that is how some critics of détente viewed U.S. negotiations with the Soviet Union during the Nixon years. The fear that by talking to our adversaries we would strengthen them and give them greater staying power has shaped our approach to negotiations. Cuba has been off-limits for years. Iraq, under Saddam Hussein, was treated the same way. Iran and North Korea have at times also been put in this category. This is not to say that we should have been talking to these countries or their leaders, or that we should be willing to talk to everyone regardless of the circumstances. There are those who deserve to be ostracized, whose behavior is so unacceptable that isolation is the only answer—not only to punish them but also for the signal it sends others about behaviors that won't be tolerated or ever accommodated. There are, however, also reasons to talk to adversaries, ranging from defusing threats and avoiding war to finding ways to change dangerous or objectionable behavior. The challenge is to know how to use negotiations for our purposes and to make good judgments on whom to talk to and when to do so.

NEGOTIATING WITH ADVERSARIES

When considering negotiations with adversaries there is a very basic question to ask: "What are you going to talk about?" Clearly, the starting point has to be deciding whether there is enough common interest for the two sides to talk. With the Soviet Union, we had one overriding reason to talk, and that was to avoid mutual annihilation. There could hardly be a more powerful common interest, though it was based more on a shared fear than a shared desire. Negotiations driven by negatives, fears more than hopes, won't necessarily resolve conflict, but they can reduce dangers; they can make relationships more predictable; they can lessen the prospect of miscalculation and conflict; and they can manage competition. That is what arms-control agreements with the Soviet Union were designed to do. By definition, such agreements channel or contain hostility; they don't remove it.

Even when deciding that there is something to talk about with an adversary, leaders will also need to ask whether the objective they hope to achieve is worth the effort and whether it can be met without doing damage to other objectives. Take Iran and its pursuit of nuclear capability. Some see the danger of an Iran with nuclear weapons as superseding any other concern, and argue that talking to Iran is necessary to get the mullahs to give up their nuclear ambitions. Others see the mullah rule in Iran as an enduring threat and are not prepared to countenance negotiating with the Iranian leaders if the price of doing so is to undercut Iranian reformers and democrats.

Whether with Iran, North Korea, or anyone else, negotiations are a two-way street. If we ask the other party to give up something, they will want to receive something they value in return. Neither Iran nor North Korea will simply surrender its nuclear ambitions or capabilities. Apart from specific economic and technological payoffs, each of these regimes seeks guarantees for its survival. Neoconservatives would have a hard time supporting such a tradeoff, believing the regimes themselves are evil, will always constitute a grave threat, and must not in any way be legitimized or safeguarded. Indeed, during the first term of President George W. Bush, neoconservatives' belief in regime change blocked the formation of any policy at all, at least with regard to Iran. Between those who favored regime change and those (around Colin Powell) who supported negotiating an agreement with the Iranian regime, there was no middle ground. So long as the president did not decide between these two divergent approaches, there was no policy, save for letting the Europeans talk to the Iranians and dissociating ourselves from those talks. It was a policy by default because the gap in the administration was never bridged or overcome.

Early in his second term, President Bush shifted course and was ready to give indirect negotiations a try. The policy became one not of joining the Europeans in the talks but of coordinating with them and permitting them to offer incentives to the Iranians. The neoconservatives in the administration associated with Vice President Cheney and Secretary of Defense Rumsfeld seemed to believe that the negotiations with the Iranians could not succeed and that when they failed, regime change would again become the preferred option.

From this standpoint, the neoconservatives continued to reject the essence of what negotiations produce—namely, something of value for both sides. For them, any gains for the Iranian regime would sustain it and dishearten its opposition, and avoiding that outcome dwarfed all other concerns, including the nuclear one.

If nothing else, this is a reminder that multiple considerations will influence how any American administration (or for that matter any political leader) is going to approach negotiations with adversaries. With Iran, there is a profound mistrust of the mullahs, and of their perceived deceit, their support for terror, and their enduring hostility to America and its friends in the Middle East. No U.S. president is going to ignore public perceptions of Iran or the possible political fallout from negotiating directly with the Iranian leadership. The politics alone might not rule out negotiations, particularly if the only other option for preventing the Iranians from going nuclear is the use of force, but domestic concerns are likely to figure prominently in how negotiations are approached, and packaged publicly. No one will be keen to be portrayed as soft on the Iranian mullahs.

Domestic political concerns have also obviously affected the readiness of different administrations to talk to Cuba. The political weight of the Cuban exile community in Florida and New Jersey, together with the wish to avoid doing anything that might strengthen Fidel Castro, has influenced presidents from Lyndon Johnson to George W. Bush.

Quite apart from these concerns, American presidents and their principal advisors must also consider how our friends and allies will be affected by our talking to those who are not only our adversaries but theirs too. It should come as no surprise that our friends typically see such talks in zero-sum terms: gains for their adversaries are losses for them. Consider, for example, the case of the Koreas. For most of South Korea's history, it feared anything that would strengthen the North or call into question the American commitment to the South. In the North, leader Kim Il Sung saw bilateral talks with the United States as a major victory and as demonstrating our recognition and acceptance of the North after the cold war. Not surprisingly, until South Korea adopted its "sunshine" policy of opening to the North, they saw U.S. bilateral talks with the North as coming at its expense.[2]

Similarly, during the 1970s and 1980s, Yasir Arafat sought to gain American recognition of the PLO, believing that would create an inexorable logic leading to Palestinian statehood. Israel, on the other hand, saw any American discussions with the PLO prior to Oslo in 1993 as a mortal threat.

In each of these examples, North Korea and the PLO, our readiness to talk would have been a mistake unless we developed a clear and meaningful objective and coordinated with the South Koreans and Israel prior to the talks. Since leaders such as Kim Il Sung and Yasir Arafat were so anxious for the direct talks, it was essential to get something of consequence in return for holding negotiations. Naturally, the anxiety that both the South Koreans and the Israelis felt would probably have led them to seek to impose onerous preconditions for our talking—preconditions amounting to a surrender of what the North Koreans and the PLO held dear. In such circumstances, our friends would likely have created conditions that made talks impossible.

While not wanting our friends to be the arbiters of whether we talk in such circumstances, the fact remains that with some negotiations we will face a dilemma. To address it, we must satisfy ourselves that the potential gains from holding talks are sufficiently high to overrule the objections of our friends. At a minimum, our objectives must be clear and important—not only on what we are trying to gain, but also on what we are likely to do if the talks fail to achieve what we want. As an example, it would have been easier to reassure the Israelis about the United States talking to the PLO if we had been very clear that nothing less than explicit recognition of Israel's right to exist as an independent, Jewish state and a renunciation of terror would be acceptable as the conditions for beginning negotiations. Instead, the United States, at the end of the Reagan administration, launched a dialogue with the PLO based on its acceptance of Security Council resolution 242 and its readiness to negotiate—a far vaguer formulation that left Israel highly suspicious of the dialogue and left the incoming Bush administration in a position of constantly having to reassure the Israelis.

Recognizing that our friends are likely to be highly fearful of talks with their adversaries, we need to avoid surprises if at all possible. However, at times, if with great secrecy a breakthrough with strategic implications for the region or internationally is possible, there is probably no choice but to keep an ally in the dark. Certainly the strategic payoff of the opening to China warranted, in the eyes of President Nixon and Henry Kissinger, keeping their secret diplomacy from the Taiwanese. In other cases, domestic considerations may argue for taking a step even if it surprises important friends. In late November 1990, for example, after the UN Security Council adopted a resolution authorizing the use of "all necessary means" to expel Iraq from Kuwait, the Saudis were taken by surprise by President Bush's announcement the next morning that he was inviting Saddam Hussein to send an envoy to Washington, and that he would be sending Secretary James Baker to Baghdad to see Saddam Hussein.

President Bush felt that he had to prove to our public that he had gone the extra mile to avoid using force, particularly if later we had to go to war. Domestically, his judgment made sense. Unfortunately, he left the Saudis out of the equation, and his announcement shocked them. The Saudi ambassador to the United States, Bandar bin Sultan, called me and, highly agitated, charged that we were giving Saddam a great victory and sawing off the limb the Saudis had gone out on to receive American forces in the kingdom. It took time and effort to reassure the Saudis, and Saudi pressure led the president to scale back his public offer, agreeing only to have Secretary Baker meet a representative of Saddam Hussein's someplace other than Iraq. Even then, the Saudis remained suspicious.[3]

Taking the Saudis into our confidence before the president's announcement might have relieved their anxiety without robbing the announcement of its desired dramatic effect. Naturally, it might also have led the Saudis to talk the president out of his plan—and that often is the real reason for reluctance to take our allies into our confidence: the concern that a president will have to overcome opposition to what he feels our interests require.

Our interests and those of our friends are not identical. But our alliances are the context for our diplomacy. So, when contemplating negotiations with the adversaries of our friends, we have to prepare the ground.

NEGOTIATING WITH HOSTILE NON-STATE ACTORS

As non-state threats or actors make themselves felt, pressures are going to build to engage them in dialogue. By definition, these groups are the spearheads of violence and terrorism, and often pose existential threats to our friends. Nonetheless, it did not take long for there to be calls for the United States to begin talking to the insurgents in Iraq in order to stop the insurgency. Similarly, the electoral successes of Hizbollah in Lebanon and Hamas in the Palestinian Territories produced calls for the United States to begin talking to them, even though each has been on our terrorism list. Imagine the reaction of the Iraqi government or the Israelis or even the Lebanese government to an American willingness to engage these groups.

Should those governments' prospective opposition prevent us from engaging any of these groups? Perhaps, but the challenge of coping with the threats they pose creates a rising chorus, especially among our European allies, calling on us to negotiate. Even if the European Union is likely to accept that Al Qaeda is not a fit partner for discussions, EU members clearly began to say that both Hizbollah and Hamas were part of the political and social reality of Lebanon and Palestine, and as such, must be dealt with. In fact, if they become acceptable partners, would it not be only a matter of time before the Muslim Brotherhood and other Islamists were seen in similar terms?

Such a prospect should give us pause, because our willingness to talk with them will legitimize them and often weaken their moderate opponents. Moussa Abu Marzouk, one of the leaders of Hamas, has declared that the outside world must recognize the growing weight of Hamas among Palestinians, even though such recognition will not change its objectives. (In a meeting in East Jerusalem with twenty local representatives of Fatah, the leading secular faction among Palestinians, I was told that American or even European meetings with Hamas would undercut them and persuade Hamas that they were winning and need not alter their behavior.)

It would be disastrous for American leaders to enter into talks with groups such as Hamas, Hizbollah, or the Muslim Brotherhood in Egypt without clear ground rules. We must establish certain preconditions for dialogue.

For starters, they must renounce violence: not only dissociate themselves from it, but also act to discredit it. It is not enough to do what Yasir Arafat did—namely, denounce terrorism but wink at the groups carrying it out, or, worse, glorify terrorism by saying that those who die while conducting terrorist acts are martyrs. Many in the Arab world will say that the term *martyr* (or *shahid*) is widely and loosely used, and is too embedded in the common parlance to be dropped. Unfortunately, that is precisely the problem; a *shahid* has done what is right, and no one questions it. How can terrorism be discredited when those who do it are honored and the term that conveys that honor can't be altered or questioned?

Thus, our criteria for dealing with Hamas or Hizbollah or the Muslim Brotherhood or others must be their unmistakable dissociation from acts of terrorism and their willingness to declare that those who persist in conducting terrorism (or glorifying it) are a threat to their cause. But we must demand that they go a step further: they must be ready to coexist with Israel and be prepared to negotiate with it. What exactly would we discuss with them if eradication of the state of Israel remained part of their political program? This is especially true at a time when they are trying to convince the Arab street that they represent the wave of the future and that there is no need to accept a two-state solution to the Israeli-Palestinian conflict.

All Palestinians and Lebanese should know that the United States will not deal with those who remain committed to violence or who rationalize it—or who are not prepared to coexist with Israel.

Finally, we must make clear that they must give up their weapons. No doubt, some will argue that this is unrealistic, and even unfair. After all, the hardest thing to do even in circumstances in which deals have been struck—as in Northern Ireland—is to get formerly underground or resistance groups to surrender their weapons. Undoubtedly, Hamas and Hizbollah supporters will argue that since Israel retains a large and well-equipped army and air force, they need to add on to their arms. The problem is that groups such as Hizbollah or Hamas and their leaders do not even pretend to have altered their agenda, at least as regards Israel. Whatever the criticisms of Gerry Adams and Sinn Féin, they committed themselves to nonviolence and a political solution with the Unionists and the British. And they also accepted the Mitchell Principles for negotiations, which included a process for the decommissioning of weapons. Neither Hizbollah nor Hamas has been willing to renounce violence or even hint at giving up its weapons, let alone embrace a peaceful resolution of the conflict. On the contrary, both have declared that they will not give up violence as a tool, and in any case, they have opted for only taking part in the political process internally in Lebanon or Palestine. The determination to maintain their arms is an indication that they seek to use them as leverage against the political process and against Israel. If they have truly joined the political process, there is no place for their weapons, except to create pressure on their political competitors or to preserve the option of withdrawing from the political process altogether. Either they are committed to being political actors or they are not.

Of course, it is not up to the United States to determine who is a politically relevant actor and who is not in the Middle East. Lebanese or Palestinians or local polities will determine that. But we can establish our principles. We should be clear that Lebanese and Palestinians can elect anyone they choose and that we will respect their choice. That does not mean, however, that we will automatically negotiate with them. We are just as entitled to make such choices as they are. And as they choose their leaders, they should know whether these groups will make it more or less likely for them to have a relationship with the United States.

It follows that there are circumstances in which we should be prepared to negotiate. If, for example, the elected members of Hamas and Hizbollah are prepared to accept civil society, forsake and condemn violence, respect the law, and coexist with Israel, we should be prepared to talk to them—again, closely coordinating with those allies or friends who are likely to be most affected or fearful of such talks. That is common sense and good statecraft.

To sum up, let me invoke the John F. Kennedy admonition: we should never negotiate out of fear, but we should never fear to negotiate. A willingness to talk is not a sign of weakness, unless we make it one. By the same token, avoiding or refusing talks with adversaries is not a sign of strength; on the contrary, often it may signal uncertainty on our part. More than anything else, it is essential to know what we want and can reasonably expect to achieve in entering negotiation.

GUIDELINES FOR NEGOTIATIONS

It seems safe to conclude that negotiations today are more complex than they once were. There will be more moving parts, and more actors with diverse interests to have to consider and reconcile. Here again, then, effective statecraft will be essential. It will be important to know when to talk to one party or another, and specifically what to talk about to align their interests with ours. Similarly, it will be essential to understand the limitations of those we are dealing with, including what they are capable of doing and what is beyond their means and inclinations.

Also, we must know, in any given situation, which actors, personalities, and governments have influence at a particular moment. And we must understand how to energize those who have the capacity to exercise influence and how to develop the circumstances in which they are willing to do so.

Of course, if we are to gain partners for our desired goals, we will have to know how to shape a public context internationally and domestically for our preferred course of action. It is a lot easier to get others to join with us, particularly in opposition to those we see as threatening peace and security, if we have fostered a broader consensus on what constitutes a threat to peace and how best to deal with that threat. As we see in chapter 4, Iraq's invasion and occupation of Kuwait was opposed internationally. That certainly made it easier to get others to accept the need for a collective response, but building a coalition for imposing sanctions was not a given. To preserve that coalition and move toward the authorization of the use of force required a constant nurturing of private and, just as important, public attitudes about what Saddam Hussein was doing in Kuwait, the implications of his noncompliance, and the limited nature of our goals.

In this sense, we are reminded of the need to constantly think of how best to position ourselves and our objectives in public. That means talking and listening to putative partners and finding out what will make it politically easier for them to join with us, then crafting an "outreach strategy" that will reach both the public and the party (or parties) with whom we are negotiating.

Looking back at the Middle East peace process during the Clinton years, I believe I was far too cautious in using the media to set a tone and convey messages to all sides and their publics. There were times when clear signs of losing patience would have created a very useful pressure on both sides. (On Hebron, I did use the media that way, but only in the endgame of the negotiations.) But I could have employed messages or signals through the media much more than I did on, for example, making clear that Palestinian nonperformance on security would lead to a suspension of U.S. mediating efforts; on pointing out that Israeli settlement activities were making our task impossible; and on putting the onus on Arab states for doing little to contribute to peace and raising the question of whether they had any serious interest in seeing an end to the conflict.

My point is that when employing negotiations as a leading tool of statecraft, there are many different pieces and activities to be managed. A practitioner will instinctively understand all the balls that have to be juggled both internally and externally.

While there is a great deal of literature on negotiations, most of it has not been written by practitioners. This is not to denigrate the value of the negotiation literature. In fact, much in this literature is especially useful for identifying and explaining the basic concepts of negotiating. Yet if one is to understand how to employ negotiations effectively as a tool of statecraft (or even in business or other walks of life), it makes sense to have a practitioner's guide to negotiations.

Why suggest a practitioner's guide to negotiations? It is not only because of the more complicated setting in which negotiations will take place as we safeguard our national security. It is also because instinct plays an integral part in how and what to do in negotiations, and is more likely to be revealed by a practitioner. Moreover, because practitioners need to be constantly mindful of their own constituencies—and those of the parties that they may be negotiating with—a practitioner's guide is more likely to reflect how these more political concerns tend to be considered or managed.

With these factors and the logic of statecraft in mind, let me turn to and explain my twelve rules for negotiations.

9.

$$\left\{ \textbf{NEGOTIATIONS} \right\}$$

Twelve Rules to Follow

In chapter 8, I discussed the "what" of negotiations as a tool—*the* tool—of statecraft. This chapter deals with the "how" of negotiations. Foreign policy will always require understanding what must be done and knowing how to do it.

What follows are twelve rules that I believe offer a good guide to the "how" of negotiations. Each of the rules offers an insight and a perspective on how to conduct negotiations, not only taking into account different constraints and pressures, but also shaping the best way to map out the talks and produce the desired results. Of course, surprises can pop up that affect any negotiation, and, unfortunately, even the most skilled negotiator may not succeed if those he or she is negotiating with are incapable or unwilling to reach agreement. If that is true, these rules will provide greater insight into what is possible and not possible. These rules can also reveal whether any deal is in the cards, and if it is not, suggest ways to reduce the costs and risks of the negotiation.

1. KNOW WHAT YOU WANT, KNOW WHAT YOU CAN LIVE WITH

Nothing would seem more obvious than this. But it is not as simple as it might seem. In a high-stakes negotiation, each side may know what it wants in the abstract, but not really have thought through what it may be able to accept. The process of negotiations can alter expectations by transforming the view of the adversary. Former Israeli prime minister Ehud Barak once said to me that if he saw the Palestinians prepared to assume certain security responsibilities, it would change his view of what Israel could ultimately afford to give up. While this may have simply been an attempt to get the Palestinians to do what they had not been doing, there can be little doubt that Barak understood that the Israeli public would alter its views if it saw Palestinians acting as genuine partners on security—or demonstrating that they would not countenance Palestinian terror against Israelis. Thus, perceived bottom lines can turn out to be less-than-irreducible goals as circumstances and the perception of the negotiating partner change.

You should anticipate such changes before entering negotiations. One way to do so is to explore different scenarios in which the other side fundamentally adopts new positions. What do you do in response? Rarely do parties ask such questions or play out such scenarios. For example, neither Israelis nor Palestinians—for most of their negotiations—were willing to ask themselves hard questions about what they could accept on Jerusalem, refugees, and borders. Even an internal discussion of these issues was deemed too sensitive. The Israelis feared that any internal discussion, no matter how private, would be leaked to the Israeli media, with explosive, even paralyzing results politically. The Palestinians dreaded incurring the wrath of Arafat, who might claim they were giving away Palestinian rights or betraying the cause.

As a result, neither side thought through their bottom lines on the core issues. There was, however, an asymmetry in the negotiations. The Israelis never could articulate, even to themselves, what their vision of the future was or what they wanted the outcome of negotiations to be. They knew that they would withdraw from territories but they did not have an idea of how much withdrawal they could accept nor did they develop a rationale for what they needed to hold on to. The Palestinians may not have thought through bottom lines, but they did develop a consistent view of what the outcome of the negotiations should be. They knew they would not get full withdrawal to the June 4, 1967, lines, with East Jerusalem as the capital of their state and the right of return for Palestinian refugees to their homes. But this vision could be repeated like a mantra; although it forestalled any hard internal discussions on concessions, it gave them a built-in advantage over the Israelis. As Israeli negotiator Oded Eran confided to me on more than one occasion, his side, unlike the Palestinians, was always limited in the negotiations by not knowing what it wanted.

Ironically, the more the Palestinians repeated their mantra on the outcome, the more problematic it became to concede any part of it. At the time that the Oslo process was agreed upon, in 1993, I have little doubt that Palestinian negotiators such as Abu Ala or Hassan Asfour (the Oslo negotiators) understood that when it came time for permanent-status talks, they would have to compromise on issues such as Jerusalem and borders. They believed the Israelis would have to concede much more, but they knew they would not escape compromise. (The fact that other leading Palestinians, including Abu Mazen, the formal head of the negotiating delegation, pleaded with me not to give up on Arafat, since he was the only one who had the moral authority to concede on the permanent-status issues, suggests that they, too, understood that compromise would be required.) But the permanent-status talks that were supposed to begin in 1996 did not begin until the end of 1999, and by that time the Palestinian posture, adopted by all its possible negotiators, was that the Palestinians had already conceded on the territorial component, including Jerusalem, by accepting the June 4, 1967, lines, which represented only a small part of mandatory Palestine.

Upon first hearing this line of argument from Palestinians such as Nabil Sha'ath and Saeb Erekat, I asked what Oslo had been about. Wasn't it supposed to have started a negotiating process? I asked: Are you now saying you made all your concessions before entering the talks? If so, do you think that Yitzhak Rabin thought that is what he was signing up to? They did not have much of an answer for me, but they had the advantage of a clear vision of an outcome, and the Israelis could not offer a comparable one. The Israelis would not say they were going to annex the territory but they could not bring themselves to say they would hold half of it.

So they put themselves at a disadvantage. The lesson is this: if you don't know what you want, your negotiating partner will develop a vision that serves his/her posture in the negotiation but not yours.

There is a common reason political leaders often go into negotiations without such vision. They enter negotiations not because they expect an agreement but because they need to reduce political pressure on them over a policy path they have chosen. Negotiations can prove that they are "doing something." As the war in Vietnam turned increasingly into a quagmire, for example, President Lyndon Johnson sought negotiations to buy time and to relieve domestic pressures. Ho Chi Minh, recognizing the Johnson administration's motives, was in no rush to go to talks. And when the North Vietnamese did go, their negotiators, first with the Johnson administration and later with the Nixon administration, showed little interest in reaching agreement. Either the United States would effectively surrender at the table or the North Vietnamese would change the realities on the battlefield and get their way.

It is certainly a mistake for any president to enter negotiations—even if he thinks they are largely for show—without a vision and an understanding of acceptable outcomes. Once in a negotiation, there are political costs for walking away. The longer a negotiating process goes on, the more it tends to justify itself—and the more one must not lose sight of its initial purpose. American presidents must assume that the other side will know what it wants, and must be no less prepared as they enter negotiations—having thought through different scenarios, having gone beyond generalities, and having determined a range of acceptable outcomes.

2. KNOW EVERYTHING THERE IS TO KNOW ABOUT THE DECISION MAKER(S) ON THE OTHER SIDE

This, too, should be obvious, but too few systematic questions are really examined about who makes decisions and who is able to influence the relevant decision maker or makers. Before negotiations, basic questions must be asked: What are the leaders' reasons for entering the negotiations? Does the other side really want a deal? If so, what kind of deal, and is it a deal (in content and scope) you can live with? Under what circumstances is the other side's view likely to be modified? Who has influence on the other side? How likely are they to exercise that influence? What pressures are most likely to affect the other side internally? What pressures from the outside might move the other side positively? What pressures will harden, not soften, their positions? What is the other side afraid of and what do they value?

Just as in rule number one, where the president ought to know why he is going into negotiations and what he can live with, he also needs to have a good picture of the other side's reasons for talking, their principal concerns, and what they want and require from the talks. Surely it is easier to produce basic answers to these questions when dealing with friends or allies—typically because we are likely to have so many more sources of information and access to those within and with ties to the leadership.

As we see in chapter 2, President George H. W. Bush found that Prime Minister Thatcher and President Mitterrand shared Mikhail Gorbachev's opposition to the reunification of Germany and its integration in NATO. But the president was in regular and personal communication with both leaders, and while working to address their concerns, he also came to understand from them that whatever their misgivings, they would not block the negotiations outright.

Negotiations conducted with friends are a challenge but a manageable one, because you can generally find out what you need to know. Knowing what you need to know before or during negotiations with adversaries is much more difficult. They are often determined to keep you from knowing by hiding critical information or misleading you.

So what can be done? Start by recognizing the problems, and then recognize that nothing is more important in negotiations than probing, listening, and testing.

With first the Soviets and then the Russians, I would have long conversations with Sergei Tarasenko and Yuri Mamedov, key aides to the then foreign ministers Eduard Shevardnadze and Andrei Kosyrev. Conversations with them revealed a great deal about what was and wasn't possible on arms control—not necessarily because I was pumping them for information, but because I asked questions that conveyed an interest in trying to understand the broader circumstances in which they had to operate.

For example, sometimes I would ask questions about how much reform was really possible. Frequently, this led to discussions about decline and malaise in the Soviet Union, the advocates and opponents of varying degrees of reform, their arguments, where arms-control agreements fit in, and their views about where we and others could either help or harm the reform process.

One essential attribute for any negotiator is to be a good listener. It's crucial to know when to talk but, more important, when to listen. You won't be learning when you are talking. You may be shaping or conditioning attitudes, but you will not be learning. You learn when you listen. Being a good listener conveys a level of interest and respect. It shows that you take seriously those with whom you are dealing. You are likely to elicit more when you convey such respect and listen actively.

By active listening, I mean listening to what is being said and then asking questions based on what you have heard. This is a respectful way to understand more about where the other side is coming from and why. It is also essential for another reason. Whether trying to learn more before entering negotiations or learning more during the negotiations themselves, oftentimes the other side will try out ideas not by explicitly giving away a major concession but by hinting at it. Listening and probing in light of what you hear is the only way you will know whether you have heard something meaningful.

When Secretary Albright and I were meeting with President Hafez al Asad in December 1999, he said, seemingly in passing, that he did not impose any conditions for negotiations. Because he was a leader who had consistently posed conditions, I sensed that this might be a signal worth probing. But I wanted the initial probing to come from the secretary, not me. To Albright's surprise, I asked Asad if the secretary and I could have a brief recess. When we were out of Syrian earshot, I told her that I thought Asad had said something new and that she should now explicitly ask him if he was ready to resume negotiations. Though Albright was not sure that he had said anything meaningful, she agreed and posed the question. Asad nodded, saying, "They never really stopped." Here, again, his comment belied the reality, and I thought this, too, might indicate a greater openness on his part to approach the negotiations differently. So I decided to press directly to see if it was possible not only to resume the talks but to raise them to the political level—and when I asked, he agreed. For nine years, he had resisted doing this.

Perhaps Asad would have revealed this without our having listened actively and probed with questions. But in negotiations, one never knows when nuggets are going to be dropped to test what the response might be. Sometimes they are just a test. Other times, they indicate a readiness, as in Asad's case, to change course. The key is always to be listening.

Testing is just as important for trying to determine what a decision maker is willing to do. One of our big mistakes with Yasir Arafat was not testing his intentions. On a strictly bilateral basis we had a need to know if he was willing or able to make a permanent-status deal. His response to our probing questions was always vague. Too often we simply interpreted this as reflecting his style and his pattern in negotiations. But we could have tested him, and should have.

To be precise, had we told him we would not play any role on permanent status if he were not prepared to condition his public for compromise on the core issues, we would have seen if he was willing to do what was necessary for an end-of-conflict deal. Arafat not only valued the relationship with us but also saw us as leveling the playing field with the Israelis. He knew that nothing was possible on the permanent-status issues unless we were actively pressing both sides to make hard—indeed, historic—decisions. So this was an excellent way to determine if he was prepared to make such decisions. However, this required us to be very concrete in terms of what we were asking: He had to say that compromise was necessary for both sides and that he understood that neither the Palestinians nor the Israelis could get 100 percent of what they wanted on Jerusalem, borders, and refugees. This would have had to be said publicly and repeatedly. With such public statements and conditioning, we would insist on beginning permanent-status negotiations; without such public positions, we would focus on interim issues and on building cooperation. His unwillingness to take this step would have revealed that he could not deal with the permanent-status issues, and we could have adjusted our approach accordingly.

Would Arafat's failure to pass this test have ended our involvement in peace promotion? No, we could still have worked to promote increasing Palestinian freedom from Israeli control, negotiated other interim steps to foster cooperation and a better environment between Israelis and Palestinians, and generally managed a process until a time beyond the Arafat era, when his successors would have been psychologically more capable of ending the conflict.

The point is that testing is an important way of determining what you don't know about the other side's leader and his or her decision-making instincts and attitudes in a negotiation. As with any other rule—especially when there is some risk involved—you have to be prepared for the results of your test. Some tests can be subtle and come with less risk, others with more. But with any test, there must be a consequence for failing to pass it. With Arafat, he would know that his unwillingness to condition his public would cost him an American role in permanent-status discussions—and probably reduce the American stakes in him.

Devising tests that are revealing and that you as a negotiator are prepared to live with is no easy task. However, they are a necessary part of learning all there is to know about a decision maker—and his/her motivations, capabilities, limitations, and psychological hang-ups.

3. BUILD A RELATIONSHIP OF TRUST WITH THE KEY DECISION MAKER

How does one build trust with the key decision maker, whether an adversary or an ally? There are several requirements. First and foremost, establish your credibility. You must never promise something and not deliver, and you must always deliver *exactly* what you promise. (The lesson here is to give promises with great care.) Second, be open and revealing. Active listening permits you to learn, but just as negotiations are a two-way street, so, too, is any dialogue. You, too, must be prepared to offer insights into the thinking of your leadership or decision maker. Third, protect confidences and never expose your counterpart. And, fourth, be prepared at a certain point to deliver something of value to your counterpart that he or she knows is difficult for you to produce—indeed, even something that may cost you something. With Sergei Tarasenko I developed such a close relationship and produced, through Secretary Baker, an easing of some of our positions on cruise missiles and bombers in the arms-control negotiations, positions that Sergei knew had been difficult to change. For his part, he was consistently overcoming a deeply resistant Soviet foreign ministry on issues ranging from arms control to German unification to producing a joint statement on Iraq after the invasion of Kuwait—a joint statement that had the Soviet Union condemning Iraq, its erstwhile ally, and supporting an arms embargo against it.

The traditional national security apparatus in the Soviet Union was deeply opposed to such a joint posture with us, and at one point, in the fall of 1990, when Gorbachev was under enormous pressure from the Soviet military and other party leaders not to be supportive of possible military responses against Iraq, he sent Yevgeni Primakov to Washington on a special mission. Earlier I referred to the back-channel and highly sensitive message Sergei sent me indicating that Shevardnadze's job and our hopes for partnership were at stake, and we must reject what Primakov was peddling.

Without an extraordinary degree of trust, Sergei would never have sent such a message that, if revealed, might have cost him more than his job. By this time, we had obviously proven our bona fides to each other. Developing such relationships is equally important with friends and allies. During this period, Robert Zoellick, then the counselor in the State Department, developed a similar relationship with Frank Elbe, the right-hand man of German foreign minister Hans-Dietrich Genscher. Genscher was from a different party than the chancellor, Helmut Kohl. He was considerably more to the left politically and less instinctively supportive of the close U.S.-German ties than Kohl. Yet the Zoellick-Elbe relationship helped to foster increasingly close cooperation between Secretary Baker and Genscher, which paid dividends on the negotiations over German unification in NATO, conventional arms control in Europe, and German logistics and economic support for us in the first Gulf War—none of which would necessarily have been predictable.

I cultivated similar relationships with Israelis and Palestinians, and like all such ties of trust, they helped at critical moments when negotiating agreements. Trust will allow a negotiator to learn much more than he would otherwise about what can and cannot work in the negotiations. So much of negotiations are about learning where there may be openings, and when the time is right to pursue them or to raise a new idea. Every new idea must generate something in response, and here, again, a good negotiator will want to test if it will. If you don't have a trusted relationship with your counterpart, the odds of producing the desired response—or at least having confidence that you can—are likely to be low.

Building trust is rarely done in formal settings. Informal settings must be created. Back channels, which I say more about in the next chapter, on mediation, should be developed and used. In such channels, informal and noncommitting discussions can take place. Ideas can be tested without fear. But they won't be useful until trust is developed, and one needs private settings to begin that process.

When we began Israeli-Syrian negotiations at the Wye River Plantation, I wanted Uri Savir and Walid Mouallem to develop a relationship; I knew each well and had become close to both. They were both deep believers in peace, but they themselves would have to recognize this in each other. I brought them together and explained why each had become a friend of mine and why I found them trustworthy. I asked them to talk about their hopes and concerns, and then I left them alone for several hours to get to know each other. Later, when they had something sensitive to discuss, they would meet alone, creating an informal channel of communication. At one point, Mouallem asked Savir to set up a demarcation group to meet on the border, which presumed agreement on the principle of withdrawal to the June 4, 1967, lines. Savir had to get Shimon Peres's approval, but was ready to do so with a proviso: that Mouallem understand that demarcating the border—even with the June 4, 1967, lines as the basis—would lead to tough fights between them about exactly where the border would be drawn. Mouallem tacitly acknowledged this, indicating that he understood this was the beginning of a tough negotiation, not the end. Had it not been for four bombs in nine days in 1996, which led to the suspension of Israel's talks with the Palestinians and Syrians and to the defeat of Peres in the May elections, I am convinced that agreement would have been reached, with Savir and Mouallem leading the negotiations. If nothing else, here is a reminder that negotiations take place in a real world of events and traumas and political pressures.

Trust is a necessary part of making negotiations work. If trust is limited only to the negotiators, it won't insulate the negotiations from outside pressures. By definition, adversaries are unlikely to have much trust beyond the negotiators—assuming such a relationship has been developed. The point is that negotiators, while striving to build a relationship of trust, will face pressures and obstacles even when they succeed in believing in each other.

Moreover, even when they do develop great personal trust, they will still hesitate to reveal highly sensitive positions prematurely. No negotiator should expect that trust alone will produce a revelation about bottom lines before the timing is right. But a relationship of trust will provide insight into which pathways will be productive and which will be destructive. And, ultimately, at the crunch point that comes in any high-stakes negotiation, trust will prove pivotal. In essence, every negotiation is about manipulation. Each side is determined to convince the other that it cannot concede on what it regards as critical. By implication the other side must concede—in effect, you are saying my redline is red, while yours is pink. But when negotiations evolve to the point where the fundamental decisions have to be made—where it truly is make-or-break—if there is trust, the negotiator or leader will be able to say that he/she can do X and not Y, and that will be believed and not seen as one more manipulation.

4. KEEP IN MIND THE OTHER SIDE'S NEED FOR AN EXPLANATION

The concept of "explanation" may be one of the most important in negotiations. No matter what the transaction, no matter what walk of life, no matter the stakes involved, in making a deal each side must be able to explain to itself or others why the agreement was in its interest. The greater the stakes involved in the negotiations, the greater the need for an explanation. Similarly, the more significant the concessions being made, the more important it becomes to be able to explain why the concessions were necessary to achieve something of greater value. Between countries—regardless of whether they are democratic or authoritarian—there will need to be an explanation, either for publics or for powerful constituencies.

A negotiator must be thinking about how the other side will explain an important concession even as he/she is pushing for it. No one is going to be open to being told that they must make a historic concession—the kind of concession that for reasons of tradition, habit, or political culture would seem unthinkable—without some major mitigating or offsetting factor accompanying the proposal. Certainly, there are times in negotiations when one or the other side may be deluding itself as to what it will ultimately have to concede and may need to be shocked into reality. But the shock may be completely disruptive or even paralyzing if not accompanied by a plan for how the concession—regardless of the difficulty—can be explained.

Once I watched Israeli negotiator Shlomo Ben-Ami introduce the idea that the Palestinians would have to accept that there would be no right of return for refugees and that there would need to be a modification of the June 4, 1967, lines; but, in return, Palestinians would be able to show their public and the Arab world that for the first time in 1,500 years there would be internationally recognized Arab (namely, Palestinian) sovereignty over East Jerusalem and the Islamic holy places. While Abu Ala, Ben-Ami's counterpart, was not about to surrender positions that had a mythical standing on the Palestinian side, he did not respond in a peremptory fashion, either. He and his colleagues were intrigued by Ben-Ami's argument, and following that meeting, Abu Ala told me, "Shlomo is a good man, and I can do business with him."

Even in negotiations in which there is an asymmetry of power and interest, and one side may need the deal more than the other, a credible explanation will be required by the weaker side, not only for the sake of concluding the deal but also to make sure it is sustainable and can be implemented. In trying to gain Gorbachev's acceptance of a unified Germany in NATO—given the deeply ingrained Russian threat perceptions of Germany and NATO—we needed to create both a process that would enable Gorbachev to say he had shaped the outcome and an outcome in which he could say that NATO's relationship had changed with the Soviet Union and it was no longer an enemy.

For the former, we devised the Two Plus Four process. For the latter, we stage-managed a NATO summit communiqué that announced with great fanfare that it was a new era and that the alliance was now being transformed.

We took Gorbachev's need for an explanation seriously. We understood the delicacy of his position internally. We had no interest in weakening him. He was challenged by those in the Soviet hierarchy who had no interest in cooperation and partnership with the United States. We worried that an issue such as Germany, which evoked such emotions in the Soviet Union, could congeal the opposition to Gorbachev and actually threaten his leadership.

In the end, Germany was unified in NATO and Gorbachev was able, in 1990, to manage the political fallout domestically because he had an explanation. His situation is a reminder that in some negotiations the weakness of the negotiating partner needs to be kept in mind.

Helping to shore up a weak but agreeable adversary—or emerging friend—will not be easy, but if it is not done, any agreement is unlikely to survive. If the agreement was important enough to negotiate, you will certainly want to see it implemented. Here, again, reconciling what is important to you with what is also significant to the other side will be critical. An explanation certainly reflects something that the other side feels it must be able to say publicly about the agreement—and being aware of that will help both sides reach a deal.

5. TO GAIN THE HARDEST CONCESSIONS, PROVE YOU UNDERSTAND WHAT IS IMPORTANT TO THE OTHER SIDE

While consistent with keeping the other side's need for an explanation in mind, this rule goes well beyond simply ensuring that the other side has something to point to as it "sells" a deal. Rule number five is about demonstrating that you know not only what is important to the other side but also why certain concessions are so painful for it. I call this the "empathy rule."

Some might consider empathy to be a form of self-sacrifice. It is not. It requires no concession other than to good sense. In a negotiation, displaying empathy may be one of the best ways to look out for one's self-interest. Consider that if you are asking the other side to do something very hard for it, you have little chance of succeeding unless you can demonstrate that you know why what you are asking is so difficult for it. This is the starting point for getting a hearing. After all, who is going to take you seriously or be willing to respond if you ask for something very difficult and indicate no clear understanding of why it is difficult?

Failing to appreciate what is hard for the other side creates two basic problems in a negotiation. First, the other side will stop listening, and second, it will go on the offensive, believing it must prove to you the high cost of proceeding down the path you have chosen.

Displaying empathy and demonstrating a clear understanding of the problems that would be created by your proposal may not yield an immediate result but it will make what might have been considered a nonstarter part of the negotiating landscape. No one was better at the empathy rule than Bill Clinton.

Clinton's effective use of the "empathy rule" was not simply a function of his ability to demonstrate that he understood the other leader's problems. It was also that he married his "empathy" with an acute understanding of the details of the issues. One is far more likely to be convincing about understanding the other side's problem if he/she speaks not in slogans but in specifics. Clinton could do that as he mastered the central issues in any negotiation and could explain them in some depth. With Boris Yeltsin, Clinton showed on NATO expansion his understanding of why Yeltsin would be under great pressure, and then used his mastery of the detail to portray how a new relationship could be forged with Russia and embodied in a "charter" to mitigate that pressure.

I saw him operate in much the same way in the Middle East. When, for example, Clinton met Hafez al Asad for the first time, in Geneva in January of 1994, he explained to Asad that he understood the significance of the land (the Golan Heights) to Syria; the importance to Asad of how his public and the Arab world perceived his getting the land back and the manner in which he did so; and how this had to be reconciled with Israeli prime minister Rabin's needs—needs Clinton also defined. Afterward, Asad grabbed me by the arm and said, "You know, I liked President Bush. But President Clinton is a real person. He speaks to you with awareness and understanding. He knows our problems better, and he is committed to solving them. I haven't felt this from an American president before." From someone who had met and held discussions with Presidents Nixon, Carter, and Bush, this was a remarkable statement.

While ultimately there was no peace agreement reached between Asad and Rabin (or later between Asad and Ehud Barak), it is interesting that when Asad stood next to Clinton at the press conference in Geneva and Clinton used terms publicly that went well beyond what Asad was prepared to say about the content of peace with Israel, Asad made no effort to soften the Clinton words. He felt that Clinton understood him and he would live with how Clinton was describing what Asad would accept when it came to peace.

In any negotiation, applying the empathy rule does not involve self-sacrifice because it is employed to gain something in return. The more you show that you will reach out and that you do understand the other side, the more you can and should create an expectation that the other side must also understand your needs and respond to them. And having proven that you understand what is so difficult to do, it becomes possible for the other side to contemplate making concessions—provided they know they have something significant to gain by doing so and something significant to lose if they do not.

6. TOUGH LOVE IS ALSO REQUIRED

Empathy is critical and must be married to an understanding of the details to make it convincing. But empathy in isolation has its limitations. While it creates an opening and a readiness for the other side to consider what might previously have been inconceivable, it is unlikely on its own to produce agreement. For that, there must also be an understanding that there is going to be a consequence. With German unification and with NATO expansion, first Gorbachev and then Yeltsin understood that they were not going to stop either process. They did not have the leverage to do so. Understanding their needs and conveying a clear appreciation of them (as well as their need for a public explanation for their acquiescence) made it easier for them to go along—and, of course, to remain in power. But understanding the consequences of their opposition also gave them an incentive to get what they could and do a deal.

In both cases, the U.S. position was one of understanding the other sides' predicament, but always with an accompanying and unmistakable message: this train is moving, and you need to be on it before it leaves the station. On German unification, this message came from both Bush and Baker, although the president tended to convey it more to the hesitant British and French leaders and Baker more to Gorbachev and Shevardnadze—the ones who most clearly had to acquiesce and who potentially would pay the most for doing so. On NATO expansion, Christopher and Talbott tended to convey the message much more clearly with Yeltsin and Kosyrev than Clinton, but the president would convey it as well, always with his customary understanding.[1]

Tough love was not President Clinton's strength. When it came to marrying his empathy to an understanding of the details, he had no peer. When it came to offering tough love—telling the other side what it had to do, what the consequence would be if it did not, how it would lose us, pay a heavy price and get nothing—this was done better by others. President Clinton tended to see the value of building his capital and nudging the other side along and embracing them as they made tough decisions. While necessary, empathy is not sufficient. In high-stakes negotiations, especially when trying to resolve historic conflicts, where leaders are asked to make the hardest decision they will ever have to make, Clinton-style empathy is essential to get them to the point of making a decision. However, to get them to cross historic thresholds, they must also feel that there will be a profound, adverse consequence if they do not do so.

Clinton's approach to Arafat in the make-or-break White House meeting on January 2, 2001, showed both the president's impulse to embrace and his instinct to shy away from playing hardball at the critical moment. In this meeting in which Arafat had to know that the president had taken the negotiations as far as he could, and Arafat's unwillingness to accept the Clinton parameters would be seen and understood by the president as proof that Arafat was incapable of settling the conflict, the president could not bring himself to say this. At two junctures in the meeting, he drew back rather than confront. First, when Arafat outlined his reservations regarding the Clinton parameters and these reservations effectively destroyed the logic of the proposals, Clinton did not call Arafat on what he was doing and say, "You have just rejected my ideas." If nothing else, such a remark would have signaled that Clinton was not fooled by Arafat's manipulation and that Arafat would not get away with dressing up a rejection as mere reservations.

Second, believing the meeting could not end with Arafat having that impression, I privately suggested to President Clinton that he become very blunt with Arafat about the consequences of what he was doing. President Clinton agreed. Unfortunately, when he assumed a blunter posture, he did so by saying that the chairman's position was "killing Barak" and there was nothing more he (the president) could do. Arafat did not care if his position would harm Israeli prime minister Barak; he rarely showed much concern about the impact of his decisions on his Israeli counterpart. His concerns were about how his positions affected his standing with Palestinians, not Israelis. What President Clinton should have said is "Your position is killing me. I have gone out on a limb for you, presented unprecedented, historic ideas to settle this conflict, and your rejection exposes me. I can only conclude that you are incapable of making peace and I will have to convey this impression to my successor."

This would at least have told Arafat that he would pay a price with the United States. The irony is that this is precisely what President Clinton told incoming President Bush about Arafat; unfortunately, Arafat left the meeting not understanding that this would be the result.

Perhaps nothing would have changed Arafat. Perhaps his inability to make an end-of-conflict deal would have trumped the best "tough love" approach by President Clinton. But by not making it clear to him the consequences of rejection, by not adopting a blunt posture with him, Clinton had no possibility of altering Arafat's calculus. Perhaps Arafat would have considered a lesser deal—or created more possibilities for alternatives being proposed by those around him who were pushing for an agreement.

Ultimately, the empathy and tough love rules go hand in hand. One might ask whether President George W. Bush might be effective in this regard. He seems to have an instinct for being blunt—but bluntness without empathy and an awareness of the details is unlikely to work. One can only wonder how effective he might have been in getting a second resolution at the UN or in getting Turkey to be a part of the coalition in the war against Iraq had he been able to communicate both awareness and tough love.

7. EMPLOY THE GOOD COP–BAD COP APPROACH CAREFULLY

It was not uncommon in negotiations during the Clinton presidency for negotiators to be seen as harder-line and tougher than the president. In no small part, that resulted from the Clinton style, which was so heavily shaped by his impulse to embrace. In his defense, he felt the predicament of other leaders and constraints imposed on them more instinctively than any of those negotiating on his behalf. Speaking for myself, it is not that I did not see the constraints; indeed, often I would be the one to explain to Clinton what Rabin was up against politically or what limited Asad and Arafat psychologically. But Clinton, as a leader and a politician, could relate to the constraints and was often reluctant to push other leaders as a result.

In these cases, I was the bad cop, and he was the good one. Usually, in negotiations, it should be the other way around: the leader should be the bad cop and the negotiator the good cop. The negotiator in the first instance is the one charged with trying to alter the behavior and positions of those with whom he is negotiating. He tries to show an understanding of their position and to explore ways of responding to their needs, but he needs them to meet him partway because he must also persuade his boss to respond to the other side's needs. It is the boss who decides, not the negotiator. Of course, the negotiator must be seen as influential and authoritative, meaning he can influence the boss and deliver on what he offers. But he must still persuade those who have made him the negotiator, meaning he must persuade his boss or bosses—and their acceptance should never be taken as a given. As I would often say in a negotiation, "help me to help you by giving me something to work with." This often worked, but was less likely when the decision maker—in this case, President Clinton—was seen as softer than the negotiator. In such circumstances, the impulse is to go around the negotiator and deal directly with the leader. Barak, seeing Clinton's reactions, began insisting on dealing with the president on nearly every issue. When a leader is willing to be so involved, he creates the equivalent of a court of appeal, weakening the negotiator and inevitably becoming the good cop.

Good cops and bad cops are naturally a part of a negotiation in which there are multiple actors on each side, and there are differences of opinion about not only what is acceptable in the talks but also what it will take to produce agreement. And in any negotiation of this sort, the other side will see who seems more sympathetic, more willing to find bridging ideas, and more committed to producing a deal. It is only natural to try to work with that individual, to try to forge common strategies, and to find ways to help that person overcome those less inclined (or even opposed) to doing a deal.

But the impulse to work with a sympathetic individual may be tempered by the fear that apparent differences are part of a manipulation. Suspicion is also a part of nearly every negotiation; the fear that the other side is trying to get the better of you is inherent in negotiations. And there is often a tendency to view the good and bad cops as contrived or designed to suggest artificial differences or pressures for the purposes of avoiding concessions. So playing the role of the good cop is likely to be convincing if you, as the good cop, can deliver in a way that makes responding beneficial to the other side.

Alternatively, the good cop, by definition, will be more credible if the constraints on his side are very clear. Convincing the other side that you need something will be far easier if reality clearly limits what you can do. Yitzhak Rabin did not have to convince Arafat that he had a problem with Israeli settlers and therefore needed some understanding of the very real pressures he faced on settler issues. The pressures were clear; the demonstrations and even the threats were apparent. Because of that, Arafat cut Rabin slack on the issue of settlement expansion. Though not usually concerned about the needs of the other side, even before the Rabin assassination, Arafat never made much of an issue of Israeli settlement activity. His aides might raise concerns with us, but Arafat rarely, if ever, did so. Rabin, in turn, was more tolerant than his security people of what he thought Arafat could and could not do against Hamas. It was as if each understood the constraints on the other and was prepared to respect certain limitations as a result. Privately communicating on domestic or internal pressures may build understanding and trust between leaders, but such private communications will ring truer if there is public evidence of the problem.

In the end, explaining constraints, what is possible, what isn't, and the circumstances under which change can take place is essential for setting a context in negotiations—and laying the groundwork for what any good cop must do to demonstrate that he needs help to prevail against the bad cops on his side.

8. UNDERSTAND THE VALUE AND LIMITATIONS OF DEADLINES

Deadlines are essential in any high-stakes negotiation. No political leader ever wants to take a decision that will expose him or her to great political cost before absolutely necessary. Deadlines are a two-way street. You also have to be prepared to make your own hardest concessions. You have to be ready to close. And you have to be willing to live with the consequences of having no deal—or at least not the one you envisioned.

The higher the stakes in a negotiation, the more a deadline is likely to be necessary to force concessions that each side is ultimately willing to make but reluctant to undertake until they become convinced that there is no choice. In negotiations, there is always reluctance to go to one's real bottom line—assuming it is truly known—for fear that playing what one sees as his/her ultimate concession will prove insufficient if the other side is not equally ready to make decisions. In such circumstances, if your side reveals its bottom line and the other still doesn't move, you will end up having little choice but to go beyond your redline or see the end of negotiations and the failure to achieve a deal.

Hafez al Asad would frequently ask me, "Are the Israelis ready to conclude a deal?" He was not asking, do they want a deal? He was trying to determine if they were ready to go to the endgame, where each side must finally put its cards on the table. I did not understand this distinction until later in the process—and when I finally did, I told Asad, "You want to know whether they are ready to close now and put their real bottom lines on the table, but your own behavior signals that you are not ready to do that. If you want to go to an endgame, prove it in terms of what you are prepared to do; give me something to show the Israelis that this is not just an attempt to draw them out without revealing anything on your side." In fact, Asad finally did this when he changed his posture on resuming negotiations, sent his foreign minister for the first time to negotiate with the Israelis, and made concessions even on borders— believing this was now the endgame. Unfortunately, Ehud Barak, suddenly believing that he must not look like he was rushing to an agreement, decided that it was not the time for the endgame after all. We had not imposed a deadline, but Asad had believed we were in an endgame and that Barak was similarly ready to decide.

Deadlines are used to force each side to decide. One should not impose them unless one is ready to live with the consequences. Similarly, deadlines should not be imposed unless you feel that you truly have played out the string, meaning that nothing more can be done and the negotiations have become a process of avoidance rather than of decisions. Richard Holbrooke and Secretary of State Christopher understood this in forging the Dayton Accords on Bosnia. George Mitchell also understood that he could not conclude the Good Friday Agreement on Northern Ireland without a deadline. In both cases, Holbrooke and Mitchell realized what it took to conclude a deal, and with a deadline, they could finally force each side to overcome its reluctance to decide and close the deal.

One other time to impose a deadline is when you believe the circumstances exist to reach a deal but may change. Sometimes a deadline is necessary not only to force decisions but also because the political context in which those decisions could be made is under pressure and not likely to be sustained. When I was negotiating the deal between the Israelis and Palestinians on Hebron, I imposed a deadline for both reasons: I could see that the gaps were bridgeable and that decisions had to be made, and at the same time, I feared that if we did not close at that time, the circumstances would change. New issues would open up, there could be an act of terrorism, and Netanyahu would lose his base or need to make a deal—and Arafat might decide that the deal no longer served his interests.

Ultimately, deadlines are derivative. They don't produce agreements where agreements are not possible, but rather they create the necessary pressure to overcome the inherent reluctance to make hard decisions. They require great nerve and a sense of timing. They are certainly necessary, but they are not sufficient for reaching agreements.

9. TAKE ONLY CALCULATED RISKS

No negotiator worth his or her salt will avoid taking risks in a negotiation. Naturally, the risks he or she takes will be calculated, but they will be risks nonetheless. Reluctance to take risks will be seen by the other side (or sides) as your needing the negotiations more than they do. Neither side in a negotiation wants to send the signal that it needs the negotiating process or deal more than its opponent, or that it fears a breakdown so much that it will make the concessions needed just to keep the other side in the game. That is surely a slippery slope.

Negotiations involve leverage. They involve convincing the other side (or sides) that while a deal should serve both sides' interests and produce a win-win outcome, you can and will walk away if your interests are not served. But no matter how well you feel you read the situation, you cannot be certain, and others on your side of the negotiations may fear the consequences of a breakdown and shy away from running the risk of bringing everything to a head. I certainly faced this when trying to close the deal on Hebron.

I had taken over the negotiations the last day, telling Prime Minister Netanyahu that his negotiators could not make the necessary moves to resolve the remaining issues—even though I had helped narrow the differences between the two sides—and I would resolve what was left with the Palestinians if he would accept my doing so. Believing that it was now or never, he said, "Go for it." After working with Abu Mazen and

Saeb Erekat until well past midnight, we reached agreement on the last issues. I told them I would sell what we had agreed to Netanyahu and they said they would do the same with Yasir Arafat.

I was able to do my part, but in the middle of the night, Saeb Erekat called me to say, "President Arafat had some questions and we need some additional discussions." I told him I was done. I had done my part and I would have no more discussions with them. In the morning, Erekat and other members of the Palestinian delegation began calling, pleading for a meeting. I instructed my team that I would have no meeting and I would not take any phone calls from the Palestinians before they acknowledged what we had agreed upon.

During the day, the Palestinians persuaded King Hussein to call me and ask me to see them. I told him I would do so only when they acknowledged our agreement—and upping the ante, I told him I would leave that night if there was no agreement. Osama al-Baz, the advisor to President Mubarak of Egypt, made a similar call, as did the Egyptian ambassador to Israel, Mohammad Bassiouny. Members of my team were nervous and suggested that I at least agree to talk to the Palestinians on the phone. I refused and put out publicly that I would be leaving at midnight.

My boss, Secretary of State Warren Christopher, called and asked if I was certain that this was the right thing to do. I convinced him that it was. But shortly after speaking to him, I got a call from Sandy Berger, the deputy national security advisor—who was about to become the national security advisor. He was concerned and, leaving no doubt that he was speaking for himself and the president, asked, "What is the harm in talking to the Palestinians?" I told him that they had to see that I was not talking anymore unless they first acknowledged the understandings from the previous night. Without that, they would reopen the issues, and everything would unravel—indeed, their desire to talk more might simply have been a test to determine if they actually had to close now. Arafat needed to understand that he had to decide now or lose our involvement and what had been achieved. Berger reluctantly, and with obvious unease, accepted my approach.

Was I so certain I was right? No, I had my doubts, but the more the pressure built on me, the more I knew there was nervousness on the Palestinian side, and the last thing I wanted to do at that moment was to relieve their anxiety. Moreover, I knew that this posture—and my withstanding pressure—would help with Netanyahu if it turned out that I had to go back to him and ask for a modification on any of the issues to close the deal. As it turned out, the Palestinians relented, acknowledged our agreement, and also met my new demand of announcing that they would host a summit with Netanyahu and me that evening to finalize the deal. When I finally met them before the summit, they asked for one minor change—which I then brought to Netanyahu saying, "With this change we have a deal." He asked, "For real, Dennis?" and when I said, "For real," we concluded the understanding on Hebron.

I ran the risk because I saw the natural hesitancy to close at a time when the gaps had effectively been bridged. I also believed there was a greater risk in not closing, and I read both sides as being ready if pushed. It was essential to show no sign of wavering on my part. In such a circumstance, a negotiator cannot run a risk if he cannot sustain the position he has adopted. Apart from the negotiator's knowing that he has the necessary backing to sustain his position, it comes back to his making a good assessment of where he is in the process and having the right sense of timing. Timing is a key for any negotiator—pushing when you should not or conceding when you need not will inevitably undercut what you want to achieve. Knowing when to run risks must be a part of the makeup of any negotiator. And being prepared as a negotiator to make threats at certain critical moments must be accompanied by a readiness to carry out what you threaten.

10. NEVER LIE, NEVER BLUFF

The most important attribute for any negotiator is his credibility. The old saying that your word must be your bond is the lifeblood for any negotiator. A negotiator's word must be trusted, his assessments and observations taken seriously, and his threats and promises always believed. Lies and bluffs will always be exposed, and once he is exposed, a negotiator may never recover his credibility. In fact, if a negotiator makes a threat on which he cannot deliver—whether because of a bluff or an inability to follow through—it will take a tremendous effort and the expenditure of real capital to recoup his losses. Even then, his credibility may never be completely reestablished. A negotiator's credibility is the one asset he must never permit to be devalued.

Upon closing the Hebron deal, I was asked on CNN, "Did you really plan to leave as you announced earlier in the day?" It was clear that the newsman asking the question thought I had simply been posturing. To his surprise, I said I would have left that night if there had been no summit and no deal. I stated very clearly that I had not been bluffing.

I would never put myself in a position of having a bluff called. If a negotiator is not prepared to act on his threats, he should not make them. Bluffs in the high-stakes game of resolving historically rooted conflicts are almost always called. The stakes are simply too high not to test how real a threat might be.

While bluffs are nearly always called, lies will also be exposed sooner or later. Too many people are involved, and the truth in any given situation is bound to be revealed by someone. A negotiator must not knowingly tell the other side something that is untrue. He can, however, qualify his assertion by making the point that he "believes" what he is saying to be the case.

When, for example, Hafez al Asad asked Warren Christopher and me whether Israel had any claims on Syrian territory at the time we were conveying from Yitzhak Rabin his readiness to withdraw from the Golan Heights, assuming Israel's needs were met, I responded, "Not that we know of." While Rabin had, in fact, not qualified his offer other than to say that his needs must be met, I did not want us to be in a position of saying something that was false. (This was fortuitous, as later we discovered that Rabin and Asad had different definitions of what full withdrawal from the Golan Heights meant.)

Yitzhak Rabin was a leader who would simply never lie. I used to say about him that he was constitutionally incapable of lying. He would literally never tell anyone something that was not true. But he was also very practiced in the art of telling the "technical truth." The technical truth is literally true but not necessarily revealing. The technical truth is certainly not the whole truth. In negotiations, especially given his expectation of Asad seeking constant advantage, the Rabin motto seemed to be that he would respond to questions from us literally but not completely.

For negotiators, there is a lesson here: while never acting in a way that might suggest bad faith, be sure always to qualify what you say in a way that ensures that you have not lied and cannot be accused of lying. One's counterpart can live with many things in a negotiation other than being lied to or deliberately misled. Make it a rule not to do either.

11. DON'T PAPER OVER DIFFERENCES

Of all the rules, none goes against basic human instinct more than this one. It is human nature to want meetings to go well or to conclude with a good feeling. But negotiations are about overcoming differences, and the differences cannot be wished away. While it is important to create a context and avoid being provocative, there are moments at which indirection does not work and when differences must be taken on directly, even if this means that a difficult, bitter meeting may be the result. Similarly, the desire to leave a meeting with good feeling or a seeming agreement can be dangerous and costly if it is based on a misunderstanding. It will always come back to haunt you.

Let me illustrate each point. Prior to going to the Wye River Plantation summit involving the Israeli and Palestinian leaders with their delegations, I knew that the Palestinians needed to know concretely, not only in generalities, what they would be asked to do on security in terms of making arrests, collecting illegal weapons, and dealing with terrorist infrastructure. Leaving this vague could provoke a shock, with claims of bad faith on our part, charges that we had invited them to the summit on false pretenses, and a retreat from positions they might otherwise be willing to adopt. So I arranged to meet with Mohammad Dahlan, the man in charge of security in Gaza and responsible for dealing with the security issues in the negotiations for the Palestinians. I let him know before the meeting we would have to go over some difficult issues, and he was in no rush to do so. When there was no putting off the task at hand, I told him I had to go over with him what would be hard for the Palestinians to accept but essential for reaching a deal. And, to be precise, I wanted to read him the points from a draft that we were planning to present at Wye.

Even though I prefaced my remarks further by explaining why I knew these points would be difficult, Dahlan could not contain himself as he listened. He exploded in anger—saying that if he had to accept these points he would look like a quisling and be unable to face his men. He got so agitated that he literally needed to walk it off for about fifteen

minutes—all the while with Gamal Helal, my advisor and Arabic inter-
preter, seeking to calm him down. When Dahlan returned to the table, I
told him that I was not trying to damage him; I was not making these
points to hurt him, even though he believed they would. But I was also
not going to mislead him and create a false promise for him. What I described would be necessary; if there were ways to say it differently to
make it easier to accept and explain in Palestinian terms, he should ad-
vise me how to do that—just so long as he understood there would be no
agreement without his side's meeting the substance of these points.

Dahlan collected himself and went over each point, explaining what
was hard but also letting me know that he was prepared to find a way to
meet the substance of each of the security concerns. In turn, he asked me
to frame each obligation in a way that would make it possible to be sold
on the Palestinian street. Ultimately, we did so. But if I had not prepared
the ground in a meeting that I knew would be confrontational, I am not
sure we would have reached agreement later.

Negotiations on hard issues will provoke harsh reactions. The trick is
not to be provocative for its own sake. Pick your moments, and don't shy
away from them. And don't disguise disagreements; make sure they are
known, even if you are not necessarily ready to take them on. The logic
of creating understanding on lesser issues and building both good faith
and momentum is a compelling one. But, again, the understandings
must be real.

Former secretary of state James Baker taught me the importance of
never leaving a meeting with a false impression or understanding, even
if it produces ill feeling. I saw him do this early in his tenure on the issue of short-range nuclear missiles in Europe. Our position at the time
emphasized modernization, and most Europeans were opposed. With
the French foreign minister suggesting there was basic agreement between us and everyone ready to adjourn one particular meeting, Baker
said he was not sure we truly were on the same page—and proceeded to
show all present that we were not really in accord at all. This was not a
small meeting; I could see from the faces on our delegation that there
was distress over the fact that Baker had chosen to highlight the differences and not let the meeting conclude with a sense of agreement. Yet
he was right. There would have been a false sense of understanding,
which would have been more painful and costly to reverse later on.

No one in my experience was more careful to avoid misunderstandings or false agreements than Baker, and it was a valuable lesson that guided me in negotiations. Once at the end of seven days of shuttling between the Israelis, Syrians, and Lebanese to stop an escalating battle between Hizbollah and Israel, I prolonged a meeting with President Asad, much to the consternation of my colleagues, after agreement had seemingly been reached on a cease-fire document. I did so because I feared there was one provision that was understood differently by the two sides, and I wanted Asad to know that if fire came from a Lebanese village against Israeli forces, under the terms of the self-defense provision the Israelis would respond against Hizbollah at the site. I wanted no surprises; I wanted no subsequent charge from Asad that he did not understand the provision that way, and I wanted to avoid an early unraveling of the accord. Notwithstanding my concerns, there was hesitancy on our side to spell this out for fear Asad would back away from the agreement—and a perception that it would be harder for him to do so once it had been finalized. I did not buy that view and acted anyway, and Asad, uncharacteristically, thanked me for pointing this out.

At a different juncture between Israelis and Palestinians, I failed to follow this rule, going against my own principles in the process, and it came back to haunt us. At the end of the Wye River Plantation summit, we had secured an agreement, but one that Prime Minister Bibi Netanyahu refused to conclude after learning that President Clinton would not release Jonathan Pollard, the American convicted of spying for Israel. Netanyahu claimed that in private meetings with the president, Clinton had understood that Bibi needed Pollard's release to sell the deal in Israel and that the president would release him. Clinton claimed he had made no such commitment. We were stuck for several hours, and after the two leaders met alone to resolve the impasse, the president told us that Bibi had thought about reducing the number of Palestinian prisoners to be released but decided he should not make Arafat pay the price for our misunderstanding; instead, he would release fewer "security" prisoners, as opposed to those who had committed petty crimes in the last phase of releases. Arafat would still get 750 prisoners released in three phases, but in the last phase, the politically sensitive prisoners would make up a smaller proportion of the releases than first planned. The president felt we might be able to change this back to the original formula if the implementation of the agreement went well. He asked Secretary Albright and me to go explain this to Arafat.

Even though I felt a vagueness that made me uneasy, I did not ask any questions. Something told me this was not quite right, but after eight days of very difficult negotiations—having spent the last forty-eight hours awake, knowing that if we did not conclude the agreement with sundown approaching on a Friday, the deal would have to be put on hold for the Sabbath and might unravel—I went along. But in doing so, we created a big problem for ourselves when it became clear within a few weeks that the two sides had totally different understandings on the meaning of the prisoner releases—a highly emotional issue for both sides. Soon the deal and the Israeli government came apart. Perhaps both would have happened anyway. But with all the pressures of the moment, I still should have made sure that we were not disguising a difference that could break the agreement later on.

The lesson is an important one. Don't rely on false understandings. They won't last, and everything that relies upon them will come apart.

12. SUMMARIZE AGREEMENTS
AT THE END OF EVERY MEETING

Clearly this rule is a logical extension of the need to avoid misunderstanding. One way to make sure that there is a common understanding of what has been agreed is to summarize the points of agreement or convergence at the end of every meeting. By summarizing, the other side will either agree or not agree on the points and their interpretation. At least then you and your counterpart will have a common appreciation of where you stand.

Clearly such summaries have a value in preventing misunderstandings. But they can also contribute in another way: I sought to create a dynamic in negotiations in which each meeting would advance the baseline of the previous one, even if only minimally. The psychology was one of advance, not retreat or merely holding the line. Summarizing the outcome at the end of each meeting always provided a clear status report. Both sides would know what the baseline was going in and coming out.

Summaries also provided a concrete basis on which to make agreements on particular issues. I was always a firm believer in resolving agreements on issues whenever possible. In my discussion on mediation in chapter 10, I describe the importance of reaching agreement where you can, but also note the circumstances under which there can be exceptions to this rule.

In any case, since misunderstandings frequently bedevil negotiations and always set them back, being careful to summarize what has been both understood and not understood on each issue at the end of a meeting is a critical rule of thumb for negotiators.

Employing these twelve rules will make it possible to use negotiations as a more effective tool of statecraft. In the complicated landscape of international conflict and diplomacy that we are facing in the twenty-first century, negotiations will be needed to create a climate that legitimizes what we want or produces partners for what we seek or changes the behaviors of those who might be a threat. Mediation, which obviously involves negotiation and many of the rules outlined above, is a related tool of statecraft that in the last several years has been increasingly neglected. It is time to employ it more extensively.

10.

⎰ MEDIATION IN A WORLD ⎱
⎱ OF LOCAL CONFLICT ⎰

Why a separate chapter on mediation? Mediation involves negotiations, and the rules outlined in the last chapter will apply in nearly any mediation effort. However, in a book about statecraft, and how best to employ it to serve America's national security interests, mediation is worthy of a separate discussion. It is not about resolving our differences with another country or seeking to get another country to accept our positions; it is about using a negotiation process to try to reconcile differences and conflicts between others. In the words of Saadia Touval and I. William Zartman, "Mediation is best thought of as a mode of negotiation in which a third party helps the parties find a solution that they cannot find by themselves."[1] By definition, our own interests are less directly engaged in a mediation process.

This is not to say that we have no interests. While our interests are less directly involved, we may still decide that we have an important stake in trying to stop or prevent a conflict between others. Maybe we see a terrible loss of life or abuse of human rights if such a conflict is not prevented. Maybe we fear destabilization of a region and the escalatory dangers of a possible war. Or maybe we decide that we have the ability to settle or at least defuse a conflict and should do so.

In such circumstances, mediation is a form of U.S. intervention to lessen conflicts. It is certainly cheaper than militarily intervening and it can be used to prevent conflicts from turning violent and bloody or to end them altogether. In recent years, it has been one form of statecraft that has been underused, or employed less ambitiously and far less intensively. And yet it is a tool that could be used to respond to conflicts around the globe. The old saying that we don't have a dog in that fight has always reflected an understandable logic: Why involve ourselves, our prestige, our diplomatic and material resources, in something that may be very hard to resolve and doesn't appear to relate to us?

In a world that was far less connected, that might make sense. It is not just that the world—as Thomas Friedman has pointed out—is flat, in which everything is connected and those around the globe can compete economically on a much more level playing surface; it is that we are now in a world in which we will find it far more difficult to insulate ourselves from conflict. For those who are still not a part of the flat world, and who are unlikely to join it any time soon, resentments run deep. Traditional sources of conflict—competing claims to power, land, and resources, and intercommunal and ethnic rivalries—will be compounded by an abiding resentment of being left out of global development, and as 9/11 proved, that will affect us sooner or later.

Thus, quite apart from our responding out of genuine humanitarian concern—an impulse that is more neoliberal than neoconservative—there are very practical reasons to involve ourselves in conflict situations through mediation. Foremost among these, many local conflicts fuel the very anger and alienation that breeds ready recruits for Al Qaeda and its offshoots. The Palestinian issue is not the source of Bin Ladenism or Jihadism, but the anger and sense of grievance that radiates from it is exploited by the radical Islamists. Not every local conflict can be so exploited, but as the appeal of jihad on its own merits wanes, its perpetrators will increasingly seek to exploit local conflicts to keep their cause alive.

Surely mediation is not the answer in every situation. But it can be a useful tool. If nothing else, actively and visibly employing it will create a far more favorable view of the role and utility of American power internationally—and building the legitimacy of what we are doing will make it easier for others to be associated with us and to embrace our purposes. It is certainly far easier to influence others if our purposes are accepted and not rejected.

MEDIATION TO PROMOTE AMERICAN ACCEPTABILITY

One objective of statecraft—indeed, one fundamental objective of our foreign policy—must be forging an international context in which what we seek is generally accepted. The more our purposes are seen as appropriate, the more others will identify with what we seek, and the more we will be able to influence others and find partners for dealing with challenges around the globe. In a world where increasingly we must act with others to be effective, it is essential that we be seen as legitimate and that our adversaries be seen as illegitimate. Richard Haass, using the concept of integrating the other leading powers into a common policy approach, goes so far as to say that we can never vanquish threats stemming from loose nukes and terrorism without having others share our basic goals and purposes.[2]

The failing of the Bush administration in its first term was to believe that persuasion was ultimately not necessary because others would adjust to the realities that we created.

In the Bush administration's second term, there has been a growing awareness that our policies were repelling more than they were attracting others. Secretary of State Rice has thus emphasized outreach and a new slogan: "practical idealism." The slogan is meant to convey that the United States will not back away from its idealistic goals but will pursue them by engaging others actively, listening to them, and taking their concerns into account. While Secretary Rice has certainly made an effort to show she is listening to others, the perception internationally is that the United States still preaches more than it seeks to persuade.

If we are to reduce the almost reflexive opposition to the United States and its purposes throughout much of the international community, we will have to do much more to change attitudes toward us. In a world of non-state actors posing threats, we need others to join with us and believe that is the right thing to do. So, transforming our image, building the acceptability of our actions, making ourselves less toxic, and having others see that we are acting selflessly are all going to be necessary parts of statecraft—particularly at a time when we must also be competing for the hearts and minds of a population in the Islamic world that has become angry and alienated from us.

And, here, mediation can be a very valuable tool. Mediation has the virtue of showing the United States at its best. It can demonstrate concern for others and an unmistakable commitment to trying to resolve conflicts. Throughout the 1990s, many in the Arab world criticized the efforts the United States was making to resolve the Arab-Israeli conflict, complaining that we were too biased toward Israel and too hard or demanding on the Arab side in the negotiations. But no one questioned that America cared about this conflict and was making a genuine effort to settle it. Indeed, as the most visible face of our mediation efforts, I found myself often approached in the Arab world and told how much my work was appreciated. Even some of my foremost Arab critics at the time, including the secretary-general of the Arab League, Amre Moussa, now bemoan the fact that I am no longer the mediator; though I believe they miss me less than they miss the emblem of America caring about the issue.

Contrast this with the Bush administration and the perception that it has simply disengaged from the conflict. Its unwillingness to pursue mediation fostered an impression throughout the Middle East that it was indifferent to a conflict that animated a basic grievance among those in the Arab and Islamic worlds. Whereas the Clinton administration got credit for genuinely caring—even if our policies then were often questioned—the Bush administration got no credit, only a deepening resentment about its purposes.

That said, mediation should be used as a tool not simply because of its effect on our image. Clearly, the main reason for mediating is to promote conflict resolution. Here, however, mediation must be approached realistically. Not every local conflict can be settled. But the measure of mediation, like diplomacy more generally, is not always what you positively achieve. It is also what you prevent, limit, contain, or defuse.

MEDIATION, CONFLICT REDUCTION, AND LEVERAGE

American mediation efforts during the years 2001–2006 were not going to end the Israeli-Palestinian conflict. This was not in the cards, especially while Yasir Arafat was alive. Nonetheless, our efforts might have limited the death, destruction, and victimization on both Israeli and Palestinian sides during the second intifada. Had we made such an effort, it would have made the resumption of peacemaking efforts far easier and far more likely to pay off. Instead, with a legacy of more than five years of warfare and an accumulated set of grievances on each side, both Israelis and Palestinians have increasingly lost faith in peacemaking.

When it comes to Middle East diplomacy, or other conflict zones, the situation is rarely static. If the process of peacemaking is not moving forward, it is usually going backward and deteriorating. Restoring faith in such a process when it is lost is not simple. Here the Bush administration failed to comprehend the price of deterioration. It came into office believing that if it could not resolve the conflict, there was little reason to do anything. However, it failed to understand the psychic costs of deterioration, and it failed to appreciate that U.S. mediation might have kept the conflict within bounds and limited the deterioration. And doing so could have bought time to get beyond Arafat while also shaping an environment that was more conducive to resuming real peacemaking at a later time.

In this sense, mediation should be seen as a tool serving different purposes ranging from containment or reduction of conflicts to their resolution. Success can be measured not by whether you resolve a conflict or fail to do so, but by whether you transform it and make resolution possible at a later point.

Obviously mediation can take multiple forms. It can be intensive and designed to broker differences, bringing the sides to the negotiating table and making proposals to bridge differences. This is what was done at certain stages in the Clinton administration on Bosnia, Northern Ireland, and the Arab-Israeli process. Alternatively, mediation can be far more passive, facilitating communication and clarifying differences but shying away from actively brokering agreements. In the early years of the Oslo process, we tended to play this role. The Norwegians were capable of only a more supportive or facilitating role, and that is the one they played in making the Oslo process possible.

To be a broker as opposed to a facilitator, one needs leverage. A country such as Norway could offer inducements but it could not offer any meaningful penalties. It could walk away from the process, but others could replace it. It wanted to be involved in the process more than the parties ultimately needed it to be involved. In this respect, Norway could play a role only when the parties wanted it to do so.

The United States is more capable of imposing itself in a negotiation if it so desires. It is far harder for parties to say no to U.S. involvement, for fear of creating problems in the relationship. Israel, for example, could never easily reject U.S. involvement in a negotiating process if an American administration pressed the issue. And yet different administrations have been reluctant to impose themselves when their presence was not sought or desired.

Typically, this reluctance to impose American mediation resulted from the perception that if there was little that was achievable, and no enthusiasm for our playing the role, what was the point of mediating? While the Bush administration has taken this to an extreme, the Clinton administration was ready to play the more ambitious mediator role only when both sides wanted it to do so—something that was true during Prime Minister Rabin's time only with Syria. (With Prime Ministers Netanyahu and Barak, there was a keen interest in an active American mediation role—and the Palestinians always sought such an American role because they believed it would level the playing field with the Israelis.)

Again, perceptions of there being a possibility to make progress, or, alternatively, a fear of serious deterioration without our efforts, have tended to drive American readiness to play a mediator's role. In Northern Ireland, it was the perception of possibility and the belief that we could make a difference that prompted an activist mediator role.

In Yugoslavia, however, our initial reluctance during the George H. W. Bush administration to assume a mediator posture resulted from a sense of hopelessness about the prospects of any settlement. We were only too willing to let the Europeans take the lead, rationalizing this behavior with the belief that this was a conflict in their backyard and one that could help define an appropriate European role in the post–cold war world.

In the first two years of the Clinton administration, we remained very hesitant about intervening in an active way—leaving mediation efforts to a UN- and European Union–led process involving former secretary of state Cyrus Vance, representing UN secretary-general Boutrous-Ghali, and David Owen, the former British foreign secretary, representing the EU. These two sides were not without leverage, but it was primarily limited to moral suasion and economic pressure. Unfortunately, when

Vance and Owen devised a plan for the resolution of the conflict, they failed to get support from the United States, and their real leverage was limited and rarely exercised. Coercion and threats against Serbia remained largely absent. When dealing with someone like Slobodan Milošević, the Serb leader, moral suasion carried little weight and even economic pressure was going to take a long time to produce an effect. Only the credible threat of hard military power (and at times its application) was likely to make a difference, and the administration was not prepared either to use it or to back the Europeans with it. The more egregious Serb behavior became—extensive ethnic cleansing, the Srebrenica massacre, the horrific mortar attack killing civilians in a Sarajevo market—the greater the pressure for us to intervene with force, and the greater our leverage became on Milošević to change his ways and accept a negotiated pathway.

The Europeans were limited in their ability to be a mediator given their inability to exert real pressure. They tended to see inducements more than sanctions as the way to change Serb behavior. Indeed, the terrible legacy of the twentieth-century wars in Europe has made coercion and the possible use of force generally unacceptable to most Europeans. Their approach to interventions to limit conflicts has thus focused far more on offering rewards rather than imposing penalties for fear that such penalties might provoke more aggressive behaviors. Inevitably their leverage tends to be more limited as a result.

This is not to say that mediators need to focus solely on penalties or sanctions. There almost always needs to be a mix of both potential penalties and rewards. Indeed, inducements or reassurance often are needed to get combatants to cross historic thresholds that otherwise might be difficult to cross. They need an explanation of what is to be gained if they are going to reverse historic positions. Still, a mediator needs leverage—the ability to affect the behavior of one or both sides because of its capacity significantly to help or hurt the position of each on its own or one in relation to the other. Usually leverage stems from the ability not just to aid one or the other side in a conflict but also to deny it what it might want. Creating enmity in a powerful outside party who could materially support one's opponent is bound to make one think twice about resisting that party's effort at mediation. Not surprisingly, those who have leverage are far more capable of being effective mediators than those who can only offer their good offices and little in terms of side payments or threats.

WHEN TO MEDIATE AND HOW TO DO SO

While leverage is critical, there also must be some reason to believe that the intervention of a mediator can make a difference. Parties to a conflict that are simply not ready to end it may be pressured to cease fire for a short period but not engage seriously in conflict reduction or resolution. The purpose of mediation in such a context will tend to be quite limited. Produce the cease-fire and try to find ways to preserve it, and hope circumstances will change to make a more enduring arrangement possible in time.

Outside parties will always be more willing to play an active mediating role if they believe the parties to a conflict are ready to end it. How does one come to such a judgment? Sometimes the parties themselves make it easy by demonstrating a clear desire for change. The readiness of the Israelis and the PLO to meet secretly and then engage in mutual recognition suggested that a historic threshold had been crossed. Dramatic changes in behavior from the past will always be convincing. At other times, one or more parties may convey to a possible mediator the readiness to change. Certainly on Northern Ireland the Clinton administration saw renewed and intensive joint efforts by the British and Irish governments—and a new attitude by Sinn Féin and Gerry Adams toward negotiations—as reason enough to believe intensive mediation might work.

From the perspective of an American policy maker, it will be important to assess whether there are openings for ending or transforming a conflict so it can be resolved or at least defused. Such assessments should be guided in the first instance by an indication that the conflict has become, in I. William Zartman's words, a "mutually hurting stalemate"— one where each side realizes that it cannot win, that the costs of conflict are less and less sustainable, that the losses themselves may threaten the hold on power of leaders, and where each side begins to look for a way out. Of course, one can also look for more positive indicators: Is a new leadership emerging that is less tied to the past, whose legitimacy does not depend on continuing the conflict, and who seems poised for change?[3]

At times the answers to these questions will be clear, and the decision to play a mediating role is relatively straightforward. At other times the answers may be far more opaque, ensuring real doubt about whether mediation can be of use. Nonetheless, from an American standpoint, our interests might still dictate a desire to transform the regional or international landscape and lead us to explore these questions or even take the initiative with the parties to see if they are open to outside help. Even assuming that we determine that they are and that mediation could help, we will still have to decide what kind of role we should be playing as mediator. Should we limit ourselves to bringing the parties together and facilitating the process of negotiations? Should we be more active and ambitious, intervening anytime there is a problem and offering proposals to overcome deadlocks in their talks? Should we try to solve all problems at once with a grand bargain and push the parties to accept it?

The right role in mediation will depend on where the parties are in the conflict-resolution process. If they are just beginning, but signal that they want to resolve their differences—and not simply have a negotiating process for its own sake—the mediator will need to explore privately with each side what it can do and how much is theoretically possible. Even if each side's intentions are sincere, they may still need to get to know one another and their respective concerns before any serious effort at resolution or at offering major proposals is attempted.

In other words, assuming the role of an activist broker is likely to make sense only when it fits the stage of the negotiations and the mindset of the parties. A more limited facilitator or supportive role may be more appropriate as a negotiating process begins. Fostering greater understanding between the two sides, trying to get each to appreciate the grievances of the other side, ensuring that neither side misinterprets what the other side is saying at the table, may be very important for setting the stage for resolving the conflict over time—and for these purposes, playing a supportive role geared toward facilitating communications may be the most fitting. Such a role is by definition limited, and does not involve brokering differences or pressing both sides to change their behaviors and adjust to what is necessary to produce agreements. A mediator is likely to start off working more as a facilitator (of communication, of meetings, and of the negotiating process generally) and then graduate into more activist roles involving either presenting bridging proposals or pressuring each side to change its posture and accept realistic tradeoffs and outcomes.

In dealing with the Arabs and Israelis, I was often probing to see what more we could do. But I had to be mindful of whether our involvement would actually help or become an excuse for the parties to avoid taking steps on their own, including offering possible compromises on their own. I had to consider whether it was appropriate to make a suggestion on the process of the negotiations (who should be negotiating and where they should be doing it) or a proposal on the substance of negotiations (perhaps to break a deadlock), and whether my very acts would be accepted or rejected. Rejection by itself was not always a bad thing, particularly if it forced the two sides together to come up with something on their own as an alternative to what I was suggesting. Of course, there were times when the views of the negotiators on each side might be one thing and of the leaders quite another. During Prime Minister Rabin's time, his negotiator with the Palestinians, Uri Savir, wanted to resolve differences without our intervention but was much more open to American activism than was Prime Minister Rabin. Rabin was leery of too much American involvement—believing that inevitably we would put more pressure on Israel than on the Palestinians and also believing that the real proof of changed Palestinian intentions would be their willingness to resolve differences directly with the Israelis and without outside help.

Whether talking of active brokering or of more limited facilitation of discussions, any mediator has to decide when to try to close on either partial or full agreements. Sometimes, as with the Dayton negotiations on Bosnia and the Good Friday negotiations on Northern Ireland, there may be an underlying readiness to close a deal, but for political and psychological reasons, the parties find it very hard to make the necessary decisions. They must be pushed to do so. They must know that if they don't they will lose an opportunity to resolve the conflict. Here the mediator, taking a measure of the parties and their readiness to reach agreement—as well as the inhibitions on doing so—must make the judgment that imposing a deadline makes sense or, as George Mitchell believed in the Northern Ireland negotiations, is the only way the parties will decide and reach agreement. Without a deadline, Mitchell reasoned that neither David Trimble nor Gerry Adams (or for that matter, British and Irish prime ministers Blair and Ahern) would muster the courage to make the historic choices, and face the inevitable challenges when they did.[4]

If the parties are truly ready but need the push or the pressure to make the hard decisions, a deadline can be quite effective, particularly because it raises the stakes and the possibility of losing important gains. On the other hand, sometimes it is less a deadline than an explanation or excuse ("the Americans insisted, and we would lose a lot if we said no") that is needed to close a deal.

In such cases, the die is cast, and the basic readiness to reach agreement exists. Before launching a mediation effort, any prospective mediator needs to assess what is possible and what difference his/her intervention can make. Again, simply because a complete resolution of a conflict is not possible is not a reason to avoid intervention. A partial deal might still be useful; it might be essential to creating conditions for a complete deal later on, or it might simply contain what is a troublesome conflict.

Mediation is thus a tool of why, what, when, and how—define why it is important to mediate, what is possible, and when and how to do it. It is interesting that there is one case where the Bush administration, though generally eschewing the mediation role, did play it and did so successfully, to end the north-south conflict in Sudan. There were several reasons why the administration chose this one place to intervene: it thought that progress might be possible, it had a ready and determined mediator available—former senator John Danforth, an ordained minister who cared about the issue—and, perhaps most important, its Christian evangelical base was putting pressure on it to do something about the great pain and suffering being inflicted on the Christians in the southern part of Sudan. All these factors helped lead to its decision to send a mediator. But in this case, the fact that the ongoing Sudanese civil war retained relatively low visibility internationally—and thus meant that the costs to American prestige in trying and failing to mediate would be low—

probably was as important to the Bush decision to mediate as was the pressure from his political base.

Though the Bush administration has not been risk averse when it comes to the use of force, it has been very chary of committing American diplomatic resources, especially to mediation efforts. The fear of failure seems to weigh heavily on it when it comes to mediation. Perhaps it felt that Clinton's efforts at mediation, especially in the Middle East, cost that administration much in the way of prestige and made it look ineffectual—something that in the eyes of those around the president translated into a loss of perceived American power. As such, mediation that failed would subtract from our power, not add to it. Also, perhaps the president and his advisors felt that any high-visibility mediation effort would inevitably require extensive presidential involvement, and this president was neither geared toward such efforts nor willing to do them. (His style is to set a course and have others implement it; getting into the nitty-gritty of issues and spending time persuading, cajoling, threatening, and brokering does not reflect who he is.)

One virtue of Sudan was that it had low visibility, involved other mediators, and generated no expectations about presidential involvement. Another was that it could show the administration's political base that it was making an effort to stop a conflict in which the Christians of southern Sudan were still being decimated by the Muslims of the north.

The Sudan civil war had been fought for more than two decades and had inflicted a terrible human cost of roughly two million fatalities and four million displaced persons. Senator Danforth's involvement did make a difference. While there were other mediators, including from the United Kingdom and Kenya, Danforth played a leading role in helping to forge power and revenue-sharing understandings that produced agreement and the prospect of ending the conflict. As in any successful mediation, Danforth and the other mediators were able to manipulate the needs and interests of the indigenous forces, while also inheriting a structural situation that made ending the conflict possible: the warring parties had reached the stage of exhaustion in which agreement made far more sense than continuing conflict, and the likely opposition within each camp (which continued to prefer ongoing struggle) no longer had the capacity or strength to disrupt an agreement.

MYTHS AND REALITIES ABOUT MEDIATION AND MEDIATORS

One of the most misleading conventional wisdoms about mediation is that it requires strict neutrality. One must be "evenhanded" and an "honest broker." Each sounds right, reflecting the understandable logic that a mediator ought not to be partial to one side. And yet reality is more complicated; for a power such as the United States and its possible mediators, it is rare that we would have such distance from a conflict that our interests between warring parties would be equal. Moreover, in most conflict situations we are likely to have more ties to one side or see one side as more at fault. In fact, in cases of historic conflict, it is almost a certainty that we will not be strictly neutral—but that has not prevented American mediators from playing effective roles, and being applauded after having done so.

To put this in perspective, John Danforth was not seen as neutral between the Christian south and the Muslim north in Sudan; Richard Holbrooke was not seen as neutral between the Muslims and the Serbs in the Balkans; George Mitchell was not seen as neutral between the Catholics and the Protestants in Northern Ireland.[5] And I was certainly not seen as neutral between Israelis and Palestinians or Syrians.

Neutrality was not what mattered. What mattered was who could affect both parties and alter their behaviors. It is not that in any of these cases there was indifference to perceived bias; rather, in such conflicts the greater concern is who has the capacity both to influence the behavior of one's adversary and/or simply to get things done. And, obviously, being close to one side in a conflict means also having influence and leverage with that side. For example, Anwar Sadat described the United States as having 99 percent of the cards in the Middle East, given its relationship with Israel. American bias was not his concern; getting the United States to use its relationship with Israel was. And that impulse of having the United States use its influence helps to explain in different cases how Danforth, Holbrooke, Mitchell, and I were seen.

To be sure, we all had something else in common: we understood that there was no way to reach agreement unless we could meet the needs of both sides, not only one side. We became effective brokers, which is the real measure. We were trusted by both sides because we were seen not as neutral, but ultimately as genuinely trying to broker an end to conflict and able to deliver on what we were attempting to do.

Being able to deliver reflects another attribute of a successful mediator—a mediator must be authoritative and have a clear mandate. In the Middle East, the different parties know immediately whether an envoy has authority or lacks it. They know power and they quickly recognize those who are limited and bound by constraints or simply unable to make decisions and act on them.

None of the envoys that the Bush administration has sent to the Middle East has been empowered with a broad mandate, and Israelis and Palestinians have understood this limitation immediately. Even Jim Wolfensohn, who was appointed to represent the "Quartet"—the United States, European Union, Russia, and United Nations—was given a mandate only for the economic aspects of the Israeli disengagement from Gaza. He used his clout as former head of the World Bank and his capacity to help produce real assistance for the Palestinians to build his leverage. But that clout was for a narrow and specific, if highly useful, purpose of Israeli disengagement from Gaza, and he did not touch any political issues.

Unfortunately, when the mandate for a mediator is very limited, parties feel no real need to respond. Mediators who can be ignored will never have any impact. Mediators must be able to impose consequences for rejection of their suggestions. Here is a reminder of why the United States, even if not strictly neutral, can have more of an effect than others. It is more likely to affect behavior because it is more capable of imposing consequences and costs.

In its first term, the Bush administration not only was unwilling to use an empowered envoy—both General Anthony Zinni and John Wolf were given very limited mandates—but the president and his secretary of state decided to disengage and not play a broker's role between Israelis and Palestinians. Here the Bush administration broke a clear pattern of U.S. mediating efforts in the region—a pattern that nearly every American president since Truman had embraced and a pattern that was frequently accompanied by complaints about American bias in favor of Israel.

In a question-and-answer session following a speech I gave in Gaza in December 2004, I responded to criticism of American bias toward Israel and to several statements that we were simply unable to be an honest broker by saying, "The United States has not been a broker for the last four years. Are you better off?" In an audience of several hundred people—none of whom had been shy about voicing their opinion—no one was prepared to say they were better off with the United States not playing the broker's role. They understood that neither the Europeans, the Russians, nor the UN—all of whom, in their eyes, would have been more "honest"—was capable of playing the role, and had demonstrated this over the preceding four years. None has the capabilities (or the will) to affect the parties. In truth, calls for an honest broker typically reflect a desire less to have an honest broker than to have the broker assume a posture more sympathetic to the side that is calling for a change.

Mediators will always be criticized. That should be no surprise. Mediation requires getting each side to adjust its behavior to what a deal is going to require. Mediation requires constant explanation of what the reality is, and of how both sides have to adjust to it. It requires explaining the needs of one side to the other—something that is never appreciated. Each side wants to see that the mediator is his or her advocate, not his adversary's. Opposition, anger, and criticism of the mediator are simply part of the territory. As I found, especially with the Palestinians, it was much easier and far less costly to criticize me. Hassan Asfour, one of the Palestinian negotiators, told me at Camp David that Arafat knew he could criticize me and we would stay involved, but that if he or his team criticized the president or the secretary, they might decide to give up the effort.

The lesson is that one needs a thick skin to be a mediator; it is impossible to make both sides happy, particularly because of the need to press them to alter their behaviors. But it is not just a thick skin that is required but also the passion to stay involved when you face criticism and resistance or setbacks. Here, again, we see another myth about mediation and mediators: dispassion is emphasized above all else. Mediators are supposed to keep their emotional distance. Becoming emotionally involved will, it is argued, cloud your judgment and make you lose your objectivity.

But those with actual mediation experience in intractable conflicts know that it is precisely their passion that sustains them in the face of the inevitable difficulties. It is passion that produces the perseverance that is so necessary when trying to resolve a historic conflict with very high stakes and deeply embedded grievances. The norm in such a process is going to be setback, not progress. If the mediator does not bring great commitment and determination to the task, he or she is likely to give up. Look at the Bush administration efforts to play a more active role between Israelis and Palestinians. Besides not empowering its envoys, the administration was quick to disengage every time it faced difficulties. Had there been a real passion or determination to transform the situation, it would not have given up each time it faced problems. What kept Clinton going—what certainly kept me going and continuing to argue that we must preserve the effort—was a deep sense of commitment to the objective of ending the Arab-Israeli conflict.

Mediators need that sense of commitment to maintain an effort that requires endurance and patience. George Mitchell writes of the constant frustrations and setbacks in the negotiations to end the conflict in Northern Ireland. The more frustrated he became, the more determined he became to overcome the problems; had he believed the cause impossible or not worth the effort, he would never have persisted. But he acted out of a profound conviction that it was time to end the suffering and to prevent the purveyors of violence from being the arbiters of the future.[6]

In any existential conflict—whether in Northern Ireland or between the Israelis and the Palestinians—a mediator with no passion will bring only a limited commitment to bear. And the more one is dealing with conflicts that go to the heart of self-definition and identity, the more one needs the kind of commitment that will produce staying power. The mediator must believe not only in peacemaking but also that the alternative to negotiating peace is completely unacceptable. There will be very little prospect of sticking with it, and thus little prospect of success, if the mediator lacks a sense of mission in trying to end such conflicts.

USING BACK CHANNELS EFFECTIVELY

To be sure, success in resolving such existential conflicts will ultimately depend on the parties' being prepared to alter their behavior and confront history and mythology. Mythologies are what allow parties in historically rooted conflicts to avoid reality. Myths are never easy to undo. They tend to be part of the story that leaders tell publics over long periods of time. They become part of the belief system, and are rarely challenged—except by those iconoclasts who are already outside the political system. The myths perpetuate conflicts by effectively denying the rights of the other side and by brooking no compromise on what is treated as an article of faith. For Palestinians, the "right of return" for refugees was one such mythology. Palestinians never questioned it—at least not publicly. It had been ground into the psychology of the PLO, and to question it was to guarantee being accused of betraying the Palestinian cause.

The Israelis have an equivalent mythology: Jerusalem, both Jewish and Arab areas, would be the "eternal, *undivided* capital" of Israel. Like the right of return for Palestinians, this was untouchable for mainstream Israelis, even though Israelis never even ventured into Arab neighborhoods of East Jerusalem such as Bayt Hanina and Shuafat. Until well into the Camp David summit, Prime Minister Barak was unwilling to talk about Jerusalem even in private with me or the president. So how does a mediator explore what is possible on mythologies?

Back channels are an essential part of any negotiation. For mediators, back channels with each side are crucial. On the mythologies and politically explosive issues, no discussion is even possible if there is not a private venue in which there is a basic ground rule: anything can be discussed and nothing will ever be permitted to leak out publicly. Being able to explore possibilities in a noncommitting, unquotable, and nonreferral fashion is the only way to see not only what might be possible on extremely sensitive issues but also how to go about acting on them. Here, again, trust and credibility are indispensable for a mediator. A mediator must cultivate these attributes and never squander them.

How does a mediator build trust and acquire credibility? Much as in any negotiation, it is essential to prove you understand what is important to each side. Only make promises you can deliver on, and never fail to deliver what you promise. Never betray a confidence, and never be responsible for exposing those you are working with on politically sensitive or embarrassing issues—without at least explaining well in advance that at some point you will have to talk about these particular issues publicly if there is to be an agreement. Finally, find ways to fix problems or deliver for each side when each knows it is not easy for you to do so.

As an example of such an approach, at one point I took a problem between the Israelis and Syrians and acted to fix it in a way that was appreciated for very different reasons by both Yitzhak Rabin and Hafez al Asad. Asad had been led to believe that President Clinton would provide him a note of assurance on the location of the final border—and the relationship of the security arrangements to it—as part of our effort to produce an agreed statement on the security issues between the two sides. Though the Israeli negotiator, Itamar Rabinovich, had not objected to this approach, Rabin belatedly did so with me, in Israel, the day before I was to deliver the note to Asad in Syria. Rabin argued that such a note would take a private commitment from Rabin to the president on Rabin's readiness to withdraw to the June 4, 1967, lines (provided his needs were met), and put it in written form without getting anything comparable from Asad in return. Rabin knew that both Secretary Christopher and President Clinton saw nothing wrong with reaffirming in a short, highly qualified written statement what we had already conveyed verbally to Asad about Rabin's commitment, and that both now feared retreating from something that had been promised to Asad and that he now expected. Yet when I accepted Rabin's point, persuaded the secretary and president to accept it, and was still able to deal with Asad and not lose the negotiations in the process, Rabin's trust in me as a mediator was greatly enhanced.

Of course, having done much to gain Rabin's confidence, I could not lose Asad's in the process. I did this by leveling with him; I explained that we had planned to present the letter to him, and that Rabin had objected. I explained that since the letter involved a commitment from Rabin to us, we had to respect his wishes, just the way we would respect Asad's wishes if he felt uncomfortable with our taking a verbal commitment from him and transforming it into a written statement without his approval. But I did more than level with him. I also produced something he considered important. I told him that since we would not be providing the letter, which would have been a device to help broker understandings, we would instead make a major effort to finalize agreements on the security statement of aims and principles by having his foreign minister come to Washington immediately after Rabin's upcoming visit. We would make it clear that the two visits were linked in our effort to broker security arrangements between the two sides. This was a first. It effectively gave Syria a new public standing in the process, and also offered a new, intensive brokering effort in Washington—something that Asad always believed was essential for any agreement. (Like Sadat, Asad always believed that only Washington could determine whether there would be agreements. Unlike Sadat, he saw Washington's actions as a substitute for his own.)

In the end, a mediator must be trusted and capable of using back channels to avoid stalemates or to overcome them or to explore more strategic tradeoffs down the road. The back channel functions best if the parties see it as a place where testing possibilities can be done safely and where it is a two-way street. Each side must have the confidence to be open in response to a mediator's questions, and be willing to ask sensitive questions of the mediator (and of each other). This also requires that those participating in the back channels must be authoritative and personally confident of their positions. They, too, must be strongly committed to conflict resolution. With someone like Shlomo Ben-Ami on the Israeli side, I had a partner who was very forthcoming because he was committed, trusted me, and felt that the United States played a role that was indispensable to their reaching an agreement. At a different stage, and with a different Israeli—Itamar Rabinovich—I was working confidentially with someone who happened to be a friend of long standing, but someone who was also much more guarded and less revealing. (Rabinovich was confident but also very mindful that Rabin had entrusted no one else on the Israeli side with the knowledge of his secret qualified commitment to us on full Israeli withdrawal from the Golan Heights.)

I found similar differences on the Palestinian side. Mohammad Rashid would be very open to exploring possibilities, and Abu Ala, whom I had known longer and was personally close to, was much more guarded. Several factors account for their differences: Timing and where you are in the process, and where your counterparts believe you are in the process; their personal stake in reaching agreement; their tactical approach to negotiations; their fear of being exposed on the issue; their readiness to run risks; their own personal standing, either with the leader or in the political system; their ambitions; and the nature of the political system in which your counterpart is operating.

Risk taking by Israelis, Palestinians, and Syrians varied. For Israelis, taking unauthorized positions that went well beyond the prime minister's could potentially cost a negotiator his job, or at least his or her responsibilities. However, I never saw anyone on the Israeli side lose his position after conveying compromises on issues that were not yet approved. True, there was a potential risk, but many (though definitely not all) Israeli negotiators tended to act in discussions as if they were nearly free agents—exploring what they thought might be possible, frequently with seemingly little fear of doing so.

That was certainly not the case with the Palestinians. But here the sense of risk was largely governed by what we were discussing. On issues *other* than Jerusalem, refugees, and borders, the negotiators would be much freer in private discussions on what might be possible. On the permanent-status issues, however, the fear of being charged with selling out the Palestinian cause was clearly inhibiting. Syrians were more guarded than either Israelis or Palestinians because of their authoritarian system, where the price of betraying what the leader wanted might be more than only losing a job. (Walid Mouallem, my Syrian back-channel partner, was very good at testing the limits but also reminding me of his own limitations—and at one point he not only lost his job but, for an extended period, was treated as a nonperson.)

Back channels may change over time. If a negotiation is not productive, particularly as you read that your counterpart is not being particularly forthcoming or able to do much, it makes sense to see whether someone else may be a more productive back-channel partner. Back channels can evolve as the players become better known, and as those who are more trustworthy and act with greater confidence reveal themselves.

Mediators, like negotiators, must assess what is possible and who can be most helpful in making things happen. Sometimes a mediator should take steps to build up his or her counterpart in the eyes of the leader. Having a leader see that that person is most likely to produce from the other side is part of the art of mediation.

Clearly, in cases of historic conflicts, mediation is going to be a time-consuming exercise. Many such conflicts have evolved in stages and can be resolved only in stages. That is certainly true for the Arab-Israeli conflict. So, it will take time.

Ultimately, using the mediation tool makes sense for many different reasons. It is right to try to settle conflicts and not let them fester; it is important, especially in the broader Middle East, to deny radical Islamists conflicts that they can exploit to play on anger and recruit new followers; it may be an essential means for dealing with the failed- and weak-state syndrome; and, finally, mediation, by showing that the United States is prepared to try to ameliorate conflicts that cause such pain, can improve our standing at a time when our purposes are increasingly questioned internationally. Knowing why it is so important to mediate, on what basis, when to do so, and what must be overcome for mediation to be effective, are the starting points for understanding how to use mediation as a tool. Having discussed them in this chapter, I now turn to a discussion of how to do mediation.

11.

{ELEVEN RULES FOR MEDIATION}

Since mediation is a form of negotiation, the rules for how to negotiate will also apply for any mediator. But the circumstances and conditions for mediation obviously differ, and as a result a mediator has to have a number of particular requirements in mind. A mediator must know the basics of negotiations and have an instinct for how to conduct them. Like any negotiator, a mediator must have a keen sense of timing and know when to run risks and when to back off. And while no negotiation or mediation can ever be run mechanically or simply "by the numbers," there are, I believe, eleven guidelines (that complement the rules for negotiations) that any practitioner ought to keep in mind when he or she enters a process of mediation.

1. IDENTIFY SHARED OBJECTIVES

The circumstances that produce mediation will heavily affect how this particular rule is employed. If the parties have either approached a possible mediator or responded to inquiries from an aspiring mediator—as in the case of the Israelis and the Palestinians with the Norwegians—then it is clear that at least some shared objectives already exist.

Even in more hopeful cases, one of the first tasks of the mediator is to determine the scope of the shared objectives, and to expand that scope where possible. Building a sense of commonality can foster a belief that both sides have shared stakes in finding solutions. Moreover, it can also enhance mutual confidence and hope, and thus help insulate the parties against inevitable disappointments or setbacks in a complicated negotiating process. (Both we and the Norwegians at different points in advance of the Oslo process focused on what we thought might be the shared objectives of reducing conflict, improving the quality of life of Palestinians in the territories, and promoting a dialogue to build mutual confidence.)

In other cases, in which it is the mediator initiating and reaching out, the only possible shared objective may be a negative one: ending bloodshed and suffering. It may be possible to get both sides to accept that and little else. Still, no mediation is going to work if there are no common objectives, and even a shared negative objective can provide a basis on which to begin discussions. So, determining whether there is a shared objective is the natural place to start with each side.

The technique for doing so is having separate discussions with the sides, with an eye toward focusing each on what it may have in common with the other. They know what separates them, but in conflict situations, they pay little attention to where their objectives might be shared or at least not in conflict. The mediator must try to cultivate the instinct to avoid conflict or draw back from it. But he/she can be successful only if conflict is feared and not desired. Early efforts at mediation in the Balkans faltered not just on distrust and the limited leverage of the outside mediators but also because leaders such as Milošević and Tudjman saw that further conflict served their objectives far more than negotiations.

The more positive the shared objectives, the more ambitious a mediator can be in setting the initial agenda for negotiations. The converse is also true. But a mediator's first challenge is to see what he or she is working with, what is possible, and how to build on common ground. That is why an exploration and identification of possible shared objectives with parties to a conflict is where a mediator's work begins.

2. ASSESS WHAT CAN BE NEGOTIATED, AND FRAME THE TALKS

This is a natural corollary to the first rule of determining what, if anything, the two sides have in common. It is not the same because it deals more with assessing where their differences might be bridgeable. If the parties have more in common than they realize, it is easier to look for ways to bridge differences and to frame the discussions about those differences. But a mediator must also assess the character of their differences and which ones lend themselves more to compromise than others.

The combination of rules one and two will shape a mediator's judgment of what can initially be discussed between two sides. Lisa Beutler is an experienced mediator who has worked on state and federal land-use issues involving many competing claimants. In responding to a question on whether the parties knew what they might achieve at the beginning of one negotiating process she mediated, she captured the essence of what mediators face at the outset of a mediation: "Oh, no. They didn't know what the agreements would be. They had no idea. They didn't even have a single topic to discuss. One of the first things I had to do was assess what could even be negotiated. I mean I didn't even know—no one even knew—what could potentially be discussed."[1]

No mediator should rush to bring the parties together before he/she knows what should be initially discussed. Optimally, parallel discussions with the sides should be held to develop an agenda for the initial three-way meetings with the mediator and the parties. The purpose is not to go for quick agreements—which in any case are not likely to be particularly meaningful—but to create a framework for discussion that both sides see as useful. At the outset of mediated discussions, the objective is to create a productive point of departure that channels the negotiations toward a useful path. The parties need to feel that they are engaging in discussions that can lead somewhere, build their hope that agreements are possible, and begin to alter for the better each side's perception of the other side's intentions.

When I became a broker—not a facilitator—for the first time between the Israelis and Palestinians on the issue of Israeli disengagement from Hebron, I focused initially, in separate discussions with the two sides, on what they wanted and what they feared. Naturally there were wide gaps in their objectives, at least as first discussed with me. Though both sides accepted what had been agreed upon in the Interim Agreement—that Hebron would be divided into two zones, one where there would be no Israeli presence (H-1), and one where there would be a limited number of Israeli settlers (H-2)—they had fundamentally different ideas about the practical implications of creating such zones. The Israelis wanted to preserve their control over security and civil matters in the sector (H-2) where four hundred Israelis would be living with twenty thousand Palestinians. The Palestinians wanted Hebron and both its sectors to be treated like any other Palestinian city in the West Bank with the same rights and responsibilities.

On the surface the gaps appeared unbridgeable, but the more I discussed the issues with the two sides the more I saw certain guiding principles that both could accept. While I did not have an agreement on these before we came together for an intensive three-way discussion, I had done some important conditioning of both in advance of the meeting. As a result, we were able to agree on a common framework of six principles, including that Hebron would be resolved consistent with the guidelines in the Interim Agreement, that special security provisions would be needed for Israeli citizens living in H-2, that those provisions should be temporary, and that if Palestinians did not act against a security threat coming from H-1, the Israelis would.

Each side's concerns were addressed in the principles—with Palestinian concerns about Hebron not becoming two different cities and about Israelis not being free to operate in H-1 being balanced by Israeli concerns about the means to protect Israeli citizens and about Palestinians assuming real security responsibilities. The principles did not suddenly mean that the negotiations would be easy—far from it. But they established boundaries within which to negotiate, and reassured each side that an agreement was possible.

As with negotiations more generally, it is essential to get an early picture of what can be negotiated and how best to do it. On Hebron, I followed the model of drawing each side out first and then bringing them together to forge a framework for the talks.

3. SENSITIZE EACH SIDE TO THE OTHER'S CONCERNS AND GRIEVANCES

While the first two rules guide what a mediator should initially set out to do in any mediation, this rule goes to the heart of what mediation is all about. In conflicts such as those in the Middle East or in the Balkans, both sides harbor deeply rooted grievances. Each side sees itself as the victim who has suffered at the hands of the other side. Its interpretation and use of history shapes its views, and too often blinds it to the hurts and grievance of the other side.

Bill Diepeveen, a Canadian with much experience as a mediator, has colloquially described many conflicts as "your grand-pappy did it to my grand-pappy." Because of that, the parties become "fixated" and "identify themselves so much in history and the bad situation, the bad relationships, that they can't see beyond it."[2]

It is the mediator's job to get them to see beyond it. Each side is self-absorbed, and a mediator must get it beyond focusing only on its own needs. Nothing is more important in a mediation than to get each side off what the mediation expert John Forester calls the "blame game" and onto being aware of what is driving the other side and why.[3] In fact, a mediator will spend most of his/her time explaining why the other side has a problem—psychologically, politically, and practically. One cannot begin to build bridges between the two sides until there is greater awareness on each side of the concerns and needs of the other.

There are few more thankless tasks as a mediator than this. In any conflict, each side wants to see that the mediator understands its needs. It won't be happy when it is subjected to a mediator spending time to explain the other side's problems and perceptions. Almost invariably this will trigger the assumption that the mediator is insufficiently focused on "our needs" and much too focused on the other side's needs—and will drive that side to believe that it must press the mediator much harder on recognizing its own needs.

I don't say this idly; at times, both Yasir Arafat and Ehud Barak accused me of being the other side's lawyer. This, too, goes with the territory, but if a mediator is going to do necessary conditioning, and get each side to be more mindful of the other's needs—which is essential for making compromise possible—the mediator has to bear the likely reaction of the two parties.

What can be done to minimize such reactions, and the related impulse to become even more demanding about each side's particular needs? First, demonstrate how well you understand the grievances, concerns, and needs of the side with whom you are talking. Always raise its particular concerns first and create a context of those concerns and how they relate to the other side's. In other words, don't treat the other side in isolation, but always in relation to the needs of the side you are talking to. In my discussions with the Syrians, for example, I would address all the reasons the land (the Golan Heights) was so important to them and then address the Israeli concerns that would have to be assuaged to make it possible for Syria to get its land back.

Second, even after demonstrating how well you understand the grievances of the side you are dealing with, don't hesitate to ask additional probing questions about its problems or concerns. Show you are still willing to learn and that you don't feel you know all you need to know about its needs. Earlier, in discussing negotiations, I speak of the importance of active listening. As a mediator, you cannot ask too many questions about why certain positions are so important. It signals genuine interest in understanding just what is so important to each side and it also offers the best chance to gain greater insight into the thinking and the logic or reasoning of each side. The latter will certainly be important when you are trying to craft possible bridging proposals.

Ultimately, mediators have to make an enormous effort to educate each side to the needs of the other so it becomes less self-absorbed and more open to possible compromises.

4. THINK OUTSIDE THE BOX WHEN FORGING CRITICAL COMPROMISES

One reason a mediator must listen actively and come to understand what is important to each side, and why it is important, is to be able to come up with ideas that can work when there are inevitable stalemates in the negotiations. In any tough process, each side is going to get locked into certain positions. The more it states certain positions privately and publicly, the more it will find it difficult to explain walking away from them.

At times, a side becomes wedded to positions for political reasons and at other times for psychological reasons. The only certainty is that a mediator will have to come up with compromises designed not just to split the differences but also to offer what amounts to a third way that reshapes the issues at stake. I explained this very concept to Ariel Sharon in 1998, when he was the foreign minister of Israel.

At that time, he and I would have private chats on how to approach permanent-status negotiations. He was desirous of getting into the negotiations but dubious that much was possible because, as he said, "We cannot do what they want, and they cannot do what we want." In response, I suggested that we had to change the model of negotiations and realize that we could not find the halfway point between the two positions on borders or the other issues; instead, we had to be open to other ways of thinking about what divided the two sides. As an example, I said, "What if we can fuzz the issue of borders by creating industrial zones or special economic zones in border areas that effectively put Israeli and Palestinian economic enterprises on both sides of what would be the border? What if, at the same time, we say that security would be handled in these areas by the Israelis? If we did, the very concept of borders would change." I told him I was not suggesting that this was necessarily the way to solve the border issue but it was an illustration that we could think unconventionally and come up with some solutions that were outside the rigid boxes of how each side now approached each permanent-status problem. He liked the approach, and might well have pursued something like it had the government he was then a part of not fallen and been replaced.

Coming up with an unconventional approach or idea is not a way to avoid having to deal with the needs of both sides. Those needs are a given; however, it is a way to meet the needs of both sides by also redefining issues or coming up with a distinctly new idea. John Major, though not the mediator, came up with a concept that George Mitchell and his colleagues used in order to find a way around the issue of decommissioning weapons as a precondition for all-party negotiations in Northern Ireland.

In trying to produce all-party negotiations, the mediator found the problem of the paramilitaries and their weapons to be a fundamental sticking point. The British position—shared by the leading Unionist parties—was that there could be no negotiations until the weapons of the paramilitaries (principally the IRA) were decommissioned or until at least some significant decommissioning had been implemented. The Republicans (those who wanted Northern Ireland to be a part of the rest of Ireland and not a part of the United Kingdom) argued that there could be no decommissioning until the completion of the negotiations. The Republican argument was driven by psychological and practical considerations: Psychologically, they felt that the British and Unionists wouldn't negotiate seriously if they knew the weapons had been given up and violence was never an option. Practically, they doubted they could get the IRA to disarm without a political solution. The British and Unionist argument was, not surprisingly, also driven by twin factors: the Republican unwillingness to decommission weapons indicated that the IRA was not prepared to change its ways and accept a nonviolent solution, and further signaled that the Republicans would hold their weapons as leverage and if they did not get what they wanted politically, they would return to violence.

Mitchell and his mediating partners from Canada and Finland developed a logical compromise built around a "split-the-difference" approach of (a) requiring all parties to the negotiations to embrace principles of democracy and nonviolence, (b) considering a parallel decommissioning weapons process (meaning that decommissioning would not precede but run parallel to the negotiations), and (c) offering a detailed process to achieve decommissioning.

I describe this as a split-the-difference approach not to denigrate it but to indicate that it logically tried to provide something that mattered to each side. This, of course, is what a mediator must do in any negotiation. However, at times, the conventional way or the existing ideas won't be sufficient, so something outside the box is required. And, in this case, Prime Minister John Major provided a third way in his response to what became known as the Mitchell Principles for negotiations. Major suggested a democratic mandate for holding all-party negotiations. While still saying that decommissioning weapons first might be one way to establish the inclusive negotiations, the other way was to have elections, and those who received a mandate could take part in the negotiations. Mitchell saw the virtue of this alternative route to negotiations, and in fact, inclusive all-party negotiations were convened following an election process.[4]

Thinking creatively will always be essential for fashioning those compromises that meet the respective needs of parties in conflict. To do so, a mediator may have to think about changing the frame of reference, by offering either entirely new concepts or ideas that seem on a different plane.

5. MAKE SURE THE PARTIES DEMONSTRATE THEIR SERIOUSNESS

The mediator cannot be the only serious party in a process designed to resolve or lessen conflict. The more the parties seek out the mediator, the easier it is to use the leverage of walking away if there is not sufficient seriousness, because the leverage of a mediator will increase the longer the process goes on. Even those parties that may not have been so enthusiastic for a mediation process initially will acquire increasing stakes in it as it survives and builds expectations of change.

Of course, mediators also build higher stakes in success. It is not so easy for mediators to walk away from a process in which they have heavily invested. While I was more inclined to threaten to walk away or put everything on hold in the Israeli-Palestinian and Israeli-Syrian negotiations, President Clinton was less so, fearing collapse, a resumption of violence, and a failure pinned on the United States.

Ironically, all parties—including the mediator—tend to have their stakes increase the longer the process of negotiations is sustained. Everyone sees risks in the process ending, and even if that reduces the mediator's readiness to walk away, it certainly still gives the mediator the ability to insist on seriousness. And, as I saw with the Israelis and Palestinians, there was a constant concern that the Clinton administration not declare publicly that one side was serious and the other was not. Precisely because expectations get raised during ongoing negotiating processes, neither side wants to be seen in its own domestic terms as being responsible for the breakdown of the process.

The more advanced a process, and the closer to dealing with core issues, the more each side will also want to be taken seriously by the mediator. In processes that are reaching a climax, each side will have an interest in proving to a mediator that it is doing all it can to reach agreement. In part, it has this impulse to avoid being blamed publicly if there is a stalemate, and in part it also doesn't want the mediator asking it for additional concessions. The desire is always to keep the onus for the next move on the other side.

It was common practice in the negotiations I was involved in, particularly with the Israelis and Palestinians, for each side to try to convince me how much it was doing and how it could not possibly be asked to contemplate additional compromises on the core questions of Jerusalem, refugees, and borders. I understood both the tactical reasons for this and the genuine difficulties each side had in revealing more about possible concessions on these existential questions. But I also understood that each side had an interest in convincing me that it wasn't being unreasonable, that it was doing its part, and that it was mindful of not only its needs but the other's as well. And I used that interest to try to draw out each side on what it might actually be able to do on the most sensitive issues.

Let me explain. Knowing that each side wanted me to believe in its seriousness and that it was not focused only on its own needs (lest I press it to be responsive to the other) and knowing as well that it did not feel that it could reveal more of its own bottom-line positions (lest those become the departure point for additional concessions), I asked the lead negotiator on each side to tell me what he thought the other could do on the core questions. In other words, I was not pressing him to reveal more to me about his own position; instead, I employed a technique of having the Palestinian negotiators tell me what they thought at the end of the day the Israelis could do on Jerusalem, refugees, and borders; and I asked the Israeli negotiators to tell me what they thought the Palestinians could ultimately accept on each of these issues.

If under these circumstances they had simply repeated maximal positions, they knew I would say, you don't understand the other side, and inevitably would have pressed them more on meeting the other's needs and concerns. As a result, each side gave an interesting account of what it thought the other in the end could accept.

It was not just the desire to prove to me they were serious—though that clearly counted for a lot. It was also their recognition that this was another way to reveal something sensitive about what they might be able to accept without having to say anything about it themselves. If, for example, the Palestinian negotiators responded, as they did on Jerusalem, that Israel could accept the division of East Jerusalem provided they could preserve the eight Jewish neighborhoods there, they were revealing something very important. After all, if their purpose was an agreement, and they said the Israelis cannot accept less than this, then their acknowledgment that the Israelis needed the eight Jewish neighborhoods also signaled what the Palestinians could accept in the end—and yet no one could accuse them of having offered a new concession.[5]

The technique of asking each side to explain what it thinks the other can accept is one that cannot be used prematurely. One must be at a stage in which much conditioning has been done on both sides' needs and also when the parties themselves have an incentive for showing the mediator that they are very serious and doing their part to produce an agreement.

6. GET EACH SIDE TO ADJUST TO REALITY

While one indispensable task of a mediator is to get each side to recognize the needs of the other (or others), he/she must also get them to adjust to reality more generally. Bear in mind that being aware of the other side's needs does not mean that a side is necessarily prepared to adjust to giving up what it wants. Conflict resolution is about meeting "needs," not "wants." Neither side can get everything it wants but it should be able to achieve its most important needs.

It is never easy to get parties to give up what they want. They must be conditioned both to the circumstances under which an agreement that meets their basic needs is possible and to the circumstances under which it is not. The starting point surely is recognizing what the other side must have in order to be able to agree. But the ending point, the point where the agreements become possible, is when each side realizes that some of what it has sought or wanted will not be achievable if there is to be an agreement.

When mediating on the road to the Wye River Agreement between the Israelis and Palestinians, I knew that the mind-sets on both sides had to be changed. It was a matter of explaining to each not just what the other side needed but also that its own concept or approach had to change. With Arafat, this required telling him before even beginning permanent-status negotiations—where borders, Jerusalem, and refugees were to be negotiated—that he was not entitled to 90 percent of the West Bank. It required undoing his view that with three unspecified Israeli force redeployments called for in the Interim Agreement, he should get 30 percent of the West Bank each time the Israelis withdrew their forces. With Netanyahu, it required telling him that while he did not have to negotiate with the Palestinians the three further Israeli redeployments, he could not satisfy Israel's obligations under the Interim Agreement by simply deciding that the redeployments would be limited—as one of his aides suggested publicly—to "a dunam, a dunam, and a dunam."[6]

Both sides saw the further redeployments and how they were carried out as giving or denying them leverage for the permanent-status negotiations. That each side would want to maximize its leverage and minimize its counterpart's was no surprise. But it was not just about leverage. The further redeployments of Israeli forces—of which there were to be three over eighteen months—were seen in fundamentally different terms and revealed a great deal about how each side saw the negotiating process and where it should lead. Neither side had a realistic view, and if we were to forge an agreement (which we did in time at Wye River), we would have to change their expectations and condition them to a different reality. And I did succeed in doing so over a period of several months, ultimately getting Bibi Netanyahu to understand that he would have to withdraw from a double-digit percentage of the West Bank, and Yasir Arafat to understand that double digits were closer to 10 percent than 30 percent.

Getting sides to adjust their expectations is a necessary part of mediation and it is never easy. But it is easier than getting them to give up their mythologies. In an existential conflict such as that between Israelis and Palestinians, an erosion of mythologies is essential for resolving their conflict once and for all. While it is prudent to try to do this over time, mythologies really become the core of the problem when you are dealing with conflict resolution, not management. It is at the stage of resolution that a mediator has to take on myths, which, as I observe earlier, have become part of the self-image of each side and what they have told themselves is so important.

In ending conflicts and actually making peace, one has to get each side to reconcile to reality. Reconciling myths is impossible; discarding myths, then, is the challenge. The best way to do so is to keep conditioning each side to what an agreement will take and constantly reminding each—and increasingly their publics—that certain outcomes are simply out of the question. President Bush's letter to Ariel Sharon in April 2004 was useful for conditioning everyone to reality: that significant Israeli population centers in the West Bank (i.e., settlement blocs) had to be taken into account in any permanent-status agreement, and that the problem of Palestinian refugees should be resolved through the creation of a Palestinian state and that Palestinian refugees should go there rather than to Israel.

The Palestinians objected mightily to each of these observations, but what was the real source of their angst? Put simply, they saw themselves as excluded from the decisions that affected their future. Once again, issues that went to the core of who they were and what they wanted as a people appeared to be being decided without them. Thus, for process reasons, they objected. Had there been parallel discussions with them, and had those discussions addressed myths on the Israeli side—such as all of East Jerusalem, including its entire Arab population of 225,000, will remain part of Israel—the Palestinian reaction might have been very different.

If nothing else, this reminds us that mythologies can be taken on and debunked, but a mediator has to create a context for doing so. One is unlikely to debunk mythologies if only one side is required to face and accept reality. Both sides must be challenged, and both sides must see that the mediator requires mutual adjustments to reality. Ultimately, no matter how much conditioning has been done, there is no escaping the need to give up mythologies, and that will always be psychologically and politically painful. However, in the Israeli-Palestinian case, there will be no agreement if the Israelis are not prepared to see through the illusion that Jerusalem, specifically East Jerusalem, can never be divided; Palestinians, for their part, must understand that reality requires them to accept that there will be no right of return to Israel for Palestinian refugees.

7. SET ASIDE EACH SIDE'S PRINCIPLES
AND FOCUS ON PRACTICALITIES

If there is a rule of thumb for any mediator, it is that one side's principle is the other side's impossibility. Principles drive each side to its most rigid positions. Who wants to look like he is conceding on his principles? Certainly not anyone I've ever worked with.

Breaking down problems, however, and looking for practical ways to overcome differences is a natural way to build bridges between two sides. In these circumstances, no one is seen as losing, and needs can be met.

A good example of solving a problem by avoiding principles—and meeting a profound need in the process—was the Israeli-Palestinian approach to water at the time of the Interim Agreement and later in the permanent-status discussions at the expert level. The Palestinians wanted the Israelis to accept the principle that the water resources were theirs and that they had a right to the aquifers in the West Bank that must be recognized. The Israeli position was that if the Palestinians as a matter of right or principle had control over these aquifers, it would fundamentally threaten the quality and quantity of the Israeli water supply—and Israel could never accept such an outcome.

For the interim period, the two sides agreed to defer the question of principle and rights and focus instead on water allocation. If the Palestinians identified the amount of water they needed, then the Israelis would do their best to ensure that they received it—with, of course, American guarantees to support these undertakings or to supplement needs if they could not be met. In the permanent-status negotiations, the negotiators came to the conclusion that they could never reach agreement on the principle of water control, but they could come up with practical arrangements that both sides could live with. Each might say that there had been no agreement on the question of water rights—so neither had to concede the point. At the same time, they would not let principle get in the way of practical allocations that could meet both sides' needs.

While mediators will want to create general principles that frame the negotiation process at the outset—or at times when the most fundamental issues are being tackled—they will eventually want to get the sides off a focus on their principles. Focusing on practicalities, and not debating each side's principles, can solve real problems, reduce differences, and build momentum for (and new baselines of) agreement.

8. MAKE AGREEMENTS WHERE YOU CAN

In my years as a mediator I always operated on the premise that it made sense to nail down understandings whenever they were available. My thinking was that firming up an understanding was useful and created new baselines from which to proceed. Oftentimes to reach an understanding or understandings on technical questions, I would remind everyone that we were operating with the proviso that nothing was agreed upon until everything was agreed. This allowed each side to reach what amounted to partial agreements, while protecting itself from having done anything that would be binding until a final agreement could be concluded.

Reaching any agreements in a deeply rooted conflict is always going to be difficult. The first understandings represent the crossing of a threshold. To cross them, a mediator has to use devices—e.g., offering inducements or guarantees or assuring each side that what they are agreeing to now won't compromise their position later in the process. The very fact of crossing a threshold has a psychological effect on each side. It conditions it to the reality that it can reach agreements. Particularly when dealing with Israelis and Palestinians, I was always mindful of the danger of an act of terrorism that might derail or set back the talks. In the back of my mind, I was trying not just to cross thresholds, but also to safeguard progress where it had been made. If we faced an act of violence or terrorism—or if an Israeli decision on settlement expansion made it difficult for Palestinians to concede in the face of such a decision—I did not want the process going back to square one. So, reaching agreements when you can is a good rule of thumb on which to operate.

Yet this rule is about concluding understandings when you can without losing sight of the bigger picture. I say this because in a negotiation in which one does not have full confidence in the purposes of the leaders, one also has to take into account the effect that each understanding is likely to have. For example, prior to reaching the Wye River Agreement, when trying to resolve the issue of the size of the further redeployment of the Israeli military in the West Bank, I would have been able to nail down Bibi Netanyahu's agreement to 13 percent (a figure Arafat had already accepted), but I chose not to do it. Normally, I would have wanted to tie this one down so as not to lose it, and yet I chose not to. Why?

Basically because I knew that Netanyahu was about to visit America and wanted to be able to say that he had agreed on the territory and that now the onus was on Arafat to agree on the security provisions. And in these circumstances, I knew that Netanyahu would likely up the ante on the security provisions in a way that would make them unachievable. If I finalized this important provision, I risked not achieving the overall agreement. Had I been completely confident at this point that Netanyahu wanted such an agreement, I would have proceeded to nail down the understanding on the 13 percent. I was not, and I needed to maintain leverage on Netanyahu.

In any mediation, one must never lose sight of the big picture. Usually every understanding that you tie down will build momentum and your leverage. But in some cases, if you are not thinking ahead, an understanding that lets one side off the hook, and in a position to make impossible demands, can be self-defeating. Most mediators would probably say this is the exception that proves the rule.

9. ACT SWIFTLY TO CONTAIN CRISES

In any delicate mediation, where trust is low or nonexistent, crises (often triggered by events outside the negotiations) must be dealt with immediately. If a mediator fails to act swiftly and decisively in such an event, he/she may see everything unravel, and the process either set back or actually undone. At a minimum, a mediator must be sensitive to the impact of such external events and not hesitate in responding—even if it means responding unconventionally.

To illustrate the point, Richard Holbrooke recounts an incident in which he had to respond immediately (and not according to protocol) lest an incident in the town of Bosanski Petrovac, in which Muslim troops killed two Croat soldiers, trigger a crisis and unravel the process he was constructing. To preserve cooperation between the Croats and Muslims—the key to changing both the realities on the ground and the Serb calculus—Holbrooke acted quickly:

> I asked Tudjman [the Croatian president] if he would agree to meet with Izetbegovic [the Bosnian president] under American auspices to forge a common position . . . the idea of an American Assistant Secretary of State convening two heads of state, who already knew each other well and met regularly, seemed both presumptuous and odd. The alarming incident at Bosanski Petrovac changed that: the explosive situation could undo everything.[7]

In the summer of 1998, following a suicide bombing in Jerusalem, I did something similar. I knew that if the Israeli government saw a Palestinian business-as-usual response to the bombing (make perfunctory condemnations and a few symbolic but meaningless arrests), the Israelis would understandably freeze all political contacts with the Palestinian Authority—and an already stalemated process would begin to unravel. I understood that the Palestinians had to act, but I knew they would not if Arafat did not see the importance of doing so and of making commitments that he felt he would have to live up to. So I asked to convene a meeting with Arafat, all of his security chiefs, and Amnon Shahak and Ami Ayalon—the heads of the Israeli Defense Forces and Shin Bet, respectively. Though this was highly unusual and had not previously been done—and certainly not with the American envoy organizing it and presiding over it—I knew that Arafat respected both Shahak and Ayalon and always wanted to be taken seriously by them. Both Arafat and Prime Minister Netanyahu agreed to my convening the meeting at Arafat's headquarters. The meeting was successful and, for a time, did make a difference.

The lesson here is that in any high-stakes mediating process, outside events can create shocks. A mediator must make a quick assessment of the damage and then decide how to respond to contain the problem or to change the focus and the subject. The luxury of passively sitting and letting the shock play itself out does not exist. An urgent intervention is often needed, and the more unconventional the better, particularly if the intervention itself creates drama and gives everyone a reason to pause and change the subject.

10. USE ANGER AS A TOOL—BUT USE IT RARELY

A mediator must know how to get the attention of each side in a way that is sharp and tough and at the appropriate moment. The mediator must make the parties aware when they have not responded and when they must; when they are asking for something outrageous and won't give it up; when they go back on their word; and when they avoid decisions or challenge the mediator's word. When they do any of these or related things, they must get both barrels from the mediator. They must know they are about to pay a serious price and they must fear that they have pushed the mediator beyond his/her endurance level. There are times when a mediator must convey that he/she has had it and is out of patience—and genuine anger is the most credible way to convey that.

For those mediators who have a low-key approach, eruptions of real anger are likely to have an effect because they are so out of character. Richard Holbrooke has described a scene between Warren Christopher and the Bosnian foreign minister, where Christopher chastised his counterpart in uncharacteristically blunt language when just before a statement of principles was to be announced publicly, he reneged on an understanding that had been reached two hours earlier, and how this was wholly unacceptable and would produce consequences that the Bosnians would regret.[8]

I witnessed a similar episode where Christopher exhibited great anger while saying little at all. At the end of a week's shuttle mission in 1996 to achieve a cease-fire between Israel, Syria, Lebanon, and Hizbollah, Christopher stood up and closed his briefcase in response to what he perceived as the Syrian president's adding a condition to what was an already sealed agreement—saying only that he was finished and there would be no agreement now. Asad was surprised because he had never seen the polite, proper, even-keeled, and meticulous secretary of state act this way.

That, of course, is precisely the point. For someone like Christopher, displays of anger were so out of character that they were bound to have an impact. Most mediators will use anger more often than Christopher, but if they use it too often, they devalue it. Here, again, the key is to be authentic; I was certainly not as fiery as someone like Richard Holbrooke; even he speaks of having a "controlled fit" when he wanted to make a particular point.[9] I used anger more sparingly, but would be far more explosive than Secretary Christopher. I would not just get angry; I would blow up. Almost every time I did it, it was planned but far less controllable than I had intended.

Usually when I blew up it was at a point of genuine exhaustion and always after someone had reneged on his word or had challenged mine. The most dramatic blowup was during the second of my twenty-three-day shuttle missions on Hebron, and came after my telling Arafat that I was not simply going to stay in the area and I needed to know what he required to close a deal. Uncharacteristically, he responded directly and systematically, ticking off the six things he would need. Just to be sure I had them right, I repeated them, got his affirmation, and I proceeded to work through the night with Netanyahu to produce what he asked for. And yet when I returned to see Arafat, he denied that he had asked for what I had now produced. When I read him back exactly what he had asked for the previous evening and was now denying he had said, he asked if I was calling him a liar. To which I said, "If the shoe fits." Then I stood up, stomped out of his office, and threw my binder across the room, inadvertently knocking over a pitcher of grapefruit juice. My team and Arafat's were literally stunned. Here was I, who never lost his cool, who was always the one to solve problems or defuse tensions or handle crises, blowing up and signaling that I had had it.

Anger should be used for those moments when it can have the greatest impact. My explosion came at a moment when an agreement was within reach and both sides had to know there could be no more games or they could lose me and the deal.

James Baker had a temper that was legendary but typically used only at particular moments. In one of the last meetings on the way to the Madrid Conference in October of 1991, Palestinians Faisal Husseini and Hanan Ashrawi were supposed to finalize with him only the outstanding issue of who would represent the Palestinians on the joint Jordanian-Palestinian delegation. Instead, they came not ready to speak about that but to reopen the Jerusalem issue—on which Baker had previously stretched further than he had intended to. Baker simply cut them off, saying, with "you people" the souk never closes. But, as he said, it had with him, and they would never get what they wanted, since he was done dealing with them. He then got up, wished them a nice life, and stalked out. They were shocked and scared and asked me what could be done— to which I told them to drop what they were now asking on Jerusalem and provide the delegates' names, and Baker soon got what he wanted.

In short, pick your moments and have the right provocation. Don't overplay the anger card; reserve it for when the parties need to know they are about to lose something they value.

11. PUT YOUR DRAFTS ON THE TABLE

At every phase, but particularly when moving toward agreements, the mediator needs to be the one to put drafts on the table for negotiation. Whatever negotiators for one side write or present to the other side, they will be invested in it and will be very reluctant to back away from it. Moreover, drafts by either side will always reflect their particular framing of the problem and will elicit reflexively negative responses from the other side—if for no other reason than the latter's seeing itself put in a disadvantaged position.

In any negotiation each side is always trying to define the terrain in which the discussion takes place. Each wants to be on the most favorable ground—ground that plays to its strengths. Each wants to fence off those issues it least wants to discuss and focus on what it most has to gain.

That is why when it comes to putting paper on the table, the mediator must be the one to frame the issues. Papers by definition create a sense of formality. To reduce that and preserve each side's deniability, a mediator may want to present a "nonpaper" that has less standing at least initially. Nonpapers help with the framing of the issues and make such framing a little easier to swallow for the parties. But whether a nonpaper or a proposed draft of general principles or the final agreement is required, it is the mediator who needs to take the initiative in defining the parameters of the negotiations and focusing the parties on what must be resolved.

Of course, there is another reason to present a paper. As important as it is to forge conceptual understandings, they must still be translated into concrete agreements that get expressed in writing. Once in black and white, everything looks more permanent. Consequently, presenting a paper without the necessary conditioning may trigger an explosively negative response. In advance of both the Wye River and Camp David summits, I tried to condition both Israelis and Palestinians to what might be coming. I was trying to reduce the potential for surprise, which almost always produces negative responses, and get each side used to possible bridging ideas.

The conditioning in the case of Wye was more successful with both sides. In part, there was much more time for conditioning, but obviously the stakes were also far lower on Wye; it was, after all, one more interim agreement. The stakes with a permanent settlement were vastly greater and triggered much greater fear of the consequences of any paper that was to be put on the table.

But the natural fear of such a paper should not necessarily prevent a mediator from presenting one. (At times, the fear of the parties can be used as leverage, creating a perfect basis on which to say, "If you don't do more on your own, we will present a paper proposing the ways to overcome your differences.") The key determinant on whether to present papers of one scope or another must be the mediator's sense of timing. If the mediator deems the time is right, either to accelerate the mediation process or to try to go for a deal, then a paper will be necessary.

Putting a paper on the table is a must in any mediation process. Whether the mediator is trying to give the negotiations a solid foundation or narrow the parameters for discussion or crystallize the points of agreement and the essential issues to be resolved—or, at the right moment, propose the actual terms of the final compromises—he/she will need to formulate and present a paper to the parties.

Note that when George Mitchell wanted to establish agreed-upon principles on which initially to negotiate in Northern Ireland or later to define the outlines of what would be the Good Friday Accord, or when I wanted to create a basis and a framework for ongoing Israeli-Syrian negotiations, or when Richard Holbrooke wanted to focus the Dayton negotiations from the outset—we all formulated and put papers on the table. There is no way to reach final agreement without the mediator shaping, channeling, and narrowing the bounds of discussion. And, typically, no final agreement can be possible unless the mediator presents a draft peace treaty that constantly gets refined by the two parties as compromises are forged and tradeoffs in language (and the key issues embodied in that language) are accepted.

Drafting such papers or proposed treaties does not guarantee success. But if mediation is required because the parties are unable or unwilling to resolve their differences without outside help, sooner or later, a mediator will be drafting papers that may include initial efforts to establish the basic goals and principles that the parties share, limited agreements on at least some of the problems, and eventually a full-fledged peace accord.

As with any negotiation, the best approach may not succeed. Some factors or developments are beyond the control of a mediator. But employing these rules will give a mediator the best possible chance for success.

12.

{PRACTICING STATECRAFT}

The Israeli-Palestinian Conflict

It is one thing to understand what goes into statecraft and how to apply some of its tools in practice. It is another to take a model of statecraft and use it to lay out how to approach current challenges in American foreign policy. Obviously, I think not only that one can but that it is time for America's decision makers to do so. In the final chapters of this book, I offer a guide to practicing statecraft, looking here at the Israeli-Palestinian conflict, the challenge of radical Islamists, the vexing question of Iran and its nuclear weapons, and contending with China as a rising power. At least with regard to the Israeli-Palestinian, Iranian, and Islamist issues, there is an unquestioned linkage.

The vision of Iran with nukes is certainly a major preoccupation of the Israelis, and at some point Israel may act militarily to forestall Iran's becoming a nuclear power. Iran is obviously aware of this, but its leadership sees value in provoking Israel, with calls to wipe it out—mostly because the Iranians believe they can put Arab regimes on the defensive and gain a greater following in the Muslim world by exploiting the region's conflict with Israel. Of course, Iranian provocation is not limited to words, as they are the leading supporter, materially and otherwise, of Hizbollah and Hamas.

The Israelis have fought a war with Hizbollah and are fully expecting that "round two" may be coming in the next year or so, either as part of a proxy war with Iran or as unfinished business stemming from the war in the summer of 2006. And Hamas, now a leading factor in the Palestinian political and social reality, represents a major impediment to peacemaking so long as it defines itself as an Islamic movement that rejects Israel's existence. Both Hizbollah and Hamas are Islamists, but unlike Al Qaeda and its offshoots, these two groups have a social agenda and compete politically. They have a political standing and use their presence in governments to limit what those governing bodies can do even while they use their militias outside the government to increase their leverage.

More generally, the Israeli-Palestinian conflict continues to affect the image of the United States and its purposes in the region. While it may not be the only challenge we face in the area—and its resolution would not be a panacea—it remains an issue that creates a deep sense of grievance in the region, one that radical Islamists exploit to promote anger and recruit new followers. From that standpoint, dealing with the Israeli-Palestinian conflict must form at least one part of our strategy for competing with radical Islamists.

These two issues or challenges are interrelated, though clearly resolving one will not make the other disappear. But dealing successfully with one will surely create a climate in which dealing with the other becomes easier.

The starting point with a statecraft model is having an objective that is clear and knowing how to act on it. Our objective in dealing with the Israeli-Palestinian conflict must not only reflect the hope for settling it but also be guided by an assessment of what is actually possible now and over time. In other words, our objective must be refined by an assessment of reality; only then can we focus on the means we have for transforming reality and working to fulfill our hopes. With that in mind, I am going to explain in some detail the background and the context in which we must presently shape realistic objectives and work to achieve them.

BACKGROUND AND CONTEXT

In a conflict that my colleague David Makovsky has described as having too much history and too little geography, one has to understand at least the recent history to evaluate what is possible.

The 1990s were characterized by intensive negotiations in which five limited interim agreements were reached. There was an active peace process in which direct dialogue between the two sides was the norm. While hopes were high, the process ultimately proved a disappointment to both sides. Israelis expected that Palestinians would give up terrorism and promote reconciliation and not the virtues of continued resistance. The Palestinians expected that the Israelis would stop controlling their lives and cease building settlements on land they expected to be part of their state.

The process came to an end with the failure at the end of the Clinton administration to negotiate a deal on all the core issues of the conflict: Jerusalem, borders, security, and refugees. As an architect of and a participant in the negotiations, I know that the gaps at the end of the negotiations were all bridgeable. I know as well that notwithstanding the disappointments and failed expectations built into the process, an agreement was possible—and both publics and both negotiating teams believed that to be the case.

Unfortunately for the Palestinians, they were led by Yasir Arafat, a revolutionary leader who could not transform himself and become a statesman. Conflict had defined him, and he could not live without claims, grievances, or a cause. He could accept a process in which he continued to have claims that he could be struggling for, but he could not end the conflict.

His strategy over the years had been to make the Palestinians into victims. But when he rejected what was available at Camp David, he lost the status of being the victim and the onus for failing to reach an agreement was put on him. In order to reestablish the Palestinians as victims of Israeli military might, he sought to exploit the intifada that erupted in the fall of 2000.

Instead, he contributed to the undoing of any peacemaking process. He supported violence against the Israelis, but in a context in which an Israeli government had been prepared to accept unprecedented concessions in the eyes of its public. When in January 2001 Arafat rejected the Clinton parameters (which went well beyond what had been on the table at Camp David), the Israeli public concluded that there was nothing that the Palestinians would accept other than Israel's disappearance. That conclusion—combined with Palestinian violence—killed the peace camp in Israel and produced a new Israeli government led by Ariel Sharon, who had vowed never to deal with Yasir Arafat.

The Israelis were not alone in their sense of grievance. Palestinians felt that the Israeli response to the intifada had been draconian, inflicting collective punishment on the people and treating them as if they were subhuman. Into this mix the new Bush administration disengaged from any effort to preserve some basis for Israeli-Palestinian cooperation and dialogue.

Ironically, the administration disengaged during a period, in the spring of 2001, when Ariel Sharon, notwithstanding his vows not to deal with Arafat, was sending his son to talk to him, even counseling his son on the need to show Arafat respect when dealing with him. As head of the opposition, Sharon had one set of responsibilities, but as prime minister he had another. He would give up on Arafat only after twenty-one Israeli teenagers were killed in the bombing of the Dolphinarium nightclub in Tel Aviv, in June 2001.

The intifada, which had involved daily violence, was transformed after the bombing into a war with far greater violence and suffering on both sides. The measure of the war could be seen in the casualties on each side. From the advent of the Bush administration in 2001 until the beginning of 2005, more than 1,100 Israelis and approximately 3,800 Palestinians were killed. For the Israelis, this number exceeded the number of fatalities suffered in two of Israel's wars with its neighboring states.

The losses were dramatically greater than those suffered during the preceding decade, when there had been a peace process. Whatever the failings of the Oslo process, Israelis and Palestinians were simply not killing one another during this period the way they would after it ended. The total number of Israeli fatalities throughout the previous ten years was less than one quarter of those suffered in the first four years of the Bush administration, and the Palestinian losses in the 1990s were roughly one third of what they were in Bush's first term.

Between Israelis and Palestinians, it is always better to have them talking rather than shooting. The Bush administration made a number of limited attempts to stop the violence. But each was marked by an absence of statecraft, not its exercise.

In November of 2001, General Anthony Zinni, the former head of

Central Command, was sent by Secretary Powell to try to produce a cease-fire. He would make a genuine effort for several months, but his mandate was limited to security issues, and he was not empowered to deal with either political or economic questions. No envoy is going to have much success when those he is dealing with know that his mandate is heavily circumscribed. Zinni's challenge would have been difficult in any case. However, the prospect of gaining Palestinian responsiveness was very poor given that he could not touch issues that mattered to them.

Later, on the eve of going to war in Iraq, the administration unveiled the Roadmap for Peace. It was supposed to constitute a performance-based path to the vision of two states coexisting side by side that President Bush had articulated in his June 24, 2002, speech. As a concept, the roadmap had promise, particularly because it was phased, required both sides to take steps, and seemingly addressed what mattered to each: for Israelis, Palestinians needed to act on security and reform, and for Palestinians, Israelis were supposed to freeze settlement activity and withdraw the checkpoints and controls on Palestinian movement.

The concept was fine, but the roadmap stood little chance of being followed because we negotiated it with everyone except those who had to implement it. The Israelis and Palestinians were supposed to act on a parallel set of obligations that, if fulfilled, would transform the realities on the ground. The administration negotiated the roadmap with the other members of the Quartet—the EU, the Russians, and the UN—but not with the Israelis and Palestinians. The result: not one of the obligations in the fifty-two-paragraph document was understood the same way by the two sides who had to carry them out. The Israelis interpreted every Palestinian obligation maximally and their obligations minimally—and the Palestinians did just the opposite.

This might still have been manageable if the United States and the other Quartet members had agreed on a common definition for what constituted performance by each side on each obligation. But that, too, was not done.

Statecraft requires a hands-on approach to working through issues. Had the administration been determined to make the Roadmap an operational (not simply a rhetorical) guide, it would have negotiated its terms with Israelis and Palestinians. Admittedly, this would have taken time and required a grinding effort. And with Yasir Arafat—whose readiness to accept commitments was often matched only by his reluctance to fulfill them—there was certainly risk to such an approach. Still, why unveil a performance-based roadmap, emphasizing its performance-based character, if there was not a readiness to try to work out actual understandings on what each obligation required and then hold up before the world which side was living up to its obligations and which side was not? If nothing else, that might have created a new dynamic, with pressures on both sides to change behaviors.

Given the costs of the intifada to Palestinians, Arafat might have found this a convenient pretext to change course. For his part, Sharon, who felt it important not to cross the U.S. administration when it demonstrated it was serious, also might have found this a way to show he had a pathway to the future. By 2004, he felt a need to break the stalemate for Israel's reasons—politically and demographically—by acting unilaterally. Might he not have found a genuine American initiative, backed not only by words but by intensive diplomacy, a better way to go—particularly because he might have gotten something from the Palestinians?

When it comes to investing in Israeli-Palestinian diplomacy, however, hesitancy has marked the Bush administration. The administration has preferred diplomacy on the cheap, with limited effort, investment, and exposure.

Unfortunately, that instinct not only doomed the roadmap, but it also meant that the openings occasioned by three historic developments would be lost, leaving the prospects even worse off for peacemaking.

A LOST OPENING FOR PEACEMAKING

In 2004 and 2005, three dramatic developments created a strong basis for resuming peacemaking efforts. First, Yasir Arafat died in November 2004. So long as he was alive, no change between Israelis and Palestinians—much less within Palestinian society or between Palestinians and the U.S. administration—was possible. Second, in January 2005, Mahmoud Abbas (Abu Mazen) was elected as president of the Palestinian Authority on a platform of nonviolence and reform. This was a first, with Abu

Mazen making clear that Palestinian interests were not served by violence, and with the Israeli public and government having a vastly more favorable view of Abu Mazen's intentions than of Arafat's. And, third, Ariel Sharon not only declared in February 2004 his intention to withdraw completely from Gaza, evacuating twenty-one settlements and pulling out the Israeli Defense Forces, but in August 2005 he implemented the withdrawal. By itself, the withdrawal had the potential to transform the stalemate between the Israelis and Palestinians by unfreezing the realities on the ground.

However, to take advantage of these developments someone had to seize the openings and develop an active, urgent game plan. To begin with, there had to be an understanding that with Arafat gone, Palestinian behavior could change, but changes had to come quickly. Abu Mazen might have won a mandate for his vision of nonviolence, but he had no inherent standing on his own. Yes, he had been elected, but he was replacing an icon, a revolutionary leader who had symbolized the Palestinian movement; unlike Arafat, Abu Mazen lacked authority and needed to build it by showing that his way—the way of nonviolence—paid off. So he had to put people back to work and gain freedom of movement—two accomplishments that would be felt by all Palestinians.

Beyond Abu Mazen being seen as delivering, there had to be a sense of urgency about producing coordination between the Israelis and Palestinians on the Israeli withdrawal from Gaza. The more the hand-off of territory and settlements could look as if it had been agreed upon or at least coordinated between the two through talks, the more "negotiations" as a vehicle for producing progress could be restored in the minds of both Israelis and Palestinians.

Lastly, in the worst case, if coordination was difficult to establish effectively—and if we found it difficult to help Abu Mazen deliver much—we still needed to be sure that life got better after the Israelis left Gaza. Ensuring this would build the Palestinian stake in preserving stability there and preventing any attacks from Gaza. It would allow the Palestinians to show the world and the Israelis that they could fulfill their responsibilities—and if they could do that in Gaza, why not in the West Bank also? But life could get better only if "security for access" arrangements were worked out before Israel left Gaza, not after. If the

Israelis felt there were inadequate security provisions, they would deny movement into and out of Gaza, and that would cripple any possibility of building an economy and improving life there.

On all three measures, our efforts were too little and too late. This is not to excuse Abu Mazen, who did very little to help and acted as if avoiding decisions rather than making them was his objective. But we had the means to do much more than we did. Abu Mazen was a known quantity. His strength was his intentions, not his decision-making instinct. He had to be pushed to make decisions, even while we delivered for him in a way that built his authority and his confidence.

I was not alone in calling for the creation of an international team to be established in his office to create a work plan, with time lines for projects and mechanisms for implementation. Such a team would have pushed Abu Mazen to decide. It would also have helped him to create a functioning office and to tackle the issue of corruption—an issue that created great anger among the Palestinian public.

Of course Abu Mazen needed more than forms and mechanisms to produce projects; he needed the financing to make them possible. Donor efforts were organized, starting even the month prior to his election. But the efforts produced pledges that were very slow to be honored. Here again someone needed to spearhead the effort in a way that produced immediate financing for projects that would put people back to work. The Palestinian per capita income had dropped by 30 percent in the years of the intifada. Had Abu Mazen produced quickly, it could have dramatically altered the political reality and context—and certainly raised the costs for those who might resist him.

One obvious place to produce quickly for him was in financing for housing. Palestinians had been the backbone of the Israeli construction industry. Now, for security reasons, they were no longer permitted to work in Israel in any appreciable numbers. Palestinian construction companies had the design and contracting wherewithal to use the financing and put large numbers of laborers to work—provided the financing was forthcoming. With Saudi Arabia, the UAE, Kuwait, and Qatar flush with cash from the rise in oil and natural gas prices, there was an obvious source for the financing that was needed. But someone had to make this a priority; someone had to make it a public issue; someone had to make it a campaign so that it would be difficult for the Gulf states not to respond.

Unfortunately, the administration did very little. It approached the Saudis and others quietly but never pushed with any insistence or specificity. Nor was there any urgency attached to making things happen on the ground.

The secretary of state appointed General William Ward to work with the Palestinians on security so the Israelis might lift checkpoints and ease Palestinian mobility, but Ward's mandate was extremely limited, and he refrained from promoting the kind of Israeli-Palestinian security cooperation that might have made a difference. And in keeping with the administration's approach in foreign policy in general, no one asked Ward hard questions or created accountability for him and his mission.

The same lack of urgency plagued the approach to forging a coordinated basis for Gaza withdrawal. To be sure, Ariel Sharon was not keen to have such coordination. In his eyes, this was an Israeli decision and he did not want the Palestinians to be able to tell him how it should be done. But we had a stake in how it came out. We had a stake in ensuring that Hamas not be the main beneficiaries of it. We had a stake in using Gaza withdrawal to restore faith in Israeli-Palestinian cooperation and peacemaking—and none of this was going to happen on its own.

Here, again, the administration made a belated effort, but its hesitancy worked against its objectives. James Wolfensohn, the outgoing president of the World Bank, was appointed as the envoy for the Quartet to help with the management of the Gaza withdrawal. But his mandate included only the economics of withdrawal, not security.

Moreover, Wolfensohn was not appointed until May 2005, a little more than two months prior to the time of Israeli withdrawal. Already that was late in the day, and though his efforts were heroic, they were largely of his own making. When he was not in the area, nothing happened.

It was as if the administration, especially in its second term, had a much better appreciation for the elements of statecraft and some of its tools, but it was easing into using them with Israelis and Palestinians at a time when the clock was ticking and time was the one thing we did not have. And its instinctive hesitancy on investing in a hands-on effort continued to hold it back.

While it may have been hesitant on investing in intensive hands-on diplomacy, it was not hesitant on its agenda for democracy promotion in the Middle East more generally. As such, it pushed an obviously reluctant Abu Mazen to hold parliamentary elections in January 2006. The administration saw elections as part of a renewal process.

But it failed to appreciate that Hamas might do very well in the elections, particularly given the anger at Fatah for its corruption and seeming indifference to the needs of the Palestinian public. While the election may have been more about voting against Fatah than voting for Hamas, the outcome, nonetheless, put Hamas in charge of the Palestinian government.

Hamas, an acronym for the Islamic Resistance Movement, rejects Israel's right to exist and remains deeply wedded to the idea of "resistance" against it. Hamas's election meant that the very premise of any peace process—namely, the outcome should be based on a two-state solution—was now rejected by those running the day-to-day affairs of the Palestinian government.

So after having three historic developments—Arafat's death, Abu Mazen's mandate for nonviolence, and Sharon's disengagement—the net result was a Hamas-led government in the Palestinian Authority. The opening that existed throughout 2005 was closed in 2006. Thus, even before the war with Hizbollah in the summer of 2006, there was little ground for peacemaking. But at least the Israeli commitment to "disengagement" still gave the administration something significant to work with, especially from the perspective of statecraft.

ISRAELI ELECTIONS AND DISENGAGEMENT

With Hamas in power, the Israeli perception that there was no Palestinian partner was more deeply cemented. If anything, that further convinced the Israeli public that negotiations were fruitless and it was time to separate from the Palestinians unilaterally. The growing consensus in Israel was shaped by the desire to "be done with the Palestinians," get out of their lives, and preserve the Jewish character of Israel by ending the occupation of the Palestinians. These motivations led Sharon to withdraw unilaterally from Gaza and dictated continued disengagement and withdrawal from a large part of the West Bank.

Kadima, the new party formed by Ariel Sharon prior to his massive stroke, had further disengagement as its raison d'être. Ehud Olmert, who had been deputy prime minister under Sharon and had joined the prime minister when he left the Likud Party to form Kadima, became Sharon's successor.

Running in the election on a platform of fulfilling the Sharon legacy, Olmert left little to the imagination in the campaign: he made clear that as prime minister he would carry out a disengagement (withdrawal) from up to 90 percent of the West Bank and even from parts of Arab East Jerusalem. While he preferred to do this with Palestinian agreement, he declared that this was unlikely after the Hamas election and therefore he would do it unilaterally if necessary. And, while his mandate might not have been as strong as some expected, his party won the largest number of votes, and the rightist parties became a clear minority—with Likud dropping from forty seats in the Knesset to twelve.

A new, untested Israeli prime minister being elected on such a platform gave the United States leverage toward the Palestinians and the Israelis. With the Palestinians, we were in a position to say that Israel is going to withdraw and can do it in a way that takes your needs into account. Or they can do it without you. Work with us, and we will press the Israelis to undertake withdrawal in a way that works with and not against you, and leaves open the possibility of negotiations on peace later on.

Olmert, on the other hand, also needed the United States. If he could not get anything from the Palestinians for withdrawing—which was his presumption—he needed something from America. He needed to show that, as he evacuated up to seventy settlements and sixty to seventy thousand settlers from the West Bank, which unlike Gaza constitutes the heartland of Jewish history, he garnered meaningful commitments from the United States. While he knew he could not get formal recognition of the new boundaries that Israel was drawing, he wanted and needed U.S. acceptance of the new settlement blocs and an open American acknowledgment that there would be no pressure from the United States to change these borders absent an unmistakable Palestinian partner ready to fulfill all of its obligations on terrorism. Olmert needed to be told that he could only gain the U.S. support he needed by working with the Palestinians at least through our mediation and with our ground rules.

Until the summer of 2006, disengagement remained the Israeli policy, and the United States had leverage to affect the situation and create a new baseline for preserving calm between Israelis and Palestinians and later pursuing peace. Unfortunately, that changed with the Lebanon war.

THE LEBANON WAR AND THE END OF DISENGAGEMENT

On July 12, 2006, Hizbollah launched a barrage of rockets across the Israeli border as cover in which to kidnap Israeli soldiers. Israel responded by trying "to destroy Hizbollah." Israel began this war with great understanding internationally, with support even from the Europeans that it was justified in responding to the Hizbollah attack, and with unquestioned backing from the Bush administration. But the indecisive conclusion to the war changed the political realities in Israel. After thirty-four days of warfare, the Israeli public saw an outcome that raised basic questions about the judgment and competence of its leadership—how, Israelis asked, could their leaders squander the extraordinary circumstances in which the war was launched; why did they not relate military plans to political objectives; and why did they equivocate in launching a ground campaign and do so belatedly at high cost?

Not surprisingly, the logic of disengagement now also seemed to lose all credibility. Why? Israel had unilaterally withdrawn from Lebanon in 2000 and Gaza in 2005. After the Lebanon war of 2006, what did the Israeli public see? Hizbollah had become stronger in Lebanon as a result of Israeli withdrawal and had built up over six years a capacity that permitted it to hit Israeli territory with roughly four thousand rockets during the course of the war. Similarly, Hamas had emerged as the power in Gaza after Israeli withdrawal, and not for one day following the Israeli withdrawal had rocket fire from Gaza into Israel ceased. True, the rockets from Gaza were far less capable in range and payload than those from Lebanon, but as Hizbollah had shown in Lebanon, that could change in time.

What the Israel body politic saw was that unilateral withdrawals had not made Israel more secure, and a comparable withdrawal from the West Bank (which is far closer to all Israel's major cities and communities than Gaza) would render all of Israel vulnerable. The bottom line: Israelis now face a conceptual vacuum when it comes to how to approach the future and relations with its neighbors.

I say this because the policies of the political "left"—negotiate and make peace with the Palestinians—were discredited by the failure of negotiations and the eruption of the intifada. The policies of the political "right"—the status quo is acceptable, and eventually the Arabs will adjust—were discredited by demographic realities and the costs of preserving the occupation. The failure of the left and the right produced the "third way"—disengagement and the construction of a separation barrier. But after Lebanon, this conceptual pathway also was discredited, at least in its unilateral form. A fourth way is needed and is likely to emerge gradually as Israelis debate their future and as the Olmert government struggles to survive and avoid elections.

While there will be political weakness in Israel, the Palestinians appear hopelessly stalemated. Today the reality among Palestinians is one of deteriorating economic and political life. A divided government, with Abu Mazen as the president of the Palestinian Authority, a Hamas prime minister, and a Hamas-dominated cabinet, has led to political paralysis. Hamas refuses to accept the terms of the Quartet of recognizing Israel, renouncing violence, and accepting all previous agreements between Israel and the Palestinian Authority, and as a result, the Palestinian government has largely been cut off from the kind of donor assistance that kept the Palestinian Authority afloat. Some limited donor monies are going to the office of the presidency, but not to the Hamas-dominated ministries.

Repeated efforts to produce a national unity government failed until the Saudis, worried about the growing violence between Hamas and Fatah, convened a summit between Abu Mazen, the head of Fatah, and Khalid Meshaal, the leader of the Hamas movement based in Damascus. The Mecca deal produced the guidelines for a national unity government. But even if they are implemented, the basic competition between Fatah and Hamas will continue and likely intensify.

Given the circumstances, and the reality of weak and divided leadership in Israel and Palestine, peace is not something that will be possible anytime soon. But preventing further deterioration and laying the foundation for progress is essential. We must start by trying to restore calm between the Israelis and Palestinians, and prevent a collapse of the Palestinian Authority. We must do so in a way that addresses the needs of Palestinians and gives them hope even while we seek to get Hamas either to change or to be supplanted by secular alternatives that believe in peace.

In addition, at a time when anger toward the United States in the Arab and Islamic worlds is increasing and the concept of peace itself is more in question than it has been since the Madrid Peace Conference in

1991—with Iran, Hizbollah, and Hamas all challenging Israel's right to exist and making that part of the Middle Eastern landscape—we have to work practically on the ground and actively with others internationally to reestablish support for a two-state solution. It is possible to explore many ambitious objectives, but they must be done carefully and with our eyes open. We do not have an interest in launching a grand initiative that proves hollow and once again leaves the impression in the region that diplomacy always fails and violence is the answer.

OUR OBJECTIVES

Promote calm between Israelis and Palestinians. Notwithstanding the weaknesses of both Israeli and Palestinian leaders, they may each see great advantage in reaching an understanding that stops Palestinian attacks against Israelis and stops the IDF from carrying out almost daily incursions into Gaza or the West Bank. Olmert (or for that matter any Israeli leadership) cannot look soft on Israeli security but would undoubtedly welcome an end to rocket fire out of Gaza and attempted suicide attacks out of the West Bank. Both Abu Mazen and Hamas leaders such as Ismail Haniya are likely to want to ease the Israeli grip on the territories and allow meaningful commerce at least out of Gaza. Both would like to show they are delivering something, and in the case of the internal Hamas leaders, there is very likely a need for a respite. The question as always is delivery: Can they deliver what they promise?

Perhaps. If they also know that Israel will stop making arrests, will stop targeted killings, and will open the crossing points into and out of Gaza, which would do much to relieve the economic squeeze, they might make an effort. Hamas is the key, because the issue is not whether it will call for an end to attacks (which it has done in the past) but whether it will agree to exert real efforts to prevent them (which it has never done).

One way to explore this would be for the United States to try to mediate an understanding between Olmert and Abu Mazen. Abu Mazen would have to deal with Haniya and Hamas, and while he could not promise them recognition from the outside, he could promise them relief from the pressure and fear of Israeli arrests and targeted killings. As part of the deal, they would probably insist on their legislators and cabinet members from the West Bank being released from jail, but if they got that, and if they knew they would be relieved of continuing pressure from the Israelis, they would have a large stake in acting.

The deal would amount to a cease-fire and would lift the closure of the crossing points for the transit of goods into and out of Gaza and, if the Palestinians were living up to all their security obligations, would also remove all checkpoints in the West Bank. For the Israelis to go along, they would have to see rocket fire stop and Hamas working with Fatah to actively preempt attacks against Israelis. In all likelihood, the Israelis would not accept such a deal until they saw some demonstrations on the ground first; however, it would not be difficult to create an agreed-upon timetable for steps on each side.

Some may say that similar initiatives have been tried in the past, including between Olmert and Abu Mazen, and obviously have been found wanting. However, there has never been an initiative that required Hamas to actively deliver. What would also separate this from any previous such efforts is that it would be a full cease-fire, affecting all attacks on the Palestinian side (as well as the smuggling of weapons) and ruling out all Israeli incursions and arrests; it would also have to make very clear what happens when there is a violation. An understanding of this would have to include what constituted a violation. It would have to have agreed-upon responses to a violation. In this respect, because the Israelis have a clear chain of command, the most likely initial violation might be from one of the groups separate from Hamas or from Fatah, for example Islamic Jihad. In the past when there was a *hudna*, or truce, it was Islamic Jihad who violated it, with no response from the PA and Abu Mazen other than words. This time around, there must be agreed-upon mechanisms for discussing what is being done by the Palestinians, the time they have to act, and what the Israelis would be entitled to do if they did not act. No issues must be left open or vague or subject to different interpretations. In other words, unlike all previous efforts at a cease-fire, this one must be the product of a serious negotiation.

The United States, as mediator, must ask Abu Mazen if he needs or desires help from the Egyptians and Jordanians—but with the condition that he and Palestinians demonstrate something on their own first. The same could be true of bringing some international forces into Gaza to help at the crossing points or in patrols of the main rocket firing areas.

As a general principle, the Palestinians need to show that they can make a commitment and fulfill it. The era of excuses must end. A political culture of accountability must replace a culture of victimization and, therefore, entitlement. In the first instance, the Palestinians need this for themselves if they are to build a state.

In the context of cementing a cease-fire and enforcing it, international forces might play a supporting role that could be expanded to deal with issues of smuggling weapons into Gaza. But, again, this must start with Palestinians establishing their own responsibilities and making clear that they will try to act on them as a condition of getting help from the outside.

A U.S.-led mediation effort would need to have a Quartet dimension to it. Multiple mediators create confusion. Inevitably, there is a slightly different take on an issue, or the parties interpret differently what they hear—sometime genuinely and sometimes to play different mediators off one another. But the United States cannot ask the Europeans, the UN, or even the Russians to play a role later if they feel they are being excluded. Therefore, they must be briefed by the United States regularly. There can be general meetings, with the United States leading and managing a discussion with Olmert and Abu Mazen (or other Israeli and Palestinian leaders or representatives), to brief Quartet representatives on where the cease-fire issues and potential problems stand. Implementation committees can be set up, and the EU in particular could assume responsibility for helping direct them.

There can thus be an international dimension and role. International forces could be tied to using the cease-fire not only to establish calm but as a building block politically. For example, should international forces be brought into Gaza, it would have to be tied not only to Palestinians' making an effort on their own but also to a set of understandings with the Israelis. Acting to make sure there is no rocket fire would be a given. But if the responsibility included stopping the smuggling of arms, it might be tied to a declaration or resolution by the UN Security Council that the Israeli occupation of Gaza has ended. This would mandate new responsibilities for the Palestinians and for the international forces there, and would require the Israelis to create a different relationship with Gaza—including ending the siege of Gaza.

For those who may argue that international forces should also be brought to the West Bank and that the Israelis could withdraw as a result, there is no prospect of this until international forces in Gaza first demonstrated over time their unmistakable effectiveness. Today the Israeli presence and freedom of action prevent nearly all acts of terror coming out of the West Bank and into Israel. No one, including the United States, will be able to persuade or pressure the Israelis into giving up such a presence until Palestinians have proven they will not tolerate terrorism—and the international community will not only insist on that but also prove that their forces are efficient at preventing it.

Much would have to happen in the region—in Iraq, especially in Lebanon, and with the behavior of Hamas and Hizbollah—before the Israelis were convinced. (International forces ineffectual in implementing UNSC resolution 1701 on Lebanon will discredit any ambitious role they might play in Gaza. Already the record on implementing 1701 in Lebanon is not impressive.) But starting with mediating a cease-fire with response mechanisms for possible violations and with a possible role for international forces in Gaza could be a building block for doing much more over time.

Preserve ties to the Palestinian people. We do not have to rule out ever dealing with Hamas. We do, however, have to make clear that Hamas must adjust its behavior to the international community's norms, not the other way around. Achieving the first objective of a cease-fire will depend on Hamas but does not require our dealing with that group. To be sure, if Hamas began to enforce a cease-fire on others, that would be a sign that it was changing. That would be a sign that it no longer regarded "resistance" as its guiding principle. So long as it does, so long as it treats any act of terrorism against Israelis as legitimate, it will rationalize conflict, not coexistence, and it cannot be a partner.

The mistake the Bush administration made was not in trying to isolate Hamas and force it to meet certain conditions. On the contrary, it was right to do so. It was right to work with the Quartet and produce a consensus requiring Hamas to accept Israel and renounce violence. This was an act of effective statecraft. Its failing, however, was not to create ties to the Palestinian people at the same time, to demonstrate our concern for their well-being not in words but in actions.

To be fair, striking the balance was going to be difficult. The more one made it clear that Hamas could not deliver on any of its promises to make life better for Palestinians unless it gave up its commitment to resistance and rejection of Israel, the more the Palestinian people had to see the day-to-day consequences of having such a leadership. And with donor assistance having largely evaporated, with the PA not being able to pay its 165,000 employees, there clearly have been consequences.

But other factors also had to be kept in mind. There was a need to ensure that the PA did not collapse, with ensuing chaos and the loss of all law and order. There was a need to show that we were not punishing the Palestinian people in an act of retribution, only a leadership that thought it could gain donor assistance from the international community while rejecting the principles of the international community. And there was a need to demonstrate that we cared about the Palestinian people and their aspirations.

So what needs to be done to square the circle? Notwithstanding the difficulties, the United States should work along two parallel paths: first, continue to hold the line on Hamas's having to make a choice on rejecting terror as a political instrument if it wants to have direct ties with and assistance from the international community; and second, establish new ways to get assistance to Palestinians outside of traditional channels.

The best way to hold the line is to work constantly with the other members of the Quartet on the ground rules for assistance to the Palestinians and to draw attention to what would benefit Hamas as opposed to the Palestinian public and its needs. It also means being quick to distinguish in public and private what constitutes a real move by Hamas and what is a feint. Acting to enforce a cease-fire by stopping or punishing those who violate it is a real move. A feint is Hamas's implicitly accepting Israel by saying it "honors" previous agreements, even while continuing to rationalize and support Israel's destruction and glorify terrorism against it.

As for establishing new mechanisms for assisting the Palestinians outside of the governing ministries run by Hamas, I would establish two mechanisms. The first would involve providing assistance directly to the president's office in the Palestinian Authority. Some donor monies are going now to the president's office. There should be a significant increase, provided the president (whether Abu Mazen or a successor) commits to peaceful coexistence and a renunciation of violence, creates the means within his office to respond to social and economic needs, and establishes the capacity to spend the money in a transparent way on identifiable projects.

The second mechanism would involve the creation of new Palestinian nongovernmental organizations (NGOs) to be the recipients of assistance. As Hassan Abu Libdeh, the former minister of social affairs and labor in the Palestinian Authority, explained to me, there has been no shortage of NGOs operating in the Palestinian areas. He observed that there were 4,200, but they were not organized in a way to serve a larger purpose, either economic or social or even political. Frequently involving only two or three people, they have had very limited effect. At a time when we need to preserve our connections with Palestinian society and have some effect as we do so, we also need a new approach to NGOs. Why not create a new, larger body of NGOs, with an international steering committee to provide oversight, to promote a network among Palestinians working at the grassroots, and to drive a multiplicity of projects? The projects could involve developmental and employment assistance as well as support for the private sector, civil society, education and health, and institution building.[1]

To give an example of what this could mean in practice, private secular schools could be financed. Hamas has financed and operated thirty private religious schools in Gaza. Why not have a secular alternative? Why not use the new Palestinian NGOs with an international steering committee to create what amounts to an alternative Dawa? Hamas used the Dawa, the provision of social services—schools, clinics, food, and nutritional programs—to build their following. They did this as an opposition, but now are unable to fund the social programs and services of the government, given their unwillingness to change their behavior.

Why not compete with them and fund alternatives, building pressure on them to adjust their behavior and credo but also an alternative to them if they don't? Truth be told, such an alternative is necessary as part of state building for the future, even if Hamas is prepared to modify its purposes and objectives.

The administration needs to spearhead this effort, using the Quartet, using the monies the Congress has appropriated for assistance to the Palestinians but frozen, and launching a new effort to try to mobilize the Arab oil states to help fund such an approach. Interestingly, whatever religious attachments some in the Gulf may have to Hamas, there is a clear understanding that Hamas makes confrontation, not conflict resolution, more likely—and the Saudis and others are not interested in seeing increased confrontation or in seeing such confrontation promote Iranian purposes. As I will explain below, we need to take advantage of the Saudi perception of Hamas being an Iranian instrument to work with the Saudis to help fund and therefore empower an alternative to Hamas or at least create incentives for Hamas to change.

The task is not a simple one. It requires very active engagement with other members of the Quartet to be sure they remain on board; it requires active public diplomacy to frame what we are doing to help Palestinians even as Hamas leaves us no choice but not to deal with them; it requires an active negotiating effort with the Gulf states to gain their support; and it requires a hands-on effort with Palestinians, pushing them to develop specific projects they can act on and engaging with a sense of urgency to get the NGOs up and running.

But the more active and visible we are in providing more assistance to the Palestinians (and in some cases investment), the more it will give credibility to all of our efforts, including the promotion of alternatives to Hamas if it continues to resist adjusting its behavior and credo.

Forge alternatives to the Islamists, and principles for settling the conflict. Clearly the act of creating an alternative Dawa is part of a strategy for fostering alternatives to Islamists. It needs to be done with the Palestinians and with the Lebanese (and, as I note in the next chapter, throughout the Muslim world more generally). At this juncture, there may be a strategic opportunity to generate the monies and support for doing so.

The war in Lebanon in 2006 revealed the opening. At the outset of the war, and throughout its first week, Saudi Arabia and the Egyptians, Jordanians, Moroccans, and members of the Gulf Cooperation Council criticized Hizbollah for provoking the war. The Saudis led the way, charging that Hizbollah was not engaging in "resistance" (a hallowed concept in the Arab world); instead the Saudis accused Hizbollah of "rash adventurism." It was not only unprecedented for the Saudis to do this but also completely out of character, especially at a time when Hizbollah was fighting Israel. Why would they have acted in this way?

In a word, the reason was Iran. The Saudis saw the Iranian hand in the Hizbollah attack. Shortly before the Hizbollah attack across the border, the Hamas leadership based in Damascus and also heavily tied to Iran was responsible for an attack across the Israeli border in which an Israeli soldier was kidnapped—and that attack came at a time when Abu Mazen and the Hamas leadership in the territories had appeared close to a unity agreement on terms that the Saudis favored. What the Saudis perceived was that Hizbollah and Hamas were acting as tools of the Iranians, threatening to make the Israel and Palestine issues—the most evocative in the region—ones that Iran could manipulate. For the Saudis, few developments would be more ominous or constitute a more profound threat: an emboldened Iran capable of mobilizing great passions on the Arab "street" through the manipulation of these, the most symbolic issues of grievance.

While the situation was sufficiently real to get the Saudis to act out of character and criticize Hizbollah publicly and in the Arab League, there should also have been no illusions. The longer the Israeli bombing of Lebanon and its infrastructure went on and the longer Arab publics in the Middle East were subjected to the images on satellite television of the suffering of Lebanese civilians as a result, the less the Saudis would keep the focus on Hizbollah and the more they would retreat in the face of an emotional backlash throughout the region. The opening provided by the Saudi criticism was real and reflected a strategic convergence of interest between the United States, Israel, and a significant part of the Arab Sunni leaderships. But the opening was bound to be short-lived, and an absence of U.S. statecraft contributed to its loss.

What should have been done? The Bush administration had to seize the opening by mediating between Israel and Saudi Arabia. The two countries had the same interest of wanting Hizbollah to lose, both for reasons of Lebanon and for their mutual desire to produce a setback for Iran. The administration should have gone to the Saudis immediately and said, we will act with the Israelis to stop their attacks, or at least shape them so they fit a more strategic political outcome in Lebanon, if you put together an Arab political plan that gives cover to the Lebanese government to act and if you move swiftly to implement it. Recall that in the first days of the conflict, Hizbollah was on the defensive in Lebanon for having provoked a war without any consideration for the country, and the Lebanese prime minister called for an Arab plan—an unmistakable signal that he was seeking an Arab cover to extend the authority of the Lebanese government at Hizbollah's expense. With such a plan in hand and the readiness to move quickly to act on it, the administration should then have gone to the Israelis, who would have declared that they would stop the bombing if the Arab plan were implemented with international forces. The Israeli bombing gave them something to trade at a time *before* Hizbollah was turned into a hero in the Arab and Islamic world—and gave the Saudis and others additional leverage to call for the immediate implementation of their plan.

As I have said so often, statecraft is not just using the tools available to counter threats; it is also having the wit and the wisdom to recognize openings when they are there, knowing where your leverage is to act on those openings, and then doing so quickly. In the case of Lebanon, the opening may have been lost during the war, but the strategic reality of the Saudi interest in seeing Iran contained has not disappeared.

The trick now is to act on the strategic reality and translate it into policies that would bolster Lebanese and Palestinian moderates as alternatives to Hizbollah and Hamas. The Saudis have an interest in seeing Hizbollah weakened in Lebanon and contained. They also have an interest in seeing Abu Mazen and the noncorrupt elements of Fatah strengthened at the expense of Hamas. Helping both Abu Mazen and Fatah deliver by providing massive funds for social and economic projects and for building the security capabilities of non-Hamas security forces is something that the Saudis and other oil-rich states of the Gulf Cooperation Council could do. Oil prices were roughly twenty-seven dollars a barrel in 2003, and even if no longer at their peak of nearly eighty dollars a barrel, they have still more than doubled. The Saudis and their Gulf partners are awash in cash, have much more money than Iran, and have a reason to help bolster those who can limit the instrumentalities of Iran's strategy in the region now.

The Gulf states may recognize their interests, but someone has to mobilize them to act, and sustain their support. Secretary of State Condoleezza Rice recognizes that something has changed in the region. While I see a strategic opening with the Saudis, other Arab leaders, and Israelis all viewing Iran as a threat, she is calling it a strategic "realignment." Perhaps at one point it could become a realignment. But for that to be the case, it must be expressed in actual behaviors and not only in words. Private expressions of interest or threat perception mean little if policies don't become aligned—and we will have to painstakingly guide such a process.

In the Saudi case, we are talking about a tremendous leap. It won't simply happen. We will need to work with them every step of the way, reassuring and at times pressuring them to stay the course. For the Saudis, the temptation at certain points may be to fall back on their instinct of trying to buy off Hamas or Hizbollah or to accommodate the Iranians. And, with the Mecca deal and Saudi discussions with Iran over Lebanon, we may already be seeing such signs.

For the Saudis not to hedge their bets or play a double game, they will have to see our staying power. Moreover, their readiness to work out a coordinated approach in which we and they act in parallel to strengthen the alternatives to Hizbollah and Hamas may be influenced by whether they believe the United States is willing to act practically, not just rhetorically, on the Palestinian problem.

While the Saudis may now be prepared to back a more assertive or even confrontational policy toward Hamas, this will still need to be tested. The reason I suggested a cease-fire option to restore calm is largely because I do not believe Abu Mazen is likely to confront Hamas. But there could be an alternative he might back. While the cease-fire approach inevitably brings Fatah and Hamas together, Abu Mazen could conceivably embrace an alternative designed to clarify the Palestinian political situation and show that Hamas does not represent what most Palestinians want. He could call for a national referendum. He could declare that such a referendum (more stark and clarifying than his previous call for new legislative and presidential elections) is needed to put the Palestinian people on record for peace, provide a mandate for negotiating on the core issues of Jerusalem, refugees, and borders, and allow the international community to end their embargo on assistance to the Palestinian Authority.

The referendum would ask for a simple yes or no on two questions: Do you support a two-state solution? Do you support empowering the Palestinian government to negotiate with Israel to achieve that outcome?

Hamas would oppose any such referendum for two reasons. First, Hamas leaders are not interested in being exposed as outside of the

Palestinian mainstream on the issues of war and peace; and second, they would not want their government, which won the legislative council elections, to be supplanted.

Unlike the cease-fire option, which basically drives Fatah and Hamas together, the referendum would drive Abu Mazen (i.e., Fatah) and Hamas apart. Two factors might lead Abu Mazen to adopt such a course: First, his seeing the Mecca deal leading in practice to increasing Hamas control of the PLO and Palestinian society, something that could well happen. And, second, knowing he would gain extensive financial backing for his security forces and also social services from the Saudis and other Gulf states, a broad Arab political umbrella backing the referendum, and an understanding that, following it, Israel would be forthcoming quickly in the ensuing negotiations.

In other words, the referendum option represents a far different course from a cease-fire and presumes that the Saudis, in particular, may favor a much more ambitious course in cutting Hamas dramatically down in size. But having such a desire or hope is not a policy. And calling for a referendum should not be treated as a mere slogan. Adopting the referendum as a pathway will require a great deal of preparatory work: first, there must be quiet consultations with Abu Mazen to see if he would be willing to do it and, if so, what he would require from others—Arabs and Israelis alike—to proceed; second, there would have to be discreet discussions with the Saudis, Egyptians, and others to see whether they would meet Abu Mazen's financial and political needs, and whether they are truly prepared to back a more confrontational posture; third, there would have to be a parallel dialogue with Israeli prime minister Olmert to see what impact a referendum in which 70 percent of the Palestinians vote for a two-state solution would have on the Israeli public. Would it create a psychological change? Would Olmert feel politically capable of responding with the offer of a major withdrawal from the West Bank early in negotiations? (In all likelihood, Abu Mazen's readiness to take on Hamas would have as much of an effect on the Israeli public and the IDF as the referendum, particularly because it might well signal a readiness finally to assume serious security responsibilities.)

All this could be moot because Abu Mazen, fearing a civil war, may not be prepared to confront Hamas under any circumstances. Similarly, the Saudi readiness to midwife the Mecca deal may suggest that they, too, are more inclined to try to wean Hamas away from Iran than to undermine them. Nevertheless, it ought to be tested.

Even if the Saudis are prepared to become more assertive or supportive of bolstering the alternatives to Hamas (and Hizbollah), it is conceivable that they will want more cover from the United States to do so. They may well want a more dramatic indicator that America is now ready to act to resolve the conflict once and for all. That could provide the Saudis an explanation for their own unusual actions—after all, Hamas for a long time received most of its private support from Islamic charities in Saudi Arabia and the Gulf.

One indicator of the new U.S. readiness to act would be for the Bush administration or its successor to offer its own central principles for settling the conflict. These would leave room for negotiation but would basically embrace something like the Clinton parameters or tradeoffs on the core issues. But before going down this road, here again, quiet testing of the Saudis, Egyptians, and Jordanians would be needed to see if they would be willing to embrace the broad principles necessary to settle the conflict. The answer is by no means obvious, particularly because the Saudis et al. may not be willing to embrace the realistic principles that meet the needs of both sides. For example:

- meet the Palestinians largely on territory by using the 1967 lines as a point of departure, but with territorial swaps to permit Israel to preserve its major settlement blocs
- balance the respective interests in Jerusalem by declaring that what is Arab in East Jerusalem will be Palestinian, and what is Jewish will be Israeli, including in the Old City
- produce credible security arrangements for the Israelis and demilitarize the Palestinian state
- make clear that Palestinians have the right of return for their refugees to their own state but not to Israel

Surrendering the right of return represents the hardest but most necessary part of the compromises for the Palestinians; for the Israelis, accepting the 1967 lines with modifications but with the principle that they will give territorial compensation or swaps to the Palestinians for the settlement blocs will be necessary and difficult.

The Saudis and others who seek cover on the Palestinian issue probably won't want that cover if it appears they are endorsing compromises that the Palestinians would be hesitant to embrace in any case but certainly before the negotiations began. The irony, of course, is that given Abu Mazen's weakness, he is the one who is likely to need Arab political cover or an umbrella to make any compromises on the core issues. Are the Saudis willing to provide such cover? They never have been in the past.

But that is why there need to be quiet consultations with the Saudis to see whether they would increase their readiness and incentive to empower alternatives to Hamas and Hizbollah. It is possible that the Saudis might favor such an American outline of principles as showing that the United States is committed in a new and meaningful way to resolving the conflict—even if they would not publicly endorse the principles.

Such discussions cannot take place in a vacuum. Similarly discreet (and parallel) consultations need to be conducted with the Israelis. Like the Saudis, the Israeli leadership (obviously depending on the politics of the moment) might also not object to America's laying out such principles, as long as they were not expected to endorse them. This would be far more likely if the Israelis knew that the Saudi position was one of at least implicit support for the U.S. move. Statecraft is often conducted by carrying out parallel, private discussions with those who either cannot talk to each other or find it difficult to do so—and, of course, can involve conveying messages that can be used to build one or the other side's interest in agreeing to a particular position. If, for example, the Israelis understood from the Saudis that such a U.S. initiative would make it possible for them to actively undermine Hamas and Hizbollah in ways that were credible to Israeli leaders, the Israeli response might be positive.

In the end, all three objectives—mediating a real cease-fire, developing ties with the Palestinians in a way that does not benefit Hamas but could alter its behavior, and bolstering those who are an alternative to Hizbollah and Hamas by playing on the strategic interest the Saudis and others have in containing Iran—require a hands-on approach by the United States. They require knowing how to coordinate the approaches of those who have converging interests.

They also require consulting and testing and tying our own willingness to take more ambitious steps to solicit particular responses or actions from each side. If, for example, the Saudis want us to take ambitious moves to try to deal with the core issues of the conflict or at least to defuse it, we need to know what they will do concretely at the same time. And, therefore, these objectives could require either a readiness on our part to articulate a new set of general principles for resolving the conflict or, alternatively, a much more practical posture in which we act to create parallel unilateral moves. The latter could involve the development and execution of a different kind of roadmap—one in which parallel steps by the Israelis, the Palestinians, and the Arab states are quietly conceived, indirectly agreed upon, and taken according to a specific choreography in terms of sequence and timing. The United States would have to be both the broker and stage manager of the agreed-upon steps and the timing of their execution.

Peacemaking may not be possible now, but the task for this administration or its successors is to create an environment where it becomes possible over time—and that is certainly within the realm of effective statecraft.

13.

{ PRACTICING STATECRAFT }

Radical Islam and the Challenge of Iran

In chapter 7, I discuss the challenge of radical Islam. Radical Islamists are those whom we are now fighting in the war on terrorism. Terrorism is their tool. They seek to legitimize it as their weapon against those whom they perceive as imposing on Islam. They try to cast their struggle as a war to save Islam from a predatory Western crusade—a crusade whose goal is to dominate the Islamic world and confiscate its land and resources, principally oil.

Osama Bin Laden and those like him play on the theme of protecting Islam, its dignity, and its precepts against those who would subvert it. In the words of Ayman al Zawahiri, Bin Laden's deputy, it is the holy warriors "who are fighting on the very front line for the dignity of Islam."[1]

The holy warriors are those who commit to jihad, carry on the struggle, and are the martyrs who frequently sacrifice themselves as suicide bombers. Bin Laden has tried to justify their acts of carnage committed against noncombatants in the West not simply by using the terminology of *holy warriors* and *martyrdom* (which strike a deep chord in Islamic history), but also by suggesting that there are no innocents in the West. After all, the blood of Muslims must be avenged and, as noted in chapter 7, Bin Laden takes credit for having been able to create a Muslim "balance of terror" with the West.

But Bin Laden goes beyond seeking to produce a metaphorical balance to justify attacks against civilians. For him, the citizens of the West bear equal responsibility; in a nod toward the representative nature of democracy, he has declared that "war is the joint responsibility of the people and the governments. While the war continues, the people renew their allegiance to their rulers and politicians and continue to send their sons to our countries to fight us."[2]

In other words, killing civilians is justified because they are equally responsible. There are no noncombatants.

Perhaps this is the area of greatest vulnerability for the radical Islamists. While they can certainly play on the anger and abiding sense of humiliation that many Muslims internationally feel, they cannot explain all attacks that kill obviously innocent people—especially when those attacks make other Muslims the prime victims. In November 2005, after three hotels in Amman were bombed and sixty people were killed—half of them from a wedding party—more than a hundred thousand Jordanians demonstrated in the streets to protest an Al Qaeda–sponsored act of terrorism. What had the victims done? What crime had they committed against Islam? What had made them bad Muslims?

Few Arab or Muslim leaders shed tears over the killing of Israelis in suicide bomb blasts, with many in the Arab media even proclaiming that the suicide bombers were the Palestinian answer to Israeli F-16 bombers. For too many Muslims, the sense of injustice suffered by Palestinians justifies acts of terrorism against Israelis. Moreover, few in the Arab world ever make any effort to justify Israel's right to exist. Israel might exist as a fact, and as such it might not be undone, but if its legitimacy was never acknowledged was it really considered illegitimate to carry out acts of terrorism against it? Truth be told, even when some in the Arab world or Palestinians condemned acts of terrorism against Israel, they tended to couch their condemnation in terms of these acts being counterproductive to the Palestinian cause—not wrong, not morally indefensible.

But the terrorist bombing of Muslims was another story, at least in Jordan. I say "at least in Jordan" because the condemnations of the hotel bombings—and the massive demonstrations that followed in Jordan—may have been related to the fact that the victims were Sunnis. As noted earlier, it is extraordinary that the bombings in Iraq, including in mosques, that kill so many Shi'a noncombatants draw almost no condemnation in other predominately Muslim countries. To many Sunnis, the Shi'a are heretical Muslims; the late archterrorist Abu Musab al Zarqawi, who was responsible for the Jordanian hotel bombings and for many terrorist bombings against Shi'a targets in Iraq, referred to the Iraqi Shi'a in one video as Rawafidh—meaning "rejecter" of Islam. In his words, "we believe that any government made up of *rejecter* or godless Kurds or people who call themselves Sunnis is only a 'collaborators' government, and that it would be a sword in the Islamic nation's body."[3] Lest one think that Zarqawi's views were restricted only to the fringe, it is worth noting the words of Abdul Rahman al-Barak, a leading Saudi cleric with ties to the royal family. He termed Shi'a "rejectionists" and said, "By and large, rejectionists are the most evil sect of the nation and they have all the ingredients of the infidels."[4]

Killing those who are rejectionists or who "have all the ingredients of the infidels" may not generate the same sense of outrage as killing those who are considered to be good Muslims. And the Sunni-Shi'a split among Muslims—with Sunnis making up 85 percent of all Muslims—may raise questions about who is a good Muslim. And yet focusing too much on the Sunni-Shi'a divide may be misleading in terms of trying to understand the areas of radical Islamist vulnerability.

Iranian leaders, who are Shi'a, have generated much instinctive support among many Arabs for seeming to stand up to and defy the United States and the West. Hizbollah (also Shi'a from Lebanon) have also done much the same in the Arab world for standing up to the Israelis in a way that no Arab armies have ever succeeded in doing. In the past, Ayatollah Khomeini may have frightened many Arab leaders (much the way Hassan Nasrallah of Hizbollah has similarly done today), but he excited many on the Arab street who identified with his defiance of the West. He captured the imagination of those throughout the Muslim world who felt powerless and looked for a champion who would represent them against the powerful. Today, the current Iranian president, Mahmoud Ahmadinejad, seeks to exploit a similar populist theme. While the Western world may find Ahmadinejad's statements calling for Israel's elimination reprehensible, many in Arab and Islamic countries are attracted to them. The deeply embedded sense of humiliation and of being imposed upon, which one finds throughout much of the Islamic world, creates a natural attraction to those prepared to humiliate those who have humiliated the Muslims for so long.

Osama Bin Laden and Al Qaeda and like-minded radical Islamists—who seek to restore a caliphate and its religious guidance to all—appeal to a yearning to restore greatness and dignity. They will not be discredited by non-Muslims. They will only be discredited by moderates within the Muslim world who take them on and describe them for what they are—the true enemies of Islam.

After Chechen terrorists killed hundreds of schoolchildren in Beslan, Abdul Rahman al Rashid, a leading Arab commentator at the time and now the director of the Al Arabiya satellite network, wrote in *Al Sharq al Awsat*, "Certainly not all Muslims are terrorists but we say with deep regret that the majority of the world's terrorists are Muslims" and we have to ask ourselves why.[5] His words not only touched a nerve but also began to attack the radical Islamists at the core of their vulnerability. Even Ayman al Zawahiri seemingly understands that there are limits to the kind of terrorist attacks to be carried out. In a letter he wrote to Abu Musab al Zarqawi dated July 9, 2005, Zawahiri warned that the beheadings of those taken hostage and the bombings of Shi'a holy places in Iraq ran the risk of alienating ordinary Muslims. Zawahiri was not telling Zarqawi to stop terrorist attacks, only to change the tactics: kill hostages by gunshot and attack U.S. and Iraqi forces.

Zawahiri wrote Zarqawi that "we are in a battle . . . for the hearts and minds of our people."[6] If Zawahiri understood this, so must we. The vulnerability of the radical Islamists stems in part from their appearing to undermine the essence of Islam, which most Muslims see as a religion of peace. Islam prohibits ever killing innocents; it forbids suicide; it calls for justice. But, of course, it also demands defense of the faith against those who threaten it.

Bin Laden and the radical Islamists cast themselves as the defenders of Islam against those who seek to subvert or corrupt it. They claim to act in self-defense and portray their Muslim critics as apostates—enemies of Islam. They wrap themselves in the cloak of self-defense and justice.

Unfortunately for us, their claims are not simply dismissed. Their charges and the mythologies they promote are often believed. Why?

WHAT WE ARE UP AGAINST

A number of factors explain this phenomenon and the instinct of large numbers of Muslims spread across many countries to believe nearly any charge that is leveled against us. First, there is a profound sense of longing for greatness lost; Islamic leaders, teachers, and empire (and their Arab vanguard) once led the world in science, mathematics, language, art, and commerce. But it has now lagged behind the non-Islamic world for a millennium, and a feeling has developed over time that greatness lost is actually greatness denied. The outside world, especially the Western world, is seen as having conspired to keep Islam down; external imposition and conspiracy are themes that resonate throughout the broader Middle East.

Second, a related part of the historical narrative, particularly among Arabs, emphasizes an abiding legacy of betrayal and humiliation. Recall that in his first video after 9/11, Osama Bin Laden referred to eighty years of humiliation. He was referring to a memory seared into the collective Arab consciousness of the British and French betraying their promise of independence for the Arabs from the Ottoman Empire if they joined in the fight against the Turks in World War I. The Arabs fulfilled their side of the bargain with the "Arab revolt," but rather than receiving independence, the Arab world was denied its destiny, its land carved up into mandates, and remained under foreign rule. Yet another betrayal in the narrative is the West's support for the creation of Israel; in Arab eyes, Germany inflicted a crime against the Jews, and the Palestinians paid the price, losing their homeland. Iranians, too, have made the U.S. and British coup against their nationalist leader Mohamad Mossadeq part of their narrative of Western imposition and betrayal—and both are feelings that the radical Islamists exploit.

Third, imposition is also felt internally. Corrupt regimes that appear largely indifferent to the local populations and who betray the tenets of Islam—at least according to the radical Islamists—are propped up by the United States and its Western allies. Bin Laden and Zawahiri have made special targets of the Saudi and Egyptian regimes, describing them as corrupt and able to remain in power only because of American support. Because many of the Arab regimes in the region have been so obviously corrupt and prone to benefiting only the leaders, their families, and their cronies, it should come as no surprise that their publics are both alienated and angry. Frustrated by the lack of opportunity and by the corruption that benefits the few at the expense of the many, Muslim publics often see American support for the regimes that impose on them as one more sign that the United States cares little about them, or its self-professed higher values, and more about narrow and selfish American interests.

Fourth, most of the regimes in the region lack legitimacy, having been imposed by coup or mandated by family heritage—they certainly are not in power because of the consent of the governed. To shift attention away from their own failings—or to avoid real reform that might deny them their power, privilege, or wealth—they have sought to focus attention on the Palestinian issue or blame all local failings on the United States, the Western world, and Israel. Nabil Khatib, the editorial director of Al Arabiya television, told me that "for fifty years Arab regimes have used Palestine as an excuse to avoid dealing with all issues—poverty, education, economy." Worse, Nabil observed, they also have no interest in settling the issue, preferring to blame others for it than to deal with it.[7] The lack of legitimacy has led to two realities: regimes, including those that we support, such as Egypt, seek to promote anger against the United States to avoid having that anger directed at them; and a culture of victimhood, not accountability, has permeated much of the Arab and Islamic world. Problems are never their fault, and it is always up to someone else to fix them. Under such circumstances, it is easy to blame us—and both the radical Islamists and our putative friends do so.

Fifth, the media, with the interesting exception today of Al Arabiya, which is now trying to take on the prevailing political culture, promotes a populist, reflexively anti-American posture. America's motives are openly or implicitly questioned; our insensitivity to Muslim needs is often highlighted; and our tendency to inflict pain on Muslims, particularly in Iraq, is a staple for much of the Arab media. One time I appeared on al Jazeera's *Crossfire*-type show; the question for the night was "Is the United States an occupier or a liberator in Iraq?" The presumption—even the way the question was posed—was designed to put the United States on the defensive. Not surprisingly, in polling the audience before we began, 94 percent of those polled declared that the United States was an occupier.

When all these factors are taken together, it should come as no surprise that our purposes are questioned and the worst is often believed about us in the broader Middle Eastern world. In a Zogby poll done in 2005, when Arabs throughout the Middle East were asked what factors drive U.S. objectives in the Middle East, nearly 80 percent said controlling oil, while just 5 percent responded spreading democracy.[8]

While we may believe we are selfless, Muslims do not generally see us that way. And our image has certainly suffered during the Bush years. Few will defend us in either the Arab or broader Islamic worlds. As Abdul Rahman al Rashid told me, "The Europeans will not defend you; obviously, the Arabs will not defend you. Only Americans can defend their point of view."[9] And Rashid's argument is, we are not doing a good job of that. At the same time, Iraq and the Palestinian issue have been effectively used against us.

Fair or not, Iraq is seen as a mess that we created; in the words of Rashid, "The invasion of Iraq obviously made it easy for the anti-Americans to prove their point." Marwan Muasher, the former foreign minister of Jordan, made a similar point to me, saying, "Everyone sees what Iraq has become and the way the Iraqi people are suffering."[10] Daily violence, bombings, kidnappings, chaos, lawlessness, sectarian warfare, marauding militias, and continued economic hardship represent the picture that others in the broader Middle East see in Iraq. When combined with the indignities and abuses that American soldiers are portrayed as having committed against Iraqi prisoners at Abu Ghraib, there can be little doubt that Iraq has made it far easier for the radical Islamists to demonize us and our purposes.

The Palestinian debacle has added to our problems. At least during the Clinton years no one questioned the U.S. commitment to resolving the conflict; the appearance of American indifference and ineffectiveness—and Palestinian suffering at the hands of Israelis—has added to the sense of grievance that many in the Islamic world feel against us and that the radical Islamists play upon. What's more, with the Hamas election victory, the Islamists are now far better positioned to become the arbiters of what is acceptable on an issue that the publics throughout the broader Middle East believe is a wrong that must be righted—and the Islamists (from Hamas to the Iranians) are clearly trying to restore the pre-1967 idiom on the so-called Arab street that the existence of Israel need not be accommodated, that the land of Palestine is an Islamic trust, and that only the United States prevents the fulfillment of Arab or Muslim destiny there.

So, is our task hopeless in competing with the radical Islamists? Not necessarily, but here, again, we have to have a strategy for transforming how we and the radical Islamists are perceived. To do so, we have to play on their vulnerabilities and use all the tools we have far more effectively. We must also focus on who our natural partners might be and how we help them to achieve our shared objective of discrediting the radical Islamists.

UNDERSTANDING THE ISLAMISTS AND MARSHALING THE TOOLS TO COMPETE WITH THEM

There can be little doubt that every tool at our disposal is going to be necessary as we try to overcome the scourge of radical Islam. If we are to succeed in tailoring an effective strategy for doing so, it is essential to understand that not all Islamists are the same.

The challenge of Hamas is different from that of Al Qaeda. While they may all seek to create an Islamic state, with sharia, or religious law, governing the state, Al Qaeda and its offshoots are far more nihilistic than the Muslim Brotherhood or even Hamas or Hizbollah.

Some Islamists have a political agenda, believing they can gradually take over the states they reside in. Entering the political process, while preserving their militias, is certainly part of the strategy that Hamas, Hizbollah, and key Iraqi political-religious factions have employed. Clearly, elections are also part of their strategy. In the case of the Muslim Brotherhood in Egypt, they have even eschewed violence and arms, something that neither Hamas nor Hizbollah is prepared to do.

So far the Muslim Brotherhood in Egypt is the only Islamist party to give up violence as a tool for its advancement. In their case, they appear to believe that it is better to use the stasis of Mubarak's regime and crackdowns by the Egyptian secret services against others (such as Egyptian judges) to build their own following.

Are the Muslim Brothers in Egypt "Islamic democrats" who believe in the rule of law, pluralism, and tolerance? Could they be a model for other Islamists who say they seek Islamic states but are prepared to coexist with others? Could they be partners in undermining the radical Islamists? Ask Khairi Abaza and Hala Mustafa, two genuine Egyptian reformers, what they think and they will say it is all a charade. So long as the Muslim Brothers are unable to supplant the Egyptian regime, they will seek common cause with others. But for both Abaza and Mustafa, the Brotherhood's purpose remains that of creating an Islamic state, with no room for secular law, multiple parties, or tolerance for minority rights, much less respect for women's rights.[11]

Whether or not Abaza and Mustafa are correct, the unwillingness of the Muslim Brotherhood to condemn violence as a tool of other Islamists should be reason enough not to treat them as potential partners or a model to be held up to others. In general, we should be skeptical that so-called moderate Islamists will become like any other party that competes for power and enables open political systems to flourish.

Such a possibility should not be ruled out in all circumstances, but American officials should not be rushing to promote the "moderate" Islamists. On the contrary, we do not want to signal that we believe they represent the wave of the future.

This is not to say that moderate Islamists should be prevented from competing in elections; anyone who meets certain basic criteria of giving up their weapons, renouncing and opposing violence, respecting the outcome of voting, and supporting the rule of law should be eligible to compete in elections, including Islamists. Under such circumstances, we should also be prepared to meet with them. But these are not the groups or individuals that we should be seeking to support as alternatives to radical Islamists and oppressive regimes. Our natural allies in the struggle with the radical Islamists will be liberal, moderate, secular elements. If there are moderate Islamists who would truly oppose radical Islamists and seek to discredit them that would be one thing—and we could revisit the idea of contact with such groups if they began to emerge. We can always work through others—liberal reformers or other third parties—who could probe such groups and see if they were prepared to reject violence as a means for pursuing their political agendas.

Understanding who the Islamists are—even if there are differences among them—and being able to explain to others internationally why there are basic criteria that they should meet before we individually or collectively deal with them will be an essential part of forging a strategy that can work to delegitimize radical Islamists. Once again, we are re-minded of the importance of framing issues and explaining them. Obvi-ously, the clearer we are with our objectives and the challenges we must overcome, the easier it will be to frame issues in a way that makes them acceptable domestically and internationally.

The starting point in competing with the radical Islamists is to recog-nize that they must be discredited and that we, in the first instance, won't be the ones to do that. Muslims in the different Arab and Islamic coun-tries must be the ones to do that. Two points will be critical in this regard: First, we have to contend with our own credibility problems, particularly because association with us should not be a liability for those pressing for liberal or moderate reforms and political transformation in the greater Middle East. And, second, we have to find a way to help reformers in Arab and Islamic countries become more capable of delivery. They must be able to deliver results on the ground and not just words or slogans that sound good.

HELPING OUR PARTNERS ACHIEVE OUR SHARED OBJECTIVES

We must support those who are pressing for reform and challenging the Islamists. However, given our credibility problems, we need to do so in a way that does not create problems for them. As former Jordanian foreign minister Marwan Muasher told me, "I am often now accused of being an American agent because I call for democracy."[12] As Muasher observes, the term *democracy* has become stigmatized. We should not be defensive about the word or necessarily shy away from using it, but so long as it has become a code word in the Arab and Islamic world for pursuing a sus-pect American agenda, we may want to work with local reformers and determine whether different terms might be more useful in promoting a genuine reform agenda. Developing *good governance, combating corruption,* building a *law-based society,* respecting *minority* and especially *women's rights,* may all be part of the necessary process of constructing demo-cratic, pluralistic societies. And these terms may also be part of using a new lexicon that helps reformers and doesn't hinder them.

Clearly that must now be one of the objectives we establish as part of the struggle with the radicals. One tool we could use to achieve that more limited objective might be initiating a strategic dialogue with reformers in each of the countries of the Arab and Islamic worlds. As Robert Satloff argues, it is important to deal with the reformers and democrats on a country-by-country basis for at least two reasons. First, the challenges and opportunities differ from country to country, with the realities in Morocco looking very different from those in Saudi Arabia and the Arabian peninsula; and, second, the radical Islamists are at war with the very idea of there being individual countries, seeking instead to promote the image of the *umma*—one large transnational community of Muslim believers that should be a "unit of Muslim political activity," and should be guided by one set of religiously based precepts that are all-encompassing and cannot be questioned.[13]

Recognizing the differences between countries and the reformers in them argues for identifying who are the most credible reformers in each country in the broader Middle East and for developing a sustained dialogue with them. This is an essential means for competing with the Islamists; through such a "strategic dialogue" we could begin to frame or package what we said and what we did in each country. Our challenge is to help those who are, in Satloff's words, the "people who carry the daily burden of confronting the Islamists."[14] Too often we unintentionally harm those we need to be helping.

The best way to help them rhetorically and practically is to develop a common strategy with them on what is most likely to benefit them. Part of the task is to make sure that what we are saying publicly is more likely to resonate positively in the area—and certainly local reformers are better arbiters of this than we are. And part of the task is to develop programs of assistance that are more likely to permit reformers to deliver results and not just rhetoric.

Reformers throughout the Arab Middle East are too often seen as elitist, addressing only a narrow stratum of the public, failing to organize at the grassroots level, and never delivering programs that might actually affect the day-to-day reality of people who are suffering and have profound needs. Wafa' Abdel Rahman, a Palestinian women's rights advocate, told me when I met her in Ramallah how "Hamas worked the grassroots and we [Palestinian reformers] were working the elites." She went on to say that she and her colleagues had ignored the "relief agenda," while Hamas was giving the people "food and helping them when they're in despair."[15]

Hamas is not unique among Islamist groups who have used the provision of social services to build an appeal. Hizbollah did the same in Lebanon, often providing the only social and economic services to the Shi'a in southern Lebanon or in southern Beirut when the government largely ignored them. The same has clearly been true for the Muslim Brotherhood in Egypt.

Islamists thus built an appealing contrast both to the corrupt, unresponsive regimes, and to reformers who too often seemed riveted on developing an abstract democratic agenda. Such an agenda might serve the long-term interests of building an inclusive, participatory society, but in the near term it has little meaning to large impoverished publics. For former secretary of state Madeleine Albright, who believes deeply in the importance of promoting democracy in the Middle East, there must be a balanced perspective on how to approach democracy building. In her words, people in impoverished areas are "more interested in eating than voting."[16] Like Wafa' Abdel Rahman, Secretary Albright sees the value in having a social and not just a political agenda.

So does Bassem Awadallah, former minister of planning in Jordan and now chief of the royal court. But he sees the problem through the lens of the demographic trends in the region. In a conversation we had in his Amman office, he put a special emphasis on the urgency of competing effectively:

> Over half the population of the Arab world is under the age of eighteen, and over 65 percent is under the age of twenty-five. There are expectations on behalf of these young people, and the quicker and more effective you are at delivery of services . . . the more successful you are going to be . . . The Islamic movements have held a huge advantage on the ground. They have the mosques and a social outreach program which is unparalleled.
>
> The Zarqawis of this world are trying to get a hold of those who are alienated, of those who are hopeless in their social and economic living conditions, and turn them into their agents as suicide bombers.[17]

For Awadallah, the lesson is clear: start delivering tangible goods (such as education, services, and jobs) on the ground to give people, especially young people, hope for the future. For me, the message is also unmistakable: take a page from the Islamists' playbook. If they use what is known as the Dawa to deliver a social safety net apart from the regimes, why not help reformers develop and deliver either a secular or an alternative Dawa apart from the nonreforming regimes? I say "the nonreforming regimes" because we need to help the reforming regimes—such as those in Jordan and Morocco—with the means to be more effective and responsive to the grass roots.

To be sure, we also need to have a clear and consistent approach to regimes, such as Egypt's, that have been traditionally friendly to the United States but have demonstrated no serious approach to reform. In Egypt, there are economic reformers who have gravitated to Gamal Mubarak, the son of President Hosni Mubarak. Gamal's circle hopes to open the economy, privatize it, free it from government regulation and management, reach a free-trade agreement with the United States, and make it possible to integrate with the global economy. Their agenda is economic and not overtly political, but they expect that economic reforms will inevitably, if gradually, foster greater political inclusion and participation.

To date, the progress on both fronts has been mixed. Privatization is proceeding slowly, but its benefits are felt mostly among the elite. While economic reform at least appears to be on the agenda, political change seems to be more of a slogan than a policy. President Mubarak's decision to permit multiparty competition in the presidential elections certainly represented a step forward, but the imprisonment of Ayman Nour, his main challenger, the postponement of municipal elections for two years, and the crackdown on judges who called attention to the fraudulent nature of the elections all signaled that the regime was not about to permit any real change politically.

After initially pushing Mubarak on reform, the Bush administration now appears to have retreated. Following the Hamas victory in the Palestinian elections, the administration seems more concerned about Islamist successes and more mindful of instability in a major country such as Egypt. Thus it offered little criticism of the Nour imprisonment and pro forma protests over the regime's crackdown on the judges and the signs of dissent. The tension between not wanting to destabilize Egypt on the one hand and, on the other, recognizing that if Egypt stifles political liberalization, it leaves only an Islamist alternative, is now being resolved in favor of near-term considerations.

While this is understandable, particularly given the importance of Egypt in the Middle East and to American interests, we must not lose sight of the longer-term consequences of blocking change and building resentment against us within the Egyptian public. Our economic and military assistance to Egypt certainly gives us leverage on the Mubarak regime, but we should apply it carefully and in a targeted fashion. Should we apply it too bluntly, we are likely to trigger a nationalist backlash that Mubarak could easily exploit. But if applied with some care, pressure from us might well achieve a desired end. What, for example, might be the result if we put a "hold" on two hundred million dollars—10 percent of our annual assistance—and announced that the hold would be released when Mubarak lifted the state of emergency, the extralegal, administrative measure he has used to put people in jail for months on end and without access to lawyers? In such circumstances, Mubarak will not find it easy to turn our posture into a test of his withstanding external pressure. The state of emergency is extremely unpopular in Egypt, and Mubarak would have a hard time explaining his position and castigating ours.

In any case, we could justify our posture as our commitment to seeing the rule of law developed in all governments, and especially so in those to which we are providing large amounts of assistance. This might be a rule or criterion we could encourage other donor countries to use to promote good governance as part of their assistance policies.

More generally, we should discuss with other donor countries how to use foreign assistance not just to promote development in the abstract but also to foster good governance with regard to regimes and reformers alike. Foreign assistance is a tool of statecraft that can and needs to be employed collectively and with a political agenda in mind. Daniel Benjamin and Steven Simon have called for making offers ("they can't refuse") of big packages of assistance that are tied to far-reaching reforms that put regimes such as Mubarak's or Bashar al Asad's in Syria in a position of being able to get major help from the outside and in a way that can "captivate key constituencies in these countries."[18]

Such generous offers are hard to imagine if there isn't also a political base developed domestically for them, or if there is not a lot of diplomatic groundwork and negotiating done with our partners internationally. Here, again, we see the value of engaging in strategic dialogues to shape common approaches. Such dialogues with our allies should be a central part of the strategy for trying to affect the behavior of friendly nonreforming regimes and perhaps also for trying to alter the behavior of regimes such as Syria's, which is stagnating and represents a threat to its neighbors.

At the same time, we cannot lose sight of where our main focus should be. Our main effort must be geared toward the reformers and reforming regimes because they are our natural partners. They share our objectives not because we want them to do so but because they believe that their own salvation is dependent on defeating and discrediting the Islamists. With them, strategic dialogues are going to be a necessary tool of our statecraft, particularly if we are to help them develop the means to compete effectively with the Islamists.

THE ART AND PURPOSE OF STRATEGIC DIALOGUES

There can be little doubt that if we and other donors are to help reformers and reforming governments provide an alternative Dawa, we will need to discuss how to do it. Such a discussion or dialogue should be used to identify particular programs or services that are most urgently needed, could be feasibly provided by reformers, and could be funded by donors. What kinds of programs might be most useful?

- after-school programs where English and computer skills could be taught
- internship programs for developing job-related or vocational skills and for offering possible paths to employment, perhaps in conjunction with private companies
- specific job-producing projects promoted with the local and international private sector and NGOs
- food-distribution centers created in the most destitute areas
- medical and dental care provided in new clinics where care has been unavailable

These represent just a small sample of what might emerge from a strategic dialogue with reformers and reforming governments. Interestingly, these suggestions fit at least in part with the findings of a Gallup poll of forty-one global Muslim communities that concluded that broad initiatives "aimed at job creation, combined with proactive support for those who wish to make change through the ballot box, will reduce the appeal of those who insist change is possible only through violence."[19]

The point is to use the dialogue to generate an activist approach, with specific programmatic suggestions built around a concept such as the development of an alternative Dawa that could attract the secular and devout alike. As with any good approach to negotiations, we should engage in active listening—probing, asking questions, demonstrating our interest in learning what can best work—while also putting the responsibility on our local partners in these dialogues to focus on practical suggestions. We should be listening more than preaching, even as we seek to ensure meaningful outcomes.

There are two other aspects to these dialogues that fit the logic of good statecraft and the exploitation of the tools we have available: we need partners not only throughout the greater Middle East, but also on the outside, who have the means to help finance these programs and have the wherewithal to help make them work. Obviously, the Europeans, the Japanese, and international financial institutions such as the World Bank can be critical in this regard. But these outside parties and institutions should be viewed as a source not only of money and expertise, but also of intelligence about who are the right partners—the real reformers—to engage in such discussions. Creating the right mix of reformers, ones who are credible and practical, will be essential to producing meaningful dialogues in each country, and we are unlikely to be able to identify the right people from each country without input from the Europeans, the Japanese, and others.

In other words, we probably need sequential and parallel strategic dialogues with those who ought to share our purpose in wanting to see alternatives to the Islamists emerge throughout the Muslim world. We need a serious discussion to forge a common approach; to make sure that approach is complementary; to create a division of labor in providing assistance and investment; to avoid divergent tactics vis-à-vis the so-called moderate Islamists; and to settle on how best to produce models of suc-

cess for the alternative Dawa in particular and for the reformers and reforming governments more generally.

None of this will happen by itself. And clearly, today, there is no such
common strategy. With the Europeans in particular, such a dialogue
might be created under the rubric of the existing United States–
European exchanges or could occur in the NATO context. But it must
be systematic and take place at a senior level—perhaps with the undersecretary of state meeting his or her counterparts, and with an ongoing
working level reporting to them. Such discussions should not be pro
forma; they can and should involve an exploration of what is possible
country by country in the Middle East, with a clear set of priorities
about which countries are most important to deal with urgently and which
are most likely to show some early results. (Again, one of the objectives
is to build exemplars of success, and to show that reformers can provide
their own delivery system.)

Such discussions should also deal with assessments of homegrown Islamist problems. As I observe in chapter 7, the Islamist threat is fed at
least in part by alienated Muslim populations in Europe; this is an intelligence problem to be dealt with not just by existing counterterrorist or
intelligence exchanges. At the political level, there needs to be a deeper
discussion of strategies. We may not have the answers, but having Europeans discuss how they see the problem, the political pressures that are
building to deal with it, and the possible public- and private-sector programmatic responses to it may deepen our collective sense of what we
are facing and how best to respond to it.

We certainly have our own emerging problem in this regard, with the
appeal of Islamists growing in U.S. prisons, and the European experience
may provide us some useful insights. By the same token, our greater
success in integrating immigrant communities (including Muslim communities) into the broader American society may also provide useful
lessons for European countries such as Belgium, the Netherlands, Den-
mark, and others now struggling to find ways to reduce the isolation and
alienation of their Muslim citizens. One possibility may be to create
parallel discussion groups as adjuncts to governmental dialogues and involve American Muslims with their European counterparts. (One young
American Muslim, the former national director of the Muslim Public

Affairs Council, Ahmed Younis, believes much could be done through such means to reduce the radicalization of younger European Muslims.)[20]

One other reason to develop a new high-level forum for such discussions is that it can also be useful for forging new and deeper bonds with our European allies at a time when our relations have frayed over the last few years. Whatever our differences, we still share important common values and basic objectives, and the threat of radical Islam plagues us all.

A common strategy for contending with it is in both our interests, and must not be limited to technical exchanges on intelligence and law enforcement, as important as those are. They are necessary tools, and much as with the use of force to defeat the Taliban or to kill, arrest, or preempt Al Qaeda operatives, there is simply no alternative. Those who believe in violence and advocate it must be defeated by violence. They must not be the answer to humiliation, but must be held responsible for producing it.

The Islamists feed on indignity and a psychic landscape of frustration and anger. To be defeated, they must be seen as producing one more source of failure. Just as we want to create models of success for the reformers, we also need the Islamists to fail. That is why Hamas must be forced to change or to fail—with change itself being a demonstration that Islamism is not the answer. You can destroy with it but not build.

Defeating the Islamists and showing that they fail is not simply a military or intelligence or law enforcement challenge. If there was understandably a need after 9/11 to apply these tools with great urgency, so too must we now organize and shape the application of the nonmilitary tools with the same sense of urgency.

That is why a strategic dialogue, first with the Europeans and Japanese, and then with reformers in the broader Middle East, is so important. Here is where we will succeed in sharpening and clarifying the objectives, framing the issues, collaborating on means, and maximizing their effect. Here is how we will manage potential differences between us and find ways to build our collective leverage. We won't agree on everything. We will probably continue to have differences on how we look at the Arab-Israeli issue. The answer is not to hide our differences, but to ensure they don't get in the way of our larger objective of defeating the radical Islamists.

Some may argue that solving the Arab-Israeli issue is our most important task. There can be little question that Islamists need grievance to exploit and mobilize passions, and few issues are as evocative throughout the Arab and Islamic world as the Palestinian cause. Should we make an effort to solve it or at least to defuse it? Of course. The Bush administration was wrong to disengage from it and wrong to apply only episodic efforts to try to defuse it. A major effort is needed to deal with it, but like any diplomacy and exercise of statecraft, such an effort must be rooted in reality.

Settling the conflict is not in the cards now. In my earlier discussion of what should be done, I point out that it is possible to create an environment that sets the stage for settling the conflict later—and we should do that. However, even if we could settle the conflict now, it would not be a panacea. The radical Islamists would not suddenly surrender. Their agenda has been to exploit the Palestinian grievance but was never driven by it alone.

Dealing with the Israeli-Palestinian conflict must be part of a smart statecraft approach to competing with the Islamists. It has the benefit of making it easier for the Europeans and others to work with us on the rest of the agenda; it will improve our image and the way our objectives and purposes are seen by others. But it is only part of the agenda.

In truth, defusing the Palestinian issue will help to create a context for doing what is more important—making reformers successful and more confident and secure in their competition with the Islamists. Much will be required to produce that:

- secular or alternative Dawas should be created and financed so that reformers are able to deliver real goods
- reformers must be protected from regime crackdowns, meaning that we and others must be prepared to make any such crackdowns an issue not just in private but in public, even with friendly regimes such as those in Egypt and Saudi Arabia
- elections should be part of the strategy for opening up oppressive political systems but not initially, when the only two alternatives are corrupt, despised regimes and Islamists
- when elections are conducted, there need to be eligibility requirements on candidacy—meaning that militias should not be permitted to run and that candidates have to clearly choose ballots over bullets

• no shortcuts should be permitted for those regimes that want
to join the WTO and the global economy, meaning that certain
standards on corruption and economic transparency have to
be met
• collective pressure should be applied to create independent
judiciaries and access for the media

None of this will happen overnight, and none of it can be done by the
United States acting on its own. All of it will take a concerted, intensive
effort using every tool of statecraft we can muster. But we come to the
task with real assets, and the Islamists come with vulnerabilities and the
failed legacy of others who have similarly sought to exploit the anguish
of a largely frustrated population throughout the broader Middle East.

Gamal Abdel Nasser wrote in 1955 about there being a "role in
search of a hero" in the Arab world. Who would be the hero to lead the
Arab world back to greatness? Nasser sought to be that hero—to be the
leader who would end the humiliation, who would get back at those who
had inflicted so much pain on Arabs, on Muslims. Others have sought to
assume this mantle: Qadhafi, Saddam Hussein, Khomeini, and now Bin
Laden. It matters little that Arab nationalism was largely secular and Bin
Ladenism is largely religious. Each movement was designed to capture
the passions and desires of those in a part of the world that felt left out
and imposed upon.

Charismatic movements depend on grievance, but in the end they
cannot succeed only by what they reject. They cannot succeed only by
tearing down and destroying. In the end, they must deliver, they must
produce. And so our strategy for competing with radical Islam must be
geared toward having the reformers deliver change and come to be seen
as the purveyors of social justice. While the objective is daunting, we and
our allies bring substantial resources to the task. If we also bring the kind
of skill and intensive and extensive effort required for executing smart
statecraft—the kind seen in past cases of statecraft done well—we will
be able to marshal those resources and succeed.

CAN WE SUCCEED WITHOUT CHANGING
THE BEHAVIOR OF THE IRANIANS?

It is impossible to take on the challenge of competing effectively with radical Islam without also finding a way to alter Iran's behavior, especially on the nuclear issue. I say that not because the nuclear issue is the only area in which we confront Iran, but because Iran with nukes will be perceived differently in the Islamic world and will act differently. An Iran with nuclear weapons is likely to feel emboldened. Its policies in and beyond the Middle East are likely to become more assertive and certainly more coercive. Its leaders will push their Islamist agenda with more confidence. And others throughout the world of Muslim states are likely to see Iran on the march, mastering the instruments of power, and capable of challenging the West successfully. Its fortunes and the fortunes of Islamists more generally will be seen as being on the rise. We need the imagery of Islamists failing, not succeeding.

To be sure, the Iranian Islamists and the radical Sunni Islamists are not the same. As I note earlier in quoting Abu Musab al Zarqawi, the radical Sunni Islamists view Shi'a as heretics. They, unlike the Iranians, look to restore a caliphate—a Sunni-led religious leadership for the *umma*—and that would surely be seen as a threat by Iran. There is a Sunni-Shi'a split, and many Sunnis would find it difficult to follow an Iranian Shi'a lead even if Iranian defiance of the United States creates a source of attraction for many Arab publics.

Aside from the Sunni unwillingness to be led by a Shi'a Iran, the Iranians also have a more particularist agenda. They have state ambitions that reflect their own brand of nationalism. They see themselves tied to a legacy with a long national history, with an ancient civilization, a superior culture, and empires whose power, wealth, and reach gave, and should continue to give, Iran a special standing throughout the Middle East. Ray Takeyh, of the Council on Foreign Relations, writes that the mullahs of today have maintained the tradition of "successive Persian monarchs and empires [who] perceived Iran as the epicenter of the region, a country that by the dint of its history and civilization was ordained to lead the Arab states."[21] Persian nationalism is thus fused with wider ambitions to spread Islamic legitimacy and the Khomeini legacy of a "revolution without borders."

The point is that the interests of the state matter. All of Iran's leaders agree on that. Some may be more hard-line, believing that the weight and power of the state is best secured by spreading Iranian influence and pursuing a confrontational style that preserves a revolutionary élan. Others are more pragmatic, preferring to build the state, its economy, and its well-being internally and are more sensitive to the costs of external confrontation.

Nonetheless, all of Iran's leaders (hard-line or pragmatic) seem to have favored political strategies to build Iran's leverage to pursue its interests. For both ideological and national reasons, Iran's leaders support Hizbollah and Hamas. Hizbollah allows them to build the basis of an Islamic state—led by Shi'a—in Lebanon, and also fight a proxy war at a safe distance against Israel. Hamas, which is a Sunni Palestinian group, gives the Iranians a similar kind of vehicle. Is it more important that Hamas seek to build an Islamic state in all of Palestine (in place of Israel) or that it wages an ongoing struggle against Israel? The Iranian leadership does not have to choose between objectives. Seeing the Israelis as an agent of the United States—the country that has sought, according to the Iranian narrative, to control Iran and deny it its regional role and destiny—Iran's leaders wage an indirect war against Israel. They see that war as also giving them leverage against Arab leaders whom they can put on the defensive for acquiescing to Israel and for not fighting or doing anything to undo the perceived injustices to the Palestinians.

The strategy of supporting militias that are also political parties is ideologically satisfying and also serves the interests of the state. We see this pattern revealed in Iranian support for Hizbollah in Lebanon, Hamas in the Palestinian Authority, and the Mahdi Army and Badr Organization in Iraq. In each case, the militias create leverage on the regimes, while the political strategy of taking part in elections legitimizes these groups as political actors and permits them to influence the governments, constrain what they can do, and potentially over time come to dominate them.

The radical Sunni Islamists reject political strategies and see elections as being inconsistent with Allah's will. What the Iranians have in common with the radical Islamists is that they both use terrorism and see the West as an oppressor and a threat to Islam. The Iranian threat is more subtle and sophisticated. But because it is driven as much by state interests as by ideology, the Iranians can be influenced and their behavior altered. The radical Sunni Islamists must be defeated; the Iranians must be redirected.

REDIRECTING THE IRANIANS

Our point of departure has to be establishing a meaningful objective that reflects both the reality of the situation and our means. Put simply, Iran must not develop nuclear weapons. An Iran with nukes is likely to destabilize the Middle East and in so doing probably trigger the fatal weakening of the nuclear nonproliferation regime. Certainly there is a high risk that the Iranians with a nuclear shield may believe that they can coerce their neighbors with impunity. The expectation that the Iranians will act more coercively with a nuclear shield already exists among the Gulf states, with the Saudis and others telling American officials that they anticipate far greater direct and indirect threats from the Iranians in such a circumstance. There is a very real danger, therefore, that a nuclear Iran will drive the Saudis, Egyptians, and others to go nuclear as a counterweight to potential Iranian threats, creating a nuclear Middle East that is both inherently dangerous and also likely to reduce the prohibition against going nuclear internationally. Already the Saudi foreign minister has declared that Saudi Arabia will develop nuclear energy, using language that echoed Iranian words on nuclear power.

While some argue that we should not exaggerate the significance of a nuclear Iran, and that Iran will understand that it can't actually use these weapons or share them with others, those who make this case inevitably overlook the destabilizing impact in the region and on the nuclear nonproliferation regime. They also ignore or dismiss the Israeli fears—fears that have been increased in the aftermath of the Lebanon war. Israel could not stop Hizbollah's rocket attacks, and the recognition of Israel's vulnerability to a nuclear attack has been made far more acute as a result. Iran's hostility is not imagined in Israel. It is real and it has been behind countless acts of terrorism in Israel. If that were not enough, Iran is constantly trying to delegitimize Israel's existence. No one should expect the Israelis to wait for Iran to have the means to threaten them existentially.

The objective of trying to prevent Iran from becoming a nuclear weapons state is the right one. Can the Iranians be persuaded to forgo it, and do we or others have the means to so persuade them? In the first instance, the Iranians clearly want nuclear weapons. They may claim they want nuclear power only for peaceful uses. But their behavior belies that claim. If they want nuclear power only for purposes of generating electricity, why keep their nuclear-related activities hidden for seventeen years—in direct violation of their treaty obligations under the NPT? Why not answer the questions of the nuclear watchdog agency (the IAEA)—one not governed or run by the United States? Indeed, even now, nearly five years after Iran's hidden activities were exposed by an Iranian opposition group, the regime still obfuscates or holds back on information to the IAEA. Why turn down offers by Russia to support Iran's conversion of uranium ore to hexafluoride gas and to enrich it and supply the fuel to Iran, provided the spent fuel is returned? Why reject the offer from the European Union to provide light water nuclear reactors that can generate electricity but have limited value for developing nuclear bombs?

It is hard to escape the conclusion that Iran seriously wants nuclear weapons. And its desire is probably driven by a number of factors—some defensive and some offensive. No doubt, it wants them as a symbol of national power. It probably sees them as providing a deterrent against us—after all, we attacked Iraq, which did not have nuclear weapons, but have avoided doing the same with the North Koreans, who may have as many as twelve. It probably also sees nuclear weapons as useful in a neighborhood where the Pakistanis and Israelis have them, where the Turks are part of NATO, and in which it has an unstable Iraq on its border. But it is not only the psychological and defensive reasons that motivate the Iranians. It is probably also their sense that by rights they should be a nuclear power—given how they see their role and natural position in the Middle East. Nuclear weapons will increase their influence, and Iran will find it easier to dominate the region with them, or so its leaders appear to believe.

The reasons are real and varied. Moreover, all the previous regimes—hard-line, pragmatic, and reformist—have pursued a nuclear program. Even if such a program is likely in the hands of more hard-line elements associated with the Revolutionary Guards, there apparently has been a "nationalist consensus" on developing the capability.[22] But that does not mean that the Iranian calculus cannot be altered or affected.

So far, there has been no price or adverse consequence for Iran for pursuing a nuclear program. The Iranian elite is not homogeneous. The pragmatists and the reformers may now be overshadowed by the hard-liners represented by the president and certainly the Supreme Leader, Ali Khamenei. But by all accounts, Khamenei does not decide by fiat.[23] On the nuclear issue in particular, according to Ray Takeyh, he seems to have broadened the "parameters of the debate to include relevant elites from across the political spectrum in the nuclear deliberations."[24] And while the pragmatists and even reformers have supported the development of the program—clearly much of the work proceeded during reformist president Muhammad Khatami's tenure—they have signaled their concerns about moving ahead if it is going to produce adverse economic and political consequences for Iran. As it became increasingly apparent that the IAEA would refer Iran to the UN Security Council for possible sanctions if it continued with its nuclear activities, some of the Iranian pragmatists began to call for restraint and even saw the value of suspending the program. Former Iranian president Akbar Hashemi Rafsanjani suggested that there was a "need for prudence on both sides," meaning not just the United States and the Europeans but the Iranians as well.[25]

Later in October 2006, when the UN Security Council actually began to discuss imposing sanctions on Iran for its nuclear program, Rafsanjani went so far as to release a secret letter that Ayatollah Khomeini had written to explain his willingness to end the war with Iraq in 1988—a decision Khomeini took in the words of one Iranian newspaper because he would not permit ideology to get in the way of "a realistic understanding of the international situation."[26] Rafsanjani and those he represented in the elite seemed to be saying, let's be mindful of what we are doing, be realistic about what we are up against, and adjust our behavior accordingly.

The critical divide seems to be whether Iran will truly pay a price, with the pragmatists very wary of the potential price and the hard-liners dubious that any real price will have to be paid. The United States and the Europeans may posture, but will they really hold together and impose sanctions on Iran that would matter, that would bite? Hard-liners basically argue that "whenever we stand firm and defend our righteous stands resolutely, they [the West] are forced to retreat and have no alternatives."[27]

The Supreme Leader signaled much the same point in a conversation he had with Joschka Fischer, the former German foreign minister. Ali Khamenei told Fischer that the West would never be willing to absorb oil prices of $140 a barrel. The message is very telling, for Khamenei was saying, you in the West don't have the will or the stamina to impose a meaningful price on us—namely, an embargo on our (Iran's) ability to sell our oil—and therefore we need not back off. In effect, Khamenei was saying, since you are not really willing to absorb any pain, you won't force us to incur any, either.

The corollary is, of course, if you were willing to absorb some pain, we would then have to worry. And that is the point. We do have the means to affect Iranian thinking on how and whether they proceed with their nuclear program. It will surely not be easy; the Iranians will go to great lengths to prove to us that they won't give in; they will try to divide the United States from its partners and threaten consequences for us, the NPT, and the oil market if we impose sanctions on them. But the vulnerability is there, and differences in the Iranian elite can be exploited.

Michael Slackman, a *New York Times* correspondent who has done frequent reporting from Iran, interviewed one unnamed Iranian pragmatist who said that he and others opposed the confrontational posture of President Ahmadinejad, but Ahmadinejad was able to correctly argue that Iran never paid a price.[28] Ultimatums have been issued but then deferred. That creates the worst of all worlds: it emboldens the Iranian hard-liners, defeats the arguments of the pragmatists, and gives the hard-liners a reason to test every move made by the international community.

Given all the warnings, it should come as no surprise that the belated adoption of very limited sanctions in December by the Security Council, designed to affect the Iranian nuclear industry but not its economy, had a limited effect on the balance of forces in the Iranian hierarchy. Indeed, limited sanctions adopted with a vague timetable for adding to them tended only to confirm the hard-line view that the West is unwilling to incur any real cost. For the hard-liners, counterthreats (e.g., the denial of visas to IAEA inspectors or the hint at withdrawing from the NPT if further pressured) would undermine the consensus internationally on imposing additional costs. Limited sanctions, rather than producing an Iranian impulse toward accommodation, instead has produced more Iranian testing and threats.

But it is not too late to change the nature of the approach. Iran has been able to enrich uranium to low-grade levels. They have experienced engineering problems with the delicate centrifuges that must spin the uranium gas at high speeds to enrich it to higher levels. They have succeeded in building a few cascades of centrifuges but still need some time to master the engineering involved in creating multiple cascades. Consequently, even though the Iranians are saying that they are assembling industrial-scale centrifuges, there is still a window of time available for affecting Iranian behavior. A new approach that employs meaningful sanctions and inducements might be able to alter the balance of forces in Iran, particularly given Iranian vulnerabilities.

Iran's leaders may think they are on a roll and that the high price of oil, and the United States being tied down in Iraq, limits our means to put pressure on them, but ultimately they know their own weaknesses better than anyone. While the high price of oil has generated much revenue for the regime—forty-five billion dollars from oil exports in 2005—nearly all of it (forty-three billion dollars) went to finance imports: raw materials, industrial machinery, refined oil products, food, consumer goods, and defense materials.[29] Subsidies help keep social peace and the economy going at a time when unemployment and inflation remain very high. Oil and natural gas exports are essential, and yet, in the coming decade, Iran's aging infrastructure will require as much as eighty billion dollars in investments, much of it from foreign countries possessing the technological know-how, if it is to sustain these exports. A serious drop in oil prices will cost Iran a major portion of its revenue. A readiness to stop exporting refined oil products to Iran will present the country with a major problem because it must import nearly 40 percent of its gasoline. A determination to cut Iran off from outside investment or financing and credit markets will mean its economy—already a source of domestic unhappiness—will face acute problems.

The vulnerabilities are real. How best to play upon them? The Bush administration lost one of its most important levers when it gave away its readiness to negotiate with Iran without getting anything meaningful for it from the Europeans, Russians, and Chinese. All of them, especially the Europeans, were desperate to get the administration to change its approach and be ready to negotiate with Iran—a posture the Bush administration had resisted from its inception. Here was a lever the administration could have used to exact an agreement on specific, weighty sanctions.

In an article in the *Washington Post* on May 1, 2006, I proposed that the administration go to the Europeans, Russians, and Chinese and tell them we would be prepared to join direct negotiations with Iran on two conditions: that we as a group work out an agreement on specific sanctions to be imposed if negotiations failed, and that we agree on what would constitute failure in the negotiations so there is an agreed trigger for the sanctions. This had to be done discreetly, and our readiness to negotiate had to be announced only after there was agreement on very specific sanctions. I was told the administration had adopted such an approach, but when Secretary Rice announced our readiness to negotiate with Iran, the only agreement the administration had was on a menu of sanctions—which, as I said at the time, meant there was no real agreement on any sanctions. When I asked administration officials why they would agree to so little for giving away what had been a big card, I was told, "this is the best we could get."

So why agree? If we had said no and made clear that our continuing with a diplomatic set of options depended on agreement on sanctions, I suspect we would have done better. Even if not, we could always have agreed to this later; we, too, had to be in the business of testing.

Ironically, coercion works not only with adversaries but with friends as well. If the Europeans and certainly the Chinese (who get roughly 13 percent of their oil from Iran) think that the military option might be employed if diplomacy were stalemated or impossible to exercise, they might be much more open to the employment of meaningful sanctions. When President Hu Jintao visited President Bush in the Oval Office in 2006, the president should have told him that China should recognize the importance of not leaving us with only military options to prevent the Iranians from going nuclear. The fact that Israel—especially after the 2006 Lebanon war—may feel the need to strike Iranian nuclear facilities militarily if it believes that the international community is prepared to live with an Iran with nuclear weapons also gives us leverage. If we can persuade the Europeans that Israel may strike Iran unless we can demonstrate that we collectively are not acquiescing in the Iranian program and are imposing a credible price that may alter Iranian behavior, we will be far more likely to get the Europeans to adopt meaningful sanctions against Iran.

Sanctions are, of course, not an end in themselves. They are the means that could be used to play on the fissures or the fault lines in the Iranian leadership. How we frame what we are doing and how we talk about our purposes will be critical not only for getting the Europeans to go along with us but also for having the desired effect on the Iranians. In both cases, the less bellicose we are rhetorically, the better the results. In private it is one thing to talk about not being left with only military options to prevent Iran from going nuclear. In public, it is something else.

The Bush administration has become far more sensitive to the effect of its rhetoric. It has certainly also sought to preserve a common position with the Europeans, and even with the Russians and the Chinese. What it has not done effectively is to focus with the Europeans (at least) on how best to play on the divides in the Iranian leadership. For the Europeans who have been dealing directly with the Iranians for the last several years on the nuclear issue, the fault lines are quite visible. We should have intensive discussions with the Europeans, asking them to explain the fissures as they see them, and asking them how best to weaken the arguments of the hard-liners and strengthen those of the pragmatists.

Inevitably, we will collectively come to the conclusion that there has to be an unmistakable consequence for the behavior of the hard-liners: that growing isolation will emerge, that access to financial markets will dry up, that investment from the outside will be harder and harder to generate, and that economic pressures will intensify—so long as Iran persists with pushing ahead with a nuclear weapons program.

The corollary must also be available: namely, that if Iran is prepared to accept only a civil nuclear program, with all the appropriate safeguards, then economic, technological, and security benefits—taking account of Iranian interests in the Gulf region—become possible. Orchestrating this combination of sticks and carrots requires at this point some obviously adverse consequences for the Iranians first. They were offered an incentives package by the Europeans, but this was always going to fall short unless the price of what the Iranians had to pay for pressing ahead on nukes was clear enough and credible enough to give the Iranian pragmatists a reason to say, in effect, the price is not worth it.

In this sense, the consequences have to be potent enough for Iranians to say, we don't want to pay that price. Now what can we get for giving up the nukes? So what sanctions—either through the Security Council or outside it—might have the desired effect? Anything that creates the impression that Iran is a pariah would be costly. The Iranian self-image is such that to be isolated would be very damaging; to become North Korea is not acceptable. Travel bans, not just on those in the nuclear industry, would be acutely felt. True, it might produce a tough Iranian response to test the limits of consensus on the outside, but any sanctions employed must be sustained.

Similarly, financial sanctions that would make it difficult for Iran to do business, or more likely that would make private companies and banks on the outside fear that if they did business in Iran they might run legal risks, could have a very strong impact in Iran. I say this not just because of Iran's vulnerabilities, but also because of the sense of isolation that would additionally be imparted.

As limited as the sanctions adopted in December were, they have already triggered overt criticism within Iran of President Ahmadinejad. The newspaper *Jomhuri Islami*, which is associated with the Supreme Leader, accused the president of using the nuclear issue to "divert" the attention of the people away from "the problems of the government." And the newspaper *Hamshahri* on the same day suggested that a number of speeches by the president made the Iranian case on the nuclear issue "once again [become] suspect."[30]

If nothing else, this suggests there is in fact sensitivity in Iran to the possibility of being isolated. The broader point is that much can be done to change the Iranian calculus short of using force. Ironically, much could be done short of employing an embargo on selling Iran gasoline or going further and imposing an embargo on Iran's ability to sell its oil and natural gas. But just as President Bush is, as he says, not taking the military option off the table, so, too, should we not be taking the embargo off the table. Iran can't generate revenues if it cannot sell its oil and natural gas.

How we speak about what we are doing vis-à-vis Iran is also critical to gaining broader support internationally. This gets back to the right way to frame an issue. We do not want to be framing the issue in a way that makes it appear that we are simply trying to deny Iran its rights. Many in the developing world sympathize with Iran when it appears that we are imposing on it and denying it rights that others are entitled to have.

Creating such an impression is not only costly with many in the so-called nonaligned movement in Asia, Africa, and the Middle East, but it also tends to play into the hands of the Iranian constituency favoring confrontation. The better way to frame the issue is that Iran has the right to have nuclear power, but it continues to violate its obligations under the terms of the NPT by continuing to hide nuclear-related activities and by refusing to answer IAEA questions about problematic weapons-related tests. Iran, we should say, seeks to mislead the international community and not respond to the IAEA the way others (e.g., Argentina) have. Why should Iran be permitted to behave differently when, unlike others, it also threatens other states?

The task of putting Iran on the defensive is not easy when the Bush administration is itself on the defensive. The administration has been wise to have others take the lead publicly. It needs to be wise as well in forging a strategy with the Europeans and the Japanese (Iran's biggest commercial partners) that draws on their expertise and advice in shaping those actions most likely to impose a cost that matters to the Iranian pragmatists. This way, Europeans and Japanese can claim ownership of these positions and be more likely to employ both formal and informal sanctions. Informal sanctions—involving private-sector banking and credit institutions—might be especially effective in cutting off Iran from the trade and investment so critical for its economy.

The virtue of the informal sanctions is that they are less overt, don't depend on the UN Security Council—where tough sanctions require Russian and Chinese acquiescence—and may come from convincing banks and businesses that they are running unacceptable risks in doing business in Iran. To be effective, the Europeans and Japanese must join in the effort. Along with the United States, they must be prepared to jawbone their leading commercial and financial interests about not doing business with the Iranians.

Already the Bush administration is using the Treasury Department to try to cut off Iranian state-owned banks such as Bank Saderat from the international banking system, charging them with funneling funds to

Hizbollah, Hamas, and Palestinian Islamic Jihad.[31] In this campaign against individual Iranian banks, the Treasury Department is invoking terrorism laws, something that can create a chilling effect on those doing business with such banks. There is certainly value in such an approach, and it could underpin the more informal effort I have in mind. The Europeans and Japanese will be more likely to join us in an effort that is less overt, certainly less public, and less obviously a campaign. In other words, reach a consensus and proceed without calling great public attention to it. Iranian leaders will get the point but will find it more difficult to mobilize a nationalist response.

Will the Europeans and Japanese join us in such an effort? Less visible steps are politically easier for the Europeans. Their publics are more chary of anything that smacks of causing confrontation and producing a slippery slope that could lead to conflict with Iran. To induce greater readiness on the parts of both the Europeans and the Japanese to pursue a path of informal sanctions, we might also enlist the Saudis and other Gulf oil states. Their financial clout, and European and Japanese financial interests in these states, certainly gives them leverage vis-à-vis the Europeans and Japanese—and the Saudi fears of the Iranian nuclear program could make them very effective partners in pressing the Europeans and Japanese on Iran. (The same is also true of the Chinese; their economic ties and investment in Saudi Arabia are likely to dwarf their interests in Iran and could also be exploited to affect the Chinese approach to Iran—something that would not be lost on the Iranian elite.)

I don't suggest that informal sanctions are preferable to formal sanctions. After all, formal sanctions by definition reflect a stronger political and legal consensus on an international basis and will highlight Iran's isolation; rather, I suggest that there are many tools and points of leverage and some do not depend on gaining support in the UN Security Council—or at least might be a natural complement to more limited Security Council sanctions.

The same is true when it comes to more covert and inherently deniable alternatives to the use of force for setting back the Iranian nuclear program and making it clear to the Iranians that they will pay a costly price for pursuing it. The Iranian nuclear program has much vulnerability, particularly given the fragility of centrifuges. Sabotage of machinery that is delicate and depends upon very pure fuel might prove very costly for the Iranians to overcome, and yet would be completely deniable. Covert options would surely not be able to set back the Iranian program for as long or as extensively as military strikes, but would be far less risky and limit the options Iran would have to respond—not to mention that such options are much less likely to coalesce the Iranian public around the regime than an open attack on the homeland.

Here, again, the point is not necessarily to argue for covert military/ intelligence options to set back Iranian nuclear efforts. Instead, it is to show that we have multiple ways to raise the costs to the Iranians and in a manner that is likely to sharpen the divide in the Iranian elite over the relative benefits of their nuclear efforts. Using only blunt instruments may not always be our best option. Finding the right mix of options, with the right mix of partners—each of whom may bring to the table different assets or points of leverage—is a test of statecraft. Certainly when it comes to the Iranian nuclear weapons program, before contemplating the use of force—which would surely inflame Muslim opinion and emotions against us and give the Islamists another grievance to exploit—we should satisfy ourselves and the world that we have credibly exhausted all other means.

Whether we are trying to stop the Iranian nuclear weapons program or are competing with the radical Islamists more generally, we have to bring all our assets to bear. We have to know how to exploit vulnerabilities; we have to know how to involve others who may be more persuasive in altering the Iranian calculus or in discrediting Islamists. We have to be able to work coherently and use all our means and our imagination in these struggles.

This is no simple challenge. But we should not forget that the United States and its allies and potential partners are far stronger than the Iranians or the radical Islamists. If there was ever a task for statecraft, this must surely be it. Given our stakes, it ought to be possible to exercise statecraft in a way that meets the challenge.

14.

{ PRACTICING STATECRAFT }

China's Rise

A quarter century ago, Deng Xiaoping, then emerging as China's preeminent leader, traveled to the United States and spoke of his determination to transform China economically by the year 2000. He said, "We in China are faced with the task of transforming our backwardness and catching up promptly with the advanced countries of the world."[1] Deng's vision has been translated into reality. China has become an economic colossus. Its gross domestic product increased from $256 billion in 1984 to $1.654 trillion in 2004; it has become the third largest economy in the world and is poised to overtake Japan and become the second (behind the United States) within the next fifteen years. Should it continue to grow at roughly 9 percent a year, as it has for the last twenty years, it could match our total economic output within thirty years.

The emergence of China as a global economic power has produced a cottage industry of concern about the political consequences of China's rise. Few would challenge the conventional wisdom that with the rise of China, there will be, in Henry Kissinger's words, "a substantial reordering of the international system. The center of gravity in world affairs is shifting from the Atlantic, where it was lodged for the past three centuries, to the Pacific. The most rapidly developing countries are in Asia, with a growing means to *vindicate their perception of the national interest* [emphasis added]."[2]

What fuels the concern is the Kissinger notion that China as a rising

319

power will now be able to "vindicate" its view of its national interest. And such vindication is likely to mean a Chinese redefinition of the rules for governing the international system to ensure that they serve Chinese needs and interests first and foremost. Historically, when powers are ascending they tend to come into conflict with those who are already the leading or transcendent power or powers. In the nineteenth and twentieth centuries, that was certainly the case between Germany and Great Britain, and later between Japan and the United States.

Is conflict inevitable? Is it going to be a defining characteristic of the new international landscape? It need not be. While it may not be within our power to control China's rise, it is in our power to understand it and shape responses that affect China's choices. The starting point for such an exercise in statecraft is to see China as it is and to be realistic about its aims and our means to influence those aims.

It is too soon to say definitively that China is either a rising power with only limited aims or, alternatively, a rising power that is determined to revolutionize the international system. Certainly, the Chinese leadership has sought to allay fears of its intentions and pretensions by speaking of its "peaceful rise." One leading Chinese scholar, Wang Jisi, has suggested that America need not be concerned, because China "must maintain a close relationship with the United States if its modernization efforts are to succeed." Indeed, those very efforts mean that a "cooperative partnership with Washington is of primary importance to Beijing."[3]

Hu Jintao, China's president, increasingly speaks of a "harmonious world" in which countries of different outlooks live cooperatively in peace. It sounds good, but it may be telling that the Chinese media portrays the phrase "harmonious world" at least in part as a rebuff to the American posture that is described as "hegemonism," a view that plays to the resentment of the United States seeking to dominate all others internationally.[4]

It is also clear that China is working to foster an environment in Asia that promotes its interests and minimizes America's. Note how the Chinese and Russians have come together and created the Shanghai Cooperation Organization (SCO), which also includes the four states of Central Asia. Significantly, the SCO has been relatively quick to challenge the U.S. military presence in Central Asia, calling, in July of 2005, for a timetable for the withdrawal of U.S. forces from the region. The Chinese also arranged for India, and subsequently Iran, to have observer status in the SCO—a group that excludes the United States.

Similarly, the Chinese have also promoted an East Asia Summit, involving the ten members of the Association of South East Asian Nations (ASEAN) plus China, Japan, South Korea, Australia, New Zealand, and India—and again the United States has been left out. Both the East Asian Summit and the SCO appear to be part of a pattern in which the Chinese use strategic relationships and beneficial terms of trade with countries in Asia—where many of the ASEAN members have trade surpluses with China—to emphasize the value of ties to China and diminish connections to the United States.

Two other behaviors paint an ambiguous picture of China's intentions. First, it remains deeply secretive about its military developments. It took more than a week even to acknowledge that it had destroyed a weather satellite in space. That China had an antisatellite weapons capability was unknown, and it set off alarm bells. Was it because the Chinese wanted to signal to us that they don't want an arms race in space and seek to negotiate a weapons ban there? Or was it because the Chinese believe they can blunt our uses of space for intelligence and force-multiplying purposes?

Second, China is aggressively reaching out to African countries, holding an impressive summit and offering low-interest loans and outright grants totaling several billion dollars. Its assistance is untied, with no conditions on transparency, good governance, or human rights behavior. Some in the West applaud China for offering African states desperately needed assistance. Others are more skeptical, seeing it as part of a larger Chinese impulse to lock down access to natural resoures, perpetuating a trade relationship that exploits Africa's resources without offering any prospect of development, and excluding Western nations in the process.

To be sure, the Chinese motivations may be defensive and designed to protect their interests and prevent the United States from being able to pursue a strategy of containing China's power and influence. Looking at it from China's standpoint, it is easy to see how it might read U.S. bases and military or security ties in Asia stretching from South Korea to Japan to Taiwan to Australia to Pakistan and into Central Asia as posing a quasi-encirclement of China. No one other than the United States is capable of thwarting China's "national rejuvenation and regional aspirations," and, not surprisingly, many Chinese believe that the United States is out to contain China out of fear that it will undermine American global dominance and the U.S. desire for "absolute security."[5]

The irony, of course, is that the United States, like China, is also hedging its bets. Just like the Chinese, we want cooperation but have our doubts about where the Chinese are headed. Consequently, even while we seek to build the Chinese stakes in key international norms and economic partnerships, we, too, are bilaterally working with others to ensure that China does not come to dominate Asia in the long term. One former Bush administration official has described the importance of developing close ties with others in Asia as a practical way to blunt China's rise: "Deepened relations with Japan, India, and key allies in Southeast Asia will create structural constraints that may discourage Beijing from abusing its growing regional power."[6] Secretary Rice, in a March 2005 speech in Tokyo, was also very clear: "I really do believe that the U.S.-Japan relationship, the U.S.–South Korea relationship, the U.S.-Indian relationship, all are important in creating an environment in which China is more likely to play a positive role than a negative role."[7]

Both the United States and China may be logical and even right to pursue what amounts to a mutual hedging strategy vis-à-vis each other. Unfortunately, when two sides pursue such a strategy, what they are hedging against may become a self-fulfilling prophecy. The Chinese could drive us to focus on containment and efforts to constrain China's role and influence in Asia and internationally. We could drive the Chinese to do all they can to limit our presence and influence in Asia. Maybe we are destined to be competitors; maybe the best we can hope for is to make our competition safe and not particularly destructive. But the task of statecraft should be not to settle for that if it is avoidable. Knowing what is possible with China must start with an assessment of China's continuing weaknesses on the one hand and the factors that are likely to drive problematic Chinese behaviors on the other.

China's weaknesses. Given China's extraordinary economic growth, it is easy to overlook the very profound domestic challenges that the Chinese themselves know they must overcome. With all its newfound wealth,

China is still a country in which the scope of its poverty is almost unimaginable. It has 800 million farmers who cannot afford to see a doctor. Of its total population of 1.3 billion, nearly half live on less than $2 a day.[8] Another 114 million who earn around $5 a day are known as the "floating population"; they are migrant workers, often undocumented and unprotected by China's labor laws. They build the skyscrapers but don't share in the wealth they help create.[9]

According to UN data, the poorest 20 percent of China's citizens account for only 4.7 percent of total income, while the richest 20 percent account for more than half—a gap that is growing every year. Similarly, the incomes in the top ten urban regions exceed those in the rural areas by more than five times.[10] Deng Xiaoping, in his drive to modernize China, may have declared that "To get rich is glorious," but most Chinese are not rich, and they see a small, very wealthy class that seems to dominate their society.

The increasing social and economic gaps are feeding profound resentments within China. The poor see an unholy alliance between the wealthy and party officials. *Study Times*, the official publication of the Central Party School, which trains party functionaries, warned in the fall of 2005 that the alliance between the party and business enterprises was a big source of income inequality and corruption. The Public Security Ministry, which must contend with a literal explosion of violent incidents in China, assessed that most of these incidents stem from economic grievances against local authorities.[11]

Whatever the reason, the Chinese government now officially acknowledges that riots and violent protests have dramatically increased and are a major issue for President Hu Jintao's government.[12]

Minxin Pei, the director of the China Program at the Carnegie Endowment for International Peace, reports that in the last decade the number of riots, demonstrations, and strikes increased by 60 percent a year.[13] Thomas Friedman, quoting China's official media, says that there were ten thousand such incidents in 1993 and seventy-four thousand in 2004. In fact, a review of *The China Statistical Yearbook* indicates that the number of such incidents may be substantially higher, exceeding a hundred thousand per year.[14]

Premier Wen Jiabao reportedly told a visiting group of U.S. officials that the surge in rural uprisings kept him awake at night.[15] Small wonder, therefore, that he and President Hu are now so heavily emphasizing the need for a "harmonious society" and "social stability."

But it is not so easy to produce such outcomes or goals when the priority has been to generate rapid growth and modernization. The economic boom in China has bred not just increasing income inequalities—and corruption—but also a terrible environmental price. China has sixteen of the most polluted cities in the world. Its major rivers are contaminated; indeed, the Yangtze, the third longest river in the world, has become so polluted that it may be "dead in five years."[16] When combined with vast tracts of farmland being lost to "erosion, desertification and industry," serious water shortages are now also looming in the foreseeable future.

The government has begun to acknowledge the public's anger over pollution, "ill-considered" industrial projects, and the urgent need to tackle China's looming environmental dangers.[17] Zhou Shengxian, the new head of China's State Environmental Protection Administration, has spoken of the "disastrous consequences" of contamination from chemical plants for the Yellow and the Yangtze rivers—the biggest in China—and that "prosperity at the expense of the environment is very superficial and very weak . . . [and is] only delaying disaster."[18] In very much the same vein, Pan Yue, China's deputy minister of the environment, gave a remarkably blunt interview in the German magazine *Der Spiegel* in which he acknowledged the problem:

> Our raw materials are scarce, we don't have enough land, and our population is constantly growing. Currently, there are 1.3 billion people living in China; that's twice as many as 50 years ago. In 2020, there will be 1.5 billion people in China. Cities are growing, but desert areas are expanding at the same time; habitable and usable land has been halved over the last 50 years . . . Half of the water in our seven largest rivers is completely useless. One-third of the urban population is breathing polluted air.
>
> We are convinced that a prospering economy automatically goes hand in hand with political stability. And I think that's a major blunder. If the gap between the poor and the rich widens, then regions within China and the society as a whole will become unstable.[19]

This bleak picture seems to be sobering Chinese leaders. With expanding urbanization and 141 cities between 1 and 2 million in population (and another 274 cities approaching 1 million people), the prospects for increasing social dislocation are quite high. The Chinese know that high growth rates alone are not the answer to preserving social peace, and yet the pace of urbanization and the need for jobs also mandates such growth—perhaps with increasing environmental safeguards and new technologies designed to conserve precious energy resources.

These new demands on the Chinese are reflected in both the next five-year plan, which makes a "harmonious society" its centerpiece, and the Chinese leadership's declared objective (and slogan) of achieving a "well-off society" by the year 2020. China does not need adventures and instability on the outside if it is going to achieve that objective. On the contrary, it needs cooperation with the United States. And President Hu Jintao is reported to have told President Bush as much, admitting that fighting corruption, rural unrest, the widening wealth gap, and severe pollution consumes nearly all his time and puts China in a position in which it has neither the will nor the means to challenge American dominance in world affairs.[20]

Nonetheless, several problem areas may yet heighten tensions between the countries.

Problem areas. Taiwan remains the most profound problem area. For China, Taiwan is an existential issue; it is seen as an integral part of China, and nothing less can ever be accepted. While seven American presidents of both parties have acknowledged as much by accepting the "one China" principle, there remains the potential for tension. The United States continues to sell arms to Taiwan and to insist that reunification must be peaceful. China has embraced the idea of a peaceful solution, but has engineered a major buildup of arms aimed across the Taiwan Straits. The Pentagon now estimates that the Chinese have deployed between 650 and 730 mobile short-range ballistic missiles on the coast facing Taiwan—and the number grows by about 100 per year.[21]

The Chinese arms buildup opposite Taiwan began in the 1990s in the face of efforts seemingly designed to promote Taiwanese independence. With their preponderance of force in the Straits, the Chinese appear to be putting themselves in the position of being able to take back Taiwan, militarily if they must, and/or to deter the Taiwanese from moving toward independence—as well as deterring the United States from intervening to protect Taiwan if there is a conflict.

The Chinese military buildup and its threats to use force against Taiwan are taken as key indicators by the United States of China's ambitions as a regional power. As then secretary of defense Donald Rumsfeld publicly asked, what threats justify the Chinese military buildup? And Secretary Rice has declared that China's force modernization "looked outsized for its regional interests."[22]

Ironically, the more the administration questions the Chinese buildup, the more the Chinese suspect U.S. intentions. How, in their eyes, can the United States challenge Chinese military modernization when it pales compared with America's? Chinese defense spending is a fraction of ours (probably 20 percent), and China lacks any serious power projection capability. When combined with U.S. support for a growing Japanese role, including a more significant military role in Asia, and the related Japanese pledge to help the United States defend Taiwan, the Chinese perceive a U.S. strategy not just of containment but also of active denial of China's rights.

And sensitivity over its rights is becoming a more acute issue for China. It is not just a history of humiliation and the belief that the Chinese have a right to fulfill their natural destiny that affects the Chinese leadership now. It is also that as Communist ideology has disappeared as a basis of the regime's legitimacy, nationalism has been increasingly used by Chinese leaders as a legitimizing agent. But nationalism is a double-edged sword, and once set in motion it often seems to have a life of its own. In 1999, the leadership may have mobilized the public to respond to the accidental U.S. bombing of the Chinese embassy in Belgrade during the Kosovo war, but the demonstrations quickly got out of hand. Similarly, China's government clearly fomented nationalistic demonstrations in 2005 against both Japanese prime minister Junichiro Koizumi's visit to the Yasukuni Shrine, the memorial for Japan's war dead, and the Japanese approval of history textbooks that were perceived to "whitewash" their wartime crimes against the Chinese. Yet, in each case, China's leaders became alarmed over the scope of subsequent rioting and the danger of its being turned against the government.

Once used and unleashed, nationalism may not be so easy to channel, especially if there are problems or crises with the United States. Will the Chinese leaders find it so easy to manage such problems if nationalist sentiment is running very hot at the time? To be sure, America has its own grievances and concerns with the Chinese, starting first and foremost with trade imbalances, and these, too, will affect the ability of American leaders to manage the relationship with China. Domestic pressures will continue to build in the United States to do something drastic about our vast trade deficit with China, to get China to revalue its currency, and to induce China to protect intellectual property, to stop pirating, and to end technological espionage.

China's almost maniacal search for oil and other commodities is bound to create one other source of problems and friction. Literally, to fuel China's growth rates, it must have increasing access to oil. Over the last four years, 40 percent of the increase in oil demand worldwide has come from China.[23] So long as China is growing at roughly 9 percent a year—and its leaders believe that such growth rate levels are critical to preserving social peace and satisfying growing consumer demands—China's appetite for oil is going to continue to increase. Even with planned conservation measures and the use of new technologies to meet industrial needs, China's transport sector is going to expand dramatically, with its 24 million vehicles in 2005 growing to as many as 140 million in the next two decades. This is one of the leading reasons why Chinese consumption of energy is expected to double by the year 2030—and most of that must come from imports.[24]

Several consequences flow from China's energy needs and consumption of commodities and natural resources. First, such needs are increasing tensions with Japan over competing claims to the East China Sea and its gas reserves. Already the Japanese Defense Agency, according to some analysts, has revised its security strategy partly on the "assumption that conflicts over resources could escalate into war."[25]

Second, its needs are making China's foreign policy increasingly motivated by a desire to lock down guaranteed access to oil and other commodities regardless of the character of the regimes with whom China is dealing. Apart from the possible effect on the oil markets, this may also increase friction with the United States as the Chinese protect regimes such as the one in Khartoum from sanctions and at the same time provide the Sudanese the arms used to spread death and destruction in Darfur. In general, China has continued to reinforce its relations with Iran, Myanmar, and Sudan, prompting Assistant Secretary of State Christopher Hill to say in congressional testimony that a major challenge for the United States and its Asian allies must be to "ensure that in its search for resources and commodities to gird its economic machinery, China does not underwrite the continuation of regimes that pursue policies seeking to undermine rather than sustain the security and stability of the international community."[26] (At a minimum, China's dependence on Iranian oil may be one of the biggest impediments to our being able to isolate Iran and raise the costs to it of becoming a nuclear power; certainly the Chinese have little stake in seeing economic sanctions passed against Iran in the UN Security Council.)

Third, China's resource needs are bound to create environmental problems elsewhere. While Chinese consumption serves the economic interests of some of those China is dealing with, others in Africa, Europe, and Latin America have become more skeptical as they see "the environmental damage being caused by Chinese companies around the world."[27] Chinese energy needs drive not only their appetite for oil and natural gas internationally but also their production of coal plants, with one a week opening in China. And certainly that is already having an impact on global warming as well as on the air quality both in China's neighborhood and as far away as the western United States.[28]

I cite some of the problem areas not to suggest that we are on an inexorable collision course with China, but rather to emphasize that the international playing field with China is complicated. It is not likely to lend itself to a linear development in our relations or in our ability to channel Chinese behavior. We will have to work at it, recognizing the pitfalls and some of the inevitable dangers along the way. But the stakes are also high in trying to fashion the proper course, and doing so will take time, effort, and the use of all the tools at the disposal of any American administration. As Robert Zoellick, former deputy secretary of state—and probably the best practitioner of statecraft in the Bush administration—said during his tenure: "Picture the wide range of global challenges we face in the years ahead—terrorism and extremists exploiting Islam, the proliferation of weapons of mass destruction, poverty, disease—and ask whether it would be easier or harder to handle those problems if the United States and China were cooperating or at odds."[29]

Zoellick is unquestionably right that cooperation with China is fundamentally in our interest. But such cooperation won't magically materialize on its own. Rather, hedging strategies that feed each other—and risk confrontation—will define the future unless we apply an integrated approach to China that exploits our various tools of persuasion. Otherwise, we may be left at the mercy of an emerging power that is also learning how to use its economic assets to contain what the United States seeks in Asia, Africa, and elsewhere around the world.

Using the right means to redirect U.S.-China relations. Not surprisingly, our most fundamental objectives toward China might be characterized as both positive and negative: Positively, ensure that China adopts complementary approaches to the transnational dangers of proliferation, radical Islam, terrorism, environmental degradation, energy shortages, global poverty, pandemics, and crime. Negatively, avoid conflict and destructive competition militarily, and otherwise, in the Asia–Pacific rim region.

How should we go about trying to achieve these objectives? First, we must help make China an integral player in an open, stable international system—meaning that it has stature, recognition, rights, but also responsibilities. When Robert Zoellick called for making China a "responsible stakeholder" in an international system that had unquestionably benefited the Chinese, he was "framing" the objective effectively.[30]

We frame issues because we want others to think about and approach those issues in a certain way. We want what we want to be accepted and embraced—in this case, getting the Chinese and the international community to see that we are in the business of respecting and recognizing Chinese rights but also to acknowledge that with rights come responsibilities. China should not be trying to lock down its oil access at the expense of others, and neither should we. China should join others in preventing acts of genocide in places such as Darfur and not protect the Sudanese because of oil interests or because China prefers always to treat matters of internal sovereignty as inviolable. Similarly, China has a stake in preventing its environmental issues from becoming problems either regionally or internationally, and the United States does as well.

Part of our challenge with China is to show that when it plays by and reinforces broad rules those rules will not be used against it. In other words, we are not using the rules in order to gain advantage either to block China from getting access to the energy resources it needs or to provide the basis to intervene domestically in a way that may unsettle the Chinese leadership.

Statecraft toward China must be designed to reassure the Chinese leaders even while engaging them in a way that takes account of their needs and the places where we have leverage (or at least unmistakable mutual needs) that can be used to influence their choices. One thing is very clear from assessing the Chinese political landscape: the Chinese leadership is riveted on generating economic growth to preserve social peace. Their "need" in this regard also means that they have a deep interest in a healthy U.S. economy that continues to have a voracious appetite for what China produces. While they may be building leverage by holding U.S. debt, it is not leverage they can exploit without weakening the U.S. economy and the very U.S. consumption of Chinese goods they need for their growth. If nothing else, this means we have mutual economic dependency or, as Larry Summers has said, a "balance of financial terror."[31]

Similarly, we share concerns about oil shortages. The United States may not want China to feel the need to lock down oil access from rogue regimes, both for the impact such an action could have on oil markets and for the adverse effect it would have on our being able to change the behavior of those regimes. Bringing the Chinese into the International Energy Agency, which works out multilateral agreements to minimize the danger of potential oil supply disruptions, would seem to reflect well on our mutual needs—while also having the benefit of proving to the Chinese that we have no interest in making life difficult for them on access to oil.

Other areas of potentially strong mutual interest could involve the mutual need to compete with radical Islamists. One of the growing concerns China has is the radicalization of ethnic Muslims in its Xinjiang region. This should be another area in which we seek to fold the Chinese into our collective efforts—our division-of-labor efforts—to identify and help those moderate Muslims in the Middle East and Asia (Thailand, Malaysia, and Indonesia) who are key to being able to discredit the radical Islamists.

My point is not to exhaustively identify the areas of mutual need that might also give us leverage or the ability to influence Chinese behavior and build their stake in mutual steps. My point is to show that effective statecraft would seek to embed an agenda of issues—oil access, radical Islam, the environment, the economy, and security—in bilateral and multilateral mechanisms shaping U.S. and Chinese behaviors and gradually reducing the perceived need to hedge.

Our own bilateral mechanisms could be upgraded, building first and foremost on the strategic dialogue launched by Robert Zoellick when he was the deputy secretary of state. Zoellick was focused on developing a common agenda and understanding how one uses such discussions to condition attitudes and habits of thinking. This forum, which has been allowed to languish, should be used as one means both to assure the Chinese and to explain to them how Americans tend to see certain Chinese behaviors—something that, of course, invites the Chinese to explain how they see American behaviors and offer their own assurances. This forum can additionally explore how best to define our respective roles and responsibilities on a global and regional level, including in Asia. In doing so, some of the roots of mistrust might be erased. One point certain to emerge is that the Chinese actually do see the continuing American military presence and alliance relationships—certainly with Japan—as having benefits insofar as that presence and those alliances limit the Japanese impulse to remilitarize its posture in Asia.

And here one can also see the value of actively creating a nexus between our bilateral security relationships and existing multilateral mechanisms such as ASEAN and the ASEAN Regional Forum. Evan Medeiros, a specialist at the RAND Corporation, has written that "actively mixing bilateral and multilateral mechanisms would improve the legitimacy of the U.S. regional role and may prod China to contribute more to regional activities."[32] Additionally, such an active mixing might also ease some of the competitive impulses in the region. Naturally, someone has to take the lead to create the connection, to explain its value, to discuss how it might work, to prepare agendas with particular issues to be addressed, and to prefigure what might be achieved in such discussions—in a word, someone has to exercise elementary statecraft.

Elementary statecraft could be employed as well to turn the six-party talks on North Korea into a regional forum for security issues in Asia. Why might this have value? It could take at least the five powers (the United States, China, Russia, Japan, and South Korea) and regularize their meetings, thereby creating a continuing structure where regional security issues could be dealt with on an ongoing basis. One benefit of doing so would be to establish a structure for consultation between those with significant forces (air and sea) in Asia. And like the mixing of the bilateral and multilateral mechanisms mentioned above, it would also further legitimize the U.S. presence, role, and alliances while giving the Chinese and others more confidence that these and regional affairs were being managed in a way consistent with their own interests.

It is always less difficult to come up with ideas than it is to transform them into reality, and in a way that serves the objective. The objective is to manage U.S.-China relations at a time of growing Chinese power and influence in a way that mitigates the inherent mistrust, the points of friction, and the naturally competitive instincts that otherwise may produce conflict. Mutual hedging is designed to protect both countries' interests but may yield a conflict that serves neither. Statecraft done well may turn the aforementioned (or other) ideas into a means to ensure that China's rise is, in fact, peaceful.

Conclusion

{ STATECRAFT RESTORED }

A Neoliberal Agenda for U.S. Foreign Policy

Statecraft starts with having objectives and being able to match available means to those objectives. During the Bush administration, the mismatch between objectives and means has been pronounced, helping to undermine our credibility at home and abroad. In describing statecraft as it relates to particular challenges, I have sought to outline how to marry our objectives with our means by using reality-based, not faith-based or ideologically driven, assessments.

That would seem elementary and obvious. But matching means to objectives should be connected to a larger purpose in American foreign policy, otherwise our actions take on a purely instrumental quality. The United States does and should stand for something. We should be for democracy; we should be for the protection and sanctity of human rights; we should be for law-based societies that are transparent and that protect minority rights; we should be for reducing international poverty and disease; we should be for a free-trade system (without subsidies in the wealthy nations that make it hard for poor states to compete agriculturally); we should act to prevent genocide; we should act against terrorism; and we should stand for preventing conflicts and actively bringing them to an end when they exist.

Standing for such values and purposes is consistent with the American ethos. Our foreign policy should be shaped and informed by such principles. It will be easier to mobilize domestic support for policies based on principles. But those policies won't be sustained if we lack the means to support the principles; if they exist only at the level of slogans; if we alienate the rest of the world in the process; and if we fail the basic test of being able to execute the policies we say we stand for.

A neoliberal foreign policy is one that would be guided by principle. Like the neoconservatives, neoliberals would be mindful of how regimes treated their people. They would care about what went on "inside" other states. But they would seek to build deeper consensus around the principles that should guide international behavior—the dos and don'ts—and build a stronger basis for responding.

Francis Fukuyama's "realistic Wilsonianism" represents in my mind the template for neoliberalism. We should not lose our ideals. We should not give up transformation as a goal internationally. We should, in Fukuyama's words, recognize "the importance of what goes on *inside* states" and better match "the available tools to the achievement of democratic ends." Our policy should "take seriously the idealistic part of the old neoconservative agenda but take a fresh look at development, international institutions, and a host of issues that conservatives, neo- and paleo-, seldom took seriously."[1]

Here is a call not just for preserving idealism but for developing the means, the tools, and the mind-set to be able to pursue idealism. Peter Beinart offers a similar call at least insofar as he believes that U.S. foreign policy must be guided by a cause—in his case, the struggle with jihadists—but it must also recognize limits to be more accepted internationally. Like Fukuyama, Beinart wants the United States to work more through international institutions. He believes that we gain credibility and our goals can become more convincing if we are prepared to limit some of our own power through investing more in international institutions and being constrained by them.[2]

Finding the right balance of exercising our power while accepting that we might not employ it if there is no consensus for its use will not necessarily be a simple task. As I say at the outset, no American president is going to let others veto our use of force if we believe our interests and security are at stake. One theoretical distinction to keep in mind for when we might be more prepared to be constrained by others on the use of force is when we are contemplating a war of choice as opposed to a war of necessity or a response to aggression. We had little difficulty convincing the international community that we had a right to go to war to root out the Taliban and Al Qaeda in Afghanistan after 9/11. Even in Iraq, an unmistakable war of choice, the international community might have viewed the war differently if we had exercised even a modicum of statecraft. Indeed, we might have gained support for a second Security Council resolution with a more considered strategy and a readiness to wait another thirty to sixty days. In other words, even with a war of choice and not necessity, the effective use of statecraft should be employed to build consensus—or at least to put us in a position in which we are not using force over the opposition of the UN Security Council.

Ultimately, neoliberals understand the value of demonstrating that the United States is mindful of the views of other leading members of the international community. We need to show respect but not necessarily obeisance toward those views. We need to work to build support by listening and not just preaching. We need, in other words, to work at winning support.

That is why framing issues effectively is so important. That is why knowing how to approach others by not putting them on the defensive or backing them into a corner is such an instrumental element of statecraft. The first Bush administration was expert at this. The George W. Bush administration has too often failed in this regard.

The basics of statecraft would seem self-evident: have clear objectives; tailor them to fit reality; frame them so they are more easily accepted by others; develop and utilize the means and the resources to act on them; quietly and openly condition attitudes and expectations about what needs to be done; recognize the key points of leverage that we and others possess; carefully consider how to get those who have influence to join us, and work to get them to apply the leverage they have; know how to wield carrots and sticks; develop a sense of timing for when to apply pressure and when to offer a way out; read how others—friends and adversaries—are interpreting what we are doing; don't leave anything to chance; and above all, follow through meticulously.

The art of negotiating is essential for mastering all these elements. It is not just that negotiations are central to all forms of statecraft, it is that how one approaches negotiations can also shape the right mind-set for carrying out statecraft. That does not mean that on every problem there is a deal waiting to be struck or that every problem can be solved. It does mean, however, that having an instinctive understanding of how to deal with others, and also how to use and exploit leverage when one has it, is essential for the conduct of foreign policy and for the exercise of statecraft.

Why has the Bush administration been so weak in conducting statecraft? It is not for lack of intelligent or thoughtful people in leading positions. Condoleezza Rice and Stephen Hadley are highly capable and serious. They certainly try to understand reality, even if they have been hamstrung by the ideology of the administration. On Iraq, Hadley has been quoted as telling a colleague in February 2005, "I give us a B-minus for policy development and a D-minus for policy execution."[3] If nothing else, this suggests a great deal of self-awareness.

The irony is that the Bush administration has been weak consistently in *execution*, and not just on Iraqi policy. The problem, I suspect, reflects the sociology of the Bush administration. Every administration develops its own routines for decision making and behaving. It develops its own way of doing business and dealing with others. And it develops its own contours of political correctness—meaning the contours or parameters in which policy can be acceptably pursued.

The Bush administration has certainly not had a negotiating mind-set for dealing with friends or adversaries. It has had an ideological mind-set insofar as it has been certain that it knows what is right and often has defined its role as telling or educating others on what is necessary. Here again, I know something about trying to "educate" others on how to adjust to reality. A negotiator or mediator has that as one of his or her main tasks. But how one goes about it has a lot to do with one's success. The more one can show an appreciation of why someone else believes what they do, and where that belief comes from, the more one has a chance to be successful in persuasion.

Too often the Bush administration has lectured others and has not tried to persuade them. Too often it has conveyed that it knows best and that others need to accept this. Too often it has thought that the essence of diplomacy is to give a speech and expect others to respond. If it is not prepared to brook much debate internally on most issues, particularly because of its ideological blinders, why would it accept questions from others?

This is the sociology that infuses the administration. Even in the second term, when there has been greater effort to work with others, the approach to negotiations is still limited. The patience is rarely there for painstaking work. The mechanisms for follow-up are almost always lacking. The level of effort from the top is either short-lived or missing in action. The instinct to ask hard questions, certainly by the president, is unmistakably absent.

One might argue that a change in administration will change all this and that effective statecraft might be possible again. But one reason for writing a book on statecraft now is to recognize that administrations, especially those in power for eight years, leave legacies. They leave legacies with regard to means; in the Bush case, the U.S. military is stretched to the bone, and its readiness and reserve capabilities are in wretched condition and will need a massive infusion of funds and manpower. Administrations also leave legacies in terms of policies that have consequences not so easy to undo; in this case, Bush's successors will have to deal with the Iraq war and our disengagement from Middle East peacemaking and the effect that has had on the region. And, significantly, administrations leave legacies in terms of people in the bureaucracies who have been conditioned to the starting points for policy and how it is pursued.

It is important to remind those in power about what it takes to do statecraft. Of course, it requires means. But it will be no less important for a new administration assuming the reins of power in 2009 to develop a sociology that puts a premium on all the elements of statecraft. And it must make a special effort to reach down into the national security bureaucracies and convey that there is a way to do the business of diplomacy, and that we can promote our interests and our values by persuading, not dictating to, others.

Maybe it is not too late to hope that even in the last stages of the Bush presidency the realities of what the administration faces will lead it to adjust some of its behaviors and its way of doing business. Iraq places limits on what the administration can do on its own. Hamas and Hizbollah have demonstrated the limits of a policy of democracy promotion guided by an abiding faith in elections but not married to a strategy for building the delivery means and capacities of reforming governments or of moderate and liberal reformers. Iran will not be prevented from going nuclear if we cannot persuade at least the Europeans and Japanese to join us in imposing a meaningful price on the Iranians as a way of altering their nuclear policy. Radical Islamists and their acts of terror may not be discredited by us, but if we want to do better in the battle for hearts and minds we must improve our own moral standing. Indeed, if we are to better our overall posture internationally, we must become more associated with what are seen as public goods worldwide. (The Bush administration has made progress in combating AIDS; maybe it can invest more and be seen as partnering more with the Bill and Melinda Gates Foundation on issues of health and clean water and with other leading nongovernmental efforts in fighting global poverty.)

Maybe this is too much to hope for in the Bush administration's final years in office. But the right policies need to be pushed from within and from outside the administration. And its successors—whether Republican or Democrat—must define our role in the world in a way that conforms to America's responsibilities and self-image. Our wealth and our power demand responsibility. Whether we like it or not—whether others internationally admit it or not—American power is indispensable for leading the world on issues of war, peace, poverty, and confronting terrorism.

We cannot take the place of others, but without us, too often little can get done. Our allies expect us to take the lead on security challenges; even a non-ally such as China expects the United States to preserve a posture in Asia that keeps Japan from remilitarizing. Peace in the Middle East may be difficult in any case, but it is unthinkable without American leadership—and the Europeans know this better than anyone. (Having often resented being on the sidelines during the Clinton years of Arab-Israeli diplomacy, the Europeans understand their own limitations and have constantly sought and pleaded for the Bush administration to take the lead again.) Whatever the challenge—whether containing regional conflicts or mobilizing donor efforts after conflicts or fighting terrorism—there is an expectation and usually a need for the United States to lead. Johns Hopkins professor Michael Mandelbaum has it right: we create an environment in which others count on the United States to regulate the international security environment in a way that makes it safe for them to pursue their own domestic agendas and economic well-being.[4] What has so unsettled many of our allies and putative allies is that the Bush administration has, in their eyes, roiled, not regulated, international security.

Bush's successors must reestablish our leadership role on a more accepted basis. Restoring statecraft in U.S. foreign policy will be essential. Done well, it will stand in stark contrast to the approach of the Bush administration and come as a welcome relief to America's allies. Here style, tone, and demonstrations of effort will count for a great deal. Perhaps also proposing and working to develop new mechanisms for action internationally could add to our credibility and effectiveness. For example, maybe it is time for us to consult discreetly with the other members of the G-8 about expanding that group to include China and perhaps India. Certainly China is already an economic giant, and if Russia qualifies to be a member of this club of world powers, the Chinese should also be included. (At this point Russia cannot lay claim to being in the G-8 because it is a democracy.)

New international mechanisms are certainly needed. Some, like an expanded G-8, may create a new forum with new working groups to create greater inclusion and responsibility for emerging powers such as China and India. Maybe such a mechanism can supplement the UN Security Council and also be more effective in dealing with practical problems related to development, poverty, and countering terrorism. All those countries in an expanded G-8 mechanism are likely to see very much eye to eye on terrorism and the need to do more to discredit it.

New mechanisms or tools are also needed here at home for our effective conduct of foreign policy. Consider that after the Lebanon war in the summer of 2006, Hizbollah had no trouble mobilizing between one thousand and two thousand engineers, electricians, plumbers, and carpenters to begin rebuilding houses in southern Lebanon. They didn't dispense just money; they dispensed contractors for rebuilding. We need to think about how we can develop a "reconstruction army of builders" that we can use in post-conflict societies or weak states. Maybe we need a new concept for the Peace Corps; people are retiring at younger ages. Maybe the demographic profile of those we should be recruiting for such programs should be changed, reflecting that an older age cohort will have the skills that are needed. Hizbollah has a strategy and tools for creating social safety networks and reconstruction, and so should we.

To do so, we also need a new mind-set at the U.S. Agency for International Development. This agency is responsible for dispensing foreign assistance. It has been overhauled many times, but in my experience it has too often been hamstrung by bureaucratic and legal restrictions to be responsive quickly by providing assistance in politically targeted ways. To be fair, there have always been good reasons to put assistance monies into institution building or civil society development or economic projects related to infrastructure—all desirable objectives.

What I have found lacking, however, is the ability to have contingency funds available for rapid reprogramming to serve the political needs of those trying to do the right things on the ground in the places familiar to me. The political level in the State Department historically, not just within the Bush administration, has been too detached from the foreign assistance process and unable to drive it. No doubt there is a risk that if the process is driven only by political, not developmental, purposes, money could be misused in the service of shortsighted goals.

Unfortunately, anyone who knows how USAID allocates its monies also knows that outside consultants—there to ensure quality control—end up absorbing too high a percentage of the assistance. I certainly don't want to do away with transparency and oversight, but I do think we need those who understand our strategic objectives, especially in key regions such as the Middle East, to have more hands-on control and an ability to steer development monies. When I was the Middle East negotiator, I was able to work a deal with the USAID administrator at the time, Brian Atwood, in which we shaped the program and created flexibility to shift monies around to produce projects designed to show that those Palestinians most determined to promote peace were also seen as delivering to their constituents.

While not a panacea, this could be a useful model for giving those on the front lines of competing with the radical Islamists or of settling local conflicts additional tools to do the job. Someone needs to be sure they have these tools. The next administration must reorganize the foreign policy apparatus with that in mind. A leading official, perhaps in the White House, must have both the responsibility and the authority to redirect and reprogram funds and people from different agencies. That official must also work with the NGO community, fashioning strategies that can draw on their skills, material resources, and—as important—their acceptability in much of the developing world. If we are going to improve statecraft, we must upgrade our tools, use them more imaginatively, and connect them more effectively with new international mechanisms.

Ultimately, statecraft requires a mind-set. It requires a readiness to take hard, candid looks at the problems or potential opportunities we face. It requires knowing how to communicate effectively with others who have their own political needs, while being capable of explaining our own needs. It requires less U.S. lecturing of others and more learning. It requires the capacity to persuade—which at times can come from knowing how to wield inducements and penalties.

But it does not require a loss of American ambition. America's ambition in the world reflects who we are and our role and responsibilities internationally. That ambition, as we have learned from the last several years, however, must be informed by reality. It must be tempered by our means. It must be harnessed to a strategy. And it must be implemented by integrating all the resources we either possess or can elicit.

We can redeem our foreign policy and our place in the world. But if we are to do so, statecraft must no longer be a lost art. It is time to rediscover it.

AFTERWORD

As I go around the country speaking about statecraft, I am struck by how hungry people seem to be for an explanation of foreign policy that makes sense to them. They certainly want to know exactly what happened in Iraq and what went wrong. But, even more important, they want to know whether we can fix our foreign policy more generally and what it will take to do it.

The starting point, I explain, is with statecraft and its main essentials: be clear on objectives and match them to our means. It sounds simple and is certainly logical. And yet as we survey the world and our biggest challenges internationally, we tend to find a wide gap between objectives and means. Why? Is it so hard to identify objectives that can be linked to means?

It should not be. But all too often our objectives tend to be at a high level of generality and not grounded in reality. Take George W. Bush on Iraq, Iran, and the Israeli-Palestinian conflict—all issues I explored at some length in this book. Toward the end of his presidency, there was a huge gap between ends and means. On Iraq, Bush's objective remained to achieve stability but he spoke in terms of succeeding and having Iraq become "our partner in the war on terror." On Iran, he continued to call attention to the grave danger that nation represents and his objective was to prevent it from acquiring nuclear weapons. On the Israelis and Palestinians, he declared himself confident we will reach "a peace treaty this year."

All those goals may sound reasonable, but do the circumstances make them achievable and, if so, do we (or others with whom we may be able to cooperate) have the means to achieve them? And even if individually

343

or collectively we may have the means, do we have a strategy for employing these means effectively to meet the objectives? Statecraft requires seeing the world as it is, not as we might like it to be. As I have explained in the preceding pages, we do not have to give up our ambition nor should we. We can still be determined to transform unacceptable realities, but we have to understand them first.

That is why I have suggested that statecraft requires reality-based, not faith-based, assessments. When I look at the policies on Iraq, Iran, and the Israeli-Palestinian issues that took root under George W. Bush, I still see faith-based or ideologically driven assessments shaping our objectives and the means we are employing. Consider Iraq: when President Bush announced the "surge" in military force in January 2007, his stated objective was to create a secure-enough environment in Baghdad to make it possible for the different sectarian leaders to forge political compromise. In other words, the military surge was the means being used to achieve political reconciliation. The administration even identified eighteen benchmarks to indicate progress toward the achievement of this objective.

By September 2007, President Bush had changed the objective from national reconciliation to local empowerment, and basically dropped all the benchmarks. In justifying this new objective, he stated: "As local politics change, so will national politics."[1] There is nothing wrong with changing objectives; after all, objectives need to be connected to reality, and adjusting to reality is a good thing.

But was the president adjusting to reality or simply revising an objective when the one we had been seeking proved to be unattainable? And was the reason it was unattainable tied to our larger problem in Iraq, which his administration had failed to address? Going forward, the problem in Iraq is that Shia and Sunnis are not building bridges or understandings between each other at either national or local levels. Until they do, it is hard to see how the reduction in violence can last.

The good news about the surge is that it improved the security situation, at least in the short term. In no small part it did so because Sunnis turned against Al Qaeda and gained the support of the United States in doing so. Nearly eighty thousand Sunnis are now in Awakening Councils, and the United States is paying each of the members of these local councils about three hundred dollars a month. For the longer term, it is essential to either integrate these newly empowered Sunnis (who are fighting Al Qaeda with us) into the government's security forces or at least make sure that the Iraqi government is paying them. Notwithstanding plans to do precisely this, the central government is continuing to drag its feet on both integrating and paying them.

Shias continue to fear that if they share power, they will lose it. They continue to suspect that the Sunnis will use their newfound power, especially military power, against them. While those in the Awakening Councils have certainly not expressed any great hopes for reconciliation with the Shia-led national government, they may yet be open to coexistence. However, someone needs to nurture it. Given the Sunni-Shia divide and the legacy of profound distrust, it won't simply happen on its own.

Local empowerment will not lead to a change in the national politics unless there is a political strategy to produce it. The shortcoming of the surge is not its approach to trying to provide greater security for Iraqi population centers; the shortcoming is that there is no parallel political surge to match the military surge. There is no political equivalent to General David Petraeus. Our ambassador, Ryan Crocker, as good and professional as he is, does not command either the resources or the authority—the political means to match the military means the surge put in place.

Absent a sound political strategy, what will happen when the United States withdraws its forces? Locally empowered groups, newly armed, will be more capable of fighting one another and will do so if the boundaries between them are not defined by any political understandings. True, as long as we are there with significant forces, we can separate Iraqis; when one looks at Baghdad, one of the facets of our strategy (along with an increased military presence) has been to build separation walls between the different sectarian neighborhoods. It may be that the Bush administration took a decision to leave this task undone, believing that U.S. forces simply need to be in Iraq for another decade. The Iraqi defense minister was in Washington in January 2008 and suggested as much.[2]

Maybe there is a strategy of simply having U.S. forces stay long enough for Iraqis to get used to living with a new situation and having us preserve internal peace until they get to that point. But is that a sustainable strategy politically in this country? Leaving aside the likely public opposition given the costs and uncertain eventual outcome, our military leaders, including chiefs of both the Army and the Marine Corps, have consistently talked about the drain on personnel and resources that Iraq is imposing on our forces.[3]

It may be late in Iraq—too late for the Bush administration, at any rate—but it may not be too late to push a political surge. There are three means that could be employed to build the necessary political understandings and achieve the objective of a "managed transition" in Iraq.

First, use withdrawal as a lever. We should be dealing with local groups and telling them that those who cooperate with one another will see that we withdraw where they want us to, when they want us to, and how they want us to—and they will get military and economic assets as this process unfolds. Conversely, we would tell those who are not prepared to cooperate with one another that we will not withdraw where, when, or how they want us to do so. They would also lose out on the military and economic goods that go to those who cooperate. To wield such incentives and disincentives, we will need someone working actively at the local levels and we will need to avoid rigid timetables for withdrawal lest we lose the necessary flexibility to use it for political purposes.

Second, we should work to convene a national reconciliation conference that brings those we are presently empowering at the local levels together with provincial and national sectarian leaders, and we should not allow this conference to disband until agreement has been reached. Prime Minister Nuri al Maliki has called together such conferences before, but they convene and disband in a day; such conferences are meant primarily for show, not for hammering out real understandings. Here again, someone must orchestrate the convening of the meeting, work out an agenda and ground rules in advance, and then actively mediate once the conference is convened.

Third, while a regional conference on Iraq has also been convened briefly twice before, no one has sought to actually broker understandings between Iraq's neighbors. Yet all of Iraq's neighbors, including Iran and Saudi Arabia, have a reason to fear a vacuum in Iraq that could lead to an endless, very expensive competition between them. So long as we are there, we keep the lid on in a way that makes it safe for everyone on the inside and the outside to avoid hard choices. Here again, withdrawal can be a lever if deployed as a means with political purposes in mind; under the umbrella of the regional conference, why not try to play on the interests of Iran and Saudi Arabia (and Turkey, Syria, and Jordan) at least to broker understandings on how to contain violence within Iraq so that it not only is more limited but also does not spill across borders. If nothing else, the Iranians know that the Saudis can finance the Sunni tribes to limit the Iranian interests in Iraq, and the Saudis know that the Iranians can insinuate themselves further in southern Iraq in a way that could be threatening to the Saudis. Such mutual fears can be a source of leverage either for supporting internal efforts to reach understandings between Shia and Sunnis or for containing conflict within the country.

The point is that there are means that could be tied to a relevant objective in Iraq. But it will take a high-powered political official, a political "four-star general," to orchestrate the three parallel sets of negotiations that need to go on at the local, national, and international levels. With the Bush administration having proven itself unwilling or unable to make this happen, President Bush's successor should. Bear in mind that his successor will be in a position to justify a new approach; a new political surge could be what our next president announces early, and with no need to surrender leverage in the process. As I have explained, withdrawal can be a form of leverage if it is not governed by too rigid a timetable. Is it not time we actually applied leverage, the essence of statecraft, in Iraq?

WHAT IS POSSIBLE WITH IRAN?

In the Iran chapter, I described Iran's vulnerabilities, especially its economic vulnerabilities, the divisions within the Iranian leadership, and the need to play upon the concerns of those in the elite who worried about the potentially high cost of pursuing nuclear weapons. While I observed that everyone in the Iranian leadership wanted nuclear status, not everyone agreed on pursuing it at any price—certainly, not if it isolated Iran and cut off its capacity to use its oil revenues to continue to maintain social peace internally.

While Iran's vulnerabilities remain, something significant has changed things since I wrote those words: the National Intelligence Estimate on Iran's Nuclear Intentions and Capabilities. Publicly released on December 3, 2007, it transformed the landscape. Here were all the intelligence agencies of the American government saying that Iran had suspended its covert nuclear weapons program in 2003. By headlining the weapons program and saying it had been suspended, it left the impression that there was no immediate threat. And, if there was no immediate threat, why pursue sanctions? Why build pressure on Iran? Why should all options, including the military, be on the table?

There was irony in the NIE's judgments. Iran had not been sanctioned by the United Nations for a covert nuclear weapons program. It had been sanctioned by the United Nations Security Council for its uranium enrichment activities which could lead to a nuclear weapons capability. The hard part of developing nuclear weapons is being able to fashion the industrial capacity, engineering know-how, and very expensive infrastructure to produce fissionable material, out of which a bomb is made. The least costly, least demanding, and least time-consuming part is weaponizing that material once you can stockpile it.

The NIE was clear that Iran was continuing in a determined way to develop enriched uranium and the means to produce fissionable material. It was the weapons part of this effort that had been put on hold. Again, the irony: Iran had put this part of the program on hold because of outside pressures. In the NIE's words, Iran stopped its weapons program in 2003 "primarily in response to international pressures" and that "indicates Tehran's decisions are guided by a cost-benefit approach."[4] And, yet the NIE, by framing its judgments in a way that emphasizes the covert nuclear weapons program rather than the overt enrichment activities, has largely reduced the ability to apply the "cost" factor in the current international approach to Iran.

I say that because the interest in adopting additional sanctions against Iran has largely dissipated after the NIE. Pre-NIE, the Russians and Chinese were ready to adopt a third UNSC sanctions resolution; post-NIE, they were hesitant and postponed its adoption for several months. Pre-NIE, French president Nicholas Sarkozy was pushing for harsher EU-wide economic sanctions on Iran that would go well beyond anything contemplated at the UN, on the grounds that anything less would fail and inevitably make it more likely that force would be the only alternative available for preventing Iran from going nuclear. Post-NIE, his posture has become softer. Pre-NIE the Saudis had gone public in pressuring Iran to adopt a Gulf Cooperation Council proposal to have all uranium enrichment for the Middle East done outside the region by an international consortium; post-NIE, the Saudis dropped any mention of the proposal.

Was this the Bush administration's intent? Hardly. President Bush, even after the NIE, declared that "Iran was dangerous, Iran is dangerous, and Iran will be dangerous if they have the knowledge necessary to make a nuclear weapon."[5] The last thing he wanted to do was take the pressure off Iran. But in a fundamental failing in the practice of elementary statecraft, his administration allowed the framing of the issue to be transformed by the NIE.

Here again there is irony: NIEs are rarely, if ever, published. It was the president's decision to publish the Iranian NIE. To be sure, there was an expectation that once the NIE was briefed to the intelligence oversight committees in the Congress, its key findings would be leaked—and the Bush administration wanted to get out in front of this. Understandable, but the White House's efforts were inept.

Instead of rushing the publication of the NIE, which the intelligence community (IC) had no expectation it would be asked to do, the Bush administration could have held off on this decision and also asked the IC not to brief the Congress until it had time to coordinate with the British, French, and Germans. The European three have taken the lead on the Iranian issue, both in terms of drafting sanctions resolutions and in negotiating with Iran.

It was important not to blindside them. It was essential to coordinate with them on how to present the findings of the NIE publicly. Unfortunately, this was not done. Once the Europeans had the chance to discuss the meaning of the NIE, they were far clearer than the Bush Administration had been in presenting the problem as enrichment and the continuing need to stop it. The administration made a muddled presentation, initially trying to focus on how the NIE had vindicated its policies of pressure rather than addressing the enrichment issue—the reason for sanctions in the first place. Had the White House employed even a small degree of statecraft, it could have coordinated a message with the Europeans and the framing would have been vastly improved.[6]

So is it now hopeless to try to alter Iran's behavior on the nuclear issue? While the handling of the NIE report has reduced the potential for exercising leverage, it has not removed it. Iran's vulnerabilities remain. Its oil output is declining at the same time its internal consumption is rising, leaving Iran with less oil for export. But that export is critical for Iran's domestic expenditures. Eighty-five percent of Iran's export earnings come from oil, and those revenues constitute half of the Iranian government's monies. Without very significant technical help from the outside, Iran will not be able to prevent the decline in oil production from existing fields, and without massive investment and technology transfer from the outside it will not be able to explore and exploit new oil and natural gas fields.

The more pressure that is applied to getting European, Japanese, South Korean, and Chinese companies to cease doing business with Iran unless it changes its behavior, the more the Iranian government will have to make hard choices. As I noted in the chapter on Iran, the Iranian economy is suffering from severe mismanagement and the misguided policies of President Ahmadinejad, who at least one very senior cleric has criticized for "heavy blows to the Iranian [economic] system."[7] Ahmadinejad promised to bring the oil revenues to every table; instead he has brought rationing of gasoline, high inflation, high unemployment, a home heating crisis (given a shortage of available natural gas), and international isolation.

While the UN Security Council (UNSC) sanctions have not touched the Iranian economy directly, unilateral American sanctions have raised fears about the risks of doing business in Iran. As a result, they have reduced investment from the outside, inhibited Iranian access to credit, and dramatically raised commodity prices in the country.[8] In the critical oil and natural gas sectors of the economy, there were no firm contracts concluded for exploring new offshore or onshore blocks for two and a half years following Ahmadinejad's becoming president.

Only in December 2007, after the NIE was released, were the first oil and natural gas contracts finally concluded with Malaysian, Chinese, and Italian companies.[9] That could signal that more companies will begin to invest in Iran, but the vulnerabilities remain and could be exploited. The problem, of course, is that the economic pressures to date have not altered Iran's behavior, and the means the Bush administration has sought to apply, particularly in the post-NIE environment, are unlikely to achieve the objective of stopping Iran from going nuclear.

Could a different strategy with a different mix of pressures and inducements change the Iranian calculus? Perhaps, but the key is to pursue a strategy that raises the costs that would matter to the Iranian leadership while also showing Iran's leaders that there is a way for Iran to gain by giving up the nuclear program—at least as currently constituted. In other words, our objective and means can be married but will require something other than a Bush-style pressure-only approach. I say this because even if the economic pressures on Iran are ratcheted up high, the Iranian leadership is unlikely to accept an outcome that leaves them humiliated and perceived as having been defeated. They must also show how they have gained by altering their approach on the nuclear issue to meet the concerns of the international community.

What is required, therefore, is a new mix of pressures and inducements. The current approach has probably run its course. Even the third UNSC resolution is too weak to add meaningful pressures on Iran, and America's unilateral sanctions—though having made European and other businesses more wary—have probably also done as much as they are likely to do. While the credit guarantees that European countries have provided to their companies have been cut back since I wrote the chapter on Iran, those guarantees still run into billions of Euros. It is pretty difficult to convince the Iranians that their economic lifeline is really going to be cut so long as credit guarantees are still available and European companies are still seeking to invest.

European hesitancy in cutting back further is driven not only by the sense of economic loss but also by the reality that Chinese companies tend to take the place of European businesses backing away. At this point, Europeans might be more willing to apply additional economic pressures if they knew that China would not take advantage of such actions. If we want to affect both the Europeans and Chinese—and have a far more dramatic effect on the Iranians in the process—we need to persuade the Saudis to exert the leverage they have on both.

We are not taking advantage of the Saudi interest in preventing Iran from going nuclear. The Saudis, after the NIE, may be charier of openly challenging Iran, but their fears about the Iranian nuclear program have not changed. Should the Saudis go privately to the European banks, investment houses, and energy companies and tell them that if they do business with Iran, they will lose the possibility of doing business in

Saudi Arabia, that would have a big effect. With the Chinese, they could basically say that it is time to make a choice: they can do business with either Saudi Arabia or Iran. China's stakes in Saudi Arabia—with major investments in the Saudi petrochemical industry, joint developments in refineries, and Saudi Arabia filling China's strategic petroleum reserve in China—dwarf those it has in Iran. Forced to make a choice, they probably would. Now, without having to do so, the Chinese will follow their largely mercantilist instincts.

Would the Saudis force such a choice? Only if they become convinced that we and others actually have a strategy and their steps are an important piece of it. We will need to explain to the Saudis how such action will ratchet up pressures on Iran and what we will and will not do to reach a deal with the Iranians. The Saudis have concerns about our being too forthcoming with Iran but also fear the possibility of the use of force against Iran that proves messy, drags on for a long time, and makes them the target of Iranian retaliation. Our readiness to spell out our strategy of pressure and inducements, as well as the likelihood that force may have to be used if there is no increased pressure on Iran, will be a necessary part of convincing the Saudis to use their financial clout with the Europeans and the Chinese.

The same approach will be required with the Europeans. They, too, fear the use of force. The NIE created the impression that the United States was no longer in a position to use force against Iran. Ironically, that could make it more likely that the Israelis, now no longer believing that the international community will prevent Iran from going nuclear and still convinced that Iran is determined to possess such weapons, will feel driven to use force against Iran's nuclear facilities. Here there would be value in having the Israelis go quietly to key European governments and explain that while they may think they can live with an Iran with nuclear weapons, Israel, facing an existential threat, cannot. The Israelis could say that if the Europeans don't raise the pressures on Iran, the Israeli government will know that it will be left with no choice but to take its own steps to set back the Iranian nuclear program.

That is likely to concentrate the European minds on the need to ratchet up the pressure. Unless they are committed to the prospect of getting the Iranians to agree to change their behavior, there is likely to be a limit on how much the Europeans will actually do. Thus, the United

States needs to make its own offer to the Europeans. In discussions with the lead EU negotiators with Iran, I have been struck by their belief that a deal is possible but only if America is also at the table. According to the Europeans, Iran seeks economic and political goods from them, but the big prize for the Iranians is the United States—and having it accept the Iranian regime and its place and interests in the Middle East.

It matters less whether the Europeans are right. What matters is that they believe our presence at the negotiating table opens up the possibility of doing a deal with Iran. So why not trade on that as well? Why not go to the Europeans and say, "We will drop our condition of Iranian suspension of uranium enrichment for us to come to the table, provided you cut off all economic credits and investment in the Iranian oil and natural gas sector." We would be doing the essence of statecraft: giving the Europeans something they want—us at the negotiating table—in return for asking them to do something that is hard for them.

This, too, would mean an abrupt, and possibly disruptive, break with the Bush administration's approach. But while Iran will be more advanced in its nuclear developments by January 2009, the dangers of an Iran with nuclear weapons will not have changed, and trying to prevent it will have to be one of the next president's top foreign policy priorities.

THE ISRAELIS AND PALESTINIANS

Since I wrote the chapter on the Israeli-Palestinian conflict, Hamas took over Gaza and the Bush administration hosted a peace conference in Annapolis. While I emphasized the importance of affecting the realities on the ground if there was to be any hope of making real progress on settling the core issues of the conflict (Jerusalem, refugees, borders, and security), the United States under President Bush kept its focus far more on generating a political horizon or political endgame than on trying to alter the realities of day-to-day life for Palestinians and Israelis.

Secretary of State Condoleeza Rice felt, particularly after Hamas's seizure of Gaza, that if she could produce a political horizon in which both sides could see the outlines of the final agreement, then Mahmoud Abbas would be able to show what the Palestinian Authority offered in terms of achieving Palestinian national aspirations and what Hamas did not—producing, in her eyes, a means to undercut Hamas's political base among Palestinians.

Unfortunately, there were three basic weaknesses to her approach: First, if daily realities for Palestinians remain bad and unchanged—they cannot move because of Israeli checkpoints and because the economy is depressed—why are the Palestinians going to believe grand promises about what they will get at some point in the future? Second, for Israelis, there is no reason to remove checkpoints if Palestinians are not acting against terror and even less reason to make far-reaching, existential concessions if Hamas can prevent implementation and may yet take over even in the West Bank. Third, even if the leaders on both sides, Prime Minister Olmert and President Abbas, are serious about wanting to negotiate the core issues, their capacity to concede on them is limited so long as their publics are cynical and disbelieving about peace.

This is why affecting the realities that shape the perceptions of both publics is so important. But this takes a strategy and means tied to more achievable objectives. It takes statecraft, not *stagecraft*—the staging of events designed to create a certain image. Stagecraft can be useful for capturing attention and changing psychology. It can help create momentum for a policy, but it cannot be the policy. Stagecraft can be a prop to support statecraft but cannot substitute for it.

The conference at Annapolis was an example of *stagecraft*. To embody statecraft, it had to be prepared substantially and a "day-after" strategy had to be prepared, too. And the Bush administration did neither. Annapolis launched formal negotiations on permanent status, but there was no agreed basis for the negotiations. If the administration was going to invite nearly fifty nations to participate, would it not have made sense to enshrine some "Annapolis principles" that all embraced as guiding the process? To be sure, that would have taken an intense diplomatic effort to produce, but then Annapolis could have been something other than merely an event. It could have been a historic development in which all the participants established their commitment to a two-state solution and agreed to the principles for achieving it.

Instead, Annapolis was, in the words of one the Israeli participants, "the mother of all photo-ops."[10] Even so, it could have been of some utility if it was then used to launch a new beginning. But that necessitated accomplishing something very quickly after Annapolis to show that this was a real departure and that life was now going to change. Here was the opportunity to give the Israeli and Palestinian publics a reason to take a fresh look at peacemaking. Opinion polls showed that each public was supportive of going to Annapolis, but highly skeptical as to whether anything would come of it. Their support showed they were paying attention, and that needed to be seized upon to produce immediate changes that could be seen and felt.

Why were there not plans to generate large numbers of jobs for Palestinians immediately after Annapolis, with the easing of Israeli controls on crossing points to facilitate commerce? Crossing points could use technology for easing the movement of goods and materials and need not have required the Israelis to take security risks by lifting checkpoints on the movement of people.

Had such steps been planned and developed in advance, Palestinians would have at least noticed that there were unmistakable economic improvements after Annapolis. In an economy in which per capita income has dropped more than 40 percent since the beginning of the intifada in 2000, this would have provided an important psychological lift.[11]

Instead, Palestinians saw no changes on the ground economically or in mobility after the Annapolis conference. While there was a donors conference held in Paris two weeks later in which large amounts of assistance were pledged to the Palestinian Authority ($7.7 billion worth of primarily projects),[12] none of those projects are likely to materialize any time soon, and, as I found in two trips to the West Bank after Annapolis, there is already grumbling about what has happened to the money.

Palestinians were not alone in not seeing anything. Israelis, too, saw business as usual on the issue that matters most to them: three Israelis were killed in two separate terrorist attacks in the West Bank and in each case those responsible for the murders were connected to the Palestinian security forces. Though the attacks were not authorized by those forces, the Israelis saw no great readiness on the part of the Palestinian security forces to admit who had been responsible until the Israelis approached with their own information. As one senior Israeli defense official said to me, "What has changed?"

Palestinians asked me the same question. Notwithstanding Secretary Rice's declaration that we would work with the parties to implement their phase-one obligations in the roadmap—obligations that required the Israelis to ease their security grip on the territories and Palestinians to act against terror and begin to dismantle terrorist infrastructure— nothing has, in fact, happened.

The gap between rhetorical goals and practical realities is growing, and rendering the achievement of a peace treaty impossible in the near term. Truth be told, it was not going to be possible given the gaps between the parties; the conviction of the Israeli military that the lessons of the last eight years and the increase in threats coming from Hizbollah and Hamas missiles make their security demands far greater than before; and the disbelief of the two publics. From that standpoint, the administration's objective was once again shaped by a faith-based assessment of the circumstances, not a reality-based assessment.

But a reality-based assessment does not need to lead to paralysis and passivity. There is something to work with: two leaders who, for the first time since Oslo, actually believe in each other's genuine commitment to reaching peace. That each is politically weak and surrounded by those far more skeptical of trying to resolve the core issues, even at a level of generality, does not militate against meaningful progress this year.

So what objectives make sense, going forward? The key is to focus on reestablishing enough belief within each public that Olmert and Abbas can feel more empowered to reach agreement on the tradeoffs, on the core issues at least at a level of principle or generality. Meaning, in other words, that Israelis accept that if they must have a Palestinian concession on the right of return, they have to respond to Palestinian needs on Jerusalem and borders. In turn, Palestinians must accept that to get what they need on Jerusalem and borders—a capital in the Arab part of East Jerusalem for the Palestinian state and borders that are based on the 1967 lines with modifications and swaps of territory—Israel must be assured that Palestinian refugees will return to their own state and not to Israel and that Israeli security concerns will be addressed practically and not only rhetorically.

It sounds simple to say, but, in fact, for each side to agree to this even at a level of principle requires both sides to take on history and mythology. Each must take on their core narratives; each must be prepared to compromise on what historically they have said they cannot compromise on—namely, Jerusalem for Israelis and refugees for Palestinians.

Maybe that is beyond the means of either leader. If so, there could be fallback objectives of an agreement in principle on borders for the Palestinian state in return for an agreed-upon process for meeting Israeli security concerns—or even a partial Israeli withdrawal in exchange for a practical (and demonstrated) approach to security.

Regardless of the objective—an agreement on the core issues in principle or a lesser agreement on land and security and an ongoing process of negotiations—both leaders need to feel empowered to take a leap. Psychologically and politically it will be hard for them to do so if they cannot give their publics a reason to take a second look at peacemaking. The more the Israeli and Palestinian publics believe again in peacemaking, the more the leaders will feel they can make concessions and have their publics accept them.

The only way to get the publics to look again at peacemaking is for each side to take steps that are politically possible in their own domestic context and still meaningful to the other side. For example, while it is beyond the capability and will of the Palestinian Authority to dismantle terrorist infrastructure at this stage, it could launch a systematic public campaign discouraging incitement against Israel in the Palestinian media, schools, and mosques. The Israeli public would see this and note that something was changing. For their part, the Israelis will not take down checkpoints, but they could dramatically ease movement through them just by opening all the lanes within each checkpoint. Similarly, they could also freeze settlement activity in all those settlements that are adjacent to Palestinian cities, towns, and villages. Each of these moves would be seen by the Palestinian public, and they would know that something was changing—indeed, that negotiations were having an effect after all.

Here are politically possible means that could be employed to change the psychology of both publics. They represent important starting points. But security also must be addressed. Without something practical happening on security, it will be difficult to negotiate even an agreement on principles. Set your sights too high and nothing will happen. Instead, a process must be started on security. Why not get the Israeli military and Palestinian security forces to reestablish a joint working group on security? All joint efforts on security stopped in 2001 as the intifada was transformed into a war.

The Israeli military, many of whose officers accepted the Oslo process and worked with Palestinian security forces at the time, felt betrayed by the intifada and don't believe that Palestinians will ever live up to their security responsibilities. They, too, must see that Palestinian security forces will not just mouth the slogans of security but act on their obligations. Start with a joint team whose mission is to develop a security plan and have it also agree on the steps for implementing that plan. If this does not succeed, there will be no agreements, and if it does, the Israeli military's stake and belief in peacemaking will be restored.

Each of these steps—or practical means—could underpin the negotiating process on the core issues and effectively empower the leaders to make compromises. Whether going for the more ambitious objective of a framework agreement or the less ambitious objective of partial agreements with ongoing negotiations, these means will make progress possible and make a contribution to Israeli-Palestinian peace.

Ultimately, statecraft is about knowing how to use our means and different forms of leverage to change behaviors. The Bush administration made it a goal for its last year to leave a more favorable legacy on Iraq, Iran, and the Israeli-Palestinian conflict and its possible resolution. Anyone who cares about America's place in the world would hope that the Bush White House would clarify its objectives and make them more realistic, marrying objectives and means on the core issues so that the new administration will inherit a less onerous legacy. Statecraft requires clear, not wishful, thinking, and over eight years the Bush administration indulged itself too often with what it wanted to be the case. The new administration will not have that luxury.

NOTES

PREFACE

1. Gordon Craig and Alexander George, *Force and Statecraft: Diplomatic Problems of Our Time*, 3rd ed. (Oxford: Oxford University Press, 1995), p. xi.

CHAPTER 1: THE BUSH FOREIGN POLICY AND THE NEED FOR STATECRAFT

1. David Sanger and Eric Schmitt, "Cheney's Power No Longer Goes Unquestioned," *New York Times*, September 10, 2006.
2. When Secretary Rice publicly speaks of our having had a policy for sixty years of sacrificing democracy for stability in the Middle East and producing neither, she certainly seems to embrace the latter mind-set.
3. "President Sworn-In to Second Term," January 20, 2005. Available at www .whitehouse.gov/news/releases/2005/01/20050120-1.html.
4. See, for example, Robert Kagan and William Kristol, eds., *Present Dangers: Crisis and Opportunity in American Foreign and Defense Policy* (New York: Encounter Books, 2000); and David Frum and Richard Perle, *An End to Evil: How to Win the War on Terror* (New York: Random House, 2003).
5. For an extended discussion on the distinctions between conservatism and neoconservatism, see Richard Lowry, "Reaganism v. Neo-Reaganism," *National Interest* (Spring 2005).
6. See Francis Fukuyama, "The Neoconservative Moment," *National Interest* (Summer 2004), and the rebuttal by Charles Krauthammer, "In Defense of Democratic Realism," *National Interest* (Fall 2004).
7. Elliott Abrams, "Israel and the 'Peace Process,'" in Kristol and Kagan, eds., *Present Dangers.*
8. Ronald Asmus and Kenneth Pollack, "The Neoliberal Take on the Middle East," *Washington Post*, July 22, 2003, p. A17.
9. While some of the leading figures in the Clinton administration were not supporters of the war, including both secretaries of state Christopher and Albright,

President Clinton, Senator Clinton, Richard Holbrooke, Sandy Berger, William Cohen, Tom Donilon, Martin Indyk, Ken Pollack, to name but a few, were supporters of the war.

10. See for example, Kenneth M. Pollack, *The Threatening Storm: The Case for Invading Iraq* (New York: Random House, 2002), particularly chapter 12, "Rebuilding Iraq"; Michael Eisenstadt and Kenneth Pollack, "Envisioning a Post-Saddam Iraqi Military," *Policy Watch* no. 681, Wash. Institute for Near East Policy, Nov. 25, 2002; Michael Eisenstadt, "Iraqi Strategy and the Battle for Baghdad," *Policy Watch* no. 733, Wash. Institute for Near East Policy, March 26, 2003; and Michael Eisenstadt and Jeffrey White, "Fighting the War to Win the Peace in Post-Saddam Iraq," *Policy Watch* no. 739, Wash. Institute for Near East Policy, April 2, 2003.

11. Francis Fukuyama, *America at the Crossroads: Democracy, Power, and the Neoconservative Legacy* (New Haven, Conn.: Yale University Press, 2006), p. 63.

12. Christopher Hitchens, "So Long Fellow Travelers," *Washington Post*, October 20, 2002, p. B1.

13. Joseph S. Nye, *Bound to Lead: The Changing Nature of American Power* (New York: Basic Books, 1990).

14. David A. Baldwin, *Economic Statecraft* (Princeton, N.J.: Princeton University Press, 1985), p. 8.

15. K. J. Holsti, quoted in Baldwin, pp. 8–9.

16. Chester A. Crocker, "A Dubious Template for American Foreign Policy," *Survival* 47, no. 1 (Spring 2005): 58–59.

17. For a detailed discussion of the definition of soft power, its importance, and its applications, see Joseph E. Nye, Jr., *Soft Power: The Means to Success in World Politics* (New York: PublicAffairs, 2004).

CHAPTER 2: CASES OF STATECRAFT: GERMAN UNIFICATION IN NATO

1. Philip Zelikow and Condoleezza Rice, *Germany Unified and Europe Transformed: A Study in Statecraft* (Cambridge, Mass.: Harvard University Press, 1995), p. 51.

2. Ibid., p. 51.

3. Ibid., p. 58.

4. Ibid., p. 62.

5. Gorbachev believed that *perestroika* (restructuring) was necessary not only in the Soviet Union but also in the countries of the Warsaw Pact. While not envisioning that they would leave the alliance or reject socialism, he also made clear that political decisions for Poland and Hungary should be made in Warsaw and Budapest, not Moscow.

6. Quoted in Zelikow and Rice, p. 99.

7. Quoted in ibid., p. 93.

8. Quoted in ibid., p. 98.

9. Quoted in ibid., p. 26, and recounted to the author by Robert Zoellick.
10. Zelikow and Rice, p. 28.
11. Robert Zoellick, "Two Plus Four," *The National Interest* (Fall 2000): p. 19.
12. Zoellick, p. 19.
13. Quoted in James A. Baker, III, *The Politics of Diplomacy: Revolution, War and Peace 1989–1992* (New York: G. O. Putnam's Sons, 1995), p. 234.
14. Quoted in Zelikow and Rice, p. 137.
15. Quoted in Baker, p. 235.
16. Quoted in Zelikow and Rice, p. 266.
17. Quoted in ibid., p. 96.
18. Quoted in ibid., p. 98.
19. Quoted in ibid., p. 207.
20. Quoted in Baker, p. 167.
21. Zelikow and Rice, p. 152.
22. Quoted in ibid., p. 204.
23. Quoted in ibid., p. 215.
24. Quoted in ibid., p. 217.
25. Quoted in ibid., p. 127. I was in the meeting, and Gorbachev's whole demeanor changed as Bush presented his initiatives and they had this exchange.
26. Baker, pp. 258–59.
27. Quoted in ibid.
28. Baker, too, quietly worked to defuse the crisis over Lithuania's declaration of independence, getting Gorbachev to open a dialogue in return for the Lithuanians' "freezing" their declaration.

CHAPTER 3: CASES OF STATECRAFT: BOSNIA

1. David Halberstam, *War in a Time of Peace: Bush, Clinton, and the Generals* (New York: Scribner, 2001), p. 29.
2. Baker, p. 636.
3. Ibid.
4. Ibid.
5. Quoted in Halberstam, p. 86.
6. Halberstam, p. 38.
7. Colin L. Powell, "Why Generals Get Nervous," *New York Times*, October 8, 1992, p. A35.
8. Halberstam, p. 126.
9. Quoted in ibid., p. 155.
10. David Owen, *Balkan Odyssey* (New York: Harcourt Brace, 1995), p. 107.
11. Quoted in Derek Chollet, *The Road to the Dayton Accords: A Study of American Statecraft* (New York: Palgrave Macmillan, 2005), p. 6.
12. Quoted in Chollet, p. 28.
13. Chollet, pp. 28–29.

14. Ibid., p. 36.
15. Madeleine Albright, *Madame Secretary* (New York: Miramax Books, 2003), p. 190, and quoted in Chollet, p. 40.
16. Quoted in Chollet, p. 60.
17. Richard Holbrooke, *To End a War* (New York: Random House, 1998), p. 191.
18. Quoted in Holbrooke, p. 195.

CHAPTER 4: CASES OF STATECRAFT: UNDOING IRAQI AGGRESSION IN KUWAIT

1. Quoted in Baker, p. 271.
2. Quoted in Baker, p. 260.
3. Baker, p. 276.
4. George Bush and Brent Scowcroft, *A World Transformed* (New York: Knopf, 1998), p. 303.
5. Bush and Scowcroft, p. 303.
6. Baker, p. 278.
7. Ibid., pp. 277–78.
8. Ibid., p. 279.
9. Baker-Aziz meeting in Geneva (January 9, 1991), in which I was a participant.
10. Bush meeting with outside experts, which I attended.
11. Quoted in Michael Watkins and Susan Rosegrant, *Breakthrough International Negotiation: How Great Negotiators Transformed the World's Toughest Post–Cold War Conflicts* (San Francisco: Jossey-Bass, 2001), p. 199.
12. Bush and Scowcroft, p. 304.
13. To create a less formal atmosphere for ministerial meetings, Baker held such meetings with Shevardnadze in Jackson Hole, Wyoming, and Shevardnadze reciprocated by hosting us at a retreat on Lake Baikal, in the Soviet hinterland.
14. Quoted in Baker, p. 2.
15. Quoted in ibid., p. 286.
16. Bush and Scowcroft, p. 378.
17. Baker, p. 304; emphasis added.
18. Ibid., p. 305.
19. Watkins and Rosegrant, p. 194.
20. Baker, p. 295. The Bush administration not only produced assistance from others but also contributed directly with additional aid to Turkey, both in real dollars and by doubling the textile quota for Turkish exports; the president angered our domestic textile industry over his decision on Turkey and similarly unleashed a torrent of questions from American farmers, who asked why he could cancel Egypt's sizable debt but not do the same for them.
21. Watkins and Rosegrant, p. 189.
22. Quoted in ibid., p. 195.
23. Bush and Scowcroft, p. 452–53.

24. Indeed, many believe that the administration's withholding of the "deconfliction" codes, the codes that would have allowed Israel and the United States to be able to identify each other's aircraft, is what prevented Israel from responding. We proved largely ineffective in finding the Scuds and bombing them or intercepting them with the Patriots.
25. Quoted in Bush and Scowcroft, p. 389.
26. Bush and Scowcroft, p. 399.
27. Baker, p. 336.

CHAPTER 5: CASES OF STATECRAFT: SADDAM, GEORGE W. BUSH, AND THE IRAQ WAR

1. Prior to this crisis, a "no-fly" zone had also been established over southern Iraq, and after Saddam backed down this time, the UN mandated that no Iraq mechanized forces could go below the thirty-second parallel, thereby limiting the forces Saddam could build up in the south.
2. Quoted in George Packer, *The Assassins' Gate* (New York: Farrar, Straus and Giroux, 2005), p. 23.
3. Ibid.
4. Michael R. Gordon and Bernard E. Trainor, *Cobra II: The Inside Story of the Invasion and Occupation of Iraq* (New York: Pantheon, 2006), pp. 13–14. According to Gordon and Trainor, Clinton suggested a different set of priorities, starting with Al Qaeda, Middle East diplomacy, North Korea, the nuclear competition in South Asia, and only then Iraq. Bush did not respond.
5. Packer, p. 36.
6. Richard A. Clarke, *Against All Enemies: Inside America's War on Terror* (New York: Free Press, 2004), p. 32.
7. Gordon and Trainor, p. 17.
8. Quoted in Packer, p. 41.
9. Bob Woodward, *Plan of Attack* (New York: Simon and Schuster, 2004), p. 2.
10. Gordon and Trainor, pp. 30–31; and Packer, p. 45.
11. Quoted in Packer, p. 45.
12. Quoted in Elizabeth Bumiller, "A Partner in Shaping an Assertive Foreign Policy," *New York Times*, January 7, 2004.
13. Brent Scowcroft, "Don't Attack Saddam," *Wall Street Journal*, August 15, 2002, p. A19.
14. The Scowcroft article fed other stories that in some cases were misleading or actually wrong. Todd Purdum and Patrick Tyler reported in *The New York Times* that Henry Kissinger and other Republicans shared Scowcroft's position and opposed the administration's course on Iraq (Todd S. Purdum and Patrick E. Tyler, "Top Republicans Break with Bush in Iraq Strategy," *New York Times*, August 16, 2006). Yet Kissinger wrote an article that, while somewhat more nuanced, basically supported the administration's posture. Baker, too, authored a

piece that emphasized the value of going to the UN as the next step in dealing with Iraq and creating more of a legitimate basis for using force against Iraq if that proved necessary to get Iraq to disarm.

15. Woodward, pp. 160–61.
16. See Woodward, p. 160; I had conversations with Scowcroft in early August about what Powell was thinking and his seeking help from the outside from those who shared his concerns.
17. Quoted in Woodward, p. 161.
18. "Remarks by the Vice President to the Veterans of Foreign Wars 103rd National Convention," Nashville, Tenn., August 26, 2002. Text available at www.white house.gov/news/releases/2002/08/20020826.html.
19. Elisabeth Bumiller, "Traces of Terror: the Strategy; Bush Aides Set Strategy to Sell Policy on Iraq," *New York Times*, September 7, 2002, p. A1.
20. "Threats and Responses; The Rationale for the UN Resolution on Iraq, in the Diplomats' Own Words," *New York Times*, November 9, 2002, p. A10.
21. The additional concession at the end of the negotiations to secure the votes and the agreement of France made it harder, not easier, to find Iraq in material breach. According to the language of the resolution, Iraq had to be guilty of a false statement or omission in its declaration *and* failure to comply with inspections. While this concession enabled the passage of the resolution, it foreshadowed the differing standards the United States and France would have to find Iraq in material breach. In other words, the Iraqi declaration could be agreed to be incomplete, but if the French interpreted Iraq as allowing further inspections, they wouldn't view Iraq as in material breach—which was precisely the dispute that arose when France pushed for a second resolution. The precise language of the resolution is: "false statements or omissions in the declarations submitted by Iraq pursuant to this resolution and failure by Iraq at any time to comply with, and cooperate fully in the implementation of, this resolution shall constitute a further material breach of Iraq's obligations and will be reported to the council for assessment."
22. Patrick E. Tyler, "Threats and Responses: The United Nations; U.S. and Britain Drafting Resolution to Impose Deadline on Iraq," *New York Times*, September 26, 2002, p. A1.
23. "Remarks by the President on the United Nations Security Council Resolution," The Rose Garden, November 8, 2002, Available at www.whitehouse.gov/news/releases/2002/11/20021108-1.html.
24. *Late Edition with Wolf Blitzer*, November 10, 2002.
25. Michael Dobbs, "Allies Slow US War Plans: British and French Urge Time for Inspectors," *Washington Post*, January 11, 2003, p. A1.
26. Karen DeYoung, "Powell 'Confident of Allies' Support for War,'" *Washington Post*, January 24, 2002.
27. Quoted in Dobbs.

28. Craig S. Smith and Richard Bernstein, "3 Members of NATO and Russia Resist U.S. on Iraq Plans," *New York Times*, February 11, 2003.
29. "In Their Words: The Security Council," *New York Times*, February 6, 2003, p. A21.
30. "President Bush Addresses the Nation," March 19, 2003: www.whitehouse.gov/news/releases/2003/03/20030319-17.html.
31. Gordon and Trainor, pp. 26–28.
32. Gordon and Trainor, p. 464.
33. Packer, p. 133.
34. Quoted in Gordon and Trainor, p. 464.
35. *The National Security Strategy of the United States of America*, The White House, September, 2002. Available at www.whitehouse.gov/nsc/nss.html.
36. *Meet the Press*, September 8, 2002.
37. *Meet the Press*, October 20, 2002.
38. "President Discusses the Future of Iraq," Washington Hilton, Washington, D.C., February 26, 2003. Available at www.whitehouse.gov/news/releases/2003/02/20030226-11.html.
39. Woodward, p. 260.
40. Author's conversation with French ambassador Jean-David Levitte, 2005.
41. Quoted in Michael Gordon and Eric Schmitt, "Threats and Response: Turkey Saying No to Accepting G.I.'s in Large Numbers," *New York Times*, December 3, 2002, p. A1.
42. James Fallows, "Blind into Baghdad," *The Atlantic Monthly*, January/February 2004.
43. Packer, pp. 111–12. The administration also ignored similar warnings from experts affiliated with the Army War College and the National Defense University; see Fallows.
44. Gordon and Trainor, p. 502.
45. Ironically, according to the interrogation of captured Iraqi generals and officials some of the evidence that Secretary Powell cited as proof of Iraqi efforts to hide their continuing WMD programs was, in fact, evidence of guidance given by Saddam to make sure that all traces of WMD residue were destroyed once and for all. See Gordon and Trainor, p. 119.
46. See, for example, "United We Stand: Eight European Leaders Are as One with President Bush," *Wall Street Journal*, January 30, 2003, p. A14.
47. Gordon and Trainor, p. 343.
48. "Briefing on Humanitarian Reconstruction Issues," Office of the Press Secretary, February 24, 2003. Available at www.whitehouse.gov/news/releases/2003/02/20030224-11.html.
49. The agencies involved with the planning were the National Security Council, the U.S. Agency for International Development, the State Department's Bureau of Population Refugees and Migration, the Pentagon Office of Reconstruction and Humanitarian Assistance, and the Office of Management and Budget.

50. Briefing on Humanitarian Reconstruction Issues, Office of the Press Secretary, February 24, 2003.
51. Jay Garner had counted on being able to move quickly into Basra but was told by General David McKiernan that there would be no forces available to help in that regard. Gordon and Trainor, p. 157.
52. John Hughes, "Bush Had Good Reason to Believe There Were WMD in Iraq," *Christian Science Monitor*, April 12, 2006, p. 9.
53. Gordon and Trainor, pp. 155–56.
54. Packer, p. 139.
55. Gordon and Trainor, p. 157.
56. Ibid., p. 155.
57. Ibid., p. 565. The full briefing is provided on pp. 565–69.
58. Ibid., p. 570; excerpts of the NIC document appear on pp. 570–71.
59. See, for example, the U.S. Army War College's Strategic Studies Institute Report, "Reconstructing Iraq: Insights, Challenges, and Missions for Military Forces in a Post-Conflict Scenario," available to the public February 1, 2003, but completed December 2002.
60. It was difficult in 1991 as well. Public opposition was well pronounced, and the foreign minister, defense minister, and chief of staff resigned in protest. I am indebted to my student Esin Erkan for pointing this out to me.

CHAPTER 6: LESSONS OF STATECRAFT FOR TODAY

1. The Nunn-Lugar program began as a $1 billion program to safeguard weapons sites in the former Soviet Union and grew over time to include financing scientists, converting nuclear materials to civilian fuel, and other broader measures of nuclear security. "NUNN-LUGAR is said to have helped to deactivate almost 6,000 nuclear warheads," according to www.nunn-lugar.com.
2. Joseph Nye, Jr., "Smart Power: In Search of the Balance Between Hard and Soft Power," *Democracy: A Journal of Ideas*, Fall 2006, 2:105.

CHAPTER 7: STATECRAFT IN A NEW WORLD

1. Walter Russell Mead, *Power, Terror, Peace, and War: America's Grand Strategy in a World at Risk* (New York: Knopf, 2004), p. 165.
2. Ibid., pp. 165–66.
3. Martin Indyk, "The Iraq War Did Not Force Gadaffi's Hand," *Financial Times*, March 9, 2004, p. 21.
4. Matthew Bunn, "Preventing Nuclear Terrorism: A Progress Update," Nuclear Threat Initiative, pp. 3–4. Available at www.nti.org/c_press/analysis_cnwmupdate_102203.pdf.
5. "A Report Card on the Department of Energy's Nonproliferation Programs with Russia," The Secretary of Energy Advisory Board, United States Depart-

ment of Energy, January 10, 2001, p. 1. Available at www.seab.energy.gov/publications/rpt.pdf.

6. George J. Tenet, Testimony to the U.S. Senate, Armed Services Committee, March 9, 2004.

7. Dan Caldwell and Robert E. Williams, Jr., *Seeking Security in an Insecure World* (New York: Rowman & Littlefield, 2005), p. 69.

8. Graham Allison, *Nuclear Terrorism: The Ultimate Preventable Catastrophe* (New York: Times Books, 2004), p. 147.

9. Caldwell and Williams, p. 63.

10. Kurt M. Campbell, Robert J. Einhorn, and Mitchell B. Reiss, eds., *The Nuclear Tipping Point: Why States Reconsider Their Nuclear Choices* (Washington, D.C.: Brookings Institution Press, 2004), p. 326.

11. Allison, p. 177.

12. Campbell and Einhorn, p. 338.

13. William Broad, "$50 Million Offer Aims at Curbing Efforts to Make Nuclear Fuel," *New York Times*, September 20, 2006, p. A14.

14. Campbell and Einhorn, p. 339.

15. Hassan M. Fattah, "Arab Nations Plan to Start Joint Nuclear Energy Program," *New York Times*, December 11, 2006, p. A10.

16. Interview with Tayseer Alouni from October 21, 2001, reprinted in Karen J. Greenberg, ed., *Al Qaeda Now* (Cambridge: Cambridge University Press, 2005), p. 197.

17. Bin Laden speech, December 26, 2001, quoted in Greenberg, pp. 213–14.

18. Ibid., p. 215.

19. Ibid., p. 213 (emphasis added).

20. Fukuyama, *America at the Crossroads*, pp. 72–73.

21. Souhelia Al-Jadda, "In French Riots, A Lesson for Europe," *USA Today*, November 9, 2005, p. 7A; Thomas Crampton, "French Police Fear That Blogs Have Helped Incite Rioting," *New York Times*, November 10, 2005, p. A12.

22. Kevin Sullivan, "E-Mail, Blogs, Text Messages Propel Anger Over Images," *Washington Post*, February 9, 2006, p. A14.

23. For an analysis of the use of the Internet by terrorist groups, see Daniel Benjamin and Steven Simon, *The Next Attack* (New York: Times Books, 2005), chapter 3.

24. George Tenet, *At the Center of the Storm* (New York: HarperCollins, 2007).

25. Zbigniew Brzezinski, "The Dilemma of the Last Sovereign," *The American Interest*, vol. 1, no. 1 (Autumn 2005), pp. 37–46.

26. See Pew Global Attitudes Project, particularly "Views of a Changing World 2003" and "A Year After Iraq War," www.pewglobal.org/reports; and "Arab Attitudes Towards Political and Social Issues, Foreign Policy and the Media," a poll conducted jointly by Professor Shibley Telhami and Zogby International, October 2005; www.bsos.umd.edu/SADAT/PUB/survey-2005.htm.

27. See Pew Global Attitudes Project, particularly "Views of a Changing World 2003" and "A Year After Iraq War."

28. Benjamin and Simon, pp. 81–95.
29. Francis Fukuyama, "The Sources of American Conduct," *The American Interest*, vol. 1, no. 1 (Autumn 2005), p. 10.
30. "From Chaos, Order; Rebuilding Failed States," *The Economist*, March 5, 2005.
31. Karen DeYoung, "World Bank Lists Failing Nations That Can Breed Global Terrorism," *Washington Post*, September 15, 2006, p. A13.
32. Quoted in ibid.
33. Nicolas van de Walle, *Overcoming Stagnation in Aid-Dependent Countries* (Washington, D.C.: Center for Global Development, March 2005), p. 71.
34. Fukuyama, *America at the Crossroads*, p. 6.
35. Josef Joffe, *Uberpower: The Imperial Temptation of America* (New York: W. W. Norton, 2006).

CHAPTER 8: NEGOTIATIONS AS AN INSTRUMENT OF STATECRAFT

1. Warren Bass, *Support Any Friend: Kennedy's Middle East and the Making of the U.S.-Israeli Alliance* (New York: Oxford University Press, 2003), chapter 3.
2. With the advent of the sunshine policy, the South Korean view changed and the Bush administration's reluctance to negotiate with the North was seen as a threat to stability, not a benefit for the South.
3. Bandar picked me up at the airport in Riyadh after we flew to Saudi Arabia from the Geneva meeting, greeting me with "You guys almost gave me a heart attack because I was sure a meeting could not go on that long with Jimmy Baker and not produce a deal."

CHAPTER 9: NEGOTIATIONS: TWELVE RULES TO FOLLOW

1. For a thorough account of U.S.-Russian relations during the Clinton administration and of President Clinton's relationship with President Yeltsin, see Strobe Talbott, *The Russia Hand: A Memoir of Presidential Diplomacy* (New York: Random House, 2003).

CHAPTER 10: MEDIATION IN A WORLD OF LOCAL CONFLICT

1. Saadia Touval and I. William Zartman, "International Mediation in the Post–Cold War Era," in Chester A. Crocker, Fen Osler Hampson, and Pamela Aall, eds., *Turbulent Peace: The Challenges of Managing International Conflict* (Washington, D.C.: United States Institute of Peace, 2001), p. 428. Jacob Bercovitch offers a more complete definition: "Mediation is . . . a process of conflict management, related to but distinct from the parties' own negotiations, where those in conflict seek the assistance of, or accept an offer of help from, an outsider (whether an individual, an organization, a group, or a state) to change their perceptions or behavior, and to do so without resorting to physical force or invok-

ing the authority of law." Quoted in Chester A. Crocker, Fen Osler Hampson, and Pamela Aall, "Is More Better? The Pros and Cons of Multiparty Mediation," in *Turbulent Peace*, p. 499.

2. Richard Haass, *The Opportunity: America's Moment to Alter History's Course* (New York: PublicAffairs, 2005).

3. Touval and Zartman, p. 437.

4. George Mitchell, *Making Peace* (New York: Knopf, 1999), p. 126.

5. Two leading Protestant leaders challenged Mitchell, and one of their deputies went so far as to say that putting Mitchell in charge of the talks "was the equivalent of appointing an American Serb to preside over talks on the future of Croatia." Quoted in Mitchell, p. 47.

6. Mitchell, pp. 98–99.

CHAPTER 11: ELEVEN RULES FOR MEDIATION

1. Quoted in John Forester, "Making Participation Work When Interests Conflict: Moving from Facilitating Dialogue and Moderating Debate to Mediating Negotiation," *Journal of the American Planning Association*, vol. 72, no. 4 (Fall 2006), p. 450.

2. Quoted in Forester, p. 448.

3. Ibid.

4. Mitchell, pp. 34–45.

5. Israeli negotiators offered similar such clues in response, by observing that the Palestinians would need the 1967 lines as the basis of withdrawal but could live with modifications and would need sovereignty in the Arab areas of Jerusalem.

6. A dunam is a quarter of an acre. This had been Dore Gold's response when asked how the Netanyahu government looked at its obligations on further redeployments in the Interim Agreement.

7. Holbrooke, *To End a War*, p. 162.

8. Holbrooke, pp. 182–83.

9. Holbrooke, p. 5.

CHAPTER 12: PRACTICING STATECRAFT: THE ISRAELI-PALESTINIAN CONFLICT

1. Author's interview with Hassan Abu Libdeh, Ramallah, April 2006. "The Battle for Arab Democracy," for which this and subsequent interviews cited in chapter 13 were conducted, aired on the FOX News Channel in June 2006.

CHAPTER 13: PRACTICING STATECRAFT: RADICAL ISLAM AND THE CHALLENGE OF IRAN

1. Quoted in Craig Whitlock, "Keeping Al-Qaeda in His Grip," *Washington Post*, April 16, 2006, p. A1.

2. Quoted in Salah Nasrawi, "Bin Laden Tape: West is at war with Islam, fighters should go to Sudan," AP, April 23, 2006.

3. Dexter Filkins, "Qaeda Video Vows Iraq Defeat for 'Crusader' U.S.," *New York Times*, April 26, 2006.

4. Quoted in Michael Slackman, "The Struggle for Iraq: News Analysis; Hangings Fuel Regional Split," *New York Times*, January 17, 2007, p. A1.

5. "Arab Commentator Decries Muslim Terror Role, Blames 'Neo-Muslims,'" BBC Worldwide Monitoring, September 6, 2004.

6. Quoted in Whitlock.

7. Author's interview with Nabil Khatib, Dubai, April 2006.

8. "Arab Attitudes Towards Political and Social Issues, Foreign Policy and the Media," a poll conducted jointly by Professor Shibley Telhami and Zogby International, October 2005. Available at www.bsos.umd.edu/SADAT/PUB/survey-2005.htm.

9. Author's interview with Abdul Rahman al Rashid, Dubai, April 2006.

10. Author's interview with Marwan Muasher, Amman, April 2006.

11. Author's interviews with Khairi Abaza and Hala Mustafa. Khairi Abaza is an activist in Egypt's Wafd party and a senior fellow at the Foundation for Defense of Democracies in Washington, D.C. Dr. Mustafa is editor-in-chief of the Egyptian quarterly *al-Dimuqratia* (Democracy Review), which is dedicated to the analysis of democratic developments worldwide.

12. Author's interview, April 2006.

13. Robert Satloff, *The Battle of Ideas in the War on Terror* (Washington, D.C.: Washington Institute for Near East Policy, 2004), p. 73.

14. Ibid., p. 75.

15. Author's interview with Wafa' Abdel Rahman, Ramallah, April 2006.

16. Author's interview with Madeleine Albright, Washington, D.C., May 2006.

17. Author's interview with Bassem Awadallah, Amman, April 2006.

18. Benjamin and Simon, *The Next Attack*, p. 228.

19. Quoted in P. W. Singer, "The 9-11 War Plus 5," Analysis Paper Number 10 (Washington, D.C.: Saban Center for Middle East Policy, The Brookings Institution, September 2006), p. 18.

20. Author's discussion with Ahmed Younis at an event sponsored by the Search for Common Ground, Washington, D.C., June 2006.

21. Ray Takeyh, *Hidden Iran* (New York: Times Books, 2006), p. 11.

22. Shahram Chubin, *Iran's Nuclear Ambitions* (Washington, D.C.: Carnegie Endowment for International Peace, 2006), p. 31.

23. Michael Slackman, "Behind Iran's Challenge to West, Cleric Cloaked in Immense Power," *New York Times*, September 9, 2006.

24. Takeyh, p. 151.

25. Quoted in Takeyh, p. 152.

26. Quoted in Bill Spindle, "In Iran, Two Power Centers Vie amid Standoff over Nuclear Fuel," *Wall Street Journal*, October 13, 2006, p. A6.

27. Former foreign minister Ali Akbar Velayati, quoted in Takeyh, p. 150.

28. Michael Slackman, "In Iran, a Chorus of Dissent Rises on Leadership's Nuclear Strategy," *New York Times*, March 15, 2006, p. A1.

29. Shmuel Even, "The Iranian Nuclear Crisis: The Implications of Economic Sanctions," *Tel Aviv Notes*, Jaffee Center for Strategic Studies, September 7, 2006, p. 2.

30. Quoted in *Akhbar Ruz*, Tehran, vol. 27, no. 229, January 9, 2007, pp. 4, 7.

31. Glenn Kessler, "U.S. Moves to Isolate Iranian Banks," *Washington Post*, September 9, 2006, p. A11.

CHAPTER 14: PRACTICING STATECRAFT: CHINA'S RISE

1. Quoted in Jim Yardley, "America and China: Partners, if Not Friends," *New York Times*, Week in Review, November 20, 2005, p. 5.

2. Henry Kissinger, "China: Containment Won't Work," *Washington Post*, June 13, 2005, p. A19 (emphasis added).

3. Wang Jisi, "China's Search for Stability with America," *Foreign Affairs* (Sept./Oct. 2005).

4. Quoted in "Aphorisms and Suspicions: China's World Order," *The Economist*, November 19, 2005.

5. Evan S. Medeiros, "Strategic Hedging and the Future of Asia-Pacific Stability," *The Washington Quarterly* (Winter 2005/2006), p. 154.

6. Ashley Tellis quoted in ibid., p. 149.

7. Condoleezza Rice, "Remarks at Sophia University," Tokyo, Japan, March 19, 2005. Available at www.state.gov/secretary/rm/2005/43655.htm.

8. Richard Florida, "Do Not Get Impaled on the Spikes of China's Success," *Financial Times*, April 7, 2006, p. 11.

9. Bay Fang, "The Floating People," *U.S. News and World Report*, June 20, 2005, p. 47.

10. Edward Cody, "China Warns Gap Between Rich, Poor is Feeding Unrest," *Washington Post*, September 22, 2005, p. A16; Florida, p. 11.

11. Edward Cody, "China Promises Equitable Growth," *Washington Post*, October 1, 2005, p. A12.

12. Cody, "China Warns Gap Between Rich, Poor Is Feeding Unrest."

13. Minxin Pei, "Time to Reflect on How Far China Has to Go," *Financial Times*, January 19, 2005, p. 19.

14. Thomas L. Friedman, "How to Look at China," *New York Times*, November 9, 2005; p. A27; *China Statistical Yearbook*, 2005, "23-12 Offense Cases Against Public Order Handled by Public Security Organs." Available at www.stats.gov.cn/tjsj/ndsj/2005/html/w2312e.htm. Regardless of the number, there can be no denying that the signs of social distress are unmistakable in what remains an authoritarian state, and China's leaders are deeply concerned about it.

15. Edward Cody, "Chinese Police Use Tear Gas on Villagers," *Washington Post*, April 15, 2006, p. A10.

16. Jane Macartney, "Pollution Has Put Yangtze on Brink of Catastrophe," *Times* (London), May 31, 2006, p. 40.

17. David Lague, "China Blames Oil Company for Benzene Spill in River," *New York Times*, November 25, 2005, p. A8; Jane Macartney, Frances Williams, "Health Risk of Air Pollution Is Global Burden, Says WHO," *Financial Times*, October 6, 2006, p. 12.

18. "China Risks Environmental Collapse, State Official Warns," Associated Press, *Washington Post*, March 12, 2006, p. A20.

19. From Pan's interview in *Der Spiegel* on March 7, 2005, quoted in Thomas Friedman, "How to Look at China," *New York Times*, November 9, 2005, p. A27. The need to act on environmental disasters quickly or otherwise pay a political price was demonstrated when Xie Zhenhua, then the chief of the state Environmental Administration and China's top environmental official since 1993, was fired in December 2005 after a slow and initially untruthful response to a chemical explosion that tainted the Songhua River and led to the shutdown for four days of the water supply of Harbin, a city of nearly 4 million people. His successor's attitudes, noted earlier, suggest that he has drawn the appropriate lessons.

20. Joseph Kahn, "In Private Candor from China, An Overture to Promote a Thaw," *New York Times*, April 17, 2006, p. A1.

21. Quoted in "Aphorisms and Suspicions: China's World Order," *The Economist*, November 19, 2005, p. 24.

22. Quoted in Medeiros, p. 159.

23. Flynt Leverett and Jeffrey Bader, "Managing China-U.S. Energy Competition in the Middle East," *Washington Quarterly* (Winter 2005/2006), p. 189.

24. Jeffrey Logan, Senior Energy Analyst and China Program Manager, International Energy Agency, "Testimony Before the U.S. Senate, Committee on Energy and Natural Resources," February 3, 2005; Leverett and Bader, pp. 189–90.

25. David Zweig and Bi Jianhai, "China's Global Hunt for Energy," *Foreign Affairs*, (September/October 2005).

26. Christopher R. Hill, Assistant Secretary for East Asian and Pacific Affairs, "Testimony Before the Senate Foreign Relations Committee, Subcommittee on East Asian and Pacific Affairs," June 7, 2005.

27. Yardley, *New York Times*, November 20, 2005.

28. Jim Yardley, "China's Path to Modernity, Mirrored in a Troubled River," *New York Times*, November 19, 2006.

29. "Whither China: From Membership to Responsibility?" Robert B. Zoellick, remarks to National Committee on U.S.-China Relations, September 21, 2005. Available at www.state.gov/s/d/former/zoellick/rem/53682.htm.

30. Ibid.

31. Lawrence H. Summers, "Speech at the Third Annual Stavros S. Niarchos Lecture," Institute for International Economics, Washington, D.C., March 23, 2004.

32. Medeiros, pp. 162–63.

CONCLUSION: STATECRAFT RESTORED:
A NEOLIBERAL AGENDA FOR U.S. FOREIGN POLICY

1. Fukuyama, *America at a Crossroads*, p. 184.
2. Peter Beinart, *The Good Fight: Why Liberals—and Only Liberals—Can Win the War on Terror and Make America Great Again* (New York: HarperCollins, 2006).
3. Quoted in Bob Woodward, "Secret Reports Countered Bush Optimism," *Washington Post*, October 1, 2006, p. A1.
4. Michael Mandelbaum, *The Case for Goliath* (New York: PublicAffairs, 2005).

AFTERWORD

1. President George W. Bush, "Address by the President to the Nation on the Way Forward in Iraq," September 13, 2007. Available at www.whitehouse.gov/news/releases/2007/09/20070913-2.html.
2. Thom Shanker, "Minister Sees Need for U.S. Help in Iraq until 2018," *New York Times*, January 15, 2008.
3. Ann Scott Tyson, "Debate Grows on Pause in Troop Cuts," *Washington Post*, February 2, 2008.
4. National Intelligence Council, "Iran: Nuclear Intentions and Capabilities," *National Intelligence Estimate*, November 2007. Available at www.dni.gov/press_releases/20071203_release.pdf.
5. President George W. Bush, "Press Conference by the President," December 4, 2007. Available at www.whitehouse.gov/news/releases/2007/12/20071204-4.html.
6. The proof of this is the British foreign minister's article in the *Financial Times* shortly after the release of the NIE. See David Miliband, "Why We Must Not Take the Pressure off Iran," *Financial Times*, December 6, 2007.
7. Farhad Pouladi, "Top Iran Cleric Makes Rare Criticism of Government," *Agence France Presse*, August 16, 2007.
8. In the words of Secretary of the Treasury Henry Paulson: "In dealing with Iran, it is nearly impossible to know one's customer and be assured that one is not unwittingly facilitating the regime's reckless behavior and conduct. The recent warning by the Financial Action Task Force, the world's premier standard setting body for countering terrorism finance and money laundering, *confirms the extraordinary risks that accompany those who do business with Iran* [emphasis added]." U.S. Department of State, "Remarks with Secretary of the Treasury Henry M. Paulson," October 25, 2007. Available at www.state.gov/secretary/rm/2007/10/94133.htm. See also Borzou Daragahi and Ramin Mostaghim, "Iran Sanctions Ripple Past Those in Power," *Los Angeles Times*, January 20, 2008.
9. See Najmeh Bozorgmehr, "Malaysia Signs $16bn Gas Deal with Iran," *Financial Times*, December 26, 2007; "Iran, China Finalise Two Billion Dollar Oil Con-

tract," *Agence France Presse*, December 9, 2007; Parisa Hafezi, "Iran, Italy's Edison Sign $107 mln Oil Deal," *Reuters*, January 9, 2008.

10. Steven Lee Myers, "Bush Offers a Nudge to Start Mideast Talks," *New York Times*, November 27, 2007.

11. World Bank, "Investing in Palestinian Economic Reform and Development; Report for the Pledging Conference," December 17, 2007.

12. "Palestinians' Donors Conference Calls for 'Further Efforts,'" *Agence France Presse*, January 22, 2008.

ACKNOWLEDGMENTS

As I began to think about how to shape this book, I had the good fortune to have a number of in-depth discussions with Rich Friman, a political scientist at Marquette University. I was teaching a course there at the time, and Rich showed patience, understanding, and great interest in the subject and my initial ramblings. He also offered some very helpful written comments that sharpened my thinking in a number of areas.

Robert Jervis did much the same, sending me extensive and extremely thoughtful comments on some initial drafts of several chapters. Karen Seitz also provided early comments and editorial advice that were immensely helpful. John Forester provided useful feedback on an early draft of the chapters on negotiations. Later David Jacobson, Joseph Nye, and Strobe Talbott also took the time and trouble to read a pre-edited draft of the book and offered suggestions that crystallized some points and led to the inclusion of others. Reading an unedited version of a lengthy manuscript is a true test of friendship, and I am deeply indebted to all of them. Many thanks as well to Andrew Exum for providing helpful comments on a final draft, and to my friend Bob Breslaver, who offered useful suggestions on how to present the negotiation and mediation chapters.

Once again, I also owe a great deal to the Washington Institute for Near East Policy. It is my base and intellectual home. Robert Satloff directs it with a deft hand and creates an atmosphere that generates serious policy-related research and scholarship. Rob and other colleagues there provide a stimulating setting for thinking, discussing, and writing—and Howard Berkowitz and Fred Lafer, the president and chairman of the Washington Institute, respectively, have been enthusiastic supporters of my work.

While I have clearly benefited from the input and comments of many people, including my students at Georgetown from the last two years, one person in particular deserves special mention. It is no exaggeration to say that this book could not have been written without Ben Fishman, my all-purpose research and executive assistant. Ben has provided essential research, comments, critiques, and suggestions

oughout the process of writing the book. He is wise beyond his years, and I look
rward to the books that he will write in the future.

Ben received help from Nathan Hodson, another talented research assistant at
the Washington Institute, and I want to thank Nathan for his meticulous assistance
on research and fact-checking.

No book such as this would be possible without a literary agent and a publish-
ing house who believe in you. I am blessed to have Esther Newberg as my agent and
my friend; she was enthusiastic about this book from my first conversations about it
with her. And once again, it has been a pleasure to work with Paul Elie at FSG. He
is much more a partner than an editor, and I look forward to future collaborations.
I feel very much the same about Jonathan Galassi, who, as Tom Friedman likes to
say, is simply the best in the business.

Finally, I need to thank my family, Debbie, Gabe, Rachel, and Ilana. Once again,
they have tolerated my tendency to be preoccupied when dealing with a project,
and once again, they were understanding and supportive as I disappeared to write.
My son, Gabe, a budding scholar in the field, dissected the manuscript and offered
valuable suggestions. And to my wife, Debbie, who also read and commented on
the unedited manuscript, I owe the most. She supports my passions, but always with
perspective and judgment. And fortunately for me, she is also my most honest
critic, telling me not what I want to hear but what I need to hear.

INDEX

Praise for *Statecraft*

"Ross's wry, intelligent and modest tone alone is an appealing contrast to the Bush administration's bombast... The consequences of the administration's flouting of elementary diplomatic principles won't be easily effaced. But if America is going to try to return to practicing statecraft, *Statecraft* shows where to begin."

—Jacob Heilbrunn, *The New York Times Book Review*

"Ross urges a return to statecraft, to the painstaking work of diplomacy and alliance building... His is the [book] that would be of the most direct use to the next administration taking office in 2009."

—Jonathan Freedland, *The New York Review of Books*

"The U.S. foreign policy community should welcome *Statecraft* as an important contribution to the vital debate about how the next president should define and implement foreign policy. One can only hope that this debate will include experienced and adult participants who will take inspiration from Ross's book."   —Chester A. Crocker, *Foreign Affairs*

"Dennis Ross has achieved a rare eminence in the diplomatic world... He has achieved this prominence because of a basic honesty in dealing with all issues, and it is that honesty that inspires trust... After years in the White House, [Ross] has returned to academia and now reflects on what he has learned working as a negotiator. He is worth listening to."

—Sol Schindler, *The Washington Times*

"Ross... makes the seemingly dreary, opaque processes of international diplomacy as coherent, absorbing and occasionally dramatic as a procedural thriller... With its call for virtuoso state craftsmanship and its detailed proposals... it could well be Ross's application for the 2009 secretary of state opening. If so, it's an impressive one, full of canny, judicious insights into the making of foreign policy."   —*Publishers Weekly*

"[Ross] writes with great understanding about the Israeli-Palestinian conflicts, Iran, Iraq and the rise of what he calls 'non-state actors,' such as Osama bin Laden ... Brimming with important ideas, well-organized and well-argued." —*Kirkus Reviews*

"Many may speak of statecraft, but few actually understand it. Dennis Ross is one of our country's best practitioners of statecraft. Now he has written about it. He offers important insights into what made for good and bad statecraft in the past, and offers an extraordinary guide for how to employ its tools. Even more important, he applies it prospectively to demonstrate what needs to be done (and how to do it) on challenges like the Israeli-Palestinian conflict and Iranian nuclear weapons. Rarely has a book been more timely or urgently needed." —Bill Clinton

"For the past two decades, Dennis Ross has been a participant in or close observer of the major events in U.S. foreign policy. His new book offers both insightful modern history and a senior practitioner's guidance on how to deploy America's multifaceted influence to achieve the nation's ends. Whether a scholar or simply someone struggling to understand America's unique ability to shape world affairs, the reader will gain from his pointed and perceptive analyses." —Robert B. Zoellick, former U.S. Trade Representative and Deputy Secretary of State